W9-BYI-238

This practical coursebook introduces all the basics of semantics in a simple, step-by-step fashion. Each unit includes short sections of explanation with examples, followed by stimulating practice exercises to complete the book. Feedback and comment sections follow each exercise to enable students to monitor their progress. No previous background in semantics is assumed, as students begin by discovering the value and fascination of the subject and then move through all key topics in the field, including sense and reference, simple logic, word meaning, and interpersonal meaning. New study guides and exercises have been added to the end of each unit (with online answer key) to help reinforce and test learning. A completely new unit on non-literal language and metaphor, plus updates throughout the text, significantly expand the scope of the original edition to bring it up-to-date with the modern teaching of semantics for introductory courses in linguistics as well as intermediate students.

JAMES R. HURFORD is Professor of General Linguistics, University of Edinburgh.

BRENDAN HEASLEY is Consultant (Postgraduate Training), Sharjah Women's College, United Arab Emirates.

MICHAEL B. SMITH is Associate Professor of Linguistics, Oakland University.

Semantics
A Coursebook

SECOND EDITION

JAMES R. HURFORD
Professor of General Linguistics, University of Edinburgh

BRENDAN HEASLEY
Consultant (Postgraduate Training), Sharjah Women's College, United Arab Emirates

MICHAEL B. SMITH
Associate Professor of Linguistics, Oakland University

CAMBRIDGE UNIVERSITY PRESS
Cambridge, New York, Melbourne, Madrid, Cape Town, Singapore, São Paulo,
Delhi, Mexico City

Cambridge University Press
The Edinburgh Building, Cambridge CB2 8RU, UK

Published in the United States of America by Cambridge University Press, New York

www.cambridge.org
Information on this title: www.cambridge.org/9780521671873

First edition © Cambridge University Press 1983
Second edition © James R. Hurford, Brendan Heasley, and Michael B. Smith 2007

This publication is in copyright. Subject to statutory exception
and to the provisions of relevant collective licensing agreements,
no reproduction of any part may take place without
the written permission of Cambridge University Press.

First edition published 1983
Second edition published 2007
6th printing 2013

Printed and bound in the United Kingdom by the CPI Group Ltd, Croydon CR0 4YY

A catalogue record for this publication is available from the British Library

ISBN 978-0-521-67187-3 Paperback

Cambridge University Press has no responsibility for the persistence or accuracy
of URLs for external or third-party internet websites referred to in this publication,
and does not guarantee that any content on such websites is, or will remain,
accurate or appropriate. Information regarding prices, travel timetables and other
factual information given in this work are correct at the time of first printing but
Cambridge University Press does not guarantee the accuracy of such
information thereafter.

To Sue and Hilda, respectively

James R. Hurford
Brendan Heasley

To my parents

Michael B. Smith

CONTENTS

PREFACE TO THE SECOND EDITION

This new edition of the text is still aimed at the same introductory audience as the first edition (as described in the preface to the first edition below). Most units contain minor changes in the form of extra examples or brief additions to the text that I feel help make the presentation of topics clearer. A major addition of this new edition is the set of exercises and questions at the end of each unit, which I developed over the years when I used the book in an introductory semantics course at Oakland University in Rochester, Michigan. In many cases they parallel similar practices in the first edition of the textbook, but there are often additional exercises and study questions that go beyond this earlier material in order to encourage the student to think about the issues from a somewhat broader perspective. The frequent practices have been kept and occasionally revised or extended in the new edition. I have not provided answers (feedback) to the new end-of-unit questions in the text itself. This is to encourage students and instructors to seek answers on their own without the easy temptation of looking them up at the back of the book. Suggested answers to most of these new exercises and questions are provided in a separate online answer key for qualified instructors (see www.cambridge.org/9780521671873).

While I agree with and have adhered to the selection of topics in the first edition, I have nevertheless tried to briefly expand or update a few sections of the text by adding selected introductory material and references on other aspects of semantics that were not included in the first edition, but which have become increasingly important in the field since that time. Consequently, I have included new discussion of topics from cognitive semantics in Units 8 through 11, which I think is accessible and of interest to an introductory audience, including additional basic material on polysemy in Unit 11, and an entirely new Unit (27) on idiomatic language, metaphor, and metonymy at the end of the book. Additional discussion was also added in parts of Unit 16 about the differences between dictionaries and encyclopaedias and why this distinction is important in semantics. The discussion of derivation in Unit 19 has been substantially expanded beyond the treatment of this topic in the first edition to include more detailed information about morphology and its relation to meaning. I have also added material on participant (thematic) roles in Unit 20, including an introduction to the roles of possessor and experiencer. With the exception of the new Unit 27, I decided to integrate this new material into appropriate existing units of the text to maintain, as far as possible, the organization of the original edition of the book, which I think is quite clear and well-designed. Finally, I have also updated and expanded the recommendations for further study at the end of the book.

Clarifying text, examples, and exercises have been added to the end of each unit.

Michael B. Smith
Department of Linguistics
Oakland University

PREFACE TO THE FIRST EDITION

This book presents a standard and relatively orthodox view of modern linguistic semantics in what we hope is a clear, stimulating, and accessible format. Our emphasis is on getting the student at every stage to think for himself, and so to proceed through the development of concepts in semantics with the confidence and conviction that comes from doing practical exercises with them. The student should not skim the practice exercises, but should try to write down the answers to each batch of questions before consulting the answers given in feedback. The labelling in the text of definitions, examples, comments, etc. should help the student to find his way around in our exposition with ease. The entry tests at the beginning of each unit should be taken seriously: they provide a way for the student to judge his own progress at each stage.

The book is suitable for first-year undergraduates in linguistics and will probably be useful to somewhat more advanced students for revision purposes. We believe that it will also be possible for a person working independently to teach himself the elements of semantics with this book. For students in taught courses, each unit, or couple of units, could provide a good basis for small-group discussion. Students should complete the units first, and discussion can focus on developing interesting and/or problematic aspects of the material.

No elementary textbook can cover everything that its authors would have wished to cover. We have been obliged to omit a number of interesting topics, including 'thematic meaning' (topic, comment, etc.), quantification in logic, tense and aspect, and the relation between syntax and semantics. We hope that the student's appetite will be sufficiently whetted by what we have covered to lead him to take an active interest in these and other more advanced topics in semantics.

ACKNOWLEDGEMENTS (SECOND EDITION)

I would like to express my gratitude to the original authors, James R. Hurford and Brendan Heasley, for entrusting me with the revision and updating of their textbook.

I would also like to thank Andrew Winnard and Cambridge University Press for inviting me to do the work in the first place.

Michael B. Smith
Department of Linguistics
Oakland University

ACKNOWLEDGEMENTS (FIRST EDITION)

We wish to express our gratitude to:

The Nuffield Foundation for two grants of £3,000 which paid part of the salary of one of the authors for two years.

The Edinburgh University Institute for Applied Language Studies and its Director, Dr Clive Criper, for generous material support in the production of this book.

The Edinburgh University Faculty of Arts research fund for grants to pay for the typing of the book.

Professor John Lyons for extremely careful and detailed critical comments on virtually the whole of the book, comments which, in the many cases where we have heeded them, definitely improve the book. In the few cases where we have not followed his advice, we fear that we may yet regret it.

The following colleagues and students, who have given helpful advice and comments: John Christie, Gill Brown, Charles Fillmore, Gerald Gazdar, Deirdre Wilson, Steve Pulman, Keith Brown.

Jaime Lass for the drawings.

HOW TO USE THIS BOOK

For all Users The coursebook develops information on the subject cumulatively. Each unit builds on previous units, so it is wise to work through it systematically from the beginning. Skipping ahead, or dipping into later units, may work, but is less likely to build up a good solid foundation for understanding all the concepts involved.

For the Student If you are new to semantics, take the practice exercises seriously, writing the answers in the spaces provided, and checking your answers with the feedback given. If there is a discrepancy between your answer and the feedback given, revisit the explanations in the book to try to understand where you went wrong. Semantics is not such a cut-and-dried subject as, say, chemistry or mathematics, so there is sometimes room for alternative answers and interpretations. But we have tried hard in this book to use unproblematic and uncontroversial examples, on which all advanced semanticists would be in broad agreement.

It always helps understanding to talk about things, so if you can work through any problematic cases with a fellow student or with your teacher, we strongly advise you to do so. As authors, we occasionally get letters from students asking us to resolve disagreements about their answers. So it is clear that the exercises provoke discussion, and also that sometimes a student needs some outside help in seeing an issue clearly. (Most of our letters from users of this book, however, seem to show that it has been successful in getting its main concepts across.)

For the Teacher We assume that you will be at least one step ahead of your students, and already familiar with more of the literature on semantics than just this book. This book is just a beginning. The further readings recommended at the end of the book open up the field to a host of intriguing questions, some of a very philosophical nature, and some of a more practical nature, to do with the study of meaning. Aim to get your students to see the concepts outlined in this book not just as ends in themselves, to be mastered rote-fashion, but as giving them a set of agreed-upon tools for discussing more advanced issues of meaning in language.

Understanding the mechanisms of meaning is vital to successful human communication, so convey to your students the everyday significance of the examples. Most of the time, the students' intuitions about the meanings of words, sentences, and utterances will be sound and consistent, but they lack the terminology to discuss meanings systematically. As noted above in our advice to students, discussion usually helps to clarify issues. Approach the questions asked by your students with an open mind, aiming to see how any misunderstandings may have arisen. And always be prepared to admit that some of the basic exercises in this book are not, ultimately, susceptible to quite such cut-and-dried answers as we have given. That is not to say that questions in semantics can't be resolved by sensible discussion, but just that the answers may sometimes be more subtle, and more interesting, than some of the cut-and-dried sample feedback answers that we have given.

1 Basic ideas in semantics

UNIT 1 ABOUT SEMANTICS

Definition SEMANTICS is the study of MEANING in LANGUAGE.

Comment The rest of this book can be regarded as an example of how one goes about investigating and understanding semantics. It may seem to you that meaning is so vague, insubstantial, and elusive that it is impossible to come to any clear, concrete, or tangible conclusions about it. We hope to convince you that by careful thought about the language you speak and the way it is used, definite conclusions CAN be arrived at concerning meaning. In the first exercise below, we ask you to start to get yourself into the habit of careful thinking about your language and the way you use it, concentrating, naturally, on instances of such words as *mean, means*, and *meaning*.

Practice Reproduced below is a well-known passage from Lewis Carroll's *Through the Looking Glass*. Pick out all the instances of the word *mean* (or *means*, or *meant*), noting which lines they occur in. (Some line numbers are given in the margin for convenience.) After the passage there are some questions for you to answer.

1 '. . . that shows that there are three hundred and sixty-four days when you might get un-birthday presents.'

'Certainly,' said Alice.

'And only one for birthday presents, you know. There's glory for 5 you!'

'I don't know what you mean by "glory," ' Alice said.

Humpty Dumpty smiled contemptuously. 'Of course you don't – till I tell you. I meant "there's a nice knockdown argument for you." '

'But "glory" doesn't mean 'a nice knockdown argument,' Alice 10 objected.

'When I use a word,' Humpty Dumpty said in rather a scornful tone, 'it means just what I choose it to mean – neither more nor less.'

'The question is,' said Alice, 'whether you can make words mean so many different things.'

15 'The question is,' said Humpty Dumpty, 'which is to be master – that's all.'

1

(1) What word is the subject of the verb *mean* in line 6?

....

(2) What is the subject of the verb *mean* in line 9?

....

(3) What is understood as the subject of the verb *mean* in line 12?

....

(4) List all the instances (by line number) where *mean, means,* or *meant* has a personal subject, e.g. *I* or *you*. (Include instances already listed in the questions above.)

....

(5) List all the instances (by line number) in which *mean,* or *means,* or *meant* is understood as having as subject something linguistic, e.g. a word, or words. (Include instances mentioned in questions above.)

....

Feedback (1) you (2) the word *glory* (3) it, or a word (4) lines 6, 8 (5) lines 9, 12, 12, 13

Comment Lewis Carroll had brilliant insights into the nature of meaning (and into the foibles of people who theorize about it). In the passage above, he is playfully suggesting that the meanings carried by words may be affected by a speaker's will. On the whole, we probably feel that Alice is right, that words mean what they mean independently of the will of their users, but on the other hand it would be foolish to dismiss entirely Humpty Dumpty's enigmatic final remark.

Lewis Carroll's aim was to amuse, and he could afford to be enigmatic and even nonsensical. The aim of serious semanticists is to explain and clarify the nature of meaning. For better or for worse, this puts us in a different literary genre from *Through the Looking Glass*. The time has come to talk seriously of meaning.

Practice (1) Do the following two English sentences mean (approximately) the same thing?   *Yes / No*
   I'll be back later and *I will return after some time*

(2) Is the answer to the previous question obvious to a normal speaker of English?   *Yes / No*

(3) In the light of your reply to (2), if I ask 'What did John mean when he said he'd be back later?', would you be giving the helpful kind of answer that I probably want if you said 'He meant that he would return after some time'?   *Yes / No*

(4) In asking 'What did John mean when he said he'd be back later?' is the questioner primarily asking

(a) what the SENTENCE *I'll be back later* means, or

(b) what JOHN meant in saying it?   *(a) / (b)*

(5) A dictionary can be thought of as a list of the meanings
of words, of what words mean. Could one make a list of
what speakers (e.g. John, you, or I) mean?   *Yes / No*

(6) Do you understand this question?   *Yes / No*

Feedback (1) Yes (2) Yes (3) No, this would be a statement of the obvious, and
therefore unhelpful. (4) asking what JOHN meant in saying it, most usually.
(5) No, speakers may mean different things on different occasions, even when
using the same words. (6) Assuming you are a competent English speaker,
yes, you do understand the literal meaning of the interrogative sentence in
question (6); but at the same time you may not clearly understand what we,
the authors, mean in asking you this question. We mean to point out that
understanding, like meaning, can be taken in (at least) two different ways.

Comment The word *mean*, then, can be applied to people who use language, i.e. to
speakers (and authors), in roughly the sense of 'intend'. And it can be
applied to words and sentences in a different sense, roughly expressed as 'be
equivalent to'. The first step in working out a theory of what meaning is, is
to recognize this distinction clearly and always to keep in mind whether we
are talking about what speakers mean or what words (or sentences) mean.
The following two definitions encapsulate this essential distinction.

Definition SPEAKER MEANING is what a speaker means (i.e. intends to convey) when
he uses a piece of language.
    SENTENCE MEANING (or WORD MEANING) is what a sentence (or
word) means, i.e. what it counts as the equivalent of in the language concerned.

Comment The distinction is useful in analysing the various kinds of communication
between people made possible by language.

Practice Read the following conversation between two people, A and B, at a bus stop
one morning. (The lines are numbered for reference.) Then answer the
questions (1)–(8).

1 A: 'Nice day'
2 B: 'Yes, a bit warmer than yesterday, isn't it?'
3 A: 'That's right – one day fine, the next cooler'
4 B: 'I expect it might get cooler again tomorrow'
5 A: 'Maybe – you never know what to expect, do you?'
6 B: 'No. Have you been away on holiday?'
7 A: 'Yes, we went to Spain'
8 B: 'Did you? We're going to France next month'

9 A: 'Oh. Are you? That'll be nice for the family. Do they speak French?'

10 B: 'Sheila's quite good at it, and we're hoping Martin will improve'

11 A: 'I expect he will. I do hope you have a good time'

12 B: 'Thank you. By the way, has the 42 bus gone by yet? It seems to be late'

13 A: 'No. I've been here since eight o'clock and I haven't seen it'

14 B: 'Good. I don't want to be late for work. What time is it now?'

15 A: 'Twenty-five past eight'

(1) Does speaker A tell speaker B anything he doesn't already know in lines 1, 3, and 5? *Yes / No*

(2) Does A's statement in line 7 give B any new information? *Yes / No*

(3) When B says 'Did you?' in line 8, is he really asking A to tell him whether he (A) went to Spain? *Yes / No*

(4) Is there any indication that A needs to know the information that B gives him about travelling to France? *Yes / No*

(5) Does A's 'That'll be nice for the family' in line 9 give B any information? *Yes / No*

(6) Do A's statements in lines 13 and 15 give B any information that he (B) needs? *Yes / No*

(7) At what point does this conversation switch from an exchange of uninformative statements to an exchange of informative statements?

....

(8) At what point does the information exchanged begin to be of a sort that one of the speakers actually needs for some purpose in going about his everyday business?

....

Feedback (1) probably not (2) Yes, probably (3) No (4) No (5) probably not (6) Yes (7) with B's enquiry in line 6 (8) with B's question in line 12

Comment All the things said in this conversation are meaningful in one way or another. But one must not equate meaningfulness with informativeness in a narrow sense. While it is true that many sentences do carry information in a straightforward way, it is also true that many sentences are used by speakers not to give information at all, but to keep the social wheels turning smoothly. Thus A and B's uninformative exchange about the weather serves to reassure them both that a friendly courteous relationship exists between them. Even when the sentences produced are in fact informative, as when B tells A about his forthcoming trip to France, the hearer often has no specific need for the information given. The giving of information is itself an act of courtesy, performed to strengthen social relationships. This is also part of communication.

The social relationships formed and maintained by the use of language are not all courteous and amicable. Speaker meaning can include both courtesy and hostility, praise and insult, endearment and taunt.

Practice   Consider the following strained exchange between husband and wife. Then answer the questions (1)–(8).

Husband: 'When I go away next week, I'm taking the car'
Wife: 'Oh. Are you? I need the car here to take the kids to school'
Husband: 'I'm sorry, but I must have it. You'll have to send them on the bus'
Wife: 'That'll be nice for the family. Up at the crack of dawn, (ironically) and not home till mid-evening! Sometimes you're very inconsiderate'
Husband: 'Nice day'

(1) This conversation includes three utterances which were also used in the polite bus stop conversation between A and B. Identify these three utterances.

   ....

(2) When the wife in the above exchange says 'Are you?' is she thereby in some sense taking up a position opposed to that of her husband?   *Yes / No*

(3) In the bus stop conversation, when A says 'Are you?' (line 9), is he in any sense taking up a position opposed to B's position?   *Yes / No*

(4) When the wife, above, says 'That'll be nice for the family', is she expressing the belief that her husband's absence with the car will be nice for the family?   *Yes / No*

(5) When A says to B at the bus stop 'That'll be nice for the family', is he expressing the belief that going to France will be nice for the family?   *Yes / No*

(6) Is A's remark at the bus stop 'Nice day' a pointed change of subject for the purpose of ending a conversation?   *Yes / No*

(7) What is the function of this remark of A's?

   ....

(8) When the husband uses these same words about the weather, above, what does he mean by it?

   ....

Feedback   (1) 'Are you?', 'That'll be nice for the family', and 'Nice day' (2) Yes (3) No (4) No, she is probably being sarcastic (5) Yes (6) No (7) part of a polite prelude to more interesting conversation (8) In the husband's case, the remark is used to end a conversation, rather than initiate one.

Comment   The same sentences are used by different speakers on different occasions
to mean (speaker meaning) different things. Once a person has mastered the
stable meanings of words and sentences as defined by the language system,
he can quickly grasp the different conversational and social uses that they can
be put to. Sentence meaning and speaker meaning are both important, but
systematic study proceeds more easily if one carefully distinguishes the two,
and, for the most part, gives prior consideration to sentence meaning and
those aspects of meaning generally which are determined by the language
system, rather than those which reflect the will of individual speakers and the
circumstances of use on particular occasions.

The gap between speaker meaning and sentence meaning is such that it is
even possible for a speaker to convey a quite intelligible intention by using a
sentence whose literal meaning is contradictory or nonsensical.

Practice   Look at the following utterances and state whether they are intended to be
taken literally (*Yes*) or not (*No*).

(1) Tired traveller: 'This suitcase is killing me'   *Yes / No*

(2) Assistant in a shop: 'We regularly do the impossible;
     miracles take a little longer'   *Yes / No*

(3) During a business meeting: 'It's a dog-eat-dog situation'   *Yes / No*

(4) During a heated argument: 'Don't bite my head off!'   *Yes / No*

(5) Hungry person at the dinner table: 'I could eat a horse!'   *Yes / No*

Feedback   (1) No (2) No (3) No (4) No (5) No

Comment   Examples such as these show that speakers can convey meaning quite
vividly by using sentences whose meanings are in some sense problematical.
To account for this, it is necessary to analyse at two levels: firstly, to show
what is 'wrong' with such sentences, i.e. why they can't be literally true,
and secondly, how speakers nevertheless manage to communicate
something by means of them. Sections of this book are devoted to both
kinds of meaning, but rather more attention is given to sentence and word
meaning.

We will now leave this topic and give some attention to the question of
how one studies meaning – to the methods of semantics.

Practice   (1) Can two people hold an ordinary conversation without
     knowing the meanings of the words they are using?   *Yes / No*

(2) Is it reasonable to say, if I use such English words as *table* and
     chair in the normal way in my conversation, communicating
     the usual messages that one does with these and other words,
     that I know the meanings of the words *table* and *chair*?   *Yes / No*

(3) If one knows the meaning of a word, is one therefore necessarily able to produce a clear and precise definition of its meaning? *Yes / No*

(4) Conversely, if several speakers can agree on the correct definition of a word, do they know its meaning? *Yes / No*

(5) Do you happen to know the meaning of the word *ndoho* in the Sar language of Chad, Central Africa? *Yes / No*

(6) Would a sensible way to find out the meaning of *ndoho* be to ask a speaker of Sar (assuming you could find one)? *Yes / No*

(7) The word *ndoho* in Sar means *nine*, so it is not a particularly rare or technical word. Would any normal adult speaker of Sar be an appropriate person to approach to ask the meaning of the word? *Yes / No*

(8) If a native speaker of Sar insists that *ndoho* means *nine* (or the number of digits on two hands, less one, or however he expresses it), while a distinguished European professor of semantics who does not speak Sar insists that *ndoho* means *ten* (or *dix*, or *zehn*, however he translates it), who do you believe, the Sar-speaker or the professor?

....

Feedback (1) No (2) Yes (3) No, being able to give the definition of the meaning of a word is not a skill that everyone possesses. (Studying semantics should considerably sharpen this skill.) (4) Yes, it would seem reasonable to say so. (5) Probably you don't. (6) Yes (7) Yes, although some speakers, possibly through shyness or embarrassment, might not be able to give you a perfectly clear answer. (8) the Sar-speaker

Comment The meanings of words and sentences in a language can safely be taken as known to competent speakers of the language. Native speakers of languages are the primary source of information about meaning. The student (or the professor) of semantics may well be good at describing meanings, or theorizing about meaning in general, but he has no advantage over any normal speaker of a language in the matter of access to the basic data concerning meaning.

English, like most languages, has a number of different dialects. Just as the pronunciation of English varies from one dialect to another, so there are also differences in the basic semantic facts from one dialect of English to another. Note that we are using 'dialect' in the way normal in Linguistics, i.e. to indicate any variety of a language, regardless of whether it has prestige or not. In this sense, every speaker, from the London stockbroker to the Californian surfer speaks some dialect.

It is not the business of semantics to lay down standards of semantic correctness, to prescribe what meanings words shall have, or what they may be used for. Semantics, like the rest of Linguistics, describes. If some of the basic semantic facts mentioned in this book don't apply to your dialect, this doesn't mean that your dialect is in any sense wrong. Try to see the point of such examples on the assumption that they are factual for some dialect of English other than your own.

Almost all of the examples in this book will be from standard English. We assume that most readers are native speakers of English and hence know the meanings of English expressions. This may seem paradoxical: if semantics is the study of meaning, and speakers already know the meanings of all the expressions in their language, surely they cannot learn anything from semantics! What can a book written for English speakers, using English examples, tell its readers? The answer is that semantics is an attempt to set up a theory of meaning.

Definition A THEORY is a precisely specified, coherent, and economical frame-work of interdependent statements and definitions, constructed so that as large a number as possible of particular basic facts can either be seen to follow from it or be describable in terms of it.

Example Chemical theory, with its definitions of the elements in terms of the periodic table, specifying the structure of atoms, and defining various types of reactions that can take place between elements, is a theory fitting the above definition. Examples of some basic facts which either follow from chemical theory itself or are describable in terms of it are: iron rusts in water; salt dissolves in water; nothing can burn if completely immersed in water; lead is heavier than aluminium; neither aluminium nor lead float in water. Chemical theory, by defining the elements iron, lead, etc., and the reactions commonly known as rusting, burning, dissolving, etc., in terms of atomic structure, makes sense of what would otherwise simply be an unstructured list of apparently unrelated facts.

In the practice section below we illustrate some particular basic facts about meaning, the kind of facts that a complete semantic theory must make sense of.

Practice Mark each of the following statements true (*T*) or false (*F*).

(1) *Alive* means the opposite of *dead*.   *T / F*

(2) *Buy* has an opposite meaning from *sell*.   *T / F*

(3) *Caesar is and* is not a meaningful English sentence.   *T / F*

(4) *Caesar is a prime number* is nonsensical.   *T / F*

(5) *Caesar is a man* is nonsensical.   *T / F*

(6) *Both of John's parents are married to aunts of mine* is in a sense contradictory, describing an impossible situation.   *T / F*

(7) If the sentence *John killed Bill* is true of any situation, then so is the sentence *Bill is alive.*   *T / F*

(8) If someone says, 'Can you pass the salt?', he is normally not asking about his hearer's ability to pass the salt, but requesting the hearer to pass the salt.   *T / F*

(9) If someone says, 'I tried to buy some rice', his hearer would normally infer that he had actually failed to buy rice.   *T / F*

Feedback   (1)T (2)T (3)T (4)T (5)F (6)T (7)F (8)T (9)T

Comment   Each of the true statements here (and the negation of the false ones) is a statement of some particular basic fact falling within the scope of semantics. (We take a rather broad view of the scope of semantics, incidentally.) Obviously, one could not expect chemical theory, for example, to illuminate any of these facts. Chemical theory deals with chemical facts, such as the fact that iron rusts in water. Semantic theory deals with semantic facts, facts about meaning, such as those stated in the true statements above.

In aiming to discover some system and pattern in an assortment of particular facts about the meanings of individual words, sentences, and utterances, it is obviously necessary to try to move from particular facts, such as those mentioned above, to generalizations, i.e. statements about whole classes of items.

Practice   Think carefully about each of the following general statements, and try to say whether it is true (*T*) or false (*F*).

(1) Proper names (like English *John* or German *Hans* or French *Jean*) have a different kind of meaning from common nouns (like English *man*, or German *Mann* or French *homme*).   *T / F*

(2) Prepositions (like English *under*, or German *unter*, or French *sous*) have a different kind of meaning from both proper names and common nouns.   *T / F*

(3) Conjunctions (like English *and* or German *und*, or French *et*) have yet a further kind of meaning from both proper names and common nouns, and prepositions.   *T / F*

(4) Articles (e.g. English *the*, German *der*, or French *le*) have a different kind of meaning from proper names, common nouns, prepositions, and conjunctions.   *T / F*

Feedback   (1)T (2)T (3)T (4)T

Comment The statements just considered are general in several ways. Firstly, they deal with whole classes of words, e.g. the whole class of prepositions, and not just with the individual examples actually mentioned. Secondly, they apply not just to English, but to human languages in general – to Arabic and Russian no less than to German and French.

We take up this point about semantic theory being applicable to all languages below. Notice that many of the particular basic facts about meaning in English mentioned in the last practice but one have clear counterparts in other languages, e.g. German and French.

Practice This practice assumes a knowledge of French and German: do as much as you can. Mark each of the following statements true (*T*) or false (*F*).

(1) In German, *lebendig* means the opposite of *tot*. *T / F*

(2) In French, *acheter* has an opposite meaning from *vendre*. *T / F*

(3) *César est et* is not a meaningful French sentence. *T / F*

(4) In German, *Caesar ist Primzahl* is nonsensical. *T / F*

(5) In French, *Et la mère et le père de Jean sont mariés à mes tantes* is in a sense contradictory, describing an impossible situation. *T / F*

(6) In German, if the sentence *Hans hat Willi getötet* is true of any situation, then so is the sentence *Willi ist tot*. *T / F*

(7) If a German speaker says, 'Können Sie mir das Salz reichen?', he is normally not asking about his hearer's ability to pass the salt, but requesting the hearer to pass the salt. *T / F*

(8) If a French speaker says, 'J'ai essayé d'acheter du riz', his hearer would normally infer that he had failed to buy rice. *T / F*

Feedback (1)–(8) T

Comment Many basic facts about English have exact parallels in other languages. The examples above illustrate some such parallels between English and German and French. Very pervasive similarities, such as these, between languages encourage semanticists to believe that it is possible to make some very general statements about all languages, especially about the most fundamental and central areas of meaning. The fact that it is possible to translate any sentence of one language (at least roughly) into any other language (however clumsily) also reinforces the conclusion that the basic facts about meaning in all languages are, by and large, parallel. This is not to deny, of course, that there are interesting differences between languages.

Practice (1) Is there an exact equivalent in French for the English word *parent*? *Yes / No*

(2) Can the English phrase *aunts of mine* (as in *married to aunts of mine*) be straightforwardly translated into French?   Yes / No

(3) Explain the difference between the two German sentences *Können Sie mir das Salz reichen?* and *Kannst Du mir das Salz reichen?*

....

(4) Can a similar nuance of meaning be straightforwardly conveyed in English?   Yes / No

Feedback   (1) No, French *parent* means something broader, translatable by English *relative* or *kinsman*. (2) No, *mes tantes* and *plusieurs de mes tantes* do not quite translate the English *aunts of mine* exactly. (3) A speaker of the first sentence would be on less intimate terms with his hearer than a speaker of the second sentence. (4) No

Comment   If we were to consider languages less closely related to English than French and German, such as Eskimo, or an Australian aborigine language, or Navaho, we would find many more such examples of differences between languages. But interesting as such differences may be as 'collector's items', semantics concentrates on the similarities between languages, rather than on the differences. Semantic theory is a part of a larger enterprise, linguistic theory, which includes the study of syntax (grammar) and phonetics (pronunciation) besides the study of meaning. It is a characteristic of Linguistics as a whole that it concentrates on the similarities between languages.

It is not possible to talk precisely and simply about meaning without using at least a small amount of the technical terminology developed by semanticists for just this purpose. Working through this book, you should learn to use some of these technical terms, and you should find, as you progress, that you get better at making precise statements about various aspects of meaning. Fortunately, the technical terminology of semantics, especially at this elementary level, is nowhere near as pervasive and difficult as the technical vocabulary of many scientific subjects, such as chemistry, biology, and mathematics. We try to avoid unnecessary jargon, and only introduce a technical term when no everyday word quite suits our purpose.

No theory, be it chemical theory, phonetic theory, mathematical theory, semantic theory, or whatever, is complete. That is, no matter how many facts a theory actually succeeds in explaining or predicting, there are always further facts in need of explanation, other facts about which the theory as yet makes no prediction (or possibly about which it makes a false prediction), and facts which do not seem to be readily describable in the terms provided by the theory. Human knowledge grows cumulatively (with occasional drastic leaps and revolutions).

Practice   Look at Hecataeus' map of the world below (after *Grosser historischer
Weltatlas*, ed. H. Bengston, 1972), originally drawn about 520 BC; then answer
the questions.

(1)   Is there enough similarity between this map and a modern
map to conclude that they are both attempts to represent
the same thing?   *Yes / No*

(2)   In what areas would a modern map coincide most closely with this?

....

(3)   In what areas would a modern map diverge most from this?

....

(4)   Does it seem reasonable to assume that a modern map is
generally a better representation of the actual geographical facts?   *Yes / No*

(5)   Is it conceivable that a modern map could be wrong in
some respects?   *Yes / No*

(6)   How must the correctness of a map ultimately be checked?

....

(7)   Are climatic conditions or geological facts represented
on a typical modern map?   *Yes / No*

(8)   Are there new techniques, invented outside the immediate
domain of the map-maker, available to the modern mapmaker,
but unavailable to the ancient mapmaker?   *Yes / No*

(9) Have the actual geographical facts changed in any way
     since 520 BC?   *Yes / No*

Feedback   (1) Yes (2) in the central areas, around the shores of the Eastern
           Mediterranean (3) in the peripheral areas, West Africa, Africa south of the
           Sahara, Northern Europe, the Far East, and the New World (4) We have no
           alternative but to assume that our modern account of the facts is more
           likely to be correct than the ancient one. (5) Yes (6) by comparing it with
           factual data gathered from the site of the map itself (7) No, these
           dimensions are usually absent, so even a modern map is far from
           representing 'all the facts'. (8) Yes, for instance, aerial photography,
           photographs from satellites, etc. (9) Very slightly – the odd river might
           have changed its course, and man-made objects, e.g. cities and canals, have
           appeared and disappeared.

Comment   The analogy between the development of semantics and the development of
           other areas of knowledge can be pressed quite far. Aristotle can be regarded as
           a forerunner of modern semantics, just as Hecataeus was a forerunner of
           modern geography. Aristotle was clearly concerned with the same general
           areas that concern modern semanticists. There are areas of meaning studied
           by modern semanticists which were *terra incognita* (Latin for 'unknown
           territory') to Aristotle. We must assume that our modern theories of meaning
           (to the extent that they agree with one another) are in some sense superior to
           Aristotle's, i.e. that in some ways Aristotle 'got it wrong', and we, with the
           benefit of more than 2,000 years' further thought, are more likely to have 'got
           it right'. Semantic theories are justified by reference to the actual semantic
           facts that they are meant to account for. As the subject has developed, new
           dimensions in the nature of meaning have begun to be described. And today's
           semanticists have at their disposal certain modern techniques (e.g. symbolic
           logic, new theories of grammar such as cognitive and generative grammar,
           and research in psychology and cognitive science, to name just a few) not
           available to the ancients. As far as we can tell, although individual languages
           have changed (Modern Greek is very different from Ancient Greek), the basic
           ways in which language is used to convey meaning have not changed at all.
               An analogy should not be pushed too far. Obviously there are also
           differences between semantics and a physical science, like geography.
               It will be seen that the semanticist has certain advantages and certain
           disadvantages in comparison to students of other subjects. He is spared the
           physical labour and inconvenience of experiments or expeditions to ascertain
           facts – he can do semantics from his armchair. (Of course he will need paper
           and pencil to formulate his theories, and he will need to go to the library to
           compare his ideas with those of other semanticists, but these are minimal

efforts.) Correspondingly, however, the mental labour, as with any theoretical discipline, can be quite arduous. The semanticist needs to be able to think in abstractions. Doing semantics is largely a matter of conceptual analysis, exploring the nature of meaning in a careful and thoughtful way, using a wide range of examples, many of which we can draw from our own knowledge.

One thing we would recommend, as you proceed through this book, is that you take a positively critical attitude to the ideas being put forward. If you disagree with the 'feedback' to some exercises, try to work out why, and discuss the problem with your instructors and fellow students. Semantics is not cut-and-dried in its final state. You can contribute to its development by active discussion of the ideas in this book, many of which may be as imperfect as Hecataeus' map.

Bon voyage!

Unit 1   Study Guide and Exercises

Directions   After you have read Unit 1 you should be able to tackle the following questions to test your understanding of the main ideas raised in the unit.

1 You should understand these terms and concepts from this unit:

semantics	linguistics
sentence (word) meaning	language
speaker meaning	components of language
native speaker (informant)	theory of semantics
'knowing' the meaning(s) of a word	

2 Try to paraphrase (restate in your own words) each of the following uses of the word *mean* as it is employed in the sentences below. Which sentences are more reflective of speaker meaning and which are more reflective of sentence meaning? Briefly explain.

   a I mean to be there tomorrow
   b A stalling car may mean a tune-up
   c *Calligraphy* means beautiful handwriting
   d It wasn't what he said but what he meant
   e What does the German word *Hund* mean?
   f Those clouds mean rain

3 Look up the words *mean* and *meaning* in any handy collegiate dictionary and find out how many senses of the words are listed there. What sense(s) of *mean* seem(s) to correspond most closely to the sense(s) that the text is concerned with?

4 What is meant by a theory of semantics? Try to explain this briefly in your own words.

5 Which of the following items appear to illustrate sentence meaning and which illustrate speaker meaning in the way these concepts were introduced in this unit? Be able to explain your choice.

a A bachelor is an unmarried man

b A red light means 'stop'

c A fine product THEY put out! (THEY is strongly emphasized)

d The sentences in the following pair appear to be opposite in meaning:

   1) The bear killed the man

   2) The man killed the bear

e My feet are killing me

6 Is meaningfulness synonymous with informativeness? Explain in your own words and supply an illustration.

7 A semantic theory should account for items like the following, which we will study in the following units. Can you guess now what aspect of meaning is involved in each example?

a The President of the United States is the Commander-in-Chief

b She can't bear children

c You're sitting in the apple-juice seat

d How long did John stay in New York?

e A tulip is a flower

f John's present wife is unmarried

g The car needs to be washed

h If *John killed Bill* is true, then so is *Bill is dead*

8 In this unit we claimed that semantics 'concentrates on the similarities between languages, rather than on the differences' (p. 11). Do you agree with this sort of focus? Does it seem too narrow? Why or why not?

9 Explain in your own words the statement that 'No theory . . . [including] semantic theory . . . is complete' (p. 11).

UNIT 2 SENTENCES, UTTERANCES, AND PROPOSITIONS

Introduction This unit introduces some basic notions in semantics. It is important that you master these notions from the outset as they will keep recurring throughout the course.

Instruction Read the following out loud:

Virtue is its own reward

Now read it out loud again.

Comment The same sentence was involved in the two readings, but you made two different utterances, i.e. two unique physical events took place.

Definition An UTTERANCE is any stretch of talk, by one person, before and after which there is silence on the part of that person.

An utterance is the USE by a particular speaker, on a particular occasion, of a piece of language, such as a sequence of sentences, or a single phrase, or even a single word.

Practice Now decide whether the following could represent utterances. Indicate your answer by circling *Yes or No.*

(1)	'Hello'	*Yes / No*
(2)	'Not much'	*Yes / No*
(3)	'Utterances may consist of a single word, a single phrase or a single sentence. They may also consist of a sequence of sentences. It is not unusual to find utterances that consist of one or more grammatically incomplete sentence-fragments. In short, there is no simple relation of correspondence between utterances and sentences'	*Yes / No*
(4)	'Pxgotmgt'	*Yes / No*
(5)	'Schplotzenpflaaaaaaargh!'	*Yes / No*

Feedback (1) Yes (2) Yes (3) Yes, even though it would be a bit of a mouthful to say in one utterance (i.e. without pauses). (4) No, this string of sounds is not from any language. (5) No, for the same reason given for (4)

16

Comment Utterances are physical events. Events are ephemeral. Utterances die on the wind. Linguistics deals with spoken language and we will have a lot to say about utterances in this book. But we will concentrate even more on another notion, that of sentences.

Definition (partial) A SENTENCE is neither a physical event nor a physical object. It is, conceived abstractly, a string of words put together by the grammatical rules of a language. A sentence can be thought of as the IDEAL string of words behind various realizations in utterances and inscriptions.

Practice Some examples will help to get the idea of a sentence across. Indicate your answer by circling *Yes* or *No*.

(1) Do all (authentic) performances of *Macbeth* begin by using the same sentence? *Yes / No*

(2) Do all (authentic) performances of *Macbeth* begin with the same utterance? *Yes / No*

(3) Does it make sense to talk of the time and place of a sentence? *Yes / No*

(4) Does it make sense to talk of the time and place of an utterance? *Yes / No*

(5) Can one talk of a loud sentence? *Yes / No*

(6) Can one talk of a slow utterance? *Yes / No*

Feedback (1) Yes (2) No (3) No (4) Yes (5) No (6) Yes

Comment Strictly, a book such as this contains no utterances (since books don't talk) or sentences (since sentences are abstract ideals). In semantics we need to make a careful distinction between utterances and sentences. In particular we need some way of making it clear when we are discussing sentences and when utterances. We adopt the convention that anything written between single quotation marks represents an utterance, and anything italicized represents a sentence or (similarly abstract) part of a sentence, such as a phrase or a word.

Example 'Help' represents an utterance.

The steeples have been struck by lightning represents a sentence.

'The steeples have been struck by lightning' represents an utterance.

John represents a word conceived as part of a sentence.

Practice (1) For each of the following label it as an utterance (*U*) or sentence (*S*), as appropriate, by circling your choice.

(a) 'The train now arriving at platform one is the 11.15 from King's Cross' *U / S*

(b) *The pelican ignores the linguist* *U / S*

17

(2) Given our conventions, say what is wrong with the following:

(a) John announced *Mary's here* in his squeakiest voice

....

....

(b) 'Mary thought *how nice John was*'

....

....

Feedback (1) (a) U (b) S (2) 'Mary's here' should be in quotation marks since it represents John's utterance, i.e. the event of his using those words on a particular occasion. (b) A sentence, which is not a physical thing, cannot be part of an utterance, which is a physical event. 'How nice John was' should not be italicized. (Alternatively the whole example should be italicized and the quotation marks removed.)

Rule We have defined a sentence as a string of words. A given sentence always consists of the same words, and in the same order. Any change in the words, or in their order, makes a different sentence, for our purposes.

Example *Helen rolled up the carpet* ⎫ different sentences
Helen rolled the carpet up ⎭

Sincerity may frighten the boy ⎫ the same sentence
Sincerity may frighten the boy ⎭

Comment It would make sense to say that an utterance was in a particular accent (i.e. a particular way of pronouncing words). However, it would not make strict sense to say that a sentence was in a particular accent, because a sentence itself is only associated with phonetic characteristics such as accent and voice quality through a speaker's act of uttering it. Accent and voice quality belong strictly to the utterance, not to the sentence uttered.

Practice (1) Does it make sense to ask what language (e.g. English, French, Chinese) a sentence belongs to? *Yes / No*

(2) What languages do the following sentences belong to?
Le jour de gloire est arrivé

....

Alle Menschen sprechen eine Sprache

....

Feedback (1) Yes (2) French, German

Comment Not all utterances are actually tokens of sentences, but sometimes only of parts of sentences, e.g. phrases or single words.

Definition A SENTENCE is a grammatically complete string of words expressing a
(partial) complete thought.

Comment This very traditional definition is unfortunately vague, but it is hard to arrive at a better one for our purposes. It is intended to exclude any string of words that does not have a verb in it, as well as other strings. The idea is best shown by examples.

Example *I would like a cup of coffee* is a sentence.
Coffee, please is not a sentence.
In the kitchen is not a sentence.
Please put it in the kitchen is a sentence.

Practice Which of the following utterances are tokens of whole sentences (*S*) and which are not (*NS*)?

(1) 'John'		*S / NS*
(2) 'Who is there?'		*S / NS*
(3) 'Mine'		*S / NS*
(4) 'It's mine'		*S / NS*
(5) 'Where shall I . . .?'		*S / NS*

Feedback (1) NS (2) S (3) NS (4) S (5) NS

Comment Utterances of non-sentences, e.g. short phrases, or single words, are used by people in communication all the time. People do not converse wholly in (tokens of) wellformed sentences. But the abstract idea of a sentence is the basis for understanding even those expressions which are not sentences. In the overwhelming majority of cases, the meanings of non-sentences can best be analysed by considering them to be abbreviations, or incomplete versions, of whole sentences.

Practice Given below are some sample conversations. In each case the second utterance is not a token of a sentence. Write out a full sentence expressing the intended meaning more fully.

(1) Magnus: 'When did Goethe die?'
Fred: 'In 1832' ....

(2) Hostess: 'Would you like tea or coffee?'
Guest: 'Coffee, please'...

(3) A: 'Who won the battle of Waterloo?'
B: 'Wellington'...

Feedback	(1) Goethe died in 1832 (2) I would like coffee please (3) Wellington won the battle of Waterloo

Comment Semantics is concerned with the meanings of non-sentences, such as phrases and incomplete sentences, just as much as with whole sentences. But it is more convenient to begin our analysis with the case of whole sentences. The meanings of whole sentences involve propositions; the notion of a proposition is central to semantics. What exactly a proposition is, is much debated by semanticists. We shall be content with a very simple definition.

Definition A PROPOSITION is that part of the meaning of the utterance of a declarative sentence which describes some state of affairs.

Comment The state of affairs typically involves persons or things referred to by expressions in the sentence and the situation or action they are involved in. In uttering a declarative sentence a speaker typically asserts a proposition.

Rule The notion of truth can be used to decide whether two sentences express different propositions. Thus if there is any conceivable set of circumstances in which one sentence is true, while the other is false, we can be sure that they express different propositions.

Practice Consider the following pairs of sentences. In each case, say whether there are any circumstances of which one member of the pair could be true and the other false (assuming in each case that the same name, e.g. *Harry*, refers to the same person).

(1) *Harry took out the garbage*
    Harry took the garbage out   *Yes / No*

(2) *John gave Mary a book*
    Mary was given a book by John   *Yes / No*

(3) *Isobel loves Tony*
    Tony loves Isobel   *Yes / No*

(4) *George danced with Ethel*
    George didn't dance with Ethel   *Yes / No*

(5) *Dr Findlay killed Janet*
    Dr Findlay caused Janet to die   *Yes / No*

Feedback	(1) No, these are always either both true or both false. We cannot imagine any situation in which one is true and the other false. (2) No (3) Yes, one could be true and the other false. (4) Yes (5) Yes, for example in the situation where Dr Findlay had caused Janet to die, but not intentionally, say by sending her to a place where, unknown to him, she was attacked. Someone else could in fact be guilty of killing her.

Comment   True propositions correspond to facts, in the ordinary sense of the word *fact*. False propositions do not correspond to facts.

Practice   In the present-day world,

(1) Is it a fact that there are lions in Africa?   *Yes / No*

(2) Is the proposition that there are lions in Africa a true proposition?   *Yes / No*

(3) Is it a fact that the state of Arkansas is uninhabited by human beings?   *Yes / No*

(4) Is the proposition that the state of Arkansas is uninhabited by human beings true?   *Yes / No*

Feedback   (1) Yes (2) Yes (3) No (4) No

Comment   One can entertain propositions in the mind regardless of whether they are true or false, e.g. by thinking them, or believing them. But only true propositions can be known.

Practice   (1) If John wonders whether Alice is deceiving him, would it seem reasonable to say that he has the proposition that Alice is deceiving him in his mind, and is not sure whether it is a true or a false proposition?   *Yes / No*

(2) If I say to you, 'If Mary came to the party, Phyllis must have been upset', do I thereby put in your mind the proposition that Mary came to the party, without necessarily indicating whether it is true or not?   *Yes / No*

(3) If I say to you, 'Was your father in the Navy?', would it seem reasonable to say that I have the proposition that your father was in the Navy in my mind, and wish to know whether this proposition is true or not?   *Yes / No*

(4) Is there something odd about the following sentence? If so, what?
Pamela considered the fact that her mother was alive and realized that it could not possibly be true.

    ....

(5) Is there something similarly odd about the following sentence? If so, what?
Pamela considered the proposition that her mother was alive and realized that it could not possibly be true.

    ....

21

Feedback (1) Yes (2) Yes (3) Yes (4) Yes, there is a kind of contradiction here, in that the same thing is said to be both 'a fact' and 'not possibly true'. (5) No, there is nothing odd about this sentence, because we stated that propositions can be either true or false.

Comment In our definition of 'proposition' we explicitly mentioned declarative sentences, but propositions are clearly involved in the meanings of other types of sentences, such as interrogatives, which are used to ask questions, and imperatives, which are used to convey orders. Normally, when a speaker utters a simple declarative sentence, he commits himself to the truth of the corresponding proposition: i.e. he asserts the proposition. By uttering a simple interrogative or imperative, a speaker can mention a particular proposition, without asserting its truth.

Example In saying, 'John can go' a speaker asserts the proposition that John can go. In saying, 'Can John go?', he mentions the same proposition but merely questions its truth. We say that corresponding declaratives and interrogatives (and imperatives) have the same propositional content.

Practice (1) In the following utterances, is any proposition asserted by the speaker?

    (a) 'Have you seen my toothbrush?' *Yes / No*

    (b) 'Get out of here this minute!' *Yes / No*

    (c) 'I'm afraid that I'll have to ask you to leave' *Yes / No*

  (2) Would you say that the members of the following sentence pairs have the same propositional content?

    (a) *Go away, will you?*
       You will go away *Yes / No*

    (b) *Pigs might fly*
       I'm a Dutchman *Yes / No*

    (c) *I am an idiot*
       Am I an idiot? *Yes / No*

Feedback (1) (a) No (b) No (c) Yes (2) (a) Yes (b) No common proposition is involved. (c) Yes

Comment The notion of propositional content will be taken up again in unit 25. Propositions, unlike sentences, cannot be said to belong to any particular language. Sentences in different languages can correspond to the same proposition, if the two sentences are perfect translations of each other.

Example English *I am cold*, French *J'ai froid*, German *Mir ist kalt*, and Russian *Mne xolodno* can, to the extent to which they are perfect translations of each other, be said to correspond to the same proposition.

Comment One may question whether perfect translation between languages is ever possible. In point of fact, many linguists disagree about this and it is likely that absolutely perfect translation of the same proposition from one language to another is impossible. However, to simplify matters here we shall assume that in some, possibly very few, cases, perfect translation IS possible.

We shall have a lot to say in later units about utterances, sentences and propositions, since these concepts are at the bottom of all talk about meaning. We shall see that we have to be very careful, when talking about meaning, to make it clear whether we are dealing with utterances or sentences. To this end we shall try summarizing the relationship between these notions.

We shall use the terms 'proposition', 'sentence', and 'utterance' in such a way that anything that can be said of propositions can also be said of utterances, but not necessarily vice versa, and anything that can be said of sentences can also be said of utterances, but not necessarily vice versa. We have already seen an example of this when we said it was sensible to talk of a sentence being in a particular language, and also sensible to talk of an utterance being in a particular language, although one cannot talk of a proposition being in a particular language.

Practice (1) Fill in the chart below with '+' or '−' as appropriate. Thus, for example, if it makes sense to think of a proposition being in a particular regional accent, put a '+' in the appropriate box; if not, put a '−'.

	Utterances	Sentences	Propositions
Can be loud or quiet			
Can be grammatical or not			
Can be true or false			
In a particular regional accent			
In a particular language			

(2) Can the same proposition be expressed by different sentences? *Yes / No*

(3) Can the same sentence be realized by different utterances (i.e. have different utterances as tokens)? *Yes / No*

Feedback (1) + − − (2) Yes (3) Yes
+ + −
+ + +
+ − −
+ + −

Comment It is useful to envisage the kind of family tree relationship between these notions shown in the diagram. For example, a single proposition could be expressed by using several different sentences (say, *Prince William will inherit the throne*, or *The throne will be inherited by Prince William*) and each of these sentences could be uttered an infinite number of times.

A proposition is an abstraction that can be grasped by the mind of an individual person. In this sense, a proposition is an object of thought. Do not equate propositions with thoughts, because thoughts are usually held to be private, personal, mental processes, whereas propositions are public in the sense that the same proposition is accessible to different persons: different individuals can grasp the same proposition. Furthermore, a proposition is not a process, whereas a thought can be seen as a process going on in an individual's mind. Unfortunately, of course, the word *thought* may sometimes be used loosely in a way which includes the notion of a proposition. For instance, one may say, 'The same thought came into both our heads at the same time.' In this case, the word *thought* is being used in a sense quite like that of the word *proposition*. The relationship between mental processes (e.g. thoughts), abstract semantic entities (e.g. propositions), linguistic entities (e.g. sentences), and actions (e.g. utterances) is problematic and complicated, and we will not go into the differences further here.

Summary
These comments are impressionistic and simplified, but we believe that they will give a beginning student in semantics an idea of the kind of motivation behind the semanticist's careful distinction between utterances, sentences, and propositions.

We have introduced a notational way of distinguishing between sentences (italic typeface) and utterances (single quotation marks). Note that we have as yet shown no way of representing propositions. One possible way will be shown in the units on logic.

Unit 2 Study Guide and Exercises

Directions After you have read Unit 2 you should be able to tackle the following questions to test your understanding of the main ideas raised in the unit.

1 You should understand these terms and concepts from this unit:

sentence	declarative sentence
utterance	interrogative sentence
proposition	imperative sentence

2 Is semantics concerned only with complete sentences? Explain.

3 Indicate the conventions used in the text to distinguish a **sentence** from an **utterance**. Give an illustration of each.

4 Indicate whether each of the following sentence pairs expresses the **same** or **different** propositions.
   a Mary read the book / The book was read by Mary
   b Fred took back the book / Fred took the book back
   c The cat chased the rat / The cat was chased by the rat
   d The chef cooked the meal / The chef had the meal cooked
   e Hondas are easy to fix / It's easy to fix Hondas

5 Explain the following from the text (p. 22): 'Normally, when a speaker utters a simple declarative sentence, he commits himself to the truth of the corresponding proposition: i.e. he asserts the proposition. By uttering a simple interrogative or imperative, a speaker can mention a particular proposition, without asserting its truth.'

6 In each of the following, indicate whether a proposition is asserted or not.
   a John left yesterday
   b Did John leave yesterday?
   c Can John leave this afternoon?
   d John, get out of here
   e John!

7 Decide whether each pair of sentences below has the same or different propositional content. If they have the same propositional content, identify the proposition that they both share.
   a Can John have some cake? / John has some cake
   b Take out the garbage / You will take out the garbage
   c Can you pass the salt? / The salt shaker is nearly empty

8 Utterances can be loud or quiet, in a particular regional accent, and in a particular language. Can you think of other characteristics of utterances?

UNIT 3 REFERENCE AND SENSE

Entry requirements SENTENCES, UTTERANCES, and PROPOSITIONS (Unit 2). If you feel you understand these notions, take the entry test below.

Entry test Answer the following:

(1) State which of the following represents an utterance (*U*) and which a sentence *S*):

John sang wonderfully last night	*S / U*
'John sang wonderfully last night'	*S / U*

(2) Can a sentence be true or false? *Yes / No*

(3) Is an utterance tied to a particular time and place? *Yes / No*

(4) Is a sentence tied to a particular time and place? *Yes / No*

(5) Can a proposition be said to be in any particular language? *Yes / No*

(6) Can an utterance be true or false? *Yes / No*

Feedback (1) S, U (2) Yes (3) Yes (4) No (5) No (6) Yes
If you have scored less than 5 correct out of 6, you should review Unit 2.
If you have scored at least 5 correct out of 6, continue to the introduction.

Introduction This unit explains some further basic notions in semantics. It is important that you master these notions from the outset as they will keep recurring throughout the course.

Comment On this page and the following ones, you will learn the difference between two quite distinct ways of talking about the meaning of words and other expressions. In talking of sense, we deal with relationships inside the language; in talking of reference we deal with the relationships between language and the world.

Definition By means of reference, a speaker indicates which things in the world (including persons) are being talked about.

Example 'My son is in the beech tree'

identifies   identifies
person   thing

26

As a further example, the second and third words of the 'comment' paragraph above form the phrase *this page*. The phrase *this page* is a part of the English language. The phrase, when it was used in the 'comment' paragraph above, actually identified a particular sheet of paper, something that you could take between your finger and thumb, a little part of the world. The actual page, the sheet of paper, is not a part of the English language, since languages are not made of pieces of paper.

Comment   So we have two things: the English expression *this page* (part of the language) and the thing you could hold between your finger and thumb (part of the world). We call the relationship between them 'reference'. That is, in the previous 'comment' paragraph, *this page* refers to the physical sheet of paper numbered 26.

Practice   Before answering these questions you should carry out the following simple instruction:

touch your left ear.

(1)   Write down the last three words in the above instruction.

....

(2)   Is the thing you touched a part of the world or a part of the language?

....

(3)   Is your answer to (1) a part of the language?   *Yes / No*

(4)   If you say to your mother 'There's a wasp on your left ear', does 'your left ear' here refer to the thing you touched in response to a previous question?   *Yes / No*

Feedback   (1) your left ear (2) A part of the world, languages do not have ears.
(3) Yes (4) No, it refers to your mother's left ear.

Comment   In the present circumstances, *your left ear* refers to the thing you touched in response to (1) above. We say that your left ear is the referent of the phrase *your left ear*: reference is a relationship between parts of a language and things outside the language (in the world).

The same expression can, in some cases, be used to refer to different things. There are as many potential referents for the phrase *your left ear* as there are people in the world with left ears. Likewise there are as many potential referents for the phrase *this page* as there are pages in the world. Thus some (in fact very many) expressions in a language can have variable reference.

Practice (1) What would be the referent of the phrase *the present President of the United States* used:

(a) in 2007?...

(b) in 1996?...

(2) Therefore we can say that the phrase *the present President of the United States* has

....

(3) What would be the referent of the phrase *the President of the United States* used in a conversation about:

(a) United States politics in 2007? ....

(b) United States politics in 1996? ....

(4) In the light of the preceding questions, does the reference of an expression vary according to (a) the circumstances (time, place, etc.) in which the expression is used, or (b) the topic of the conversation in which the expression is used, or (c) both (a) and (b)? Circle your choice.

Feedback (1) (a) George W. Bush (b) Bill Clinton (2) variable reference (3)(a) George W. Bush (b) Bill Clinton (4) (c)

Comment There are cases of expressions which in normal everyday conversation never refer to different things, i.e. in most everyday situations that one can envisage, have constant reference.

Practice Imagine two different everyday situations in which separate couples are having separate conversations about what they refer to with the phrase *the moon*.

(1) Would they be talking about the same object (i.e. does *the moon* normally have constant reference)?   *Yes / No*

(2) Does *The People's Republic of China* normally have constant reference?   *Yes / No*

(3) Does *Angola* normally have constant reference?   *Yes / No*

(4) Does *Halley's Comet* normally have constant reference?   *Yes / No*

Feedback (1) Yes (2) Yes (3) Yes (4) Yes

Comment In fact, there is very little constancy of reference in language. In everyday discourse almost all of the fixing of reference comes from the context in which expressions are used. Two different expressions can have the same referent. The classic example is *the Morning Star* and *the Evening Star*, both of which normally refer to the planet Venus.

Practice   (1) In a conversation about the United States of America in 2007 can *the President* and the *Leader of the Republican Party* have the same referent?   *Yes / No*

(2) If we are talking about a situation in which John is standing alone in the corner, can *John* have the same referent as *the person in the corner?*   *Yes / No*

Feedback   (1) Yes (2) Yes

Definition   To turn from reference to sense, the SENSE of an expression is its place in a system of semantic relationships with other expressions in the language. The first of these semantic relationships that we will mention is sameness of meaning, an intuitive concept which we will illustrate by example. We will deal first with the senses of words in context.

Practice   Say whether the pairs of words in the curly brackets in the sentences below have approximately the same meaning (*S*) or a different meaning (*D*).

(1) *I* $\left\{ \begin{array}{l} almost \\ nearly \end{array} \right\}$ *fell over*   *S / D*

(2) *It is* $\left\{ \begin{array}{l} likely \\ probable \end{array} \right\}$ *that Raymond will be here tomorrow*   *S / D*

(3) *Your gatepost doesn't seem to be quite* $\left\{ \begin{array}{l} vertical \\ upright \end{array} \right\}$ *S / D*

(4) *He painted the fireplace* $\left\{ \begin{array}{l} aquamarine \\ vermilion \end{array} \right\}$ *S / D*

(5) *I'll see you on* $\left\{ \begin{array}{l} Wednesday \\ Thursday \end{array} \right\}$ *S / D*

Feedback   (1) S (2) S (3) S (4) D (5) D

Comment   We can talk about the sense, not only of words, but also of longer expressions such as phrases and sentences.

Practice   Intuitively, do the following pairs mean the same or nearly the same thing?

(1) *Rupert took off his jacket*
Rupert took his jacket off   *Yes / No*

(2) *Harriet wrote the answer down*
Harriet wrote down the answer   *Yes / No*

(3) *Bachelors prefer redheads*
Girls with red hair are preferred by unmarried men   *Yes / No*

Feedback   (1) Yes (2) Yes (3) Yes (You may not have agreed, but it's not too important, as we are dealing with a quite rough-and-ready concept at this stage. Try to see the ways our answers fit the questions.)

Comment   In some cases, the same word can have more than one sense.

Practice   Does the word *bank* have the same meaning in the following sentence
pairs?

(1) *I have an account at the Bank of Scotland*
We steered the raft to the other bank of the river   Yes / No

(2) *The DC-10 banked sharply to avoid a crash*
I banked the furnace up with coke last night   Yes / No

Feedback   (1) No (2) No, we say that *bank* has a number of different senses
(at least 4).

Comment   We use the term 'word' here in the sense of 'word-form'. That is, we find it
convenient to treat anything spelled with the same sequence of letters and
pronounced with the same sequence of phonemes (distinctive sounds) in a
standard dialect as being the same word. Thus, for example, we treat *bank*
in the practice above as a single word with many senses. This is the way
most non-semanticists use the term 'word'. We mention this because some
semanticists, including almost all compilers of dictionaries, would regard
bank, for example, as several different words. In an ordinary dictionary
there are several different entries for the word *bank*, sometimes distinguished
by a subscript, e.g. $bank_1$, $bank_2$, etc. No confusion will arise from our
relatively non-technical use of the term 'word'. This matter will be taken
up again in a later unit, when we discuss HOMONYMY and POLYSEMY
(Unit 11).

One sentence can have different senses too, as the following practice
section illustrates.

Practice   (1) Write down two sentences bringing out clearly the two different
meanings of *The chicken is ready to eat.*

....

....

(2) Write down two sentences bringing out clearly the two different senses
of *He greeted the girl with a smile.*

....

....

(3) Do likewise for *He turned over the field.*

....

....

Feedback   (1) The chicken is ready to be eaten vs The chicken is ready to eat something (2) Smiling, he greeted the girl vs He greeted the smiling girl (3) He changed direction over the field vs He turned the field over (where *he* = a pilot or *he* = a ploughman or a farmer)

Comment   On the relationship between sense and reference: the referent of an expression is often a thing or a person in the world; whereas the sense of an expression is not a thing at all. In fact, it is difficult to say what sort of entity the sense of an expression is. Intuitively, it is sometimes useful to think of sense as that part of the meaning of an expression that is left over when reference is factored out. It is much easier to say whether or not two expressions have the same sense. (Like being able to say that two people are in the same place without being able to say where they are.) The sense of an expression is an abstraction, but it is helpful to note that it is an abstraction that can be entertained in the mind of a language user. When a person understands fully what is said to him, it is reasonable to say that he grasps the sense of the expressions he hears.

Rule   Every expression that has meaning has sense, but not every expression has reference.

Practice   Do the following words refer to things in the world?

(1) *almost*   Yes / No

(2) *probable*   Yes / No

(3) *and*   Yes / No

(4) *if*   Yes / No

(5) *above*   Yes / No

Feedback   None of the above words refers to a thing in the world. Nevertheless all these words, *almost, probable, and, if,* and *above* have some sense.

Practice   (1) When you look up the meaning of a word in a dictionary, what do you find there, its referent, or an expression with the same sense?

....

(2) Is a dictionary full of words or full of things, like a box or a sack?

....

(3) Could a foreigner learn the meanings of his very first words of English by having their typical referents pointed out to him?   Yes / No

(4) Could a foreigner learn the meanings of his very first words of English by looking them up in an English dictionary?   Yes / No

31

Feedback (1) an expression with the same sense (2) full of words (3) Yes (4) No

Comment   There is something essentially circular about the set of definitions in a
          dictionary. Similarly, defining the senses of words and other expressions
          often has something of this circular nature. This is not necessarily a bad
          thing, and in any case it is often unavoidable, since in many cases (e.g. cases
          of expressions that have no referents: *and*, etc.) there is no way of indicating
          the meaning of an expression except with other words.

          Just as there is something grammatically complete about a whole
          sentence, as opposed to a smaller expression such as a phrase or a single
          word, there is something semantically complete about a proposition, as
          opposed to the sense of a phrase or single word. One might say, roughly,
          that a proposition corresponds to a complete independent thought.

Practice Are the senses of the following expressions propositions?

          (1) *Johnny has got a new teacher*   *Yes / No*

          (2) *A new teacher* (not understood as an elliptical
               sentence-fragment)   *Yes / No*

          (3) *Johnny* (not understood as an elliptical sentence-fragment)   *Yes / No*

          (4) *This is the house that Jack built*   *Yes / No*

Feedback (1) Yes (2) No (3) No (4) Yes

Comment   To the extent that perfect translation between languages is possible (and this
          is a very debatable point, as mentioned earlier), essentially the same sense can
          be said to belong to expressions in different languages.

Practice (1) Do *M. Berger s'est rasé ce matin* and *M. Berger shaved
               himself this morning* express the same proposition?   *Yes / No*

          (2) Do the two sentences in (1) have the same sense?   *Yes / No*

          (3) Do the expressions *ce matin* and *this morning* have the
               same sense?   *Yes / No*

          (4) Do the expressions *s'est rasé* and *shaved himself*
               have the same sense?   *Yes / No*

          (5) Does *ein unverheirateter Mann* have the same sense
               as *an unmarried man*?   *Yes / No*

Feedback (1) Yes, perhaps. One might well object, however, that *s'est rasé* in French
          is not a perfect translation of *shaved*, since it could also be rendered as *has
          shaved*. (2) Yes, with the same reservations as for question (1). (3) Yes
          (4) Perhaps (5) Yes, assuming that *unverheiratet* in German has essentially
          the same meaning as *unmarried* in English.

Comment   Just as one can talk of the same sense in different languages, so one can talk of expressions in different dialects of one language as having the same sense.

Practice   (1)   Do *pavement* in British English and *sidewalk* in
American English have the same sense?   *Yes / No*

(2)   Do *pal* and *chum* have the same sense?   *Yes / No*

(3)   Can expressions with entirely different social connotations have the same sense? For example, can the following have the same sense?
People walking in close spatio-temporal proximity
People walking near each other   *Yes / No*

Feedback   (1) Yes (2) Yes (3) Yes

Comment   The relationship between reference and utterance is not so direct as that between sense and proposition, but there is a similarity worth pointing out. Both referring and uttering are acts performed by particular speakers on particular occasions.

Practice   Imagine that a friend of yours says to you, 'John is putting on weight these days', and imagine that a friend of ours (i.e. the authors of this book) happens to utter the same sentence to us one day.

(1)   Would this be a case of one utterance or two?

....

(2)   Would the John referred to be the same John or two different Johns?

....

Feedback   (1) two (2) almost certainly, two different Johns

Comment   In the two separate utterances above, there are two separate acts of referring. In fact, most utterances contain, or are accompanied by, one or more acts of referring. An act of referring is the picking out of a particular referent by a speaker in the course of a particular utterance.

Although the concept of reference is fundamentally related to utterances, in that acts of reference only actually happen in the course of utterances, we will find it useful to stretch a point and talk about reference in connection with sentences, or parts of sentences. What we are really doing in cases like this is imagining a potential utterance of the sentence or expression in question.

In everyday conversation the words *meaning, means, mean, meant*, etc. are sometimes used to indicate reference and sometimes to indicate sense.

Practice   What is intended by the word *mean, meaning*, etc. in the following examples, reference (*R*) or sense (*S*)?

(1) When Helen mentioned 'the fruit cake', she meant that
     rock-hard object in the middle of the table   *R / S*

(2) When Albert talks about 'his former friend' he means me   *R / S*

(3) Daddy, what does *unique* mean?   *R / S*

(4) *Purchase* has the same meaning as *buy*   *R / S*

(5) Look up the meaning of *apoplexy* in your dictionary   *R / S*

(6) If you look out of the window now, you'll see who I mean   *R / S*

Feedback   (1) R (2) R (3) S (4) S (5) S (6) R

Comment   The study of sense demands, as you may have noticed, a degree of idealization of the facts about meaning. In other words, sometimes we claim to be more certain than we perhaps should be about questions like 'Does this expression have the same sense as that one?' It is worth going along with this idealization. We will not let it lead us astray unduly. In later units we will deal with some problems with the notion of sense.

Summary   The notions of sense and reference are central to the study of meaning. Every further unit in this book will make use of one or another of these notions. The idea of reference is relatively solid and easy to understand. The idea of sense is more elusive: it's a bit like electricity, which we all know how to use (and even talk about) in various ways, without ever being sure what exactly it is. Even semanticists aren't sure exactly what sense is, but you'll find that your grasp of it and your appreciation of the usefulness of the concept will grow as you study more. (The importance of the sense/reference distinction was most influentially demonstrated by the German philosopher Gottlob Frege.)

Unit 3 Study Guide and Exercises

Directions   After you have read Unit 3 you should be able to tackle the following questions to test your understanding of the main ideas raised in the unit.

1 You should understand these terms and concepts from this unit:

   sense   context
   reference   dialect
   referent   proposition

2 Can different expressions have the same referent? Give an example not found in this unit.

3 Can the same expression have different referents? Give an example not found in this unit.

4 Give an example of an expression not found in this unit that has an invariable referent and of one that has no referent.

5 Explain this sentence from this unit in your own words: 'Every expression that has meaning has sense, but not every expression has reference'.

6 Characterize a typical dictionary definition of a word. Does the definition include everything a typical native speaker knows about the word's meaning? Is it possible to write such an entry which is complete?

Comment on the following examples, making reference to concepts introduced in this unit.

7 *the Evening Star / the Morning Star*

8 *the President of the United States / the Commander-in-Chief / the Leader of the Republican Party*

9 *Visiting relatives can be boring*

10 *the planet Mars*

11 *Smoking grass can be dangerous*

2 From reference . . .

UNIT 4 REFERRING EXPRESSIONS

Entry requirements REFERENCE and SENSE (Unit 3). If you feel you understand these notions, take the entry test below. If not, review Unit 3 before continuing.

Entry test Answer the following questions:

(1) Give an example of an expression that might be used to refer to the President of the United States in 2007.

....

(2) Give an example of an expression that could have variable reference.

....

(3) Give an example of an expression that always (in normal everyday conversation) has constant reference.

....

(4) Give an example of different expressions having one referent.

....

(5) Give an example of an expression that has no reference.

....

(6) Which of the following is a correct description of 'reference'? Circle your choice.
   (a) a relationship between expressions and other expressions which have the same meaning
   (b) the set of all objects which can potentially be referred to by an expression
   (c) a relationship between a particular object in the world and an expression used in an utterance to pick that object out

Feedback (1) George W. Bush, the former Governor of Texas, etc. (2) *my car, this page*, etc. (3) *England, the sun*, etc. (4) *the Morning Star* and *the Evening Star*, etc. (5) *and, if*, etc. (6)(c)

If you got at least 5 out of 6 correct, continue to the introduction. Otherwise, review Unit 3 before proceeding.

Introduction   In this unit we develop the notion of reference (introduced in Unit 3), and consider more closely the range of expressions that speakers may use to refer to some object or person in the world. We will see that some expressions can only be used as referring expressions, some never can, and some expressions can be used to refer or not, depending on the kind of sentence they occur in. We introduce a notion (equative sentence) that is closely bound up with the idea of referring expressions.

Definition   A REFERRING EXPRESSION is any expression used in an utterance to refer to something or someone (or a clearly delimited collection of things or people), i.e. used with a particular referent in mind.

Example   The name *Fred* in an utterance such as 'Fred hit me', where the speaker has a particular person in mind when he says 'Fred', is a referring expression.

     Fred in 'There's no Fred at this address' is not a referring expression, because in this case a speaker would not have a particular person in mind in uttering the word.

Practice   Could the following possibly be used as referring expressions? Circle the answer of your choice.

(1)	*John*	*Yes / No*
(2)	*My uncle*	*Yes / No*
(3)	*and*	*Yes / No*
(4)	*the girl sitting on the wall by the bus stop*	*Yes / No*
(5)	*a man*	*Yes / No*
(6)	*my parents*	*Yes / No*
(7)	*send*	*Yes / No*
(8)	*under*	*Yes / No*

Feedback   (1) Yes (2) Yes (3) No (4) Yes (5) Yes, as in 'A man was in here looking for you'. (6) Yes (*My parents* refers to a pair of things. For convenience at this point we use the idea of reference to include clearly delimited collections of things.) (7) No (8) No

Comment   The same expression can be a referring expression or not (or, as some would put it, may or may not have a 'referring interpretation'), depending on the context. This is true of indefinite noun phrases.

Practice   (1)   When a speaker says, 'A man was in here looking for you last night' is *a man* being used to refer to a particular man?   *Yes / No*

        (2)   So, in the above example, is *a man* a referring expression?   *Yes / No*

37

(3)   When a speaker says, 'The first sign of the monsoon is
a cloud on the horizon no bigger than a man's hand', is
a man being used to refer to a particular man?   *Yes / No*

(4)   Is *a man* in this example a referring expression?   *Yes / No*

(5)   Is *forty buses*, used in 'Forty buses have been withdrawn from
service by the Liverpool Corporation', a referring expression?   *Yes / No*

(6)   Is *forty buses*, used in 'This engine has the power of forty
buses', a referring expression?   *Yes / No*

Feedback   (1) Yes (2) Yes (3) No (4) No (5) Yes, assuming that the speaker has 40 specific buses in mind (6) No

Comment   In the above examples the linguistic context often gave a vital clue as to whether the indefinite noun phrase was a referring expression or not. But it does not always give a clear indication.

Practice   Are the following referring expressions? (Imagine normal circumstances for the utterance.)

(1)   *a Norwegian*, used in 'Nancy married a Norwegian'   *Yes / No*

(2)   *a Norwegian*, used in 'Nancy wants to marry a Norwegian'   *Yes / No*

(3)   *a car*, used in 'John is looking for a car'   *Yes / No*

(4)   *a man with a limp*, used in 'Dick believes that a man
with a limp killed Bo Peep'   *Yes / No*

(5)   *a man with a limp*, used in 'A man with a limp killed Bo Peep'   *Yes / No*

(6)   *a swan*, used in 'Every evening at sunset a swan flew
over the house'   *Yes / No*

Feedback   (1) Yes (2) Yes and No: the sentence is ambiguous. It depends on whether the speaker has in mind a particular person whom Nancy wants to marry. (3) Yes and No: the sentence is ambiguous. It depends on whether the speaker has a particular car in mind. (4) Yes and No (5) Yes, it can be. (6) Yes and No

Comment   All of the ambiguities in the above examples could in fact be resolved by the use of the word *certain* immediately following the indefinite article *a*, as in, for example: 'Nancy wants to marry a certain Norwegian' or 'John is looking for a certain car'.

All of the above examples involve indefinite noun phrases. It is clear that, given our definitions, which allude to what is in the mind of the speaker on a particular occasion of utterance, indefinite noun phrases can be referring expressions. Other definitions could yield different results. What the above examples show is that, in our terms, whether an expression is a referring expression is heavily dependent on linguistic context and on circumstances of utterance.

We turn now to the case of definite noun phrases.

Practice   Are the following referring expressions? (Imagine normal circumstances for the utterances.)

(1) *John* in 'John is my best friend'   *Yes / No*

(2) *he* in 'He's a very polite man', said by a husband to his
     wife in a conversation about their bank manager   *Yes / No*

(3) *it* in 'It's sinking!' used in a conversation about a battleship
     which has just been attacked   *Yes / No*

(4) *the man who shot Abraham Lincoln* in 'The man who shot
     Abraham Lincoln was an unemployed actor'   *Yes / No*

Feedback   (1) Yes (2) Yes (3) Yes (4) Yes

Comment   These straightforward examples show how definite noun phrases of various kinds, proper names (e.g. *John*), personal pronouns (e.g. *he*, *it*), and longer descriptive expressions (as in question (4)) can all be used as referring expressions. Indeed, definite noun phrases such as these most frequently are used as referring expressions. But, even with definite noun phrases, there are examples in which they are not (or not clearly) referring expressions.

Practice   Are the following expressions referring expressions?

(1) *he* in 'If anyone ever marries Nancy, he's in for a bad time'
     (meaning that whoever marries Nancy is in for a bad time)   *Yes / No*

(2) *it* in 'Every man who owns a donkey beats it'   *Yes / No*

(3) *the person who did this* in 'The person who did this
     must be insane', spoken by someone on discovering a
     brutally mutilated corpse, where the speaker has no
     idea who committed the crime   *Yes / No*

(4) *Smith's murderer* in 'Smith's murderer must be insane', uttered
     in circumstances like the above, where the corpse is Smith's   *Yes / No*

Feedback   (1) No, the speaker has no particular individual in mind as Nancy's possible future husband. (2) No, *it* doesn't refer to any particular donkey here. (3) Not such a clear case, but it could be argued that *the person who did this* is not a referring expression in this example. (4) Similarly, an unclear case, but again it could be argued that *Smith's murderer* is not a referring expression here.

Comment Such examples show that the notion 'referring expression' is not always easy
to apply. Part of the difficulty encountered in the last two examples stems
from the fact that it is not clear what we mean when we say that a speaker
must have a particular individual in mind in order to refer. We shall not try
to resolve this issue here. But note that in the case of definite noun phrases
also, the question of whether they are used as referring expressions is very
much dependent on the context and circumstances of use.

We now move to a different topic, starting with consideration of definite
noun phrases, but linking eventually with some of the previous examples
involving indefinite noun phrases.

Practice (1) Would the phrase *the President of the United States* used in a
conversation about American politics in 2007 have the same
referent as the expression *the Leader of the Republican Party*
in the same conversation?   *Yes / No*

(2) Take the schematic utterance 'X hasn't a hope of winning
the next election'. If we replace X by either 'the President'
or 'the Leader of the Republican Party', will the two
resultant utterances be equivalent in meaning, i.e. both
describe exactly the same state of affairs? (Assume still the
context of a conversation about American politics in 2007.)   *Yes / No*

(3) Assume a situation in which John is standing alone in
the corner. Would *John* and *the person in the corner* refer
to the same individual in a conversation about this situation?   *Yes / No*

(4) In the conversation about the situation in which John
is alone in the corner, would the following two utterances
make exactly the same claim?

'John looks as if he's about to faint'

'The person in the corner looks as if he's about to faint'   *Yes / No*

Feedback (1) Yes (2) Yes (3) Yes (4) Yes

Comment Normally, one expects that utterances which differ only in that they use
different expressions referring to the same thing (or person) will have the
same meaning, as in the above examples. Indeed, this normally is the case.
But there is a class of exceptions to this generalization. This is the class of
examples involving opaque contexts.

Definition An OPAQUE CONTEXT is a part of a sentence which could be made into a
complete sentence by the addition of a referring expression, but where the
addition of different referring expressions, even though they refer to the same
thing or person, in a given situation, will yield sentences with DIFFERENT
meanings when uttered in a given situation.

Example The incomplete sentence *Laura Bush thinks that . . . is a genius* constitutes an opaque context, because, even in a conversation about American politics in 2007, the following two utterances would make different claims:

A: 'Laura Bush thinks that the President is a genius'
B: 'Laura Bush thinks that the Leader of the Republican Party is a genius'

If, for example, Laura Bush believes erroneously that the President is not the Leader of the Republican Party, then A and B will mean different things.

Practice (1) In a conversation about a situation where John is standing alone in the corner, do 'John' and 'the person in the corner' have the same referent? *Yes / No*

(2) Consider the following two utterances:
'Dick believes that John killed Smith'
'Dick believes that the person in the corner killed Smith'

Assume that Dick does not know that John is the person in the corner; could one of these two utterances be true and the other false? *Yes / No*

(3) Is *Dick believes that . . . killed Smith* an opaque context? *Yes / No*

(4) The Morning Star is the Evening Star: they are both in fact the planet Venus. Assuming that Nancy does not know this, do the following make the same claim about Nancy's wishes?
'Nancy wants to get married when the Morning Star is in the sky'
'Nancy wants to get married when the Evening Star is in the sky' *Yes / No*

(5) Is *Nancy wants to get married when . . . is in the sky* an opaque context? *Yes / No*

(6) Imagine a situation in which the last banana on the table is the prize in a game of charades, but that Gary, who came late to the party, is not aware of this. Do the following make the same claim in this situation?
'Gary took the last banana'
'Gary took the prize' *Yes / No*

(7) Is *Gary took . . .* an opaque context? *Yes / No*

Feedback (1) Yes (2) Yes (3) Yes (4) No (5) Yes (6) Yes (7) No

Comment The term 'opaque' is especially appropriate because these contexts seem to 'block our view' through them to the referential interpretations of referring expressions.

Notice that opaque contexts typically involve a certain kind of verb, like *want, believe, think,* and *wonder about.* Note that it was often in the context of such opacity-creating verbs that indefinite noun phrases could be ambiguous between a referring and a non-referring interpretation, as in 'Nancy wants to marry a Norwegian'.

Turning away now from the question of opacity, and back to the more basic notion of referring expressions, we define a further notion, that of equative sentence.

Definition An EQUATIVE SENTENCE is one which is used to assert the identity of the referents of two referring expressions, i.e. to assert that two referring expressions have the same referent.

Example The following are equative sentences:
Tony Blair is the Prime Minister
That woman over there is my daughter's teacher

Practice Are the following equative sentences?

(1)	*John is the person in the corner*	Yes / No
(2)	*Henry the Eighth is the current President of the USA*	Yes / No
(3)	*Cairo is not the largest city in Africa*	Yes / No
(4)	*Cairo is a large city*	Yes / No
(5)	*Dr Jekyll is Mr Hyde*	Yes / No
(6)	*Ted is an idiot*	Yes / No

Feedback (1) Yes (2) Yes, equative sentences can be false. (3) No (4) No, this sentence does not state identity of reference. (5) Yes (6) No

Comment A feature of many equative sentences is that the order of the two referring expressions can be reversed without loss of acceptability.

Example *The largest city in Africa is Cairo*
Cairo is the largest city in Africa

Comment The 'reversal test' applied here is not a perfect diagnostic for equative sentences, however. In *What I need is a pint of Guinness, a pint of Guinness* is not a referring expression, because a user of this sentence would not have any particular pint of Guinness in mind, but the sentence is nevertheless reversible, as in *A pint of Guinness is what I need*. And the sentence *That is the man who kidnapped my boss* definitely is equative, but it is not reversible, as *The man who kidnapped my boss is that* is unacceptable.

Summary At first sight the notion of reference as a relation between expressions used in utterances and people and objects in the world seems straightforward enough. But stating simple generalizations about when an expression is actually a referring expression and when it is not, is, to say the least, difficult. Both indefinite and definite noun phrases can be ambiguous between referring and non-referring interpretations, with the appropriate interpretation being highly dependent on linguistic context (i.e. the surrounding words) and the circumstances of the utterance. The existence of opaque contexts also provides interesting complications to the contribution of referring expressions to meaning.

Unit 4 Study Guide and Exercises

Directions After you have read Unit 4 you should be able to tackle the following questions to test your understanding of the main ideas raised in the unit.

1 You should understand these terms and concepts from this unit:
referring expression   opaque context
indefinite noun phrase   equative sentence
definite noun phrase

2 Which of the following could be used as referring expressions? Be able to explain why or why not.
a my table   e or
b a unicorn   f Mary
c no love   g a book
d travel   h Abraham Lincoln

For sentences 3–6 below decide whether the italicized noun phrases are referring expressions or not, and explain why (or why not). If the sentence is ambiguous explain why it is ambiguous.

3 His father married *a dancer*

4 John wants to marry *a dancer*

5 *The whale* is the largest mammal

6 *The man who shot Kennedy* was Lee Harvey Oswald

7 Explain the ambiguity in: *I am looking for a pencil*

8 Create a set of circumstances under which the sentence *Dan believes that . . . signed the bill* is an opaque context. Use the referring expressions *George W. Bush* and *the President of the United States* in your answer.

9 Which of the following are equative sentences? Explain why.
a Fred is the man with the gun
b William the Conqueror is the current King of England
c Detroit is a nearby city
d Mary is a genius
e A box of cookies is what I would like
f Detroit is not the largest city in the USA

10 Consider the sentence *It's a tree*. Assume that this sentence is uttered by a particular person on a particular occasion to pick out a particular tree. Briefly explain how each of the following technical terms introduced so far in this book apply to the utterance of this example sentence: sentence, utterance, reference, referent.

UNIT 5 PREDICATES

Entry requirements REFERENCE and SENSE (Unit 3) and REFERRING EXPRESSIONS (Unit 4).
If you feel you understand these notions, take the entry test below. If not, review Units 3 and 4.

Entry test (1) Which of the following is the phrase a *tall tree*? Circle your answer.
  (a) a referring expression
  (b) not a referring expression
  (c) sometimes a referring expression and sometimes not, depending on context and circumstances of use

(2) Is the following statement correct (*Yes*) or incorrect (*No*)?
Whether a sentence contains any referring expressions or not
depends on the time and place at which the sentence occurs.   *Yes / No*

(3) Which of the following sentences is equative? Circle your answer.
  (a) *Mahmoud is an Egyptian*
  (b) *I was telling you about Mahmoud the Egyptian*
  (c) *Mahmoud is the Egyptian I was telling you about*
  (d) *Mahmoud is a genius*

(4) Does *if* have sense in the same way that *dog* has sense?   *Yes / No*

(5) Do the expressions *big* and *large* have essentially the same
sense in the following sentences?
I live in a big house
I live in a large house   *Yes / No*

(6) Circle those of the following words which can be referring
expressions (in normal everyday English).
John, below, Venus, swims, round, beautiful, under, went.

Feedback (1)(c) (2) No: replace 'sentence' by 'utterance' to get a correct statement.
(3) (c) (4) No (5) Yes (6) *John, Venus*
If you have scored less than 5 correct out of 6, you should review the relevant
unit. If you have scored at least 5 correct out of 6, continue to the introduction.

Introduction We start by examining the semantic structure of simple declarative sentences,
such as *My dog bit the postman* or *Mrs Wraith is waiting for the downtown*

bus. Typically such sentences contain one or more referring expressions, plus some other words that do not form part of any of the referring expressions. It is on these other words that we shall now concentrate.

Practice   In the following sentences, delete the referring expressions and write down the remainder to the right of the example. We have done the first one for you.

(1) *My dog bit the postman* .... *bit*

(2) *Mrs Wraith is writing the Mayor's speech* ....

(3) *Cairo is in Africa* ....

(4) *Edinburgh is between Aberdeen and York* ....

(5) *This place stinks* ....

(6) *John's car is red* ....

(7) *Einstein was a genius* ....

Feedback
(2) *Mrs Wraith is writing the Mayor's speech*	*is writing*
(3) *Cairo is in Africa*	*is in*
(4) *Edinburgh is between Aberdeen and York*	*is between, and*
(5) *This place stinks*	*stinks*
(6) *John's car is red*	*is red*
(7) *Einstein was a genius*	*was a genius*

Comment   The 'remainders' written in the right-hand column are quite a varied set. But in each case it is possible to discern one word (or part of a word) which 'carries more meaning' than the others. For instance, *write* in example (2) carries more specific information than *is* and the suffix *-ing*. If one strips away such less meaningful elements, one is left with a sequence of words, which, though ungrammatical and inelegant, can still be understood as expressing a proposition. The result is a kind of 'Tarzan jungle talk', e.g. *Boy bad* for *The boy is bad*, or *Woman write speech* for *The woman is writing the speech*.

Practice   Listed below are the remainders from the above examples. In each case, write down the single word (or part of a word) which carries the most specific information. We have done the first one for you.

(1) *is writing* .... *write*

(2) *is in* ....

(3) *is between, and* ....

(4) *stinks* ....

(5) *is red* ....

(6) *was a genius* ....

Feedback (2) *in* (3) *between* (4) *stink* (5) *red* (6) *genius*

Comment   The words we have just isolated from their original sentences we call the predicators of those sentences.

Definition   The PREDICATOR of a simple declarative sentence is the word (sometimes a
(partial)   group of words) which does not belong to any of the referring expressions and which, of the remainder, makes the most specific contribution to the meaning of the sentence. Intuitively speaking, the predicator describes the state or process in which the referring expressions are involved.

Example   *asleep* is the predicator in *Mummy is asleep* and describes the state *Mummy* is in.
love is the predicator in *The white man loved the Indian maiden* and describes the process in which the two referring expressions *the white man* and *the Indian maiden* are involved.
wait for is the predicator in *Jimmy was waiting for the downtown bus* and describes the process involving *Jimmy* and *the downtown bus*.

Comment   Note that some of the elements that we have stripped away in isolating the predicator of a sentence do carry a certain amount of meaning. Thus the indicators of past and present tense are clearly meaningful. The semantics of tense is interesting, but its contribution to the meaning of a sentence is of a different type from the contribution made by the predicator, and will not be pursued here. Notice also that the verb *be* in its various forms (*is, was, are, were, am*) is not the predicator in any example sentence that we have seen so far.

Practice   Strip away referring expressions and the verb *be* (and possibly other elements) to identify the predicators in the following sentences:

(1)   *I am hungry*   ....

(2)   *Joe is in San Francisco*   ....

(3)   *The Mayor is a crook*   ....

(4)   *The man who lives at number 10 Lee Crescent is whimsical*   ....

(5)   *The Royal Scottish Museum is behind Old College*   ....

Feedback   (1) *hungry* (2) *in* (3) *crook* (4) *whimsical* (5) *behind*

Comment   The predicators in sentences can be of various parts of speech: adjectives (*red, asleep, hungry, whimsical*), verbs (*write, stink, place*), prepositions (*in, between, behind*), and nouns (*crook, genius*). Despite the obvious syntactic differences between these different types of words, semantically they all share the property of being able to function as the predicators of sentences. Words of other parts of speech, such as conjunctions (*and, but, or*) and articles (*the, a*), cannot serve as predicators in sentences.

47

The semantic analysis of simple declarative sentences reveals two major semantic roles played by different subparts of the sentence. These are the role of predicator, illustrated above, and the role(s) of argument(s), played by the referring expression(s).

Example   *Juan is Argentinian*   predicator: *Argentinian*, argument: *Juan*
Juan arrested Pablo   predicator: *arrest*, arguments: *Juan, Pablo*
Juan took Pablo to Rio   predicator: *take*, arguments: *Juan, Pablo, Rio*

Practice   In the following sentences, indicate the predicators and arguments as in the above examples:

(1)   *Dennis is a menace*

       predicator: ....   argument(s): ....

(2)   *Fred showed Jane his BMW*

       Predicator: ....   argument(s): ....

(3)   *Donald is proud of his family*

       predicator: ....   argument(s): ....

(4)   *The hospital is outside the city*

       predicator: ....   argument(s): ....

Feedback   (1) pred: *menace*, arg: *Dennis* (2) pred: *show*, args: *Fred, Jane, his BMW*
(3) pred: *proud*, args: *Donald, his family* (4) pred: *outside*, args: *the hospital, the city*

Comment   The semantic analysis of a sentence into predicator and argument(s) does not correspond in most cases to the traditional grammatical analysis of a sentence into subject and predicate, although there is some overlap between the semantic and the grammatical analyses, as can be seen from the examples above. We shall be concerned almost exclusively in this book with the semantic analysis of sentences, and so will not make use of the notion 'grammatical predicate (phrase)'. But we will use the term 'predicate' in a semantic sense, to be defined below, developed within Logic.

Definition   A PREDICATE is any word (or sequence of words) which (in a given single sense) can function as the predicator of a sentence.

Example   *hungry, in, crook, asleep, hit, show, bottle,* are all predicates; *and, or, but, not,* are not predicates.

Practice   Are the following predicates?

(1)   *dusty*   *Yes / No*

(2)   *drink*   *Yes / No*

(3)	*woman*	*Yes / No*
(4)	*you*	*Yes / No*
(5)	*Fred*	*Yes / No*
(6)	*about*	*Yes / No*

Feedback (1) Yes (2) Yes (3) Yes (4) No (5) No (6) Yes

Comment The definition of 'predicate' above contained two parenthesized conditions. The first, '(or sequence of words)', is intended to take care of examples like *wait for*, *in front of*, which are longer than one word, but which it seems sensible to analyse as single predicates.

The second parenthesized condition, '(in a given single sense)', is more important, and illustrates a degree of abstractness in the notion of a predicate. A 'word', as we use the term, can be ambiguous, i.e. can have more than one sense, but we use 'predicate' in a way which does not allow a predicate to be ambiguous. A predicate can have only one sense. Normally, the context in which we use a word will make clear what sense (what predicate) we have in mind, but occasionally, we shall resort to the use of subscripts on words to distinguish between different predicates. (We do this especially in Unit 16 'About dictionaries'.)

Example The word *bank* has (at least) two senses. Accordingly, we might speak of the predicates *bank*$_1$ and *bank*$_2$.

Similarly, we might distinguish between the predicates *man*$_1$ (noun) = human being, *man*$_2$ (noun) = male adult human being, and *man*$_3$ (transitive verb) as in *The crew manned the lifeboats.*

Comment Notice that 'predicate' and 'predicator' are terms of quite different sorts. The term 'predicate' identifies elements in the language system, independently of particular example sentences. Thus, it would make sense to envisage a list of the predicates of English, as included, say, in a dictionary. The term 'predicator' identifies the semantic role played by a particular word (or group of words) in a particular sentence. In this way, it is similar to the grammatical term 'subject': one can talk of the subject of a particular sentence, but it makes no sense to talk of a list of 'the subjects of English': similarly, one can talk of the 'predicator' in a particular sentence, but not list 'the predicators of English'. A simple sentence only has one predicator, although it may well contain more than one instance of a predicate.

Example *A tall, handsome stranger entered the saloon*

This sentence has just one predicator, *enter*, but the sentence also contains the words *tall*, *handsome*, *stranger*, and *saloon*, all of which are

49

predicates, and can function as predicators in other sentences, e.g. *John is tall*, *He is handsome*, *He is a stranger*, and *That ramshackle building is a saloon*.

Practice (1) In which of the following sentences does the predicate *male* function as a predicator? Circle your choice.

    (a) *The male gorilla at the zoo had a nasty accident yesterday*

    (b) *The gorilla at the zoo is a male*

    (c) *The gorilla at the zoo is male*

(2) In which of the following sentences does the predicate *human* function as predicator?

    (a) *All humans are mortal*

    (b) *Socrates was human*

    (c) *These bones are human*

Feedback (1) (b), (c) (2) (b), (c)

Comment We turn now to the matter of the degree of predicates.

Definition The DEGREE of a predicate is a number indicating the number of arguments it is normally understood to have in simple sentences.

Example *Asleep* is a predicate of degree one (often called a one-place predicate)
Love (verb) is a predicate of degree two (a two-place predicate)

Practice (1) Are the following sentences acceptable?

    (a) *Thornbury sneezed*   Yes / No

    (b) *Thornbury sneezed a handful of pepper*   Yes / No

    (c) *Thornbury sneezed his wife a handful of pepper*   Yes / No

(2) So is *sneeze* a one-place predicate?   Yes / No

(3) Are the following sentences acceptable in normal usage?

    (a) *Martha hit*   Yes / No

    (b) *Martha hit the sideboard*   Yes / No

    (c) *Martha hit George the sideboard*   Yes / No

(4) So is *hit* a one-place predicate?   Yes / No

(5) Is *die* a one-place predicate?   Yes / No

(6) Is *come* a one-place predicate?   Yes / No

(7) Is *murder* (verb) a one-place predicate?   Yes / No

Feedback (1)(a) Yes (b) No (c) No (2) Yes (3) (a) No (b) Yes (c) No (4) No (5) Yes (6) Yes (7) No

Comment   A verb that is understood most naturally with just two arguments, one as its subject, and one as its object, is a two-place predicate.

Example   In *Martha hit the parrot, hit* is a two-place predicate: it has an argument, *Martha,* as subject and an argument, *the parrot,* as direct object.

Practice   (1)   Are the following sentences acceptable?

        (a)   *Keith made* Yes / No

        (b)   *Keith made this toy guillotine* Yes / No

        (c)   *Keith made this toy guillotine his mother-in-law* Yes / No

    (2)   So is *make* a two-place predicate? Yes / No

    (3)   Is *murder* a two-place predicate? Yes / No

    (4)   Is *see* a two-place predicate? Yes / No

Feedback   (1) (a) No (b) Yes (c) No (2) Yes (3) Yes (4) Yes

Comment   There are a few three-place predicates; the verb *give* is the best example.

Practice   For each of the following sentences, say whether it seems somewhat elliptical (i.e. seems to omit something that one would normally expect to be mentioned). Some of these sentences are more acceptable than others.

    (1)   *Herod gave* Yes / No

    (2)   *Herod gave Salome* Yes / No

    (3)   *Herod gave a nice present* Yes / No

    (4)   *Herod gave Salome a nice present* Yes / No

    (5)   How many referring expressions are there in Sentence (4) ....

Feedback   (1) Yes (2) Yes (3) Yes: one would normally mention the receiver of a present. (4) No (5) three

Comment   We have concentrated so far on predicates that happen to be verbs. Recall examples such as *Cairo is in Africa, Cairo is dusty, Cairo is a large city.* In these examples *in* (a preposition), *dusty* (an adjective), and *city* (a noun) are predicates.

    In the case of prepositions, nouns, and adjectives, we can also talk of one-, two-, or three-place predicates.

Practice   (1)   How many referring expressions are there in
Your marble is under my chair? ....

    (2)   Is *Your marble is under* acceptable in normal usage? Yes / No

    (3)   Is *Your marble is under my chair the carpet* acceptable
in normal usage? Yes / No

(4) So, of what degree is the predicate *under* (i.e. a how-many-
place-predicate is *under*)?   ....

(5) Of what degree is the predicate *near*?   ....

(6) Is *Dundee is between Aberdeen* acceptable?   *Yes / No*

(7) Is *Dundee is between Aberdeen and Edinburgh* acceptable? *Yes / No*

(8) Of what degree is the predicate *between*?   ....

Feedback (1) two (2) No (3) No (4) two (5) two (6) No (7) Yes (8) three

Comment We will now turn our attention to adjectives.

Practice (1) How many referring expressions are there in
Philip is handsome?   ....

(2) Is *Philip is handsome John* (not used when
addressing John) acceptable?   *Yes / No*

(3) Of what degree is the predicate *handsome*?   ....

(4) Of what degree is the predicate *rotten*?   ....

(5) Of what degree is the predicate *smelly*?   ....

Feedback (1) one (2) No (3) one (4) one (5) one

Comment In fact, the majority of adjectives are one-place predicates.

Practice (1) Is *John is afraid of Fido* acceptable?   *Yes / No*

(2) Does *John is afraid* seem elliptical
(i.e. does it seem to leave something unmentioned)?   *Yes / No*

(3) Could *afraid* be called a two-place predicate?   *Yes / No*

(4) Is *Your house is different from mine* acceptable?   *Yes / No*

(5) Does *Your house is different* seem elliptical?   *Yes / No*

(6) Of what degree is the predicate *different*?   ....

(7) Of what degree is the predicate *identical*?   ....

(8) Of what degree is the predicate *similar*?   ....

Feedback (1) Yes (2) Yes (3) Yes (4) Yes (5) Yes (6) two (7) two (8) two

Comment You may have wondered about the role of the prepositions such as *of* and
from in *afraid of* and *different from*. These prepositions are not themselves
predicates. Some adjectives in English just require (grammatically) to be
joined to a following argument by a preposition. Such prepositions are
relatively meaningless linking particles. You might want to think of the
combination of adjective plus linking particle in these cases as a kind of

complex or multi-word predicate with basically one unified meaning. Notice that one can often use different linking prepositions with no change of meaning, e.g. (in some dialects) *different to*, or even *different than*.

We now turn to predicates which are nouns.

Practice   (1) How many referring expressions are there in
John is a corporal?   ....

(2) Is *John is a corporal the army* acceptable?   *Yes / No*

(3) Of what degree is *corporal?*   ....

(4) Of what degree is *hero?*   ....

(5) Of what degree is *crook?*   ....

(6) How many referring expressions are there in
This object is a pitchfork?   ....

(7) Of what degree is *pitchfork?*   ....

Feedback   (1) one (2) No (3) one (4) one (5) one (6) one (7) one

Comment   Most nouns are one-place predicates. But a few nouns could be said to be 'inherently relational'. These are nouns such as *father, son, brother, mother, daughter, neighbour*.

Practice   (1) Does *John is a brother* seem somewhat odd?   *Yes / No*

(2) Is *John is a brother of the Mayor of Miami* acceptable?   *Yes / No*

(3) Could *brother* be called a two-place predicate?   *Yes / No*

(4) Could *sister* be called a two-place predicate?   *Yes / No*

Feedback   (1) Yes, it would be completely acceptable only in a somewhat unusual context. (2) Yes (3) Yes (4) Yes

Comment   Sometimes two predicates can have nearly, if not exactly, the same sense, but be of different grammatical parts of speech. Typically in these cases the corresponding predicates have the same degree, as in the following examples. See if you can determine the degree of the predicates in these sentences.

Example   *Ronald is foolish, Ronald is a fool*
Timothy is afraid of cats, Timothy fears cats
My parrot is a talker, My parrot talks

Comment   We conclude this unit by discussing one special relation, the identity relation. This is the relation found in equative sentences (Unit 4, p. 42). In English, the identity of the referents of two different referring expressions is expressed by a form of the verb *be*.

Example   *George W. Bush is the 43rd President of the United States*
The 43rd President of the United States is George W. Bush

Practice   All of the following sentences contain a variant of the verb *be*. In which sentences does a form of *be* express the identity relation? Circle your choices.

(1)   *This is a spider*

(2)   *This is my father*

(3)   *This is the person I was telling you about at dinner last night*

(4)   *The person I was telling you about at dinner last night is in the next room*

(5)   *The person I was telling you about at dinner last night is the man talking to Harry*

(6)   *The whale is a mammal*

Feedback   The identity relation is expressed by a form of *be* in sentences (2), (3), and (5).

Comment   The identity relation is special because of its very basic role in the communication of information. In English, one must analyse some instances of the verb *be* (e.g. those in sentences (2), (3), (5) above) as instances of the identity predicate. Other instances of the verb *be*, as we have seen, are simply a grammatical device for linking a predicate that is not a verb (i.e. an adjective, preposition, or noun) to its first argument, as in *John is a fool* or *John is foolish*. The verb *be* is also a device for 'carrying' the tense (present or past) of a sentence.

Summary   The predicates of a language have a completely different function from the referring expressions. The roles of these two kinds of meaning-bearing element cannot be exchanged. Thus *John is a bachelor* makes good sense, but *Bachelor is a John* makes no sense at all. Predicates include words from various parts of speech, e.g. common nouns, adjectives, prepositions, and verbs. We have distinguished between predicates of different degrees (one-place, two-place, etc.). The relationship between referring expressions and predicates will be explored further in the next unit.

Unit 5   Study Guide and Exercises

Directions   After you have read Unit 5 you should be able to tackle the following questions to test your understanding of the main ideas raised in the unit.

1   You should understand these terms and concepts from this unit:

predicator	degree of a predicate
predicate	ellipsis (elliptical)
argument	identity relation

2 Indicate the arguments and predicator(s) in each sentence.
  a John is a linguist
  b John loves Mary
  c Mary loves John   (Are arguments ordered?)
  d John gave Mary a ring
  e Chicago is between Los Angeles and New York
  f Jane is Mary's mother
  g Jones is the Dean of the College
  h John stood near the bank
     (How should the ambiguity be handled?)
  i Ed is a fool
  j Ed is foolish

3 Indicate the degree of the predicates used as predicators in each sentence in item 2 above.

4 How does the concept of **predicate** in the semantic sense differ from the concept of **grammatical predicate**? Does one seem to be more revealing than the other?

5 In this unit we said that the prepositions *from* and *of* in the two-part adjectives *different from* and *afraid of* 'are not themselves predicates . . . (and that they) are relatively meaningless linking particles'. Do you agree with this statement? Consider a sentence such as *The letter is from my uncle* before reaching a conclusion.

6 What are the functions of the verb *be* in these sentences (i.e. does it function as an identity predicate or as a grammatical device for linking a non-verbal predicate to its first argument)? Do all instances of *be* carry tense?
  a Mary is happy
  b A tulip is a flower
  c George W. Bush is the US President
  d God is

7 Does it make sense to say that the verb *be* has a meaning of its own, independent of whether it is used as a linking device or as the identity predicate? Speculate about what it could mean, and don't be concerned if your answer is quite abstract. Many lexical items in the world's languages have very abstract meanings.

UNIT 6 PREDICATES, REFERRING EXPRESSIONS, AND UNIVERSE OF DISCOURSE

Entry requirements REFERRING EXPRESSION (Unit 4) and PREDICATE (Unit 5). If you feel you understand these notions, take the entry test below. Otherwise, review Units 4 and 5.

Entry test (1) Say which of the following sentences are equative (*E*), and which are not (*N*).

    (a) *My parrot is holidaying in the South of France*   *E / N*

    (b) *Dr Kunastrokins is an ass*   *E / N*

    (c) *Tristram Shandy is a funny book*   *E / N*

    (d) *Our next guest is Dr Kunastrokins*   *E / N*

  (2) Circle the referring expressions in the following sentences.

    (a) *I am looking for any parrot that can sing*

    (b) *Basil saw a rat*

    (c) *These matches were made in Sweden*

    (d) *A dentist is a person who looks after people's teeth*

Feedback (1) (a) N (b) N (c) N (d) E (2) (a) *I* (b) *Basil, a rat* (c) *these matches, Sweden* (d) None

If you have scored less than 4 out of 4 correct in (1), you should review 'Predicates' (Unit 5). If you have scored less than 4 out of 4 correct in (2), you should review 'Referring Expressions' (Unit 4). If you got the test completely right, continue to the introduction.

Introduction We explore further the distinction and the relationship between referring expressions and predicates. We will see how the same word can be used for the radically different functions of reference and predication. And we will begin to see how these two functions fit together in the overall language system.

Comment Some expressions are almost always referring expressions no matter what sentences they occur in.

Practice (1) Can the proper name *Mohammed Ali* ever be used as the predicator of a sentence?   *Yes / No*

  (2) Can the proper name *Cairo* ever be used as a predicator of a sentence?   *Yes / No*

56

(3) In general, can proper names ever be used as predicators? *Yes / No*

(4) Can the verb *hit* ever be used as a referring expression? *Yes / No*

(5) Can the preposition *on* ever be used as a referring expression? *Yes / No*

(6) In general, can any verb or preposition be used to refer? *Yes / No*

Feedback (1) No (2) No (3) No (We would analyse cases like *That man is an Einstein* as being figurative for *That man is similar to Einstein*, where the real predicate is *similar*, and not *Einstein*, but this analysis could conceivably be challenged.) (4) No (5) No (6) No: they are always predicates and can never be used as referring expressions.

Comment The distinction between referring expressions and predicates is absolute: there is not a continuum running from proper names at one end, through 'borderline cases' to verbs and prepositions at the other. Either an expression is used in a given utterance to refer to some entity in the world or it is not so used.

There are some phrases, in particular indefinite noun phrases, that can be used in two ways, either as referring expressions, or as predicating expressions.

Practice (1) Is *a man* in *John attacked a man* a referring expression? *Yes / No*

(2) Is *a man* in *John is a man* a referring expression? *Yes / No*

Feedback (1) Yes (2) No

Comment *A man* can be either a referring expression or a predicating expression, depending on the context. The same is true of other indefinite NPs. On the face of it, this may seem startling. How are we able to use the same expressions for different purposes? We will try to untangle this riddle.

Practice (1) Imagine that you and I are in a room with a man and a woman, and, making no visual signal of any sort, I say to you, 'The man stole my wallet'. In this situation, how would you know the referent of the subject referring expression?

....

(2) If in the situation described above I had said, 'A man stole my wallet', would you automatically know the referent of the subject expression *a man*? *Yes / No*

(3) So does the definite article, *the*, prompt the hearer to (try to) identify the referent of a referring expression? *Yes / No*

(4) Does the indefinite article, *a*, prompt the hearer to (try to) identify the referent of a referring expression? *Yes / No*

Feedback (1) By finding in the room an object to which the predicate contained in the subject referring expression (i.e. *man*) could be truthfully applied (2) No (3) Yes (4) No

Comment   The presence of a predicate in a referring expression helps the hearer to identify the referent of a referring expression. Notice that we have just drawn a distinction between referring and identifying the referent of a referring expression. We will explore this distinction.

Practice   (1) Can the referent of the pronoun *I* be uniquely identified
             when this pronoun is uttered?   *Yes / No*

           (2) Can the referent of the pronoun *you* be uniquely identified
             when this pronoun is uttered?   *Yes / No*

           (3) Imagine again the situation where you and I are in a room
             with a man and a woman, and I say to you (making no visual
             gesture), 'She stole my wallet'. Would you be able to identify
             the referent of *She*?   *Yes / No*

Feedback   (1) Yes (if equating it with the speaker of the utterance is regarded as sufficient identification). (2) In many situations it can, but not always. (We usually, but not always, know who is being addressed.) (3) Yes (that is, in the situation described, if I say to you, 'She stole my wallet', you extract from the referring expression *She* the predicate *female*, which is part of its meaning, and look for something in the speech situation to which this predicate could truthfully be applied. Thus in the situation envisaged, you identify the woman as the referent of *She*. If there had been two women in the room, and no other indication were given, the referent of *She* could not be uniquely identified.)

Comment   To sum up, predicates do not refer. But they can be used by a hearer when contained in the meaning of a referring expression, to identify the referent of that expression. Some more examples follow:

Practice   (1) Does the phrase *in the corner* contain any predicates?   *Yes / No*

           (2) Is the phrase *the man who is in the corner* a referring
             expression?   *Yes / No*

           (3) Do the predicates in the phrase *in the corner* help to identify
             the referent of the referring expression in (2) above?   *Yes / No*

           (4) Is the predicate *bald* contained in the meaning of *the
             bald man*?   *Yes / No*

           (5) Is the predicate *man* contained in the meaning of *the
             bald man*?   *Yes / No*

Feedback (1) Yes (*in* and *corner*) (2) Yes (We say that the phrase *in the corner* is embedded in the longer phrase.) (3) Yes (4) Yes (5) Yes

Comment Speakers refer to things in the course of utterances by means of referring expressions. The words in a referring expression give clues which help the hearer to identify its referent. In particular, predicates may be embedded in referring expressions as, for instance, the predicates *man*, *in*, and *corner* are embedded in the referring expression *the man in the corner*. The correct referent of such a referring expression is something which completely fits, or satisfies, the description made by the combination of predicates embedded in it.

We now introduce the notion of a generic sentence. So far, we have developed an analysis of a very common sentence type, containing a subject, which is a referring expression, and a predicate (and possibly other expressions). Not all sentences are of this type.

Practice (1) In *The whale is the largest mammal* (interpreted in the most usual way) does *the whale* pick out some particular object in the world (a whale)?   Yes / No

(2) So is *The whale* here a referring expression?   Yes / No

(3) In *The whale is the largest mammal* does *the largest mammal* refer to some particular mammal?   Yes / No

(4) So are there any referring expressions in *The whale is the largest mammal*?   Yes / No

Feedback (1) No (2) No (3) No (4) No

Definition A GENERIC SENTENCE is a sentence in which some statement is made about a whole unrestricted class of individuals, as opposed to any particular individual.

Example *The whale is a mammal* (understood in the most usual way) is a generic sentence.
That whale over there is a mammal is not a generic sentence.

Comment Note that generic sentences can be introduced by either *a* or *the* (or neither).

Practice Are the following generic sentences?

(1) *Gentlemen prefer blondes*   Yes / No

(2) *Jasper is a twit*   Yes / No

(3) *The male of the species guards the eggs*   Yes / No

(4) *A wasp makes its nest in a hole in a tree*   Yes / No

(5) *A wasp just stung me on the neck*   Yes / No

Feedback   (1) Yes (2) No (3) Yes (4) Yes (5) No

Comment   Language is used for talking about things in the real world, like parrots, paper-clips, babies, etc. All of these things exist. But the things we can talk about and the things that exist are not exactly the same. We shall now explore the way in which language creates unreal worlds and allows us to talk about non-existent things. We start from the familiar notion of reference.

Our basic, and very safe, definition of reference (Unit 3) was as a relationship between part of an utterance and a thing in the world. But often we use words in a way which suggests that a relationship exactly like reference holds between a part of an utterance and non-existent things. The classic case is that of the word *unicorn*.

Practice   (1) Do unicorns exist in the real world?   *Yes / No*

(2) In which two of the following contexts are unicorns most frequently mentioned? Circle your answer.
(a) in fairy stories
(b) in news broadcasts
(c) in philosophical discussions about reference
(d) in scientific text books

(3) Is it possible to imagine worlds different in certain ways from the world we know actually to exist?   *Yes / No*

(4) In fairy tale and science fiction worlds is everything different from the world we know?   *Yes / No*

(5) In the majority of fairy tales and science fiction stories that you know, do the fictional characters discourse with each other according to the same principles that apply in real life?   *Yes / No*

(6) Do fairy tale princes, witches, etc. seem to refer in their utterances to things in the world?   *Yes / No*

Feedback   (1) No (2) (a) and (c) (3) Yes (4) No, otherwise we could not comprehend them. (5) Yes (6) Yes

Comment   Semantics is concerned with the meanings of words and sentences and it would be an unprofitable digression to get bogged down in questions of what exists and what doesn't. We wish to avoid insoluble disagreements between atheist and theist semanticists, for example, over whether one could refer to God. To avoid such problems, we adopt a broad interpretation of the notion referring expression (see Unit 4) so that any expression that can be used to refer to any entity in the real world or in any imaginary world will be called a referring expression.

60

Practice   According to this view of what counts as a referring expression, are the following possible referring expressions, i.e. could they be used in utterances to refer (either to real or to fictitious entities)?

(1) *God*   Yes / No

(2) *and*   Yes / No

(3) *Moses*   Yes / No

(4) *that unicorn*   Yes / No

Feedback   (1) Yes (2) No (3) Yes (4) Yes

Comment   Notice that we only let our imagination stretch to cases where the things in the world are different; we do not allow our imagination to stretch to cases where the principles of the structure and use of language are different. To do so would be to abandon the object of our study. So we insist (as in (2) above) that the English conjunction *and*, for example, could never be a referring expression.

The case of unicorns was relatively trivial. Now we come to some rather different cases.

Practice   (1) If unicorns existed, would they be physical objects?   Yes / No

(2) Do the following expressions refer to physical objects?

(a) *Christmas Day 1980*   Yes / No

(b) *one o'clock in the morning*   Yes / No

(c) *when Eve was born*   Yes / No

(d) *93 million miles*   Yes / No

(e) *the distance between the Earth and the Sun*   Yes / No

(f) *'God Save the Queen'*   Yes / No

(g) *the British national anthem*   Yes / No

(h) *eleven hundred*   Yes / No

(i) *one thousand one hundred*   Yes / No

Feedback   (1) Yes; it's difficult to conceive of them in any other way. (2) (a)–(i) No

Comment   So far we have mainly kept to examples of reference to physical objects, like *John, my chair, the cat*, and *Cairo*. What are we to make of expressions like *tomorrow* and *the British national anthem*, which cannot possibly be said to refer to physical objects? It is in fact reasonable to envisage our notion of reference in such a way that we can call these referring expressions also, because language uses these expressions in many of the same ways as it uses the clear cases of referring expressions.

Even though expressions like *tomorrow, the British national anthem, eleven hundred, the distance between the Earth and the Sun,* etc. do not indicate physical objects, language treats these expressions in a way exactly parallel to referring expressions. We call them referring expressions along with *John, the roof,* and *Cairo.* We say that *the British national anthem* is used to refer to a particular song, that *eleven hundred* is used to refer to a particular number, *one o'clock* to a particular time, *93 million miles* to a particular distance, and so on.

Language is used to talk about the real world, and can be used to talk about an infinite variety of abstractions, and even of entities in imaginary, unreal worlds.

Definition   We define the UNIVERSE OF DISCOURSE for any utterance as the particular world, real or imaginary (or part real, part imaginary), that the speaker assumes he is talking about at the time.

Example   When an astronomy lecturer, in a serious lecture, states that the Earth revolves around the Sun, the universe of discourse is, we all assume, the real world (or universe).

When I tell my children a bedtime story and say 'The dragon set fire to the woods with his hot breath', the universe of discourse is not the real world but a fictitious world.

Practice   Is the universe of discourse in each of the following cases the real world (as far as we can tell) (*R*), or a (partly) fictitious world (*F*)?

(1) Newsreader on April 14th 1981: 'The American space-shuttle successfully landed at Edwards Airforce Base, California, today'   *R / F*

(2) Mother to child: 'Don't touch those berries. They might be poisonous'   *R / F*

(3) Mother to child: 'Santa Claus might bring you a toy telephone'   *R / F*

(4) Patient in psychiatric ward: 'As your Emperor, I command you to defeat the Parthians'   *R / F*

(5) Doctor to patient: 'You cannot expect to live longer than another two months'   *R / F*

(6) Patient (joking bravely): 'When I'm dead, I'll walk to the cemetery to save the cost of a hearse'   *R / F*

Feedback   (1) R (2) R (3) F (4) F (5) R (6) F, dead people do not walk in the real world

Comment   These were relatively clear cases. Note that no universe of discourse is a totally fictitious world. Santa Claus is a fiction, but the toy telephones he might bring do actually exist. So in examples like this we have interaction between fact and fiction, between real and imaginary worlds. When two people are 'arguing at cross-purposes', they could be said to be working within partially different universes of discourse.

Example Theist: 'Diseases must serve some good purpose, or God would not allow them'
Atheist: 'I cannot accept your premisses'
Here the theist is operating with a universe of discourse which is a world in which God exists. The atheist's assumed universe of discourse is a world in which God does not exist.

Practice In the following situations, are the participants working with the same universe of discourse (*S*), or different universes (*D*), as far as you can tell?

(1) A: 'Did Jack's son come in this morning?'
B: 'I didn't know Jack had a son'
A: 'Then who's that tall chap that was here yesterday?'
B: 'I don't know, but I'm pretty sure Jack hasn't got any kids'
A: 'I'm sure Jack's son was here yesterday'   *S / D*

(2) Time traveller from the eighteenth century: 'Is the King of France on good terms with the Tsar of Russia?'
Twenty-first-century person: 'Huh?'   *S / D*

(3) Optician: 'Please read the letters on the bottom line of the card'
Patient: 'E G D Z Q N B A'
Optician: 'Correct. Well done'   *S / D*

Feedback (1) D: in A's universe of discourse Jack's son exists; in B's he does not.
(2) D (3) S

Comment Assuming the same universe of discourse is essential to successful communication. The participants in questions (1) and (2) are in a sense talking about different worlds. Assuming different universes of discourse is not the only reason for breakdown of communication: there can be other causes – both participants' assuming that exactly the same entities exist in the world, but referring to them by different words (an extreme case of this would be two participants speaking different languages) – or, of course, sheer inarticulacy.

Summary In the course of a sequence of utterances, speakers use referring expressions to refer to entities which may be concrete or abstract, real or fictitious. The predicates embedded in a referring expression help the hearer to identify its referent. Semantics is not concerned with the factual status of things in the world but with meaning in language. The notion of universe of discourse is introduced to account for the way in which language allows us to refer to non-existent things.

Unit 6 Study Guide and Exercises

Directions After you have read Unit 6 you should be able to tackle the following questions to test your understanding of the main ideas raised in the unit.

1 You should understand these terms and concepts from this unit:
generic sentence
universe of discourse

2 Which of the following are generic sentences? Explain.
a Americans like to eat apple pie
b Fred likes to buy Uzis
c A bird lays eggs
d My pet finch just laid an egg

3 Comment on the italicized items below in light of the points made in this chapter.
a John wants to marry *a* girl with green eyes
b I am looking for *a* pencil
c *The* whale is the largest mammal
d *The* whales at Seaworld entertain visitors

4 Language can create unreal worlds. Explain and give an illustration different from those discussed in this unit.

5 How was the question of the existence of God resolved with respect to the notion **referring expression**? How are we able to resolve the apparent difficulty of dealing with such referring expressions as *yesterday, four hundred,* and *the distance between Detroit and Chicago,* etc.?

6 How is it that we can understand speech and writings about non-existent, imaginary worlds?

7 Construct a short example of a conversational exchange different from the ones given in this unit which illustrates that the participants are working within partially different universes of discourse.

8 Why is it that 'no universe of discourse is a totally fictitious world'? What would happen if this were the case?

UNIT 7 DEIXIS AND DEFINITENESS

Entry requirements UTTERANCE (Unit 2), IDENTIFYING THE REFERENT OF A REFERRING EXPRESSION and UNIVERSE OF DISCOURSE (Unit 6). If you feel familiar with these ideas, take the entry test below. If not, review the appropriate units.

Entry test (1) Is an utterance tied to a particular time and place?   *Yes / No*

(2) Is a sentence tied to a particular time and place?   *Yes / No*

(3) Circle the referring expressions in the following utterance: 'Neil Armstrong was the first man on the Moon and became a hero'

(4) Who does 'I' refer to in the following utterance? 'I will never speak to you again'

....

(5) When a speaker says to someone, 'A man from Dundee stole my wallet', would he usually be assuming that the hearer will bring to mind a particular man from Dundee and be able to IDENTIFY him by associating him with facts already known about him?   *Yes / No*

(6) As question (5), but with the utterance, 'The man from Dundee stole my wallet'.   *Yes / No*

(7) Can a universe of discourse be partly fictitious?   *Yes / No*

(8) If perfect communication is to take place between speaker and hearer on any topic, is it necessary that they share the same universe of discourse?   *Yes / No*

Feedback (1) Yes (2) No (3) 'Neil Armstrong', 'the first man on the moon' (4) the speaker of the utterance (5) No, not usually (6) Yes (7) Yes (8) Yes

If you got less than 7 out of 8 correct, review the relevant unit. Otherwise, continue to the introduction.

Introduction Most words mean what they mean regardless of who uses them, and when and where they are used. Indeed this is exactly why words are so useful. Only if we assign a (fairly) constant interpretation to a word such as *man*, for example, can we have a coherent conversation about men. Nevertheless, all languages do contain small sets of words whose meanings vary systematically according to who uses them, and where and when they are used. These words are called deictic words: the general phenomenon of their occurrence is called deixis. The word *deixis* is from a Greek word meaning *pointing*.

Definition   A DEICTIC word is one which takes some element of its meaning from the context or situation (i.e. the speaker, the addressee, the time and the place) of the utterance in which it is used.

Example   The first person singular pronoun *I* is deictic. When Ben Heasley says 'I've lost the contract', the word *I* here refers to Ben Heasley. When Penny Carter says 'I'll send you another one', the *I* here refers to Penny Carter.

Practice   (1) If Wyatt Earp meets Doc Holliday in Dodge City and says, 'This town ain't big enough for the both of us', what does *this town* refer to?

....

(2) If a television news reporter, speaking in Fresno, California, says, 'This town was shaken by a major earth tremor at 5 a.m. today', what does *this town* refer to?

....

(3) In general, what clue to the identity of the referent of a referring expression is given by the inclusion of the demonstrative word *this*? Formulate your reply carefully, mentioning the notion 'utterance'.

....

(4) If, on November 3rd 2005, I say, 'Everything seemed to go wrong yesterday', what day am I picking out by the word *yesterday*?

....

(5) If, on May 4th 2005, my daughter says to me, 'Yesterday wasn't my birthday', what day is being picked out by the word *yesterday*?

....

(6) To summarize in a general statement, what day does *yesterday* refer to?

....

Feedback   (1) Dodge City (2) Fresno, California (3) A referring expression modified by *this* refers to an entity (place, person, thing etc.) at or near the actual place of the utterance in which it is used. (4) November 2nd 2005 (5) May 3rd 2005 (6) *Yesterday* refers to the day before the day of the utterance in which it is used.

Comment   These exercises show that the words *this* and *yesterday* are deictic.

Practice Are the following words deictic?

    (1) *here*   Yes / No

    (2) *Wednesday*   Yes / No

    (3) *place*   Yes / No

    (4) *today*   Yes / No

    (5) *you*   Yes / No

Feedback (1) Yes (2) No (3) No (4) Yes (5) Yes. (The referent of *you* is the addressee(s) of the utterance in which it is used and is therefore dependent upon the particular context.)

Comment So far, all of our examples of deictic terms have been referring expressions, like *you*, *here*, and *today*, or modifiers which can be used with referring expressions, like the demonstrative *this*. Such deictic terms help the hearer to identify the referent of a referring expression through its spatial or temporal relationship with the situation of utterance. There are also a few predicates which have a deictic ingredient.

Example The verb *come* has a deictic ingredient, because it contains the notion 'toward the speaker'.

Practice Look at the following utterances and decide whether the speaker gives any indication of his location (*Yes*), and if so, where he is (or isn't):

    (1) 'Go to the hospital'

        Yes / No..

    (2) 'The astronauts are going back to Earth'

        Yes / No..

    (3) 'Please don't bring food into the bathroom'

        Yes / No..

    (4) 'Can you take this plate into the kitchen for me?'

        Yes / No..

Feedback (1) *Yes:* not at the hospital (2) *Yes:* not on Earth (3) *Yes:* in the bathroom (4) *Yes:* not in the kitchen

Comment Some examples involve a 'psychological shifting' of the speaker's view-point for the purpose of interpreting one of the deictic terms.

Practice (1) If I say to you, 'Come over there, please!' while pointing to a far corner of the room (i.e. far from both of us), could you reasonably infer that I intend to move to that corner of the room as well?   *Yes / No*

(2) In this instance, would it seem correct to say that the speaker
is anticipating his future location when he uses the word *come*
(i.e. is *come* in this case 'stretched' to include 'toward where
the speaker will be')?   *Yes / No*

(3) If I say to you, over the telephone, 'Can I come and see you
some time?' do I probably have in mind a movement to the
place where I am, or to the place where you are?

....

Feedback (1) Yes (2) Yes (3) the place where you are

Comment This psychological shifting of viewpoint just illustrated is an example of the
flexibility with which deictic terms can be interpreted. In our definition of
deixis, 'time of utterance' and 'place of utterance' must generally be taken
very flexibly. Sometimes these are interpreted very broadly, and sometimes
very narrowly and strictly.

In addition to deictic words (such as *here*, *now*, *come*, and *bring*), there are
in English and other languages certain grammatical devices called tenses for
indicating past, present, and future time, which must also be regarded as
deictic, because past, present, and future times are defined by reference to the
time of utterance.

Practice (1) If Matthew said (truthfully) 'Mummy, Rosemary hit me', when did
Rosemary hit Matthew, before, at, or after the time of Matthew's
utterance?

....

(2) If Matthew (truthfully) says, 'Mummy, Rosemary is writing on the living
room wall', when is Rosemary committing this misdemeanour, before, at,
or after the time of Matthew's utterance?

....

(3) If I say (truthfully) 'I'm going to write a letter to the President', when do
I write to the President?

....

(4) In each of the following utterances, what can you deduce about the date
of the utterance?

(a) 'I first met my wife in the year 1993'

....

(b) 'The 1936 Olympic Games will be held in Berlin'

....

Feedback   (1) before the utterance (2) at the time of the utterance (Perhaps before and after as well, but, strictly, Matthew isn't saying anything about what happens before or after his utterance.) (3) after the time of my utterance (4) (a) This utterance can only truthfully be made in or after the year 1993. (b) This utterance must have been made in or before 1936.

Comment   Although tense is definitely deictic, as illustrated above, the issue is complicated by the fact that there are a variety of different ways of expressing past, present, and future time in English, and these different methods interact with other factors such as progressive and perfective aspect. We will not delve into these details here.

A generalization can be made about the behaviour of all deictic terms in reported speech. In reported speech, deictic terms occurring in the original utterance (the utterance being reported) may be translated into other, possibly non-deictic, terms in order to preserve the original reference.

Example   John: 'I'll meet you here tomorrow.'
Margaret (reporting John's utterance some time later):   'John said he would meet me there the next day.'
In this example, five adjustments are made in the reported speech, namely:
I → he, 'll (= will) → would, you → me, here → there, tomorrow → the next day

Practice   Use an utterance of your own to report each of the following utterances from a vantage point distant in time and space, changing all the deictic terms to preserve the correct relationships with the situation of the original utterance. Assume that John was speaking to you in each case.

(1)   John: 'I don't live in this house any more'

   ....

(2)   John: 'I need your help right now'

   ....

(3)   John: 'Why wouldn't you come to London with me yesterday?'

   ....

Feedback   (1) 'John said that he didn't live in that house any more' (2) 'John said that he needed my help right then' (3) 'John asked why I wouldn't go to London with him the day before'

Comment   These changes in reported speech arise by the very nature of deictic terms. Since deictic terms take (some of) their meaning from the situation of utterance, an utterance reporting an utterance in a different situation cannot always faithfully use the deictic terms of the original utterance.

The function of deixis in language can be better understood by asking the question, 'Could there be a language without deixis, i.e. without any deictic expressions?' Let us consider this question by means of some examples.

Practice   Imagine a language, called Zonglish, exactly like English in all respects, except that it contains no deictic terms at all, i.e. all English deictic terms have been eliminated from Zonglish.

(1) Is *I would like a cup of tea* a wellformed Zonglish sentence?   *Yes / No*

(2) Given that a Zonglish speaker could not say 'I would like a cup of tea', would it be possible for him to inform someone that he would like a cup of tea by saying, 'The speaker would like a cup of tea'?   *Yes / No*

(3) In a language like Zonglish, with no deictic terms, could one rely on one's hearers interpreting 'the speaker' when uttered as referring to the utterer?   *Yes / No*

(4) Given a speaker of Zonglish named Johan Brzown, and given that no other individual is named Johan Brzown, could he inform someone that he wanted a cup of tea by uttering 'Johan Brzown want a cup of tea'?   *Yes / No*

(5) Ignoring the problem that tense is a deictic category, could Johan Brzown inform anyone of any fact about himself if his hearer does not happen to know his name?   *Yes / No*

(6) Assuming that Johan Brzown carries a clearly visible badge announcing his name to all his hearers, how could he make it clear to his hearer that he wants a cup of tea at the time of utterance, not earlier, and not later?

....

(7) If Johan Brzown wants a cup of tea at 5.30 pm on November 9th 2006, could he inform his hearer of this by uttering, 'Johan Brzown want a cup of tea at 5.30 pm on November 9th 2006'?   *Yes / No*

Feedback   (1) No (2) No, see answers to next questions for reasons. (3) No, if 'the speaker' were to be conventionally understood as referring to the utterer of the utterance in which it occurred, it would in effect be a deictic expression, and therefore outlawed in Zonglish. (4) Using the proper name *Johan Brzown* would get over the problem of referring to the speaker. Every speaker of Zonglish would have to use his own name instead of the personal pronoun *I*. But since tense is a deictic category, Johan Brzown still has the problem of informing his hearer that he wants the cup of tea at the time of utterance, not in the past, and not in the future. (5) No (6) By using some non-deictic description of the actual time of the utterance, like, for example, at *5.30 pm on November 9th 2006* (7) Yes, with this utterance, Johan Brzown would be able to get his message across.

Comment The point about an example like this is to show that there are good reasons for all languages to have deictic terms. A language without such terms could not serve the communicative needs of its users anything like as well as a real human language. (Of course, all real human languages do have deictic terms.) Deictic expressions bring home very clearly that when we consider individual sentences from the point of view of their truth, we cannot in many cases consider them purely abstractly, i.e. simply as strings of words made available by the language system. The truth of a sentence containing a deictic expression can only be considered in relation to some hypothetical situation of utterance.

Practice (1) Can you tell by itself whether the sentence *You are standing on my toe* is true or false? *Yes / No*

(2) What would you need to know in order to be able to tell whether the sentence just mentioned is true or false?

....

(3) Can one tell whether the sentence *There are lions in Africa*, not considered in relation to any particular time, is true or false? *Yes / No*

Feedback (1) No (2) You would need to know who said it to whom and whether the hearer was in fact standing on the speaker's toe at the time of utterance. (3) No

Comment The relationship of the truth of sentences to hypothetical times and situations of utterance is brought out most vividly by deictic terms.

The is traditionally called the definite article, and *a* the indefinite article. But what exactly is definiteness? An answer can be given in terms of several notions already discussed, in particular the notion of referring expression, identifying the referent of a referring expression, and universe of discourse. A new notion is also needed, that of context.

Definition The CONTEXT of an utterance is a small subpart of the universe of discourse shared by speaker and hearer, and includes facts about the topic of the conversation in which the utterance occurs, and also facts about the situation in which the conversation itself takes place.

Example If I meet a stranger on a bus and we begin to talk about the weather (and not about anything else), then facts about the weather (e.g. that it is raining, that it is warmer than yesterday, etc.), facts about the bus (e.g. that it is crowded), and also obvious facts about the two speakers (e.g. their sex) are part of the context of utterances in this conversation. Facts not associated with the topic of the conversation or the situation on the bus (e.g. that England won the World Cup in 1966, or that kangaroos live in Australia) are not part of the context of this conversation, even though they may happen to be known to both speakers.

Comment The exact context of any utterance can never be specified with complete certainty. The notion of context is very flexible (even somewhat vague). Note that facts about times and places very distant from the time and place of the utterance itself can be part of the context of that utterance, if the topic of conversation happens to be about these distant times and places. Thus, for example, facts about certain people in Egypt could well be part of the context of a conversation in Britain five years later.

Practice According to the definition of context,

(1) Is the context of an utterance a part of the universe of discourse?   *Yes / No*

(2) Is the immediate situation of an utterance a part of its context?   *Yes / No*

(3) Draw a diagram with three circles and label the circles 'universe of discourse', 'context of utterance', and 'immediate situation of utterance' in such a way as to indicate what is included in what.

Feedback (1) Yes (2) Yes (3)

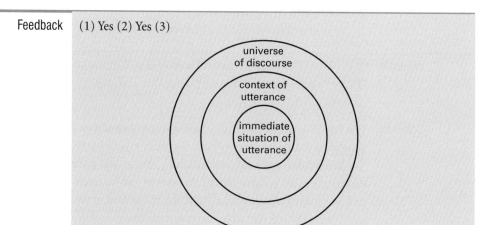

Comment Now we relate the notion of context to the notion of definiteness.

Rule If some entity (or entities) (i.e. person(s), object(s), place(s), etc.) is/are the ONLY entity (or entities) of its/their kind in the context of an utterance, then the definite article (*the*) is the appropriate article to use in referring to that entity (or those entities).

Practice If I carry on a conversation with a friend about the time, five years earlier, when we first met in Egypt (and we are now holding the conversation in the garden of my house in Britain):

(1) Which of the following two utterances would be more appropriate? Circle your answer.

(a) 'Do you remember when we met at the university?'

(b) 'Do you remember when we met at a university?'

(2) Which of the following two utterances would be more appropriate?
    (a) 'Shall we go into a house now?'
    (b) 'Shall we go into the house now?'

(3) In the context we are considering, would it be appropriate to
    use the referring expression *the elephants* (as far as you can
    tell from what we have told you about this context)?   *Yes / No*

(4) In this context, would it be appropriate to use the referring
    expression *the printer* (again, as far as you can tell)?   *Yes / No*

Feedback (1) (a) (2) (b) (3) No (4) No

Comment The appropriateness of the definite article is dependent on the context in
which it is used. The expressions judged inappropriate in the previous practice
would be quite appropriate in other contexts. Think of such contexts for
practice.

Contexts are constructed continuously during the course of a conversation.
As a conversation progresses, items previously unmentioned and not even
associated with the topics so far discussed are mentioned for the first time
and then become part of the context of the following utterance. Eventually,
perhaps, things mentioned a long time previously in the conversation will
'fade out' of the context, but how long it takes for this to happen cannot be
specified exactly.

When something is introduced for the first time into a conversation, it is
appropriate to use the indefinite article, *a*. Once something is established in
the context of the conversation, it is appropriate to use *the*. But the definite
article *the* is not the only word which indicates definiteness in English.

Definition DEFINITENESS is a feature of a noun phrase selected by a speaker to convey
his assumption that the hearer will be able to identify the referent of the
noun phrase, usually because it is the only thing of its kind in the context of
the utterance, or because it is unique in the universe of discourse.

Example *That book* is definite. It can only appropriately be used when the speaker
assumes the hearer can tell which book is being referred to.

The personal pronoun *she* is definite. It can only appropriately be used when
the speaker assumes the hearer can tell which person is being referred to.

The Earth is definite. It is the only thing in a normal universe of discourse
known by this name.

Practice (1) We reproduce below a passage from *Alice in Wonderland*. Pick out by
    underlining all the expressions which clearly refer to something the
    reader is supposed to be aware of at the point in the passage where they
    occur, i.e. all the expressions referring to things which must be assumed

to be already present in the context of the passage. You should find 15 such definite expressions altogether.

1   There was a table set out under a tree in front of the house, and the March Hare and the Hatter were having tea at it; a Dormouse was sitting
3   between them, fast asleep, and the other two were using it as a cushion, resting their elbows on it, and talking over its head. 'Very uncomfort-
5   able for the dormouse', thought Alice; 'only, as it's asleep, I suppose it doesn't mind.'

(2)   The word *it* occurs 5 times in this passage. To which different things does it refer?

....

(3)   Is there ever any doubt in this passage about the referent of any occurrence of *it*?   *Yes / No*

(4)   Who does *them* in line 3 refer to?

....

(5)   Four things (or people) referred to by definite referring expressions in this passage must be presumed to be already in the context at the very beginning of the passage, i.e. they are not introduced during the passage. Which are they?

....

(6)   Two things referred to by definite referring expressions in this passage are actually introduced into the context during the passage. Which are they?

....

Feedback   (1) line 1, *the house*; line 2, *the March Hare, the Hatter, it*; line 3, *them, the other two, it*; line 4, *their elbows, it, its head*; line 5, *the dormouse, Alice, it, I, it* (2) the table and the dormouse (3) No (4) the March Hare and the Hatter (5) the house, the March Hare, the Hatter, and Alice (6) the table and the dormouse

Comment   This passage from *Alice in Wonderland* is written in a very simple straightforward narrative style, in which things are introduced into the context by means of indefinite expressions, e.g. *a table, a tree, a dormouse*, and subsequently referred to with definite expressions, e.g. *it, the dormouse*. This kind of structure is actually only found in the simplest style. More often, authors begin a narrative using a number of definite referring expressions. This stylistic device has the effect of drawing the reader into the narrative fast, by giving the impression that the writer and the reader already share a number of contextual assumptions. We give an example in the next exercise.

Practice   Given below are the opening sentences of John Fowles' novel *The Collector*.

When she was home from her boarding-school I used to see her almost every day sometimes, because their house was right opposite the Town Hall Annexe. She and her younger sister used to go in and out a lot, often with young men, which of course I didn't like. When I had a free moment from the files and ledgers I stood by the window and used to look down over the road over the frosting and sometimes I'd see her.

(1) Is the reader given any idea who 'she' is before she is introduced?   *Yes / No*

(2) Does the mention of 'their house' give the impression that 'they' are in some way already known to the reader?   *Yes / No*

(3) Does mention of 'the files and ledgers' give the impression that the reader should know which files and ledgers are being referred to, or at least give the impression that the reader should know more about them than just that they are files and ledgers?   *Yes / No*

(4) In normal conversation, if a person was recounting some story, would he usually begin a narrative using *she* without indicating in advance who he was talking about?   *Yes / No*

(5) Is the use of definite referring expressions in the above passage different from conventional usage in the opening stages of everyday conversations?   *Yes / No*

Feedback   (1) No (2) Yes (3) Yes (4) No (5) Yes

Comment   Novelists typically use definiteness in strikingly abnormal ways in the opening passages of novels – 'abnormal', that is, from the point of view of everyday conversation.

The three main types of definite noun phrase in English are (1) Proper names, e.g. *John, Queen Victoria*, (2) personal pronouns, e.g. *he, she, it*, and (3) phrases introduced by a definite determiner, such as *the, that, this* (e.g. *the table, this book, those men*). By contrast, expressions like *a man, someone*, and *one* are all indefinite.

It follows from our definition of definiteness (p. 73) that all definite noun phrases are referring expressions. But you must be careful not to assume that every noun phrase using the so-called 'definite article' *the* is necessarily semantically definite. In generic sentences (Unit 6), for example, and in other cases, one can find a phrase beginning with *the* where the hearer cannot be expected to identify the referent, often because there is in fact no referent, the expression not being a referring expression.

Practice (1) In the sentence *The whale is a mammal,* as most typically used, which particular whale is being referred to?

....

(2) Is *the whale* in the sentence just mentioned a referring expression?   *Yes / No*

(3) Is the phrase *the whale* semantically definite in the sentence mentioned (i.e. would a user of this sentence presume that the hearer would be able to identify the referent of the expression)? *Yes / No*

(4) Take the utterance 'If anyone makes too much noise, you have my permission to strangle him'. On hearing this, could the hearer be expected to identify the referent of *him*?   *Yes / No*

(5) In the utterance just mentioned, is *him* semantically definite? *Yes / No*

(6) Which particular donkey does *it* refer to in *Every man who owns a donkey beats it*?

....

(7) Is *it* in *Every man who owns a donkey beats it* semantically definite?   *Yes / No*

Feedback (1) none at all (2) No (3) No, because there is in fact no referent. (4) No (5) No (6) No particular donkey (7) No

Comment Finally, we consider the question of truth in relation to definiteness. Does definiteness contribute in any way to the truth or falsehood of a sentence considered in relation to a given situation? We will compare the effects of the definite and indefinite articles *the* and *a* with referring expressions.

Practice I am working in the garden, and accidentally stick a fork through my foot. I tell my wife, who knows I have been gardening and knows the fork I have been working with.

(1) Which would be the more appropriate utterance (to my wife) in this situation, (a) or (b)?
(a) 'I've just stuck the fork through my foot'
(b) 'I've just stuck a fork through my foot'   ....

(2) I telephone the doctor, to tell him of the accident. The doctor knows nothing about my gardening tools. Which of the two utterances just mentioned would it be more appropriate to use? ....

(3) In the situation envisaged, do the two utterances mentioned both describe exactly the same state of affairs?   *Yes / No*

Feedback (1) (a) (2) (b) (3) Yes

Summary Deictic expressions are those which take some element of their meaning directly from the immediate situation of the utterance in which they are used (e.g. from the speaker, the hearer, the time and place of the utterance). Examples of deictic words are *I, you, here, now, come.* The availability of such expressions makes language a much more 'portable' instrument than it would otherwise be: we can use the same words on different occasions, at different times and places.

Definite and indefinite referring expressions may be more or less appropriate in different contexts. But utterances which differ only in that one contains a definite referring expression where the other has an indefinite referring expression (provided these expressions have the same referent) do not differ in truth value. Considered objectively, the referent of a referring expression (e.g. *a / the fork*) is in itself neither definite nor indefinite. (Can you tell from close inspection of a fork whether it is a 'definite' or an 'indefinite' fork?) The definiteness of a referring expression tells us nothing about the referent itself, but rather relates to the question of whether the referent has been mentioned (or taken for granted) in the preceding discourse. The definiteness of a referring expression gives the hearer a clue in identifying its referent.

Unit 7 Study Guide and Exercises

Directions After you have read Unit 7 you should be able to tackle the following questions to test your understanding of the main ideas raised in the unit.

1 You should understand these terms and concepts from this unit:
deictic words (deictics)   context
reported speech   definiteness

2 What parts of speech can function as **deictics**? List them and give an example or two of each, preferably different from the ones given in this unit.

3 Are deictics a useful device in language, or are they a burden to the speaker? Explain and illustrate.

4 Identify all the deictic expressions in the following sentences and be able to explain why they are decitic.
a You noticed me standing there
b This book was written by that author over there
c Just set your briefcase to the right of mine
d Now we have to make plans for next week
e Her best friend was standing behind John
f All the guests arrived two hours ago

5 Use an utterance of your own to report the following utterances from a vantage point distant in time and space. Be sure to change the deictic expressions as needed. Assume the people are speaking to you.

a Fred: 'I will do that assignment tomorrow.'

b Mary: 'I don't see any good books here.'

c Fred: 'Why couldn't you help me last week?'

6 Is it possible to know the truth value of a sentence with a deictic expression independently of the context in which it is uttered? Give an example and explain.

7 When is it appropriate to use the definite article *the*? When is it appropriate to use the indefinite article *a*?

8 Think of a context in which it would be appropriate to use the following utterances, and one in which it would be inappropriate.

a 'I have to read an article for class tomorrow.'

b 'Mary wants to check out the book.'

c 'Did you meet her at a university?'

9 Is the definite article *the* the only word that signals definiteness? Explain and illustrate.

10 Are all definite noun phrases referring expressions? Is every noun phrase with the definite article semantically definite? Give examples.

11 Suppose you accidentally drive the family car through a plate glass window late at night and that your parents know you have been driving the car. You first call your parents, then the police, to report the accident. Which of the following utterances would you most likely say to each party?

a 'I just drove a car through a plate glass window.'

b 'I just drove the car through a plate glass window.'

c 'I just drove a car through the plate glass window.'

d 'I just drove the car through the plate glass window.'

12 Which utterance in question 11 would you most likely say to the owner of the store whom you contact after calling the police? Explain.

13 Does the change of articles affect the truth value of the utterances in 11 above?

14 Consider the following sentences and try to determine what factor the speaker uses in choosing the italicized verb in each. Also comment on the difference in meaning in the choice of different verbs with respect to the speaker's perspective on the scene.

a I just called to see if you will be *coming* to see me tomorrow

b I just called to see if you will be *going* to see me tomorrow

c She asked me to *come* to her party, but I didn't *go*

d Please *come* in

e Please *go* in

f Don't *bring* any food with you

UNIT 8 WORDS AND THINGS: EXTENSIONS AND PROTOTYPES

Entry requirements SENSE and REFERENCE (Unit 3), PREDICATE (Unit 5), IDENTIFYING the REFERENT of a REFERRING EXPRESSION and UNIVERSE of DISCOURSE (Unit 6). If you feel you understand these notions, take the entry test below. If not, review the relevant unit(s).

Entry test (1) Which of the following most appropriately describes reference? Circle your preference.
  (a) Reference is a relationship between sentences and the world.
  (b) Reference is a relationship between certain uttered expressions and things in the world.
  (c) Reference is a relationship between certain uttered expressions and certain things outside the context of the utterance.

(2) Which of the following is a correct statement about sense?
  (a) All words in a language may be used to refer, but only some words have sense.
  (b) If two expressions have the same reference, they always have the same sense.
  (c) The sense of an expression is its relationship to semantically equivalent or semantically related expressions in the same language.

(3) How do hearers identify the referent of a referring expression (other than a proper name) –
  (a) by seeking in the context of the utterance some object to which the predicates in the referring expression apply?
  (b) by sharing with the speaker a conventional system according to which each possible referring expression has a single agreed referent?
  (c) by telepathy – reading the speaker's mind?

(4) Which of the following words are predicates? Circle your choices. *Henry, square, expensive, and, under, not, love*

(5) Which of the following is correct?
  (a) The universe of discourse is a part of the context of an utterance.
  (b) The context of an utterance is a part of the universe of discourse.
  (c) The universe of discourse is the whole real world.

Feedback (1) (b) (2) (c) (3) (a) (4) *square, expensive, under, love* (5) (b)

If you have scored at least 4 out of 5 correct, continue to the introduction. Otherwise, review the relevant unit.

Introduction We have outlined the basic distinction between sense and reference (Unit 3) and explored details of the use of reference (Units 4–7). In subsequent units (9–11) we will develop the idea of sense in similar detail. The present unit will act as a bridge between the preceding units on reference and the following units on sense, introducing several notions, including extension and prototype, which in certain ways bridge the conceptual and theoretical gap between sense and reference. In other words, we are going to try to pin down more specifically how the notions of sense and reference are related to each other in determining the meaning of a linguistic expression.

To show what we mean when we talk of a 'gap' between reference and sense, we look first at the question of how much a knowledge of the reference of referring expressions actually helps a speaker in producing and understanding utterances which describe the world he lives in.

Practice (1) In the case of expressions with constant reference, such as *the Sun* or *the Moon*, could a speaker be said to know what they refer to simply by having memorized a permanent connection in his mind between each expression and its referent? Yes / No

(2) In the case of expressions with variable reference, such as *the man* or *the middle of the road*, could a speaker be said to know what they refer to by having memorized a permanent connection in his mind between each expression and its referent? Yes / No

(3) How, in a given situation, would you know that in saying 'the cat' I was not referring to a man sitting in an armchair, or to a book in his hand, or to the clock on the mantelpiece? (Remember, from your answer to question (2), that it cannot be because you have memorized a connection between the expression *the cat* and some particular object, a cat, in the world.)

"the cat" can only be referring to a cat (man ≠ cat).

(4) Might it seem reasonable to say, in the case of a referring expression with variable reference, such as *the cat*, that a speaker has memorized a connection between the expression and a set, or type, of the expression's potential referents? Yes / No

(5) How many potential referents are there for the expression *the cat*?

as many cats as there are in the world (a lot).

Feedback | (1) Yes (2) No, because for such expressions there is no single referent with which the speaker could establish a permanent connection in his mind. (3) Because you know that the expression *the cat* can only refer to a cat, and not to anything which is not a cat, and you know that men, books, and clocks are not cats. (4) Yes (5) As many as there are (or have been, or will be) cats in the world – certainly a very large number.

Comment | The point that we are spelling out here is that someone who knows how to use the word *cat* has an idea of the potential set of objects that can be referred to as cats, i.e. he has some concept of the set of all cats. (This idea or concept may only be a vague, or fuzzy, one, but we will come back to that point later.) This leads us to the notion of the extension of a predicate.

Definition (partial) | The EXTENSION of a one-place predicate is the set of all individuals to which that predicate can truthfully be applied. It is the set of things which can POTENTIALLY be referred to by using an expression whose main element is that predicate.

Example | The extension of *window* is the set of all windows in the universe.
The extension of *dog* is the set of all dogs in the universe.
The extension of *house* is the set of all houses.
The extension of *red* is the set of all red things.

Comment | In the case of most frequent common nouns, at least, an extension is a set of physical objects. Thus, extension contrasts with sense, since a sense is not a set of anything. And extension contrasts with referent, since a referent is normally an individual thing, not a set of things. Beside these contrasts, the notion of extension has similarities to that of sense, on the one hand, and to that of reference, on the other. Extension is like sense, and unlike reference, in that it is independent of any particular occasion of utterance. Speakers refer to referents on particular occasions, but words which have sense and extension have them 'timelessly'. On the other hand, extension is like reference and unlike sense, in that it connects a linguistic unit, such as a word or expression, to something non-linguistic (i.e. outside language) be it a set of physical objects or an individual physical object, or a set of abstract entities (e.g. songs, distances) or an individual abstract object (e.g. a particular song, a specific distance).

Practice | (1) In the light of the above comment, fill in the chart with '+' and '−' signs to indicate the differences and similarities between these three concepts.

	Sense	Extension	Reference
Involves a set	−	+	−
Independent of particular occasions or utterance	+	+	−
Connects language to the world	−	+	+

81

(2) A B

Which of the two pictures would more informatively be
captioned: 'part of the extension of the word *cat*'?   A /(B)

(3) Might the other picture appropriately be captioned: 'the
referent of "Jaime Lass' present eldest cat", uttered on
January 1st 1983'? (Assume that there is someone named
Jaime Lass who owned cats at that time.)   (Yes)/ No

(4) Could the expression *her cat*, uttered on different occasions
with different topics of conversation, have a number of
different referents?   (Yes)/ No

(5) Would each object (each separate animal, that is) referred
to by the expression *her cat* on separate occasions belong
to the extension of the word *cat*?   (Yes)/ No

(6) Could both pictures actually be labelled: 'part of the
extension of the word *cat*' (though to do so might not
immediately clarify the notions involved)?   Yes / No

Feedback   (1) − + −
         + + −
         − + +
(2) B (3) Yes (4) Yes (5) Yes (6) Yes, since any individual cat belongs to the
set of all cats.

Comment The notions of reference and extension are clearly related, and are jointly
opposed to the notion of sense. The relationship usually envisaged between
sense, extension, and reference can be summarized thus:

(1) A speaker's knowledge of the sense of a predicate provides him with an
idea of its extension. For example, the 'dictionary definition' which the
speaker accepts for *cat* can be used to decide what is a cat, and what is
not, thus defining implicitly the set of all cats. Some semanticists
describe this relationship between sense and extension by saying that the
sense of a predicate 'fixes' the extension of that predicate.

(2) The referent of a referring expression used in a particular utterance is an
individual member of the extension of the predicate used in the
expression; the context of the utterance usually helps the hearer to identify
which particular member it is. For example, if any English speaker, in any

situation, hears the utterance 'The cat's stolen your pork chop', he will think that some member of the set of cats has stolen his pork chop, and if, furthermore, the context of the utterance is his own household, which has just one cat, named *Atkins*, he will identify Atkins as the referent of 'the cat'.

Now we will consider further the idea that a speaker of a language in some sense knows the extensions of the predicates in that language, and uses this knowledge to refer correctly to things in the world.

Practice (1) The cat I had as a child is long since dead and cremated, so that that particular cat now no longer exists. Is it possible to refer in conversation to the cat I had as a child? Yes / No

(2) Does it follow that the extension of the predicate *cat* includes the cat I had as a child, which now no longer exists? Yes / No

(3) New cats are coming into existence all the time. Does it seem reasonable to say that a speaker is continually updating his idea of the set of all cats, to include the newcomers? Yes / No

(4) Or does it seem more reasonable to define extensions in such a way as to include objects in the future, as well as in the present and the past? Yes / No

(5) Is it possible to refer to the cat which you may own one day in the distant future, a cat which does not yet exist? Yes / No

Feedback (1) Yes (2) Yes (3) No (4) Yes (5) Yes

Comment Since clearly one can refer to things which no longer exist and to things which do not yet exist, and since the notion of the extension of a predicate is defined as a set of potential referents, we are forced to postulate that extensions are relative to all times, past, present, and future. Thus, the extension of *window*, for example, includes all past windows, all present windows, and all future windows. Similarly, the extension of *dead* includes all things which have been dead in the past (and presumably still are, if they still exist), which are dead now, and which will be dead in the future. Predicates are tenseless, i.e. unspecified for past, present, or future.

In actual use, predicates are almost always accompanied in sentences by a marker of tense (past or present) or a future marker, such as *will*. These have the effect of restricting the extensions of the predicates they modify, so that, for example, the extension of the phrase *is dead* could be said to be the set of all things which are dead at the time of utterance. Correspondingly, the extension of the phrase *is alive* could be said to be the set of all things alive at the time of utterance. Thus the extensions of *is dead* and *is alive* are different in the appropriate way at any particular time of utterance. This restricting of the extensions of predicates is an example of a more general fact. The extension of a combination of several predicates is the intersection of their respective extensions, or in other words, it is the set of things common to all of the extensions of the individual predicates.

Practice   Study the drawing. Imagine a very impoverished little universe of discourse containing only the objects depicted.

Practice   Assuming that the predicates *two-legged, four-legged, striped, mammal, creature,* etc. have their normal English meanings, draw circles on the drawing as follows:

(1) Enclosing all four-legged things, and nothing else (i.e. the extension, in this little universe, of the predicate *four-legged*)

(2) Enclosing the extension of the predicate *creature*

(3) Enclosing the extension of *mammal*

(4) Enclosing the extension of *two-legged*

(5) Did the intersection of the first two circles you drew enclose just the set of four-legged creatures?   (Yes)/ No

(6) Did the intersection of the last two circles you drew enclose just the set of two-legged mammals?   (Yes)/ No

(7) In this little universe, is the extension of *non-human mammal* identical to that of *four-legged creature*?   (Yes) No

(8) In this little universe, does the extension of the expression *striped human* have any members at all?   Yes / (No)

Feedback   (1) The circle encloses the table, the chair, the cow, and the tiger. (2) It encloses the man, the bird, the cow, and the tiger. (3) It encloses the man, the cow, and the tiger. (4) It encloses the man and the bird. (5) Yes (6) Yes (7) Yes (8) No, the extension of *striped human* has no members. It is technically called 'the null (or empty) set'. Logicians allow themselves to talk of a set with no members.

Comment It has tempted some philosophers to try to equate the meaning of a predicate, or combination of predicates, simply with its extension, but this suggestion will not work. Classic counterexamples include the pairs *featherless biped* vs *rational animal*, and *creature with a heart* vs *creature with a kidney*. The only featherless bipeds, so it happens apparently, are human beings, and if we assume that human beings are also the only rational animals, then the phrases *featherless biped* and *rational animal* have the same extensions, but of course these two phrases do not mean the same thing. It also happens to be the case that every creature with a heart also has a kidney, and vice versa, so that the extensions of *creature with a heart* and *creature with a kidney* are identical, but again, these two phrases do not mean the same thing. Philosophers and logicians who have developed the idea of extension have been very resourceful and ingenious in adapting the idea to meet some of the difficulties which have been pointed out. We will not discuss such developments here, because they seem to carry to an extreme degree a basic flaw in the essential idea of extensions. This flaw can be described as the undecidability of extensions. We bring out what we mean by this in practice below.

Practice We will try to solve the well-known 'chicken-and-egg' problem. To do so we make the following assumptions: (a) the only kind of egg that a chicken can lay is a chicken's egg, and (b) the only thing that can hatch from a chicken's egg is a (young) chicken.

(1) Do the assumptions given allow the following as a possibility? The first chicken's egg, from which all subsequent chickens are descended, was laid by a bird which was not itself a chicken, although an ancestor of all chickens. Yes / No

(2) Do our initial assumptions allow the following as a possibility? The first chicken was hatched from an egg that was not a chicken's egg. Yes / No

(3) Now imagine that, miraculously, a complete fossil record was available of all the birds and eggs in the ancestry of some modern chicken, going back to clear examples of non-chickens and non-chickens' eggs. Would it be possible, by careful inspection of this sequence of eggs and birds, to solve the chicken-and-egg problem empirically by pointing either to something that was clearly the first chicken, or alternatively to something that was clearly the first chicken's egg? Yes / No

(4) Try to explain the reasons for your answer to question (3).

Evolution is to subtle to tell when the 1ˢᵗ true chicken was hatched.

Feedback | (1) Yes (2) Yes (3) No (4) Evolution proceeds in such minute stages that one has the impression of a continuum. We do not have a clear enough idea of what is and what is not a chicken (or a chicken's egg) to be able to tell with any certainty which one in a long line of very subtly changing objects is the 'first' chicken('s egg).

Comment | The point is that even people who can reasonably claim to know the meaning of *chicken* cannot draw a clear line around the set of all chickens, past, present, and future, separating them from all the non-chickens. In short, the extension of chicken is not a clear set. It is a 'fuzzy set', and fuzziness is far from the spirit of the original idea of extensions. This fuzziness is a problem which besets almost all predicates, not only *chicken* and *egg*.

Practice | (1) If all the ancestors of some modern cat, going back as far as pre-cats, were available for inspection, do you think it would be possible to tell clearly which one of them was 'the first cat'? Yes / No

(2) Is the extension of *cat* a clearly defined set? Yes / No

(3) Can you imagine finding some creature in the woods and, despite thorough inspection, not being able to decide whether it should be called a 'cat' or not? Yes / No

(4) Is the 'present extension' of *cat* (what we have called the extension of *is a cat*) a clearly defined set? Yes / No

(5) Could a potter make some object which was halfway between a cup and a mug? If so, what would you call it?
Yes, "mug" or "cug" (since you wouldn't know what to call it 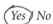 a cup or mug)

(6) Could a whimsical carpenter make an object that was halfway between a table and a chair? If so, what would you call such an object?
Yes, hard to know what to call it.

Feedback | (1) No (2) No (3) Yes, this situation is imaginable. (4) No (5) Yes; it would be hard to know whether to call it a cup or a mug. (6) Yes; it would be hard to know whether to call it a chair or a table.

Comment | In practice, certain kinds of predicates present more difficulties than others. It is unusual, in everyday situations, for there to be much problem in applying the predicates *cat*, or *chicken*. Cats and chickens are natural kinds, which the world obligingly sorts out into relatively clear groups for us. But in the case of some other kinds of predicates, it is obvious that everyday language does not put well-defined boundaries around their extensions. A good example of this is the difficulty people often have in deciding what the boundary is between two similar colours, as shown in the following practice.

Practice (1) Have you ever argued with another English speaker
about whether or not to call some object blue?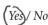

(2) Have you ever been in doubt yourself, as an individual,
about whether to call something pink or orange?

(3) Have you ever been in doubt about whether to call
something a tree or a shrub?

(4) Is there a clear difference for you between what can be
called a book and what can be called a pamphlet?

(5) Is there a clear difference between what can be called paper
and what can be called card?

Feedback   (1) Yes, probably (2) Yes, probably (3) Yes, probably (4) No, probably not
(5) No, probably not

Comment   The original motivation for the idea of extension was to explain the ability of
speakers of a language to group entities having similar characteristics, such as
cats or chickens, into distinct mental categories and to refer to these objects
in the world, using linguistic expressions containing predicates. In addition,
the idea of extension was to explain their ability as hearers to identify the
referents of referring expressions containing predicates, and their ability to
make and understand descriptive statements using predicates, as in *Atkins is a
cat*. But speakers are in fact only able to do these things in normal situations.
The idea of extension is too ambitious, extending to all situations. In fact, a
speaker does not have a perfectly clear idea of what is a cat and what is not a
cat. Between obvious cats and obvious non-cats there is a grey area of doubt,
as we see in the following sketches.

In order to get around such difficulties with the idea of extension,
semanticists have introduced the two closely related notions of prototype and
stereotype.

Definition   A PROTOTYPE of a predicate is an object which is held to be very TYPICAL
of the kind of object which can be referred to by an expression containing
the predicate. In other words, the prototype of a predicate can be thought of
as the most typical member of the extension of a predicate.

Example   A man of medium height and average build, between 30 and 50 years old,
with brownish hair, with no particularly distinctive characteristics or defects,
could be a prototype of the predicate *man* in certain areas of the world.

87

A dwarf or a hugely muscular body-builder could not be a prototype of the predicate *man.*

Practice   For each of the drawings (1)–(7), say whether the object shown could be a prototype of the predicate given below it for an average person living in Europe or North America.

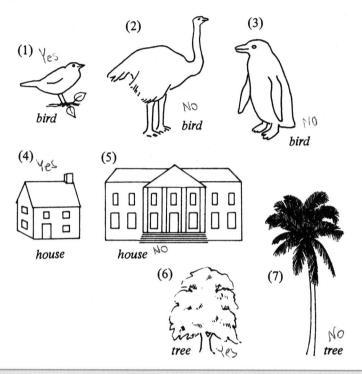

(1) Yes
bird

(2) No
bird

(3) No
bird

(4) Yes
house

(5) No
house

(6) Yes
tree

(7) No
tree

Feedback   (1) Yes (2) No (3) No (4) Yes (5) No (6) Yes (7) No

Comment   Since we are not especially interested in the language of any one individual, but rather in, say, English as a whole, we will talk in terms of shared prototypes, i.e. objects on which there would be general agreement that they were typical examples of the class of objects described by a certain predicate. In a language community as wide as that of English, there are problems with this idea of prototype, due to cultural differences between various English-speaking communities. Consider these examples.

Practice   (1)   Could a double-decker bus (of the kind found in British cities) be a prototype for the predicate *bus* for a British English-speaker?   Yes / No

(2)   Could such a bus be a prototype for the predicate *bus* for an American English-speaker?   Yes / No

(3)   Could a skyscraper be a prototype for the predicate *building* for an inhabitant of New York City?   Yes / No

(4) Could a skyscraper be a prototype for the predicate
building for someone who had spent his life in Britain
(outside London)?　　　　　　　　　　　　　　　　Yes / No

(5) Could a palm tree (like that pictured in a practice above)
be a prototype for someone who has lived since birth on
a tropical island, say in Hawai'i?　　　　　　　　Yes / No

(6) Could a parrot (or other similar large brightly coloured
bird) be a prototype for someone who has lived her life
in the rain forest?　　　　　　　　　　　　　　　Yes / No

Feedback　(1) Yes (2) No, probably not (3) Yes (4) No (5) Yes (6) Yes

Comment　You will be able to think of other examples of cultural differences leading to
different prototypes.

　The idea of a prototype is perhaps most useful in explaining how people
learn to use (some of) the predicates in their language correctly. Recent
research on the acquisition of categories in human language indicates that
the prototypical members of the extension of a predicate are usually learned
earlier than non-prototypical members. Predicates like *man, cat, dog* are often
first taught to toddlers by pointing out to them typical examples of men, cats,
dogs, etc. A mother may point to a cat and tell her child 'That's a cat', or point
to the child's father and say 'Daddy's a man'. This kind of definition by
pointing is called ostensive definition. It is very plausible to believe that a
child's first concepts of many concrete terms are induced by ostensive
definition involving a prototype. Obviously, however, not all concepts can be
learned in this way.

Practice　(1) Could the predicate *bottle* be defined ostensively, by
pointing to a prototypical bottle?　　　　　　　　Yes / No

(2) Is it likely that the predicate *battle* would be learned
by ostensive definition?　　　　　　　　　　　　Yes / No

(3) Are predicates for various external body-parts, e.g.
chin, nose, eye, leg, elbow, most probably first learned
from ostensive definitions?　　　　　　　　　　　Yes / No

(4) Are colour predicates, such as *red, blue, green, yellow*,
probably first learned from ostensive definitions?　Yes / No

(5) Could the meaning of *ambition* be learned from a simple
ostensive definition (i.e. by someone pointing to an
ambitious man and saying 'That's ambition' or
even 'He's an ambitious man')?　　　　　　　　　Yes / No

(6) Could the meaning of *electricity* be defined ostensively?　Yes / No

Feedback (1) Yes (2) No, although one might just possibly learn the meaning of *battle* from being shown a battle in a movie. (3) Yes (4) Yes, most likely (5) No, someone who doesn't know the meaning of *ambition* couldn't identify the relevant quality just by being shown an ambitious man. (6) No, it's difficult to see how this could happen.

Comment Some predicates which do not have clearly defined extensions (e.g. colour terms like *red* and *blue*) do in fact have clear prototypes. Influential research in the 1960s by Brent Berlin and Paul Kay demonstrated that although one cannot be sure exactly where red shades off into pink or orange, for example, there is general agreement in the English speech community about the central, focal, or prototypical examples of red. Thus the idea of prototype has at least some advantage over that of extension. But in other cases, such as abstract mass terms (e.g. *ambition*) there is about as much difficulty in identifying the prototype of a predicate as there is of identifying its extension.

We conclude by repeating definitions of referent, extension, and prototype below.

Definition The REFERENT of a referring expression is the thing picked out by the use of that expression on a particular occasion of utterance.

The EXTENSION of a predicate is the complete set of all things which could potentially (i.e. in any possible utterance) be the referent of a referring expression whose head constituent is that predicate.

A PROTOTYPE of a predicate is a typical member of its extension.

Comment We make a distinction between prototype and stereotype: we will define stereotype in the next unit. In other texts, the two terms are often used interchangeably. A further term, which we will have an occasional use for, is 'denotation'. In many cases denotation can be thought of as equivalent to extension. Thus, for example, the predicate *cat* can be said to denote the set of all cats. But often the term is used in a wider, essentially vaguer, sense, especially in connection with predicates whose extensions are problematical. Thus one may find statements about meaning such as '*redness* denotes the property common to all red things', or '*ambition* denotes a human quality', or 'the preposition *under* denotes a spatial relationship'.

Summary Reference, extension, and prototype all focus attention on the relationship between words and things. Clearly, language does not exist in a vacuum. It is used to make statements about the world outside, and these three notions are useful in an analysis of exactly how the relationship between language and the world works.

Unit 8 Study Guide and Exercises

Directions   After you have read Unit 8 you should be able to tackle the following
questions to test your understanding of the main ideas raised in the unit.

1   You should understand these terms and concepts from this unit:
extension   fuzzy set
extension of a one-place predicate   ostensive definition
prototype   denotation

2   Is the difference between **reference** and **sense** clear-cut or not? Explain and
illustrate.

3   Explain the notion of **potential referents** in connection with the phrase
the book.

4   What term introduced in this unit describes the set of potential referents of
a referring expression such as the noun phrase *the book* in 3 above?

5   Distinguish between **referent** and **extension**.

6   Make sure you understand the chart on page 81 in which the differences
and similarities between sense, extension, and reference are described. In
what way are **sense** and **extension** alike, and unlike **reference**? In what way
are **extension** and **reference** alike, and unlike **sense**?

7   In this unit we said that 'A speaker's knowledge of the sense of a predicate
provides . . . an idea of its extension'. In other words, we noted that sense
fixes (determines) extension. Explain as best you can in your own words.

8   Do you think it would be possible for the extension of a predicate to fix
(determine) the sense of that predicate? Why or why not?

9   Describe briefly the extension of *car*.

10 What is meant by the statement that 'extensions are relative to all times,
past, present, and future'? How can we restrict the extension of a
predicate?

11 In this unit we noted that **extension** and **meaning** cannot be equated (cf.
featherless biped and *rational animal*). Why not?

12 What is the basic flaw in the idea of extensions? What are **fuzzy sets** and
how is this notion supposed to resolve the problem? Give your own
example.

13 What role does the notion of **natural kind** play with respect to the notion
of **extension**? What originally motivated the notion of an extension?

14 Briefly describe **prototypical** examples of the following entities, along with
one or two non-prototypical examples that could also be referred to by each
predicate. Explain why the non-prototypical examples diverge from the
prototype.

a bird   d dog
b book   e flower
c furniture   f chair

15 What does the concept **prototype** have to do with meaning? How is it related to the learning of the meanings of certain expressions?

16 In this unit we gave several examples in which cultural differences can lead to different prototypes. Think of some more examples not mentioned in the book.

17 Give some examples not in the book which would probably be learned via **ostensive definition** and some which are probably not likely learned that way.

3 . . . to sense

UNIT 9 SENSE PROPERTIES AND STEREOTYPES

Entry requirements ONE-, TWO-, and THREE-PLACE PREDICATES (Unit 5), EXTENSION and PROTOTYPE (Unit 8). If you feel unfamiliar with any of these ideas, review the appropriate unit. Otherwise, take the entry test below.

Entry test (1) Which of the following are two-place predicates? Circle your answer.
below, smother, sleep, come, annihilate, vanish, afraid (of)

(2) Write the terms 'referent', 'extension', and 'prototype' in the appropriate boxes in the chart below:

	(Set of things that could be referred to using a particular predicate)
(Thing referred to on a particular occasion of utterance)	....
	(Thing typically referred to using a particular predicate) ....

Feedback (1) *below, smother, annihilate, afraid of*

(2) Referent | Extension
              | Prototype

If you have answered both questions correctly, continue to the introduction. Otherwise, review the relevant unit.

Introduction It is sometimes hard to distinguish a factual (or 'ontological') question from a semantic one.

Practice (1) Have you ever been asked an apparently factual question about something (call it 'X'), and found it necessary to say to your questioner 'Well, it depends on what you mean by X'?   *Yes / No*

(2) Have you ever been involved in an argument with someone over an apparently factual matter, only to discover that some particularly crucial word in the argument had a different meaning for the other person?   *Yes / No*

(3) In a case where someone says, 'Well, it depends what you mean by X', is it often possible, once the meaning of X has been agreed by both parties, for the original factual question to be answered straightforwardly?   *Yes / No*

(4) If two people can be said to agree on the meanings of all
     the words they use, must any remaining disagreements between
     them be regarded as disagreements about matters of fact?   *Yes / No*

(5) If we could not agree about the meanings of any of the words
     we use, could any disagreement about matters of fact even be
     formulated, let alone resolved?   *Yes / No*

Feedback   (1) Probably, almost everyone has been in this situation. (2) again,
           probably Yes (3) Yes (4) Yes (5) No

Comment   In order to be able to talk meaningfully about anything, it is necessary to
          agree on the meanings of the words involved. This is a truism. In everyday
          life, people reach practical agreement on the meanings of almost all the
          words they use, and effective and successful communication takes place as a
          result. If a person wants to hinder or obstruct communication, he can begin
          to quibble over the meanings of everyday words. Although there may be
          disagreement about the fine details of the meanings of words 'around the
          edges', we find in the everyday use of language that all words are understood
          by speakers as having an indispensable hard core of meaning.

Practice   Given below are three conversations which get stuck. In each one, speaker B
           seems to ignore some particular convention about the meaning of one of the
           words involved, a convention universally accepted in everyday English. For
           each conversation, write out a statement about the meaning of the word
           concerned, a statement that speaker B seems not to accept.

(1) A: 'I saw something strange in the garden this morning.'
     B: 'Oh! What was it?'
     A: 'An animal perched on top of the clothes pole.'
     B: 'How do you know it was an animal?'
     A: 'I saw it. It was a cat.'
     B: 'You might have seen a cat, but how can you be sure it was an
          animal?'
     A: 'Well, of course it was an animal, if it was a cat.'
     B: 'I don't see how that follows.'

     ....

(2) B: 'My neighbour's child is an adult.'
     A: 'You mean he was a child and is now grown up?'
     B: 'No. He is still a child, even though he's an adult.'
     A: 'You mean that he's a child who acts in a very grown up way?'
     B: 'No. He's just an adult child, that's all.'

     ....

(3) B: 'I finally killed Ben's parrot.'
     A: 'So it's dead, then?'
     B: 'No, I didn't say that. Just that I killed it.'
     A: 'But if you killed it, it must be dead.'
     B: 'No. I was quite careful about it. I killed it very carefully so it's not dead.'

....

Feedback   (1) The meaning of *cat* includes that of *animal*. (2) The meaning of *adult* excludes the meaning of *child*. (3) The meaning of *kill* is related to that of *dead* in such a way that anything killed is necessarily dead.

Comment   The kind of meaning we are talking about here is obviously the kind associated with words and sentences by the language system, and not the speaker meaning (see Unit 1) specifically associated with utterances made by speakers on particular occasions. This kind of meaning we call sense.

Definition (partial: The SENSE of an expression is its indispensable hard core of meaning.
see also Unit 3)

Comment   This definition deliberately excludes any influence of context or situation of utterance on the senses of expressions. (Thus it is problematic to talk of the senses of deictic words (Unit 7), but we will not go into that problem here.)
    The sense of an expression can be thought of as the sum of its sense properties and sense relations with other expressions. For the moment, we will concentrate on three important sense properties of sentences, the properties of being analytic, of being synthetic, and of being contradictory.

Definition   An ANALYTIC sentence is one that is necessarily TRUE, as a result of the senses of the words in it. An analytic sentence, therefore, reflects a tacit (unspoken) agreement by speakers of the language about the senses of the words in it.
    A SYNTHETIC sentence is one which is NOT analytic, but may be either true or false, depending on the way the world is.

Example   Analytic: *All elephants are animals*
The truth of the sentence follows from the senses of *elephant* and *animal*.
Synthetic: *John is from Ireland*
There is nothing in the senses of *John* or *Ireland* or *from* which makes this necessarily true or false.

Practice   (1) Label the following sentences either *T* for true, *F* for false, or *D* for don't know, as appropriate.

           (a) *Cats are animals*   *T / F / D*

           (b) *Bachelors are unmarried*   *T / F / D*

95

(c)	*Cats never live more than 20 years*	*T / F / D*
(d)	*Bachelors cannot form lasting relationships*	*T / F / D*
(e)	*Cats are not vegetables*	*T / F / D*
(f)	*Bachelors are male*	*T / F / D*
(g)	*No cat likes to bathe*	*T / F / D*
(h)	*Bachelors are lonely*	*T / F / D*

(2) Were you able to assign *T* or *F* to all the above sentences?   *Yes / No*

(3) Which of the above sentences do you think ANY speaker of English could assign *T* or *F* to?

....

(4) Which of the sentences in (a)–(h) above would you say are true by virtue of the senses of the words in them?

....

(5) Which of the sentences above would you say might be true or false as a matter of fact about the world?

....

Feedback   (1) (a) T (b) T (c)–(d) Actually we, the authors, don't know the answers for these sentences. (e) T (f) T (g)–(h) We don't know the answers for these, either. (2) Perhaps you were; we weren't. (3) (a),(b),(e),(f) (4) (a),(b),(e),(f) (5) (c),(d),(g),(h)

Comment   Sentences (a),(b),(e),(f) are analytic. Sentences (c),(d),(g),(h) are synthetic.

Practice   Here are some more sentences. Circle *A* for analytic, or *S* for synthetic, as appropriate. For some, you will have to imagine relevant situations.

(1)	*John's brother is nine years old*	*A / S*
(2)	*John's nine-year-old brother is a boy*	*A / S*
(3)	*Sam's wife is married*	*A / S*
(4)	*Sam's wife is not German*	*A / S*
(5)	*My watch is slow*	*A / S*
(6)	*My watch is a device for telling the time*	*A / S*

Feedback   (1) S (2) A (3) A (4) S (5) S (6) A

Comment   Analytic sentences are always true (necessarily so, by virtue of the senses of the words in them), whereas synthetic sentences can be sometimes true, sometimes false, depending on the circumstances. We now come to contradiction.

Definition   A CONTRADICTION is a sentence that is necessarily FALSE, as a result of
the senses of the words in it. Thus a contradiction is in a way the opposite of
an analytic sentence.

Example   *This animal is a vegetable* is a contradiction.
This must be false because of the senses of *animal* and *vegetable*.
Both of John's parents are married to aunts of mine is a contradiction.
This must be false because of the senses of *both parents, married*, and *aunt*.

Practice   Circle the following sentences *A* for analytic, *S* for synthetic or *C* for
contradiction, as appropriate. For some you will have to imagine relevant
situations.

(1)	*That girl is her own mother's mother*	A / S / C
(2)	*The boy is his own father's son*	A / S / C
(3)	*Alice is Ken's sister*	A / S / C
(4)	*Some typewriters are dusty*	A / S / C
(5)	*If it breaks, it breaks*	A / S / C
(6)	*John killed Bill, who remained alive for many years after*	A / S / C

Feedback   (1) C (2) A (3) S (4) S (5) A (6) C

Comment   Analytic sentences can be formed from contradictions, and vice versa, by the
insertion or removal, as appropriate, of the negative particle word *not*.
   We pay no attention here to the figurative use of both analytic sentences
and contradictions. Taken literally, the sentence *That man is not a human
being* is a contradiction. This very fact is what gives it its power to
communicate a strong emotional judgement in a figurative use (stronger
than, say, the synthetic *That man is very cruel*).
   We will now mention a limitation of the notions analytic, synthetic, and
contradiction. Remember that these notions are defined in terms of truth.
Imperative and interrogative sentences cannot be true or false, and so they
cannot be analytic (because they cannot be true), or synthetic, because
'synthetic' only makes sense in contrast to the notion 'analytic'.
   You will have noticed that synthetic sentences are potentially informative in
real-world situations, whereas analytic sentences and contradictions are not
informative to anyone who already knows the meaning of the words in them.
It might be thought that the fact that semanticists concentrate attention on
unusual sentences, such as analytic ones and contradictions, reflects a lack of
interest in ordinary, everyday language. Quite the contrary! Semanticists are
interested in the foundations of everyday communication. People can only
communicate meaningfully about everyday matters, using informative
synthetic sentences, because (or to the extent that) they agree on the meanings

97

of the words in them. This basic agreement on meaning is reflected in analytic sentences, which is what makes them of great interest to semanticists.

The notions analytic, synthetic, and contradiction each apply to individual sentences. Analyticity, syntheticity, and contradiction are, then, sense properties of sentences.

Example   *That man is human* has the sense property of analyticity (or of being analytic). *That man is tall* has the sense property of syntheticity (or of being synthetic). *That man is a woman* has the sense property of being a contradiction.

Practice   (1) Does the analyticity of *That man is human* depend in some crucial way on a semantic relationship between the sense of *man* and that of *human*?   *Yes / No*

(2) Which of the following statements seems to express this semantic relationship between *man* and *human* correctly? Circle your choice.

(a)   The sense of *man* includes the sense of *human*.

(b)   The sense of *human* includes the sense of *man*.

(c)   The sense of *man* is identical to the sense of *human*.

(3) Does the semantic relationship that exists between *man* and *human* also exist between *man* and *tall*?   *Yes / No*

(4) Does the absence of this semantic relationship between *man* and *tall* account for the fact that *This man is tall* is not analytic, like *This man is human*?   *Yes / No*

Feedback   (1) Yes (2) (a) (3) No (4) Yes

Comment   Note the interdependence of sense relations and sense properties. Sense properties of sentences (e.g. analyticity) depend on the sense properties of, and the sense relations between, the words they contain. The sense relation between the predicates *man* and *human* is known as hyponymy, a kind of sense inclusion relationship between predicates which we will explore further in Unit 10. The sense relation between the predicates *man* and *woman* is a kind of antonymy, or oppositeness, which we will explore further in Unit 11. The sense structure of a language is like a network, in which the senses of all elements are, directly or indirectly, related to the senses of all other elements in these and other kinds of ways.

For the rest of this unit, we will explore a limitation in the idea of sense, a limitation which is quite parallel to a limitation in the idea of extension, pointed out in the previous unit (Unit 8). For convenience, we repeat below our statement of the relationship usually envisaged between sense and extension.

A speaker's knowledge of the sense of a predicate provides him with an idea of its extension. We said earlier that another way of talking about this relationship is that the sense of a predicate determines or 'fixes' the extension of that predicate. For example, the 'dictionary definition' which the speaker accepts for *cat* can be used to decide what is a cat, and what is not, thus defining, implicitly, the set of all cats.

Now we'll consider the implications of this envisaged relationship more closely. We need to recognize the concepts of necessary and sufficient conditions.

Definition   A NECESSARY CONDITION on the sense of a predicate is a condition (or criterion) which a thing MUST meet in order to qualify as being correctly described by that predicate.

A SUFFICIENT SET OF CONDITIONS on the sense of a predicate is a set of conditions (or criteria) which, if they are met by a thing, are enough in themselves to GUARANTEE that the predicate correctly describes that thing.

Example   Take the predicate *square*, as usually understood in geometry. 'Four-sided' is a necessary condition for this predicate, since for anything to be a square, it must be four-sided.

'Plane figure, four-sided, equal-sided, and containing right angles' is a sufficient set of conditions for the predicate *square*, since if anything meets all of these conditions, it is guaranteed to be a square.

'Four-sided and containing right angles' is not a sufficient set of conditions for *square*. Many non-square shapes, such as rectangles and trapezoids, meet these conditions.

'Three-sided' is not a necessary condition for *square*.

Practice   (1) Is 'three-dimensional object' a necessary condition for
the predicate *sphere*?   *Yes / No*

(2) Is 'three-dimensional object' a necessary condition for
the predicate *circle*?   *Yes / No*

(3) Is 'three-dimensional object and circular in cross-section'
a sufficient set of conditions for *sphere*?   *Yes / No*

(4) Is 'three-dimensional object and with all points on surface
equidistant from a single point' a sufficient set of conditions
for *sphere*?   *Yes / No*

(5) Is 'male' a necessary condition for *bachelor*?   *Yes / No*

(6) Is 'adult, male, human, and unmarried' a sufficient set of
conditions for *bachelor*?   *Yes / No*

Feedback   (1) Yes (2) No (3) No (e.g. a cylinder) (4) Yes (5) Yes (6) Yes, for us, though some would debate the point, arguing, for example, that a monk or a Catholic priest meets these conditions but could not correctly be called a bachelor. For us, monks and priests are bachelors.

Comment   Obviously, we are stating conditions on predicates in terms of other predicates in the language. Henceforth, we will drop the quotation marks, and envisage necessary and sufficient conditions as relationships between predicates. Thus we shall say, for example, that *animal* and *cat* are semantically related in such a way that the applicability of the former is a necessary condition for the applicability of the latter. (Nothing can be a cat without being an animal.) In fact it is possible to give complete definitions of some predicates in the form of a 'necessary and sufficient list' of other predicates. Kinship predicates and shape predicates are well-known examples.

Practice   (1) Is *father* adequately defined as male parent?   *Yes / No*

(2) Is *female spouse* an adequate definition of *wife*?   *Yes / No*

(3) Is *parent's father* an adequate definition of *grandfather*?   *Yes / No*

(4) Is *hexagon* adequately defined as *five-sided plane figure*?   *Yes / No*

Feedback   (1) Yes (2) Yes (3) Yes (4) No

Comment   The idea of defining predicates by sets of necessary and sufficient conditions can be evaluated from a practical point of view. The parallel with the undecidability of extensions is very close. Just as in a large number of cases it is implausible to postulate the existence of perfectly clearly defined sets of things, such as the set of all cats, the set of all tables, etc., so too the idea that there could be satisfactory definitions in the form of sets of necessary and sufficient conditions for such predicates as *cat*, *table*, etc. is clearly misguided.

One of the best-known arguments (by the philosopher Ludwig Wittgenstein) against the idea that definitions of the meanings of words can be given in the form of sets of necessary and sufficient conditions involves the word *game*.

Practice   Given below are two definitions of the word *game*, taken from dictionaries of modern English. For each definition, give, if possible, (a) the name of at least one game (e.g. *football*, *chess*) not covered by the definition, and (b) at least one thing that is not a game (e.g. *piano-playing*, *watching television*) but which falls within the given definition.

(1) An amusement or diversion

(a) ....   (b) ....

(2) A contest, physical or mental, according to set rules, undertaken for amusement or for a stake

(a) ....   (b) ....

Feedback (1) (a) We can think of no examples of games which are not amusements or diversions. (b) piano-playing, watching television, fishing, embroidery (2) (a) cat's-cradle (not a contest), patience or solitaire (also not contests, except in a vacuous sense) (b) a 100-metre footrace, high-jump, pole-vault (such events are not normally called 'games' but rather 'races', 'contests', or 'competitions'), musical competitions

Comment Wittgenstein's example of *game* cuts both ways. On the one hand, one must admit that a set of necessary and sufficient conditions for *game* to cover all eventualities (including games played in the past and games yet to be invented) cannot be given. On the other hand, one has to admit that some of the definitions offered by dictionaries, while imperfect, do cover a large number of cases, and are in fact helpful.

It is possible to give at least some necessary and/or sufficient conditions for all predicates in a language. If there were a predicate for which we could give no necessary or sufficient condition, we would have to admit that we literally had no idea what it meant.

Practice (1) Is the sense of *activity* a necessary part of the sense of *game* (i.e. must something be an activity to be a game)? *Yes / No*

(2) Is the sense of *game* a necessary part of the sense of *tennis* (i.e. must some activity be a game to be tennis)? *Yes / No*

(3) Is the sense of *chess* a sufficient part of the sense of *game* (i.e. is the fact that something is chess sufficient evidence to call it a game)? *Yes / No*

(4) A witty literary lady coined the memorable sentence, *A rose is a rose is a rose*, implying that definition could go no further. One can actually go at least a little further. Is the sense of *flower* a necessary part of the sense of *rose*? *Yes / No*

Feedback (1) Yes (2) Yes (3) Yes (4) Yes

Comment Except in a few cases, complete definitions of the meanings of predicates cannot be given, but nevertheless it is possible to give, for every predicate in a language, at least some necessary and/or sufficient ingredients in its meaning. Later units (10–11, and the whole chapter on word meaning, Units 16–20) will explore in more detail just how far one can go in giving definitions of the meanings of words, but it is clear in advance that definitions of many terms will be quite sketchy indeed. It seems reasonable to suppose that speakers of a language have in their heads not only an idea of the bare sense of any given predicate, but also a stereotype of it.

Definition The STEREOTYPE of a predicate is a list of the TYPICAL characteristics or features of things to which the predicate may be applied.

Example   The stereotype of *cat* would be something like:

> Quadruped, domesticated, either black, or white, or grey, or tortoise-shell, or marmalade in colour, or some combination of these colours, adult specimens about 50 cm long from nose to tip of tail, furry, with sharp retractable claws, etc., etc.

Practice   (1) Suggest four characteristics which should be included in the stereotype of the predicate *elephant*. (Be sure not to include any more basic term, properly belonging to the SENSE of *elephant*.)

....

....

(2) Give two characteristics which should be included in the stereotype of *mother*.

....

....

(3) Give four characteristics which should be included in the stereotype of *cup*.

....

....

(4) Give four characteristics which should be included in the stereotype of *building*.

....

....

Feedback   (1) e.g. grey, very thick-skinned, virtually hairless, with a trunk and two tusks, adult specimens weighing several tons, etc. (2) e.g. caring for her young, living with their father, etc. (3) e.g. between 3 and 6 cm high, round in cross-section, wider at the top than at the bottom, of china, with a handle, made to fit a saucer, etc. (4) e.g. containing upward of three or four rooms, built of a durable material, such as concrete, wood, stone, with a roof, doors, and windows, used regularly by human beings, etc.

Comment   A stereotype is related to a prototype (see previous unit) but is not the same thing. A prototype of *elephant* is some actual elephant, whereas the stereotype of *elephant* is a list of characteristics which describes the prototype. The stereotype of a predicate may often specify a range of possibilities (e.g. the range of colours of typical cats), but an individual prototype of this predicate will necessarily take some particular place within this range (e.g. black).

Another important difference between prototype and stereotype is that a speaker may well know a stereotype for some predicate, such as *ghost*, *witchdoctor, flying saucer,* but not actually be acquainted with any prototypes of it. Stereotypes of expressions for things learnt about at second hand, through descriptions rather than direct experience, are generally known in this way.

The relationships between stereotype, prototype, sense, and extension are summarized very briefly in the chart. The notions of prototype

	Thing (or set of things) specified	Abstract specification
Pertaining to all examples	EXTENSION	SENSE
Pertaining to typical examples	PROTOTYPE	STEREOTYPE

and stereotype are relatively recent in semantics. We have in fact given definitions which sharpen up the difference between the two terms, which are sometimes used vaguely or even interchangeably. Important though the notion of stereotype is in everyday language, it is obviously not so basic to meaning as the idea of sense, which we have defined as an indispensable hard core of meaning. In this book we will deal no further with the notions of prototype and stereotype, but we will give a lot of attention to sense.

Summary   The sense of an expression can be thought of as the sum of its sense properties and sense relations. Sense properties of sentences include those of being analytic, synthetic, and a contradiction.

With the exception of a few predicates such as *bachelor, father, square, sphere,* etc. it is not possible to give complete definitions of the sense of most predicates by sets of necessary and sufficient conditions. Stereotypes defined in terms of typical characteristics account for the fact that people usually agree on the meanings of the words they use.

Unit 9   Study Guide and Exercises

Directions   After you have read Unit 9 you should be able to tackle the following questions to test your understanding of the main ideas raised in the unit.

1   You should understand these terms and concepts from this unit:

sense	synthetic sentences
analytic sentences	contradiction
set of sufficient conditions	necessary condition
sense properties of sentences	stereotype (feature)

2   Assume that John is the same person in each of the following sentences. Now, if the sentence *John is a bachelor* is true, then is it true or false that:

a   John is male   c   John is human

b   John is unmarried   d   John is adult

We can say that the sentence *John is a bachelor* entails (a–d) if the truth of (a–d) necessarily follows from the proposition contained in the sentence

John is a bachelor. The notion of entailment will be explored in greater detail in Unit 10.

For questions 3–7 indicate whether each sentence is **analytic**, **synthetic**, or a **contradiction**. If you are not sure about a sentence, try to explain why it is not a clear-cut case.

3   a   All bachelors are unmarried   c   All bachelors are married
    b   All bachelors are happy

4   a   All misers are stingy   c   All misers waste money
    b   All misers are rich   d   All misers are miserable

5   a   All carnivores eat meat
    b   All mammals produce live young

6   a   My unmarried sister is married to a bachelor
    b   This stool has a broken back

7   a   Kings are monarchs
    b   Kings are male
    c   Kings are fathers
    d   George Washington was the first president
    e   Witches are wicked
    f   My brother is an only child
    g   Puppies are human

8   Explain why synthetic sentences are potentially informative whereas analytic sentences and contradictions are not.

9   Give some necessary conditions for the following lexical items.
    a   table   c   sister
    b   car   d   teacher

10   Is it possible to list a set of necessary and sufficient conditions to fully and adequately characterize the lexical item *mother*? Try to come up with a couple of such sets of conditions and then explain why they are insufficient. (Hint: think of all the current terms which contain the word *mother*, including *birth mother, surrogate mother, stepmother, biological mother, adoptive mother, natural mother, foster mother, unwed mother, genetic mother*, etc.)

11   What is the difference between **prototype** and **stereotype** (or semantic feature) as set forth in this unit?

UNIT 10 SENSE RELATIONS (1)
IDENTITY AND SIMILARITY OF SENSE

Entry requirements SENSE (Units 3 and 9) and ANALYTICITY (Unit 9). If you feel you understand these notions, take the entry test below. Otherwise review the relevant units.

Entry test Words such as *mean, meaning, meant*, etc. are used ambiguously in everyday language to indicate either sense or reference.

(1) Do the words *mean* and *meant* indicate sense (*S*) or reference (*R*) in the utterance:
'I'm sorry to have disturbed you – when I said 'Will you move your chair?', I didn't mean you, I meant Patrick here.'   *S / R*

(2) Does the word *means* indicate sense or reference in:
'If you look up *ochlocracy*, you'll find it means *government by the mob*.'   *S / R*

(3) Which of the following is correct? Circle your answer.
(a) The sense of any word is its dictionary definition, in the form of a complete set of necessary and sufficient conditions for its use.
(b) The sense of a predicate is the set of all things it can be correctly applied to.
(c) The sense of a predicate is its indispensable hard core of meaning.

(4) Are the following sentences analytic (*A*), synthetic (*S*), or a contradiction (*C*)?
(a) *John is simultaneously a man and not a human being*   *A / S / C*
(b) *Mussolini was an Italian*   *A / S / C*
(c) *Every female dog is a bitch*   *A / S / C*

Feedback   (1) R (2) S (3) (c) (4) (a) C (b) S (c) A
If you had only one incorrect answer or had all correct, proceed to the introduction. If not, review Units 3 and 9 before continuing.

Introduction In previous units you were introduced to the notion of sense. We now proceed to the examination of sense relations. What we have referred to previously as the sense of an expression is the whole set of sense relations it contracts with other expressions in the language. We shall be mainly concerned with the sense relations which involve individual predicates and whole sentences.

Definition SYNONYMY is the relationship between two predicates that have the same **(partial)** sense.

Example In most dialects of English, *stubborn* and *obstinate* are synonyms.
In many dialects, *brigand* and *bandit* are synonyms.
In many dialects, *mercury* and *quicksilver* are synonyms.

Comment Examples of perfect synonymy are hard to find, perhaps because there is little point in a dialect having two predicates with exactly the same sense. Note that our definition of synonymy requires identity of sense. This is a stricter definition than is sometimes given: sometimes synonymy is defined as similarity of meaning, a definition which is vaguer than ours. The price we pay for our rather strict definition is that very few examples of synonymy, so defined, can be found. But the strict definition is useful as an ideal and we will still use it and assume that relatively good instances of synonymy are possible for the purpose of furthering our investigation into how to describe sense relations.

Practice In the following sentences, do the capitalized pairs of words have the same (or very nearly the same) sense in the ways they are used here?

(1) *The thief tried to CONCEAL/HIDE the evidence*   Yes / No

(2) *I'm going to PURCHASE/BUY a new coat*   Yes / No

(3) *These tomatoes are LARGE/RIPE*   Yes / No

(4) *This is a very LOOSE/SHORT definition*   Yes / No

(5) *You have my PROFOUND/DEEP sympathy*   Yes / No

(6) *It is a very WIDE/BROAD street*   Yes / No

Feedback (1) Yes (2) Yes (3) No (4) No (5) Yes (6) Yes

Comment Clearly the notions of synonymy and sense are interdependent. You can't understand one without understanding the other. These concepts are best communicated by a range of examples. In general, when dealing with sense relations, we shall stick to clear cases. (We admit the existence of many genuinely unclear, borderline cases.) In considering the sense of a word, we abstract away from any stylistic, social, or dialectal associations the word may have. We concentrate on what has been called the cognitive or conceptual meaning of a word.

Example *How many kids have you got?*
How many children have you got?

Here we would say that *kids* and *children* have the same sense, although clearly they differ in style, or formality.

Practice   In the following sentences, do the pairs of words in capitals have the same sense? (They do seem to differ in their dialectal, stylistic, or social associations.) Circle *S* for 'same' or *D* for 'different'.

(1)   *He comes to see us every FALL/AUTUMN*   *S / D*

(2)   *Nothing is more precious to us than our FREEDOM/LIBERTY*   *S / D*

(3)   *The body was found in the BOOT/TRUNK of the car*   *S / D*

(4)   *We've just bought a new HOUSE/APARTMENT*   *S / D*

(5)   *John got a bullet wound in his HEAD/GUTS*   *S / D*

(6)   *A BLOKE/CHAP I know has pickled onions for breakfast*   *S / D*

Feedback   (1) S (2) S (3) S (4) D (5) D (6) S

Comment   Synonymy is a relation between predicates, and not between words (i.e. word-forms). Recall that a word may have many different senses; each distinct sense of a word (of the kind we are dealing with) is a predicate. When necessary, we distinguish between predicates by giving them subscript numbers. For example, *hide₁* could be the intransitive verb, as in *Let's hide from Mummy*; *hide₂* could be the transitive verb, as in *Hide your sweeties under the pillow*; *hide₃* could be the noun, as in *We watched the birds from a hide*; and *hide₄* could be the noun, as in *The hide of an ox weighs 200 lbs*. The first three senses here (the first three predicates) are clearly related to each other in meaning, whereas the fourth is unrelated. It is because of the ambiguity of most words that we have had to formulate practice questions about synonymy in terms of sentences. The sentence *The thief tried to hide the evidence*, for example, makes it clear that one is dealing with the predicate *hide₂* (the transitive verb). *Hide₂* is a synonym of *conceal*.

Practice   The following pairs of words share at least one sense in common, but do not share all their senses (i.e. they are like *hide* and *conceal*). For each pair: (a) give a sentence in which the two words could be used interchangeably without altering the sense of the sentence – use a slash notation, as we have done in practice above; (b) give another sentence using one of the words where a different sense is involved. As a guide, we have done the first one for you.

(1)   *deep/profound*

(a)   *You have my deep/profound sympathy* ....

(b)   *This river is very deep* (*This river is very profound* is unacceptable.)

107

(2) *ripe/mature*

  (a) ....

  (b) ....

(3) *broad/wide*

  (a) ....

  (b) ....

(4) *earth/soil*

  (a) ....

  (b) ....

(5) *side/edge*

  (a) ....

  (b) ....

Feedback   The following are just some possibilities: (2) (a) *After dinner we had a ripe/mature Camembert cheese,* (b) *She's a very mature person* (not *a ripe person*) (3) (a) *The river is very broad/wide at this point,* (b) *He speaks with a broad Scottish accent* (not *a wide accent*) (4) (a) *They filled the hole with good soft earth/soil,* (b) *The rocket fell back to earth when its motors failed* (not *back to soil*) (5) (a) *The house stands at the side/edge of the lake,* (b) *Britain and Australia are on opposite sides of the world* (not *edges*)

Comment   The definition of synonymy as a relationship between the senses of words requires a clear separation of all the different senses of a word, even though some of these senses may be quite closely related, as with *hide₁*, *hide₂*, and *hide₃*, mentioned in the last comment.

All the examples so far have been of synonymy between predicates realized grammatically by a word of the same part of speech, for example between adjective and adjective, as with *deep* and *profound*. But the notion of synonymy can be extended to hold between words of different parts of speech, for example between the verb *sleeping* and the adjective *asleep*. Examples like these are not the kind usually given of synonymy, but they help to make the point that the sense of a word does not depend entirely on its part of speech. Grammar and meaning are separate though closely related aspects of language.

Let us now investigate how the notion of 'sameness' of meaning, which we referred to as synonymy in the case of individual predicates, can be extended to entire sentences in a language.

Definition   A sentence which expresses the same proposition as another sentence is a PARAPHRASE of that sentence (assuming the same referents for any referring expressions involved). Paraphrase is to SENTENCES (on individual interpretations) as SYNONYMY is to PREDICATES (though some semanticists talk loosely of synonymy in the case of sentences as well).

Example   *Bachelors prefer redhaired girls* is a paraphrase of *Girls with red hair are preferred by unmarried men*

Comment   Look at the following pair of sentences, which are paraphrases of each other.
(A) *John sold the book to a grandson of W.B. Yeats*
(B) *A grandson of W.B. Yeats bought the book from John*
   It is not possible for (A) to be true while (B) is not (assuming that we are dealing with the same John and the same grandson of W.B. Yeats). Thus (A) has the same truth value as (B), so that if (A) is true, (B) is true, and vice versa; also, if (A) is false, then (B) is false, and vice versa.

Practice   Are the following pairs paraphrases of each other (assuming that the referents of the names and other referring expressions remain the same)? Indicate your answer by circling either *P* (paraphrase) or *NP* (not a paraphrase).

(1) *John is the parent of James*
     James is the child of John   *P / NP*

(2) *John is the parent of James*
     James is the parent of John   *P / NP*

(3) *My father owns this car*
     This car belongs to my father   *P / NP*

(4) *The fly was on the wall*
     The wall was under the fly   *P / NP*

(5) *Some countries have no coastline*
     Not all countries have a coastline   *P / NP*

(6) *Fred sent Mary a new book*
     Fred sent a new book to Mary   *P / NP*

(7) *Jerry took out the garbage*
     Jerry took the garbage out   *P / NP*

Feedback   (1) P (2) NP (3) P (4) NP (5) P (6) P (7) P

Definition   HYPONYMY is a sense relation between predicates (or sometimes longer phrases) such that the meaning of one predicate (or phrase) is included in the meaning of the other.

Example   The meaning of *red* is included in the meaning of *scarlet*.
Red is the superordinate term; *scarlet* is a hyponym of *red* (scarlet is a kind of red).

Comment   Note that the superordinate term, *red*, is more general or inclusive in meaning than its hyponym *scarlet*, which is much more specific in the kind of colour it describes. In other words, the predicate *red* describes a particular region in colour space whose prototype (or focal) examples are fairly distinct from those of other colours, though we have seen that more peripheral members of the extension of *red* tend to fade into other colours. But the term also subsumes (includes) more specific kinds of *red* within this region of colour space, some of which have their own predicates to describe the narrower sort of hue, including *scarlet*, *crimson*, etc. In general, sense relationships involving hyponymy are usually structured in this way, with the superordinate term more abstract, general, or schematic than its hyponyms. This will become apparent as we examine more examples of hyponymy.

Practice   Look at the following, and fill in some missing hyponyms.

(1)   *pig*

  sow
....

(2)   *tree*

  beech
....

(3)   *virtue*

  honesty
....

(4)   *emotion*

  fear
....

(5)   *strike* (transitive verb)

....

(6)   *pleasant*

....

Feedback   (1) *piglet, boar* (2) *oak, ash, sycamore, fir,* etc. (3) *patience, wisdom, prudence, generosity,* etc. (4) *love, anger, happiness, sadness,* etc. (5) *kick, hit, butt, thump,* etc. (6) *tasty, pretty, soothing,* etc.

Comment   We have dealt with the clear cases. Note that even in the case of abstract nouns, there are some quite clear things that we can say about their meanings, or senses.

Before we leave the discussion of hyponymy, a note should be made of its relationship with extension (Unit 8). Hyponymy is a sense relation. Another term for sense, preferred by logicians, is intension, a term deliberately chosen for its implicit contrast with extension. Hyponymy is defined in terms of the inclusion of the sense of one item in the sense of another. We say, for example, that the sense of *animal* is included in the sense of *cow*. This inclusion can be shown roughly by a diagram giving a list of the 'sense-components' of *cow*. It will be seen that this list includes the component 'animal'. But paradoxically

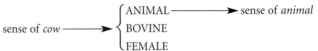

perhaps, if we draw a diagram of the extensions of *cow* and *animal*, the inclusion relationship appears the other way around.

Practice (1) Which of the following descriptions is the more specific?
  (a) A man, 5ft 8in tall, with black hair, moustache, no beard, wearing a beige duffle coat, blue jeans, and lace-up shoes
  (b A man in a duffle coat   *(a) / (b)*

(2) Which of the above descriptions gives more information?   *(a) / (b)*

(3) Which of the above descriptions describes more men?   *(a) / (b)*

(4) In general, does giving more information increase or reduce the range of things described?   ....

Feedback   (1) (a) (2) (a) (3) (b) (4) It reduces the range of things described.

Definition We define HYPONYMY in such a way that SYNONYMY counts as a special case of hyponymy. For example, given two synonyms, such as *mercury* and *quicksilver*, we say for convenience that these also illustrate the hyponymy relationship, and that *mercury* and *quicksilver* are hyponyms of each other. Thus synonymy can be seen as a special case of hyponymy, i.e. SYMMETRICAL HYPONYMY.

Rule If X is a hyponym of Y and if Y is also a hyponym of X, then X and Y are synonymous.

Comment Earlier in this unit we saw that it is possible to extend the notion of 'sameness' of meaning between predicates (synonymy) to sameness of meaning between propositions that are expressed by sentences (paraphrases). Similarly, the notion of hyponymy, which involves meaning inclusion between individual predicates, can be extended to a particular kind of meaning inclusion between propositions in a language involving truth conditions called 'entailment'. We investigate this below.

Definition A proposition X ENTAILS a proposition Y if the truth of Y follows necessarily from the truth of X. We extend this basic definition in terms of propositions

111

to cover SENTENCES in the following way. A sentence expressing proposition X entails a sentence expressing proposition Y if the truth of Y follows necessarily from the truth of X.

Example   *John ate all the kippers* (X) entails *Someone ate something* (Y).
John killed Bill (X) entails *Bill died* (Y).

It is not possible to think of any circumstances in which sentence X is true and sentence Y false.

Comment   In all of our exercises on entailment it must be remembered that the truth of sentences (and of propositions) is relative to particular sets of circumstances, or states of affairs. Thus when we say, for example, that *John killed Bill* entails *Bill died*, we are in fact envisaging these sentences being uttered in circumstances where both instances of *Bill* have the same referent and the time indicated by the use of the past tense (in *killed* and *died*) is related to the same hypothetical time of utterance. Obviously *Bill died* could not be true any time before it was true that *John killed Bill*.

Practice   Look at the following and circle the statements of entailment as correct (*C*) or incorrect (*I*).

(1) *John cooked an egg* entails *John boiled an egg*.   *C / I*

(2) *John boiled an egg* entails *John cooked an egg*.   *C / I*

(3) *I saw a boy* entails *I saw a person*.   *C / I*

(4) *John stole a car* entails *John took a car*.   *C / I*

(5) *His speech disturbed me* entails *His speech deeply disturbed me*.   *C / I*

Feedback   (1) I (2) C (3) C (4) C (5) I

Comment   Entailment applies cumulatively. Thus if X entails Y and Y entails Z, then X entails Z. (Technically, entailment is a transitive relation. See Unit 18.)

Example   X, *Some boys ran down the street* entails Y, *Some kids ran down the street*
Y, *Some kids ran down the street* entails Z, *Some kids went down the street*
Therefore,
X, *Some boys ran down the street* entails Z, *Some kids went down the street*.

Definition   Two sentences may be said to be PARAPHRASES of each other if and only if they have exactly the same set of ENTAILMENTS; or, which comes to the same thing, if and only if they mutually entail each other so that whenever one is true the other must also be true.

Comment   Note how this relationship between propositions neatly parallels the one we described earlier between individual predicates with respect to synonymy and hyponymy.

Example *John and Mary are twins* entails *Mary and John are twins;*
Mary and John are twins entails *John and Mary are twins.*
Therefore,
John and Mary are twins is a paraphrase of *Mary and John are twins.*

Practice Look at the following pairs of sentences and see if they have the same set
of entailments (*Yes*) or not (*No*) (i.e. see if they are paraphrases of each
other).

(1) *No one has led a perfect life*
Someone has led a perfect life   Yes / No

(2) *We've just bought a dog*
We've just bought something   Yes / No

(3) *The house was concealed by the trees*
The house was hidden by the trees   Yes / No

(4) *I ran to the house*
I went to the house   Yes / No

(5) *It is hard to lasso elephants*
Elephants are hard to lasso   Yes / No

Feedback (1) No (2) No (3) Yes (4) No (5) Yes

Comment The relationship between entailment and paraphrase is parallel to the
relationship between hyponymy and synonymy, as you will have noticed. Just
as synonymy is symmetric (i.e. two-way) hyponymy, paraphrase is symmetric
(i.e. two-way) entailment.

Practice Fill in the chart with the words *entailment, paraphrase, hyponymy,* and
synonymy in the appropriate boxes, thus summarizing their relationship.

	Relation between pairs of sentences	Relation between pairs of words
Not necessarily symmetric (i.e. can be 'one-way')		
Symmetric (i.e. 'both ways')		

Feedback

entailment	hyponymy
paraphrase	synonymy

Comment Now we explore further the relationship between hyponymy and entailment.

Practice (1) In terms of the concepts you have now learned, what can you say about
the relationships between the words in column A below and those in
column B?

A	B
tulip	*flower*
sheep	*animal*
steal	*take*
square	*rectangular*

....

(2) What can you say about the relationship between the A sentences and the B sentences below?

A	B
Henry was chewing a tulip	*Henry was chewing a flower*
Denis got savaged by a sheep	*Denis got savaged by an animal*
David stole a pound of beef	*David took a pound of beef*
Mary climbed through a square hole in the roof	*Mary climbed through a rectangular hole in the roof*

....

Feedback   (1) The A words are hyponyms of the B words. (2) The A sentences entail the B sentences.

Comment   In simple cases such as these, there is a clear rule that can be stated about the relation between hyponymy and entailment.

Practice   Given below are three attempts at stating this rule. Only one of them is actually correct. Which is the correct rule? Circle your choice.

(a) Given two sentences A and B, identical in every way except that A contains a word X where B contains a different word Y, and X is a hyponym of Y, then sentence B entails sentence A.

(b) Given two sentences A and B, identical in every way except that A contains a word X where B contains a different word Y, and Y is a hyponym of X, then sentence A entails sentence B.

(c) Given two sentences A and B, identical in every way except that A contains a word X where B contains a different word Y, and X is a hyponym of Y, then sentence A entails sentence B.

Feedback   The rule is correctly formulated in (c). We will call this rule the Basic Rule of Sense Inclusion.

Comment   The Basic Rule of Sense Inclusion does not work in all cases. There are systematic exceptions when certain logical words, such as *not* and *all*, are involved. We look first at cases with *not* (and *n't*), i.e. cases of negative sentences.

114

Practice (1) What is the relationship between the A sentences and the B sentences below?

A   B

Henry was not chewing a tulip   *Henry was not chewing a flower*
Denis didn't get savaged by a   *Denis didn't get savaged by an*
  sheep   *animal*
David didn't steal a pound of beef   *David didn't take a pound of beef*
Mary didn't climb through a square   *Mary didn't climb through a*
  hole in the roof   *rectangular hole in the roof*

....

(2) Below is an unfinished version of a rule of sense inclusion for negative sentences. Finish the statement of the rule correctly.

Given two negative sentences A and B, identical in every way except that A contains a word X where B contains a different word Y, and X is a hyponym of Y, then

....

Feedback (1) In this case, the B sentences entail the A sentences. (For example, if it is true that Henry was not chewing a flower, then it must be true that he was not chewing a tulip.) (2) The correct completion of the rule is: 'sentence B entails sentence A'.

Practice Now we look at sentences involving the word *all*. What is the relationship between the A sentences and the B sentences below?

A   B

Henry chewed up all my tulips   *Henry chewed up all my flowers*
All Denis's sheep have foot-rot   *All Denis's animals have foot-rot*
Mary coloured all the square   *Mary coloured all the rectangular*
  shapes purple   *shapes purple*

....

Part of the answer is: the B sentences entail the A sentences. But there is an important qualification that must be added to this. Can you think what it is?

....

Feedback The B sentences entail the A sentences. However, the entailment from B to A only holds when the set of things referred to by the phrase including *all* actually exists. For example, *All Denis's animals have foot-rot* entails *All Denis's sheep have foot-rot* only if Denis actually has some sheep, i.e. if some of his animals are in fact sheep.

115

Comment   Obviously a (somewhat complicated) rule of sense inclusion for sentences involving *all* could be formulated, but we will not go into the details of it here.
Clearly, rules stating the relationship between hyponymy and entailment are somewhat complex, although most of the logical principles involved are well enough understood. We will mention one more case which presents problems, the case of gradable words, like *big, tall, small, expensive*, etc. We will learn more about the gradability of words like these in the next unit. For now just focus on the fact that the meanings of adjectives such as *big* and *small* are not invariably fixed with respect to some absolute scale, but vary depending upon the kind of noun they modify.

Practice   What are the entailment relations between the following sentences?

A	B
John saw a big mouse	*John saw a big animal*
A tall pygmy came in	*A tall person came in*
We went in a small bus	*We went in a small vehicle*
That was an expensive sandwich	*That was an expensive meal*

Feedback   There are no entailment relations between these sentences. Thus although a mouse is an animal, a big mouse is not a big animal. The presence of gradable words upsets the normal relationship between hyponymy and entailment.

Summary   Hyponymy and synonymy are sense relations between predicates. The latter is a special, symmetric, case of the former. Entailment and paraphrase are sense relations between sentences, the latter being a special, symmetric case of the former. The sense relations between predicates and those between sentences are systematically connected by rules such as the basic rule of sense inclusion. These sense relations are also systematically connected with such sense properties of sentences as ANALYTICITY and CONTRADICTION.

Unit 10   Study Guide and Exercises

Directions   After you have read Unit 10 you should be able to tackle the following questions to test your understanding of the main ideas raised in the unit.

1   You should understand these terms and concepts from this unit:

synonymy/synonym	intension
paraphrase	symmetrical hyponymy
hyponymy/hyponym	entailment
superordinate term	transitive relation
Basic Rule of Sense Inclusion	co-hyponyms
sense relations	

2 Do you think it is easier to learn words as unique items, or as part of a system involving various kinds of sense relationships? That is, is it easier to learn words when we can relate them in systematic ways or when we learn them separately? Briefly explain.

3 What is meant by **synonymy**? Why is it difficult to define this term? Do most synonyms have identical or just similar meanings (or senses)? Do you think true synonymy exists? Try to support your answer with appropriate examples.

4 Identify in the following sentences the pairs of words in upper-case letters which appear to share the same (or nearly the same) sense. In some (or all) cases it may be difficult to decide, so be ready to explain the difficulty.
   a Fred always sleeps on the SOFA/COUCH
   b The neighbours have a BIG/LARGE family
   c The winning horse TROTTED/RAN to the finish line
   d This table is very SMOOTH/FLAT
   e That is a very HIGH/TALL building
   f That is a very FLAT/SLIPPERY road

5 Synonyms usually share some but not all senses. This becomes evident in certain of their uses. For each apparent synonym pair below supply sentences in which the two words can be used interchangeably without altering the sense of the sentence, and then give another sentence using one of the words in a different sense (where no interchange is possible with the same meaning).
   a small/little   e cheap/inexpensive
   b hard/difficult   f bright/well-lit
   c long/extended   g sad/dejected
   d lady/woman   h rob/steal
   i Do the same for the synonym pairs you identified in 4 above.

6 A special kind of synonymy falls under the heading of **euphemism**, whereby a culturally or socially disagreeable word is replaced by a more agreeable one with essentially (though not exactly) the same meaning. For each term below try to find several euphemisms which are less harsh, offensive, or explicit. For item (h) try to think of several additional examples.
   a war   f toilet
   b crazy   g poor
   c damn   h crippled
   d fired from a job i stupid
   e blind   h ....

7 Sometimes synonyms can have either positive or negative connotations, as shown by the first set below. Try to complete the other examples. A thesaurus may be helpful.

NEUTRAL TERM	POSITIVE	NEGATIVE
careful	scrupulous	keep a sharp eye on
save money	....	....
reserved	....	....
levelheaded	....	....
....	inquisitive	_____
....	....	lagging
laugh	....	....
talk	....	....
old	....	....
....	....	immature

8 What is a **paraphrase**? How are the notions of **synonymy** and **paraphrase** distinguished in semantics?

9 Supply as many paraphrases as you can for each of the following sentences. Remember that each paraphrase must have the same set of entailments as the original sentence.
a I gave the book to my friend
b Your child took out the garbage
c It is likely that Fred will win the race
d John is easy to please
e The sales clerk received the money from me
f Some students have a job

10 What is meant by **hyponymy**? When predicates are organized according to their hyponymic relationships with each other the resulting tree diagram is sometimes called a **taxonomy**.

11 Organize each of the following groups of words into a taxonomy in which the superordinate terms and their hyponyms are properly arranged with respect to each other. Be sure to identify which terms are superordinate and which are hyponyms (and which are co-hyponyms). Identify any problems you might have in organizing the data, and supply additional data if you can think of them. It may be helpful to sketch a tree diagram. Are you aware of any other disciplines in which such taxonomies are used?
a hammer, screwdriver, wrench, awl, tool, pliers
b carpenter, electrician, craftsman, plumber
c mammal, human, animal, amphibian, reptile, frog, snake
d shatter, crack, break, smash, fracture
e man, woman, husband, bachelor, wife, human, widow

12 Explain what it means to say that hyponymy involves entailment.

13 For each sentence below give another sentence which the first one entails, and then give one which the first does NOT entail.

  a John is a bachelor
  b John is a widower
  c Mary is divorced
  d This is a tulip

14 Hyponymy and synonymy refer to relations between pairs of words, while
    entailment and paraphrase refer to relations between pairs of sentences.
    Supply the correct terms in the blanks.
    Hyponymy is to .... as synonymy is to ....

15 What does the Basic Rule of Sense Inclusion have to say about the
    entailment relationship between the following two sentences?
    a Mary bought a house
    b Mary bought a building

16 Why does the Basic Rule of Sense Inclusion NOT work for the following
    pairs of sentences? How must it be amended to work here?
    a Mary did not buy a house
    b Mary did not buy a building

    c Mary bought all the houses in town
    d Mary bought all the buildings in town

17 Consider the following pair of sentences. Is there any entailment relation
    existing between them? Explain why or why not.
    a Mary bought a big house
    b Mary bought a big building

UNIT 11 SENSE RELATIONS (2)
OPPOSITENESS AND DISSIMILARITY OF SENSE AND AMBIGUITY

Entry requirements   SENSE (Unit 3), ANALYTIC, SYNTHETIC, and CONTRADICTION (Unit 9), and SENSE RELATIONS (1), (Unit 10). If you feel you understand these notions, take the entry test below. Otherwise review the relevant units.

Entry test   (1)   Analyticity is which of the following? Circle your choice.
   (a)   a sense relation between sentences
   (b)   a sense property of sentences
   (c)   a sense relation between predicates
   (d)   a sense property of predicates
(2)   The sentence *John is older than himself* is:
   (a)   analytic
   (b)   synthetic
   (c)   a contradiction
(3)   The relationship between the sentences *I detest semantics* and *I am not fond of semantics* is that:
   (a)   They are paraphrases of each other.
   (b)   The first entails the second.
   (c)   The second entails the first.
   (d)   The first is a hyponym of the second.
(4)   Which of the following statements is correct?
   (a)   All analytic sentences are paraphrases of each other.
   (b)   All contradictions are paraphrases of each other.
   (c)   Given two sentences, identical except that one has a predicate X where the other has a predicate Y, where X is a hyponym of Y, then the sentence containing X is a paraphrase of the sentence containing Y.
   (d)   If a sentence X entails a sentence Y and sentence Y also entails sentence X, then X and Y are paraphrases of each other.
(5)   Which of the following is correct?
   (a)   Synonymy is to entailment as hyponymy is to paraphrase.
   (b)   Synonymy is to paraphrase as hyponymy is to entailment.
   (c)   Synonymy is to hyponymy as entailment is to paraphrase.

Feedback   (1) (b) (2) (c) (3) (b) (4) (d) (5) (b)

120

If you scored at least 4 out of 5 correct, continue to the introduction. Otherwise, review Units 9 and 10 before continuing.

Introduction   In this unit we complete our introductory review of sense relations. Our topics include what has been termed 'oppositeness of meaning', an area that traditionally was viewed in rather simple terms. Modern semanticists, as you will see, have explored and mapped many areas within this area of meaning that go well beyond the simple traditional 'oppositeness' notion.

A traditional view of antonymy is that it is simply 'oppositeness of meaning'. This view is not adequate, as words may be opposite in meaning in different ways, and some words have no real opposites.

Practice   Quickly, what would you say are the opposites of the following words?

(1) *hot* _____

(2) *thick* _____

(3) *buy* _____

(4) *lend* _____

(5) *male* _____

(6) *dead* _____

(7) *lunch* _____

(8) *liquid* _____

Feedback   (1) *cold* (2) *thin* (3) *sell* (4) *borrow* (5) *female* (6) *alive* (7) no real opposite (*breakfast, dinner*?) (8) no real opposite – part of a three-termed system, with *solid* and *gas*

Comment   *Hot* is not the opposite of *cold* in the same way as *borrow* is the opposite of *lend*. *Thick* is not the opposite of *thin* in the same way as *dead* is the opposite of *alive*.

We will not talk of simple 'oppositeness of meaning', but will define four basic types of antonymy (or semantic incompatibility). The first we define is binary antonymy (sometimes also called complementarity).

Definition   BINARY ANTONYMS are predicates which come in pairs and between them exhaust all the relevant possibilities. If the one predicate is applicable, then the other cannot be, and vice versa. Another way to view this is to say that a predicate is a binary antonym of another predicate if it entails the negative of the other predicate.

Example   *true* and *false* are binary antonyms.

If a sentence is true, it cannot be false. If it is false, it cannot be true. Alternatively, if something is true, this entails that it is not false. If it is false, this entails it is not true.

121

Practice   Are the following pairs of predicates binary antonyms?

    (1) *chalk – cheese*   *Yes / No*

    (2) *same – different*   *Yes / No*

    (3) *copper – tin*   *Yes / No*

    (4) *dead – alive*   *Yes / No*

    (5) *married – unmarried*   *Yes / No*

    (6) *love – hate*   *Yes / No*

Feedback   (1) No, if something is not chalk, it is not necessarily cheese. (2) Yes, if two things are the same, they are not different: if they are not the same, they are different. (3) No (4) Yes (5) Yes (6) No, if I don't love you, I don't necessarily hate you.

Comment   Sometimes two different binary antonyms can combine in a set of predicates to produce a four-way contrast.

Practice   (1) Place the words *man, boy, woman, girl* in the appropriate boxes in this chart.

	Male	Female
Adult		
Non-adult		

    (2) Fill in the words *bachelor, spinster, husband, wife* in the chart below.

	Male	Female
Married		
Unmarried		

Feedback   (1) | man | woman | (2) | husband | wife |
            | boy | girl | | bachelor | spinster|

Practice   (1) In the first chart, *girl* was diagonally opposite to *man*.
        Would one normally think of *girl* as the antonym of *man*?   *Yes / No*

    (2) In the second chart, *wife* was diagonally opposite to *bachelor*.
        Would one normally think of *wife* as the antonym of *bachelor*?   *Yes / No*

Feedback   (1) No, one could normally think of either *woman* or *boy*. (2) No, one would usually think first of either *spinster* or possibly *husband*, or *married man*.

Comment   We see that combinations of binary antonyms produce more complicated (e.g. four-way) systems of contrast, but that within such systems the most

122

natural way to pair off pairs of antonyms is along the same dimension, e.g. *man* vs *woman* (along the male/female dimension), but not *man* vs *girl* (cutting across both dimensions).

Definition   If a predicate describes a relationship between two things (or people) and some other predicate describes the same relationship when the two things (or people) are mentioned in the opposite order, then the two predicates are CONVERSES of each other.

Example   *Parent* and *child* are converses, because *X is the parent of Y* (one order) describes the same situation (relationship) as *Y is the child of X* (opposite order).

Practice   Are the following pairs of expressions converses?

(1) *below – above*	Yes / No
(2) *grandparent – grandchild*	Yes / No
(3) *love – hate*	Yes / No
(4) *conceal – reveal*	Yes / No
(5) *greater than – less than*	Yes / No
(6) *own – belong to*	Yes / No

Feedback   (1) Yes, if X is below Y, Y is above X. (2) Yes (3) No (4) No (5) Yes (6) Yes

Comment   The notion of converseness can be applied to examples in which three things (or people) are mentioned. The case of *buy* and *sell* is one such example.

Practice
(1) If John bought a car from Fred, is it the case that Fred sold a car to John?	Yes / No
(2) Are *buy* and *sell* converses?	Yes / No
(3) Are *borrow* and *lend* converses?	Yes / No
(4) Are *give* and *take* converses?	Yes / No
(5) Are *come* and *go* converses?	Yes / No

Feedback   (1) Yes (2) Yes (3) Yes, if X borrows something from Y, Y lends that thing to X. (4) No, if X takes something from Y, Y does not necessarily give that thing to X (for example, X might take it without Y's permission), so *give* and *take* are not exact converses, although they almost meet the definition. (5) No, if Mohammed goes to the mountain, the mountain does not come to Mohammed.

Comment   In both types of antonymy discussed so far, binary antonymy and converseness, the antonyms come in pairs. Between them, the members of a pair of binary antonyms fully fill the area to which they can be applied. Such areas can be thought of as miniature semantic systems. Such semantic systems are sometimes known as 'semantic fields'.

Thus, for example, *male* and *female* between them constitute the English sex system, *true* and *false* are the two members of the truth system etc. Other such systems (or fields) can have three, or four, or any number of members, depending upon the way in which the system is organized.

Practice (1) What would you call the system of oppositions to which the words *Spring* and *Summer* both belong?

....

(2) How many members does this system have altogether?

....

(3) What would you call the system to which *solid* and *gas* belong?

....

(4) How many members does this system have?

....

(5) Can you think of an example of a seven-member system? (Hint: you use it every day of the week.)

....

(6) Four-member systems are quite common. How many can you think of?

....

Feedback (1) The 'season system' would be a natural name. (2) four (3) It could be called the 'physical-state system'. (4) Three: *liquid, solid,* and *gas.* (5) The system that includes *Monday, Tuesday, Wednesday,* etc. (6) *hearts, clubs, diamonds, spades; earth, air, fire, water; North, East, South, West* (although this last one is frequently boosted to a system with more members, such as *South-West, North-East-by-North,* etc.).

Comment What these systems have in common is that (a) all the terms in a given system are mutually incompatible, and (b) together, the members of a system cover all the relevant area. For instance, a playing card cannot belong to both the hearts suit and the spades suit. And besides hearts, clubs, diamonds, and spades, there are no other suits. Systems such as these are called systems of multiple incompatibility. There are large numbers of open-ended systems of multiple incompatibility.

Practice (1) How many English colour words (like *red, grey*) are there?

....

(2) How many names of plants are there in English (e.g. *holly, daffodil*)?

....

(3) How many names of different metals are there in English (e.g. *brass, tin*)?

....

(4) Think of three further examples of such open-ended systems of multiple incompatibility.

....

....

Feedback   (1)–(3) an indefinite number (4) the vehicle system (*car, bus, train*, etc.); the animal system (*bat, bear, tiger*, etc.); the flower system (*pansy, primrose, poppy*, etc.); the furniture system (*table, chair, bed*, etc.), and many, many more.

Definition   Two predicates are GRADABLE antonyms if they are at opposite ends of a continuous scale of values (a scale which typically varies according to the context of use).

Example   *Hot* and *cold* are gradable antonyms.
   Between *hot* and *cold* is a continuous scale of values, which may be given names such as *warm, cool,* or *tepid*. What is called *hot* in one context (e.g. of oven temperatures in a recipe book) could well be classed as *cold* in another context (e.g. the temperatures of stars).

Practice   Are the following pairs gradable antonyms?

(1) *tall – short*	*Yes / No*
(2) *long – short*	*Yes / No*
(3) *clever – stupid*	*Yes / No*
(4) *top – bottom*	*Yes / No*
(5) *love – hate*	*Yes / No*

Feedback   (1) Yes (2) Yes (3) Yes (4) No (5) Yes, intermediate expressions on the scale include *like, dislike, be indifferent to.*

Comment   A good test for gradability, i.e. having a value on some continuous scale, as gradable antonyms do, is to see whether a word can combine with *very*, or *very much*, or *how?* or *how much?* For example, *How tall is he?* is acceptable, but *How top is that shelf?* is not generally acceptable.

Practice   Apply this test to the following words to decide whether they are gradable (*G*) or not (*NG*).

(1) *near*	*G / NG*
(2) *cheap*	*G / NG*

(3) *beautiful*	*G / NG*
(4) *electrical*	*G / NG*
(5) *triangular*	*G / NG*

Feedback (1) G (2) G (3) G (4) NG (5) NG

Practice To sum up these exercises in antonymy and incompatibility, classify the following pairs as binary antonyms (*B*), multiple incompatibles (*M*), converses (*C*), or gradable antonyms (*G*).

(1) *cat – dog*	*B / M / C / G*
(2) *easy – difficult*	*B / M / C / G*
(3) *good – bad*	*B / M / C / G*
(4) *better than – worse than*	*B / M / C / G*
(5) *deciduous – evergreen*	*B / M / C / G*
(6) *pass – fail*	*B / M / C / G*
(7) *urban – rural*	*B / M / C / G*

Feedback (1) M (Both cat and dog belong to the open-ended English animal name system.) (2) G (3) G (4) C (The relationship between *better than* and *worse than* is one of converseness, even though both *better* and *worse* are themselves gradable terms, since, for example, *very much better* or *how much worse?* are acceptable expressions.) (5) B (6) B (7) a debatable case – probably B for some people, G for others.

Comment We saw in the previous unit that certain relationships between predicates, such as hyponymy and synonymy, could be paired off with certain relationships between sentences (or more precisely, between propositions expressed by sentences) such as entailment and paraphrase. Antonymy is a relationship between predicates, and the corresponding relationship between sentences is contradictoriness.

Definition A proposition is a CONTRADICTORY of another proposition if it is impossible for them both to be true at the same time and of the same circumstances. The definition can naturally be extended to sentences thus: a sentence expressing one proposition is a contradictory of a sentence expressing another proposition if it is impossible for both propositions to be true at the same time and of the same circumstances. Alternatively (and equivalently) a sentence contradicts another sentence if it entails the negation of the other sentence.

Example *This beetle is alive* is a contradictory of *This beetle is dead.*

Practice Say whether the following pairs are contradictories (i.e. contradict each other) or not. Assume constancy of reference of all referring expressions.

(1) *John murdered Bill*
    Bill was murdered by John   Yes / No

(2) *John murdered Bill*
    John did not kill Bill   Yes / No

(3) *Bill died*
    James can't swim   Yes / No

(4) *Mary is Ann's parent*
    Mary is Ann's child   Yes / No

(5) *Room 404 is below this one*
    Room 404 is above this one   Yes / No

(6) *This doorhandle is brass*
    This doorhandle is plastic   Yes / No

Feedback (1) No (2) Yes (3) No (4) Yes (5) Yes (6) Yes

Comment Below is a suggested statement of the relationship between contradictoriness and antonymy (and incompatibility). We will see whether this statement actually works correctly for all the types of antonymy and incompatibility that we have discussed.

Statement A
Given two sentences, both identical except that: (a) one contains a word *X* where the other contains a word *Y*, and (b) *X* is an antonym of *Y* (or *X* is incompatible with *Y*), then the two sentences are contradictories of each other (i.e. contradict each other).

Notice that the formulation of this statement is exactly parallel to what we called the Basic Rule of Sense Inclusion in Unit 10, the rule relating hyponymy to entailment in basic cases. Let us see whether the above statement of the relation between antonymy and contradictoriness is as successful.

Practice Do the following pairs of examples conform to Statement A?

(1) *This cat is male*
    This cat is female   Yes / No

(2) *John hates Californians*
    John loves Californians   Yes / No

(3) *This mouse is dead*
    This mouse is alive   Yes / No

(4) *John owns three male cats*
    John owns three female cats   Yes / No

(5) *Some people love Californians*
     Some people hate Californians   *Yes / No*

(6) *I found a dead mouse in the shower*
     I found a live mouse in the shower   *Yes / No*

Feedback (1) Yes (2) Yes (3) Yes (4) No, John might own three male and three female cats. (5) No (6) No, I might have found two mice, one dead, one alive.

Comment In the first three examples the two sentences are identical except for a pair of antonyms (or incompatibles), and the sentences contradict each other. These examples, then, conform to Statement A. In the last three examples the two sentences are identical except for a pair of antonyms or incompatibles, but the sentences do not contradict each other. They are therefore counterexamples to Statement A, and we must conclude that Statement A is wrong. What, then, is the correct statement of the relation between contradictoriness and antonymy? Indeed, is there any single statement that correctly captures this relationship? We shall not pursue the matter here, but a correct formulation seems to need to make use of the concepts of referring expression, predication, and quantification. (See Units 4 and 5 for the first two of these.)

One of the goals of a semantic theory is to describe and explain ambiguities in words and in sentences.

Definition A word or sentence is AMBIGUOUS when it has more than one sense. A sentence is ambiguous if it has two (or more) paraphrases which are not themselves paraphrases of each other.

Example *We saw her duck* is a paraphrase of *We saw her lower her head* and of *We saw the duck belonging to her*, and these last two sentences are not paraphrases of each other. Therefore *We saw her duck* is ambiguous.

Practice The following sentences are all ambiguous. For each one give two paraphrases which are not paraphrases of each other. Be very careful to make sure that your answers are exact paraphrases of the original sentence, as far as this is possible.

(1) *The chicken is ready to eat*

     ....

     ....

(2) *Visiting relatives can be boring*

     ....

     ....

(3) *They passed the port at midnight*

....

....

(4) *The thing that bothered Bill was crouching under the table*

....

....

(5) *The captain corrected the list*

....

....

Feedback   (1) The chicken is ready to be eaten vs The chicken is ready to eat some food (2) It can be boring to visit relatives vs Relatives who are visiting can be boring (3) They passed the seaport at midnight vs They passed the port wine at midnight (4) It was crouching under the table that bothered Bill vs The creature that bothered Bill was crouching under the table (5) The captain corrected the inventory vs The captain corrected the tilt

Comment   Some semanticists adopt a definition of 'sentence' according to which a sentence cannot be ambiguous. For such scholars, a sentence is a particular string of words associated with one particular sense. According to this usage, for example, *The chicken is ready to eat* is not one sentence, but represents two different sentences. We adopt a usage that has been current in recent Linguistics, and according to which sentences like *The chicken is ready to eat* (and the others given above) are single ambiguous sentences. This is essentially a matter of terminology.

Definition   In the case of words and phrases, a word or phrase is AMBIGUOUS if it has two (or more) SYNONYMS that are not themselves synonyms of each other.

Example   *Trunk* is synonymous with *elephant's proboscis* and with *chest*, but these two are not synonyms of each other, so *trunk* is ambiguous. Similarly *coach* is synonymous with *trainer* and with *charabanc* (or *bus*) but these two are not synonyms of each other, so *coach* is ambiguous.

Practice   Each of the following words is ambiguous. For each one, give two synonymous words or phrases that are not themselves synonymous. You might find it helpful to use a dictionary for this exercise.

(1) *bust* .... vs ....

(2) *plane* .... vs ....

(3) *crop* .... vs ....

(4) *pen* .... vs ....

(5) *sage* .... vs ....

Feedback	(1) sculpture of a person's head, shoulders and chest vs broken (2) aeroplane vs flat surface (3) harvest vs handle of a riding whip (4) handwriting instrument using ink vs enclosure (5) wise vs herb (*Salvia officinalis*)

Comment   We use the term 'word' in the sense of 'word-form'. That is, anything spelled and pronounced the same way (in a given dialect) is for us the same word. Some semanticists work with a more abstract notion of word, in which a word-form is associated with a particular sense, or group of related senses, to give a 'word'. For such semanticists, for example, *sage* corresponds to two different words, whereas for us *sage* is a single word with different senses, i.e. an ambiguous word. We use 'predicate' for 'word-in-a-particular-sense'. Predicates cannot be ambiguous, according to this definition.

In the case of ambiguous words, a distinction is sometimes made between polysemy and homonymy. This distinction has basically to do with the closeness, or relatedness, of the senses of the ambiguous words.

Definition   A case of HOMONYMY is one of an ambiguous word whose different senses are far apart from each other and not obviously related to each other in any way with respect to a native speaker's intuition. Cases of homonymy seem very definitely to be matters of mere accident or coincidence.

Examples   *Mug* (drinking vessel vs gullible person) would be a clear case of homonymy. *Bank* (financial institution vs the side of a river or stream) is another clear case of homonymy.

There is no obvious conceptual connection between the two meanings of either word.

Definition   A case of POLYSEMY is one where a word has several very closely related senses. In other words, a native speaker of the language has clear intuitions that the different senses are related to each other in some way.

Example   *Mouth* (of a river vs of an animal) is a case of polysemy.

The two senses are clearly related by the concepts of an opening from the interior of some solid mass to the outside, and of a place of issue at the end of some long narrow channel.

Polysemy in nouns is quite common in human languages. Some additional examples will be given for you to think about in the exercises at the end of this unit.

Example   *Run* is another more complicated case of polysemy in which the word has more than one related sense. Note that in this case we have an example of polysemy with a verb (at least in most of its senses). So polysemy is not restricted to just one part of speech.

The multiple senses of *run* are related to each other in a somewhat more abstract way than in the case of the senses of *mouth*. Some uses of *run* which bring out a few of its complex interrelated senses include: *run a race (on foot), run for office, this road runs from east to west, the motor is running, the water is running down the roof, run a computer program, a run in a stocking,* etc. Can you determine how these various senses are related to each other?

Practice The following are all polysemous words. For each one, we have indicated two closely related senses. What you have to do is to say how these senses are related, i.e. what they have in common. To show you the way, we have done the first one for you.

(1) *chimney* (pipe or funnel-like structure on a building for smoke to escape through vs narrow vertical space between rocks up which a climber can wriggle by pressing against the sides)

Both senses contain the concept of a narrow vertical shaft in some solid material

(2) *cup* (drinking vessel vs brassiere cup)

....

....

(3) *guard* (person who guards, sentinel vs solid protective shield, e.g. around machinery)

....

....

(4) *ceiling* (top inner surface of a room vs upper limit)

....

....

(5) *Earth/earth* (our planet vs soil)

....

....

(6) *drive* (as in *drive a nail* vs as in *drive a car*)

....

....

Feedback (2) Both senses have the concept of container with a particular round shape. (3) Both contain the concept of protection against danger. (4) Both contain the concept of a maximum upper boundary. (5) Both contain the concept of land at different levels of generality (earth as land, not sky;

earth as soil, not water). (6) Both contain the concept of causing something to move in a particular direction.

Comment   Many linguists are beginning to realize that polysemy is probably much more common in human language than was previously thought. It is probably more true than not that most words have related variations in sense that depend on the particular linguistic context in which they are used. In practice, however, it is nearly impossible to draw a clear line between homonymy and polysemy. As a matter of fact, it appears that homonymy and polysemy occupy places along a graded continuum of meaning with homonymy at one extreme and vagueness at the other extreme, with polysemy falling somewhere in between. A word is said to be 'vague' when it appears to have one basic sense (monosemy) which is nevertheless flexible enough to allow for minor variations in meaning or use which are not particularly entrenched in the mind of the speaker. The English word *aunt* is often cited as an example of vagueness, since most speakers feel it has one fairly unified sense in spite of the fact that it can be used to refer to distinct members of a person's family: the sister of either a person's father or his or her mother. However, as usual in these units on sense and sense relations, we will try to concentrate on clear cases, where there is no difficulty in drawing the distinction.

Practice   Decide whether the following words are examples of homonymy (*H*) or polysemy (*P*).

(1) *bark* (of a dog vs of a tree)   *H / P*

(2) *fork* (in a road vs instrument for eating)   *H / P*

(3) *tail* (of a coat vs of an animal)   *H / P*

(4) *steer* (to guide vs young bull)   *H / P*

(5) *lip* (of a jug vs of a person)   *H / P*

(6) *punch* (blow with a fist vs kind of fruity alcoholic drink)   *H / P*

Feedback   (1) H (2) P (3) P (4) H (5) P (6) H

Comment   To simplify matters we will concentrate on clear cases of homonymy from now on and not mention polysemy further. But you will have the opportunity to consider another example of polysemy in the exercises at the end of this unit.

You will have noticed that it is not always possible to find an exactly synonymous phrase for a given word. For example, in the case of *sage* above, we had to resort to the Latin botanical label, which was, strictly speaking, cheating, since synonymy is usually thought of as a relation between words (and phrases) in the same language. Where exact synonyms are not available, it is possible to indicate different senses of a word by giving different environments in which the word may be used.

Example *Grass* has two senses which are indicated by the following environments:
(a) *Please keep off the grass*
(b) *The informer grassed on his partners-in-crime*

Practice For each of the following words, give two full sentences which include them and which bring out distinct senses of the word.

(1) *rock* ....

....

(2) *hard* ....

....

(3) *file* ....

....

Feedback Here are some possible answers: (1) The ship hit a rock and sank; I will buy an electric guitar and become a rock star (2) This wood is hard; Playing the violin is hard (3) We will open a file for our overseas contracts; I sharpened the scissors with a file

Comment In many cases, a word used in one sense belongs to one part of speech, and used in another sense, it belongs to a different part of speech.

Example *long* in the sense of *yearn* is a verb and in the sense of *not short* is an adjective

Practice Disambiguate the following ambiguous words simply by giving two or more parts of speech.

(1) *sack* ....

(2) *fast* ....

(3) *flat* ....

Feedback (1) verb vs noun (2) verb vs noun vs adjective vs adverb (3) noun vs adjective

Practice Below are four suggested statements of the relationship between ambiguous sentences and ambiguous words. Only one of them is actually correct. Think carefully about them and about actual examples of ambiguous words and sentences and say which statement is correct. Take some time over this exercise before checking your answer.

Statement A
All sentences which contain one or more ambiguous words are ambiguous, and every sentence which contains no ambiguous words is unambiguous.

Statement B
Some sentences which contain ambiguous words are ambiguous while others
are not, and some sentences which contain no ambiguous words are
ambiguous while others are not.

Statement C
Some sentences which contain ambiguous words are ambiguous while some
are not, but all sentences which contain no ambiguous words are
unambiguous.

Statement D
All sentences which contain ambiguous words are ambiguous, but some
sentences which contain no ambiguous words are also ambiguous while
others are not.

Feedback	Statement B is the correct one.

Comment We will now go in detail through the reasoning which leads to the conclusion
that statement B is the correct one.

Practice (1) Below are some sentences containing ambiguous words. (The ambiguous
words are given in capitals.) In each case say whether the sentence is
ambiguous (*A*) or not ambiguous (*NA*).

    (a) *A KIND young man helped me to CROSS the road*   *A / NA*

    (b) *A pike is a KIND of fish*   *A / NA*

    (c) *I'm very CROSS with you*   *A / NA*

(2) Your answers to these questions should enable you to eliminate two of
the statements A–D above. Which two?

Feedback	(1) (a) NA (b) NA (c) NA (2) Statements A and D are shown to be incorrect by these examples.

Comment This leaves just statements B and C as possibilities. Let us see how we can
eliminate one of them.

Practice For each of the following sentences, say (a) whether the sentence contains any
ambiguous words, and (b) whether the sentence is ambiguous.

(1) *I observed John in the garden*   (a) *Yes / No*
    (b) *Yes / No*

(2) *We had to decide on the bus*   (a) *Yes / No*
    (b) *Yes / No*

(3) *Fred said that he would pay me on Thursday*   (a) *Yes / No*
                                                    (b) *Yes / No*

(4) Your answers to these questions should enable you to eliminate
either statement B or statement C above. Which one?   ....

Feedback   (1) (a) No (b) Yes (2) (a) No (b) Yes (3) (a) No (b) Yes (4) Statement C is
eliminated by these examples, which are not compatible with the second
half of it.

Comment   This leaves statement B. Of course, the fact that statements A, C, and D are
wrong does not prove that statement B is right. We still need to test statement
B against the linguistic facts. Statement B predicts the existence of four
different types of examples, as illustrated in the chart below:

	Ambiguous sentence	Unambiguous sentence
Sentence containing ambiguous words		
Sentence containing no ambiguous words		

Practice   Given below are five sentences. Put the numbers (1)–(5) in the chart above.

(1) *Semantics is a subdiscipline of Linguistics*

(2) *Semantics is a branch of the study of language*

(3) *John sawed a rotten branch off the ash tree*

(4) *The drunken visitor rolled up the carpet*

(5) *Cinderella watched the colourful ball*

Feedback   (5) | (2)   (3)
           (4) | (1)

Definition   A sentence which is ambiguous because its words relate to each other in
different ways, even though none of the individual words are ambiguous, is
STRUCTURALLY (or GRAMMATICALLY) AMBIGUOUS.

Example   *The chicken is ready to eat* (and many of the other sentences we have used) is
structurally ambiguous.

Definition   Any ambiguity resulting from the ambiguity of a word is a LEXICAL
AMBIGUITY.

Example   *The captain corrected the list* is lexically ambiguous.

Comment   Structural ambiguity is basically a question of 'what goes with what' in a sentence, and this can be shown by diagrams of various sorts. We will mention one such diagramming technique, constituency diagrams, which we will present with square brackets around the relevant parts of the sentence (or phrase).

Example   The phrase *old men and women* is structurally ambiguous. It is synonymous with *women and old men* and with *old men and old women*. We represent these two senses with square brackets thus:

(1)   [old men] and women
        old [men and women]

The first diagram indicates that *old* modifies only *men*, and the second indicates that *old* modifies the whole phrase *men and women*.

Comment   As you learn more semantics, you will learn in more detail of more accurate ways to represent meaning and, hence, of describing ambiguity. The material in this unit is just a start. Ambiguity of various kinds is never far from the centre of our attention in semantics.

To end this unit, we will mention some things that must not be confused with ambiguity.

Definition   A phrase is REFERENTIALLY VERSATILE if it can be used to refer to a wide range of different things or persons. This is very similar to the notion of vagueness mentioned earlier in this unit.

Example   The pronoun *she* can be used to refer to any female person. On a given occasion *she* might be used to refer to Mary, on another occasion to Lucy, etc., but this does NOT mean that *she* is ambiguous, because although it is used to refer to different people this is not a matter of a difference in sense.

Comment   We must also mention again referential vagueness. Some nouns and adjectives are gradable. Examples are *tall* and *short* (adjectives) and *mountain* and *hill* (nouns). Just as there is no absolute line drawn in the semantics of English between *tall* and *short*, there is no absolute distinction between *mountain* and *hill*. What is referred to on one occasion with *that mountain* might be called *that hill* on another occasion. Hence expressions such as *that hill* and *that mountain* are referentially vague. Referential vagueness is not the same thing as ambiguity. We saw that this was also the case when we considered the word *aunt*, which does not seem to have more than one sense, even though it can be used to refer to more than one distinct member of a kinship system.

Summary   Binary antonymy, converseness, and gradable antonymy are sense relations between predicates which fit a simple pretheoretical notion of 'oppositeness of meaning'. Multiple incompatibility, though not traditionally thought of as

136

a kind of oppositeness, is formally similar to binary antonymy, the main difference being in the number of terms (i.e. 2 or more than 2) in the system concerned. Contradictoriness is a sense relation between sentences (and propositions), related in an apparently complicated way to the sense relations mentioned above.

Lexical ambiguity depends on homonymy (senses not related) and polysemy (senses related). To show the relationship between ambiguous sentences and ambiguous words we proposed the following statement: some sentences which contain ambiguous words are ambiguous while others are not, and some sentences which contain no ambiguous words are ambiguous while others are not. We then discussed the differences between grammatical ambiguity and lexical ambiguity and suggested ways of representing grammatical ambiguity. Finally we distinguished referential versatility and referential vagueness from ambiguity.

Unit 11   Study Guide and Exercises

Directions   After you have read Unit 11 you should be able to tackle the following questions to test your understanding of the main ideas raised in the unit.

1 You should understand these terms and concepts from this unit:
types of antonymy
binary antonymy (complementarity)
converses/converseness (relational opposites)
systems of multiple incompatibility
gradable antonyms
contradictoriness (said of sentences)
ambiguity (structural and lexical)
homonymy
polysemy
referential versatility & vagueness vs ambiguity

2 Be sure you understand why oppositeness of meaning is not as simple as it sounds. Try to restate the issue in your own words. What seems to be necessary in order for two words to be classed as antonyms of any type?

3 A test for binary antonyms is that the negative of one term must be equivalent to (or entail) the other: thus, *dead* and *alive* are binary antonyms because if something is not dead then it must be alive. Use this test to determine which of the following pairs of predicates are binary antonyms. If some (or all) are uncertain, identify and explain them.

a wood/metal	e happy/sad
b big/small	f give/receive
c awake/asleep	g present/absent
d honest/dishonest	h in/out

4 Binary antonyms can be thought of as incompatible terms which are members of two-term sets (the 'miniature semantic systems' we described in the text). This notion can be extended to other groups of words which are not so much opposites as they are incompatible members of a larger (multiple-term) semantic system (or **semantic field**), such as the days of the week, the seasons of the year, etc. Note that the members of such larger sets are co-hyponyms and that the term which refers to the field itself is a superordinate term. Think of a few additional such systems of multiple incompatibility (with varying numbers of members) that were not mentioned in this unit.

5 Identify the type of antonymy or incompatibility (binary, gradable, converses, or multiple incompatibles) for each pair of words below.
   a high/low   f legal/illegal
   b punch/slap   g lessor/lessee
   c husband/wife   h expensive/cheap
   d higher/lower   i table/chair
   e pregnant/not pregnant   j parent/offspring

6 Explain the difference between a **contradiction** (a sense property of a sentence) and **contradictoriness** (a sense relation between sentences).

7 Which of the following pairs of sentences are **contradictories**?
   a Max baked the cake / The cake was baked by Max
   b Max is Sam's father / Max is Sam's child
   c This class begins at 9:45 a.m. / This class begins at 8:45 p.m.
   d Jane died / Jane is still alive

8 We said in this unit that 'a sentence contradicts another sentence if it entails the negation of the other sentence'. Show that this is true for the contradictories you found in item 7 above.

9 Give an example different from the ones in the text in which two sentences which are identical except for a pair of antonyms or incompatibles DO contradict each other, and an example in which they do NOT contradict each other.

10 Disambiguate the following **ambiguous** sentences by supplying paraphrases which are not themselves paraphrases of each other.
   a Climbing plants can look strange
   b Jane waited by the bank
   c They are moving sidewalks
   d The English history teacher knows a lot
   e The minister married my sister
   f She's selling synthetic buffalo hides
   g The long drill was boring

h The boy saw the man with a telescope

i He gave me a punch

j The grass was very expensive

11 Identify which sentences in exercise 10 above are examples of **structural ambiguity** and which are examples of **lexical ambiguity**.

12 For each polysemous word below identify several common senses and try to show how they are related to each other. Try to find some other examples for item (j).

a iron   f around

b conductor   g flight (fly)

c eye   h go

d face   i hand

e foot   j ....

13 Go back to the various senses of the word *run* that were mentioned earlier in this unit. Try to see if you can come up with a few more uses that are different from the ones given previously, and then try to figure out how the various senses of the word are related to each other. (**Hint:** You might want to start by identifying the sense that seems most concrete, basic, or prototypical, based on native speaker intuitions, and then work from there to figure out how the other senses could have developed from that basic sense. But don't be surprised if the common thread linking the senses of *run* is fairly abstract and not every sense of *run* shares exactly the same set of abstract characteristics. It's usually sufficient for the polysemous senses of a word to be related to each other as long as they share at least some characteristics in common.)

14 Explain why it is difficult to draw a clear line between **homonymy** and **polysemy**. Give an example to illustrate this difficulty. Why is this an important question for lexicographers (dictionary makers)?

15 Now try your hand at figuring out how the various polysemous senses of the English preposition *over* are related to each other. As we did for the word *run*, here are some examples to get you started, but you will need to come up with additional examples of your own to get a full picture of the complexity of the related senses of this word.

a The lamp is over the table

b Mary put the painting over the couch

c Frank walked over the log

d Jan put a table cloth over the table

e The plane flew over the city

f They live over the river from us

g The movie is now over

h The baby put her hands over her face
i There were soldiers stationed all over the field
j The spider walked all over the wall

16 In this unit we discussed the relationship between ambiguous sentences and ambiguous words. Give an example (other than ones in the book) of a sentence containing one or more ambiguous words
   a that is unambiguous
   b that is ambiguous

17 Give an example of a sentence (other than the ones in the book) of a sentence containing NO ambiguous words
   a that is unambiguous
   b that is ambiguous

18 A test for referential vagueness vs referential ambiguity is that it is possible to negate one of the senses of an ambiguous lexical item while asserting another sense at the same time and in the same context of discourse. This is not possible with vagueness, as is shown in the following examples, in which *punch* is ambiguous but *bird* is vague. The star (*) notation indicates that sentence (b) below is unacceptable.
   a I punched the paper but I didn't punch the paper
   b *There is a bird (i.e. a robin) on the lawn
       but there isn't a bird (i.e. a penguin) on the lawn.

   What different senses of *punch* are possible in (a)? Show how this test can be used to demonstrate that *pig* is also ambiguous.

4 Logic

UNIT 12 ABOUT LOGIC

Entry requirements PROPOSITION (Unit 2), SENSE RELATIONS and SENSE PROPERTIES, especially those of SENTENCES, i.e. ENTAILMENT, PARAPHRASE, AMBIGUITY, ANALYTICITY, and CONTRADICTION (Units 9–11)

Entry test (1) Which of the following correctly distinguishes sentences from propositions? Circle your choice.

(a) A proposition is an act of proposing something, usually performed by uttering some sentence.

(b) A sentence is the abstract representation of a particular meaning whereas a proposition is a string of words expressing that meaning in a particular language.

(c) A proposition is the abstract meaning of a declarative sentence, when that sentence is used to make an assertion.

Consider the following eight sentences:

(a) *John passed the hammer and saw through the window*

(b) *John saw through the window and passed the hammer*

(c) *John passed the hammer and the saw through the window*

(d) *John passed the saw and the hammer through the window*

(e) *John passed the hammer*

(f) *John saw through the window*

(g) *The hammer which John saw was not a hammer*

(h) *A saw is a tool*

(2) Say which of the above sentences is ambiguous ....

(3) Two other sentences in this set are in a paraphrase relationship. Which two? ....

(4) Which sentence is entailed by sentence (d) but does not entail it? ....

(5) Which of the above sentences is analytic? ....

(6) Which of the above sentences is a contradiction? ....

Feedback (1) (c) (2) (a) (3) (c) and (d) (4) (e) (5) (h) (6) (g)
If you scored at least 5 correct out of 6, continue to the introduction. Otherwise, review the relevant unit.

141

Introduction *Logic* is a word that means many things to different people. Many everyday uses of the words *logic* and *logical* could be replaced by expressions such as *reasonable behaviour* and *reasonable*. You may say, for instance, 'Sue acted quite logically in locking her door', meaning that Sue had good, well thought-out reasons for doing what she did. We shall use the words *logic* and *logical* in a narrower sense, familiar to semanticists. We give a partial definition of our sense of *logic* below.

Definition LOGIC deals with meanings in a language system, not with actual behaviour
(partial) of any sort. Logic deals most centrally with PROPOSITIONS. The terms 'logic' and 'logical' do not apply directly to UTTERANCES (which are instances of behaviour).

Practice Using this partial definition, do the following statements use the words *logic, logical, logically,* and *illogical* in our narrow sense, or not?

(1) It's not logical to want to kill oneself.   *Yes / No*

(2) Harry is so illogical: first he says he doesn't want to come, and
     then he changes his mind.   *Yes / No*

(3) The truth of the proposition that Socrates is mortal follows
     logically from the fact that Socrates is a man and the fact that
     all men are mortal.   *Yes / No*

(4) *Max is not coming* is, logically, the negation of *Max is coming*.   *Yes / No*

(5) The logic of Churchill's tactics in the Eastern Mediterranean
     was quite baffling.   *Yes / No*

Feedback (1) No (2) No (3) Yes (4) Yes (5) No

Comment There is an important connection between logic (even in our narrow sense) and rational action, but it is wrong to equate the two. Logic is just one contributing factor in rational behaviour. Rational behaviour involves:

(a) goals

(b) assumptions and knowledge about existing states of affairs

(c) calculations, based on these assumptions and knowledge, leading to ways of achieving the goals

Example Goal: to alleviate my hunger
(of rational Assumptions and knowledge:
behaviour)   Hunger is alleviated by eating food.
                Cheese is food.
                There is a piece of cheese in front of me.
                I am able to eat this piece of cheese.

Calculations:

> If hunger is alleviated by eating food and cheese is food, then hunger is alleviated by eating cheese.
>
> If hunger is alleviated by eating cheese, then my own hunger would be alleviated by eating this piece of cheese in front of me, and
>
> eating this piece of cheese would alleviate my hunger, and my goal is to alleviate my hunger, so therefore eating this piece of cheese would achieve my goal.

(Rational) action: eating the cheese

Comment Eating the piece of cheese in such circumstances is an example of entirely rational behaviour. But the use of the word *logic* here restricts the logic to the 'calculations' aspect of this behaviour. The goals, assumptions, knowledge, and final action are in no way logical or illogical, in our sense.

Practice In the light of this comment:

(1) If the word *cheese* in the above example were replaced throughout by the word *chalk*, would the calculations lead to the conclusion that I should eat a piece of chalk?   *Yes / No*

(2) Regardless of whether you think eating a piece of chalk in these circumstances would be rational or not, would there be anything illogical (in the narrow sense) in the conclusion that I should eat a piece of chalk?   *Yes / No*

(3) Is the statement that chalk is food in itself logical (*L*), illogical (*I*), or neither (*N*), according to the semanticist's use of these terms?   *L / I / N*

(4) Is it logical, illogical, or neither to wish to alleviate one's hunger?   *L / I / N*

(5) Say I were to calculate thus: If hunger is alleviated by eating cheese and cheese is food, then hunger is not alleviated by eating cheese. Would you say that this calculation is illogical?   *Yes / No*

Feedback (1) Yes (2) No, the calculations are as valid (i.e. logical) for chalk as they are for cheese. (3) N (4) N (5) Yes

Comment Logic, then, tells us nothing about goals, or assumptions, or actions in themselves. It simply provides rules for calculation which may be used to get a rational being from goals and assumptions to action. There is a close analogy between logic and arithmetic (which is why we have used the word *calculation*).

'Arithmetical fact' does not mean just fact involving numbers in some way, but rather fact arising from the system of rules defining addition, subtraction, multiplication, and division. A similarity between arithmetic and logic is the unthinkability of alternatives.

Example '2 + 2 = 5' is unthinkable. We can say the words easily enough, but there is no way that we can put together the concepts behind '2', '+', '=', and '5' so that they fit what '2 + 2 = 5' seems to mean. This is an arithmetical contradiction.

All men are mortal and some men are not mortal is unthinkable in the same way. This is a logical contradiction.

Practice Given below are a number of sentences. Each one expresses either a logical contradiction or a necessary truth of logic. (Sentences expressing necessary truths of logic are a type of analytic sentence.) Mark each sentence for contradiction (*C*) or for analytic (*A*) as appropriate.

(1) *John is here and John is not here*   *C / A*

(2) *Either John is here or John is not here*   *C / A*

(3) *If John is here, John is here*   *C / A*

(4) *If everyone is here, no one isn't here*   *C / A*

(5) *If someone is here, then no one is here*   *C / A*

Feedback (1) C (2) A (3) A (4) A (5) C

Comment The concepts of contradiction and analyticity are fundamental to logic, so that logic and the study of sense relations to a large extent share the same outlook and goals. But there is a difference of emphasis. The above examples are all centred around a small set of words, namely *and, or, not, if, every,* and *some*. It is the concepts behind these words that logicians have singled out for special attention. These words are thought of as belonging to a small set constituting the logical vocabulary. We will try to see what is special about these words, what sets them apart from other words. First we will compare them with the familiar semantic word-types, names and predicates, and with referring expressions.

Practice (1) Names are referring expressions, i.e. can be used to pick out individuals in the world. Can the word *and* (in normal English) be used in this way?   *Yes / No*

(2) Can the word *or* be used as a referring expression, to pick out some individual?   *Yes / No*

(3) Is *not* a referring expression?   *Yes / No*

(4) Predicates express relations between individuals (e.g. *under*) or properties of individuals (e.g. *asleep*). Can *and* be used to express a property of an individual (e.g. *John is and*, or *John ands*)?   *Yes / No*

(5) Can *and* be used to express a relation between individuals, as the
predicate *under* does? (For example, is *John and Mary* a sentence
telling us of some relationship between John and Mary? Think
whether *John and Mary* (taken out of context) actually tells you
anything about John and Mary.)   *Yes / No*

(6) Is *and* a predicate?   *Yes / No*

(7) Is *or* a predicate?   *Yes / No*

(8) Is *not* a predicate? Does *Not John* or *John is not* (again taken
out of context) tell you anything at all about John?   *Yes / No*

Feedback   (1) No (2) No (3) No (4) No (5) No – *and* by itself tells you nothing about
the relation between John and Mary; some predicate is needed before any
information is actually conveyed, e.g. *John and Mary are asleep*, which
attributes the same property to the two individuals, or *John and Mary are
married*, which expresses a relationship between the two individuals. But
the word *and* by itself does not express either a property or a relation.
(6) No (7) No (8) No – as with *and* and *or*, some predicate is needed
before *Not John* or *John is not* can be meaningful.

Comment   Words such as *and, or,* and *not* are not predicates and cannot be used as
referring expressions. Logic calls such words connectives. We will learn much
more about the meaning properties of these words in the next few units, but
it is easy enough to see now that, intuitively speaking and as their name
suggests, the main purpose of the connectives *and* and *or* is to 'connect'
individual propositions with other propositions. (The word *not* functions in
a somewhat different way and will be explained further in Unit 15.) The kind
of meaning that is involved is structural, i.e. it deals with the whole structures
of propositions and how they are related to each other, rather than with
individual items within propositions, such as names and predicates. It is
possible to talk of the extensions (or, more loosely, the denotations) of names
and predicates taken in isolation, but it is not possible to imagine extensions
or denotations for words such as *and, or, if,* and *not,* taken in isolation. It
follows from the special structural nature of the meanings of connectives that
they are topic-free and hence more basic, or general. A topic-free meaning is
one that can be involved in discourse or conversation on any topic whatever,
without restriction.

Although one may, of course, take a legitimate interest in the meanings
of individual predicates such as *red, round,* or *ruthless* (as linguists and
dictionary-writers do), an understanding of the meanings of such basic
words as *and, if, or,* and *not* is more central to the enterprise of semantics,
the study of meaning. An early book on logic was called *The Laws of
Thought,* and this is the view we take of the subject. Logic analyses the basis

of so-called logical thought. (Propositions can be grasped by the mind, i.e. they can be the objects of thought.) Thoughts are notoriously difficult things to talk about, since we can't physically experience them; correspondingly, it is difficult to talk clearly and systematically about propositions, as the logician tries to do. We will bring out the nature of some of these difficulties in practice.

Practice
(1) Have we, in this book, adopted a standardized way of representing sentences (as opposed to, say, utterances)? *Yes / No*

(2) And have we yet adopted any standardized way of representing propositions? *Yes / No*

(3) Can a declarative sentence be ambiguous? *Yes / No*

(4) Using the terms 'proposition' and 'sentence' as we have, if a declarative sentence is two-ways ambiguous, how many different propositions correspond to it? ....

(5) Is it desirable, in trying to talk clearly about propositions, to have some way of showing which propositions we are talking about? *Yes / No*

(6) What problem would be encountered if one adopted, say, sentences printed in a bold typeface as a method for representing propositions?

....

Feedback
(1) Yes, italic typeface (2) No (3) Yes (4) Two (5) Yes (6) There would be no way, with this proposal, or distinguishing the different propositions involved in the case of ambiguous sentences.

Comment
The initial difficulty in talking about propositions is that we need to invent a way of representing them unambiguously. One needs a notation that will provide, for example, two clearly different representations for the two different meanings of a two-ways ambiguous sentence, and three different representations in the case of a three-ways ambiguous sentence, and so on.

In the units that follow, we will introduce a logical notation, a specially developed way of representing propositions unambiguously. The notation will include a few special symbols, for example **&, V, ~**, and you will learn some rules for putting logical formulae together correctly, using these symbols. (To set such logical formulae off clearly from the rest of the text, they will be printed in bold type.)

Example
John and Mary are married is ambiguous, being paraphrasable either as:
John and Mary are married to each other or as
John is married to someone and Mary is married to someone

In logical notation, the first interpretation (proposition) here could be represented by the formula:

(j MARRIED TO m) & (m MARRIED TO j)

and the second interpretation would be represented by the formula:

(∃x (j MARRIED TO x)) & (∃y (m MARRIED TO y))

Comment Do not try at this stage to work out exactly how this notation applies to the examples just given. The notation will be explained gradually and in detail in the following units.

In addition to providing a means for representing the various meanings of ambiguous sentences, logical notation brings another advantage, that its formulae can be used much more systematically than ordinary language sentences for making the calculations that we mentioned at the beginning of this unit. We illustrate below some of the difficulties that arise when trying to state the rules for logical calculations in terms of ordinary language sentences.

Practice (1) Do the following two sentences have parallel grammatical structures?
Stan and Oliver worked conscientiously
Stan and Oliver worked together   Yes / No

(2) Does the first of these two sentences entail *Stan worked conscientiously?*   Yes / No

(3) Say we try to set up a 'rule of logical calculation' working on ordinary English sentences as follows: a sentence of the form noun-*and*-noun-verb-adverb entails a sentence of the form noun-verb-adverb (keeping the same nouns, verbs, and adverbs, or course); would this rule actually give the correct result in the case of *Stan and Oliver worked conscientiously?*   Yes / No

(4) Does the sentence *Stan and Oliver worked together* entail *Stan worked together?*   Yes / No

(5) Would the calculation rule given in question (3) predict that *Stan and Oliver worked together* entails *Stan worked together?* (Assume that *together* is an adverb.)   Yes / No

(6) Would the rule given in question (3) actually make a correct prediction in this case?   Yes / No

Feedback (1) Yes (2) Yes (3) Yes (4) No, in fact *Stan worked together* doesn't make literal sense. (5) Yes (6) No

Comment The problem is that pairs of sentences with similar or identical grammatical forms may sometimes have different logical forms. In order to state rules of calculation, or 'rules of inference', completely systematically, these rules have to work on representations of the logical form of sentences, rather than on the grammatical forms of the sentences themselves. Here are some examples:

Practice (1) Does the truth of the third sentence below follow necessarily from the truth of the first two?
A plant normally gives off oxygen
A geranium is a plant therefore
A geranium normally gives off oxygen   *Yes / No*

(2) Does the truth of the third sentence below follow necessarily from the truth of the first two?
A plant suddenly fell off the window-sill
A geranium is a plant therefore
A geranium suddenly fell off the window-sill   *Yes / No*

(3) Are the two trios of sentences above of similar grammatical form?   *Yes / No*

(4) The crucial difference between the two cases above lies in their first sentences. In terms of distinctions met earlier (Units 4 and 6), is *A plant gives off oxygen* a generic sentence (*G*), an equative sentence (*E*), or neither (*N*)?   *G / E / N*

(5) Is *A plant fell off the window-sill* a generic sentence, an equative sentence, or neither?   *G / E / N*

Feedback (1) Yes (2) No (3) Yes (4) G (5) N

Comment Generic sentences have a different logical form from non-generic sentences. The two sentence types express logically different types of proposition. They would therefore be represented by different types of formulae in logical notation and the logical rules of inference working on these formulae would arrive at different conclusions in the two cases, as is appropriate.

An analogy may again be made between logic and arithmetic. The Arabic notation used in arithmetic is simple, useful, and familiar. Logical notation is equally simple, equally useful in its own sphere, and can become equally familiar with relatively little effort or difficulty. As with arithmetic, learning to use the system sharpens up the mind. In particular, learning to translate ordinary language sentences into appropriate logical formulae is a very good exercise to develop precise thinking about the meanings of sentences, even though the logical form of a sentence does not express every aspect of meaning of that sentence. (Of course, logic does not involve any specific numerical ability.)

A system of logic, like a system of arithmetic, consists of two things:

a notation (in effect, a definition of all the possible proper formulae in the system)

a set of rules (for 'calculating' with the formulae in various ways)

To conclude this unit, we will give some informal examples of the kind of rules of calculation that it is necessary to include (or to exclude) in a logical system which captures the essence of rational human thought.

Practice Given below are a number of arguments, or logical calculations. Some of these actually reach logically invalid conclusions, and some of the arguments are valid. Mark each argument invalid (*I*) or valid (*V*), as appropriate.

(1) If John bought that house, he must have got a loan from the bank.
He did buy that house, so therefore he did get a loan from the bank. *I / V*

(2) If John bought that house, he must have got a loan from the bank.
He did buy the house, so therefore he didn't get a loan from
the bank.   *I / V*

(3) If John bought that house, he must have got a loan from the bank.
He didn't get a loan from the bank, so therefore he didn't buy that
house.   *I / V*

(4) If John bought that house, he must have got a loan from the bank.
He didn't buy that house, so therefore he must not have got a loan
from the bank.   *I / V*

(5) John is a Scot, and all Scots are drunkards, so John is a drunkard. *I / V*

(6) No one is answering the phone at Gary's house, so he must be at
home, because whenever Gary's at home, he never answers the
phone.   *I / V*

Feedback (1) V (2) I (3) V (4) I (John could have got a loan from the bank even
though he didn't buy that house.) (5) V (6) I

Comment The cases of valid argument here are examples of basic rules of logical
inference. The cases of invalid argument are examples of some well-known
logical fallacies. Obviously, a logical system should not permit any fallacious
arguments. The first example in the above practice makes use of a logical rule
generally known by the Latin name 'modus ponens'.

Rule MODUS PONENS is a rule stating that if a proposition P entails a
proposition Q, and P is true, then Q is true. Put in the form of a diagram,
Modus Ponens looks like this:

$$\frac{\begin{array}{l} \mathbf{P \rightarrow Q} \\ \mathbf{P} \end{array}}{\mathbf{Q}}$$

Comment The formulae above the line in this diagram represent the propositions which
are the premises of the argument, and the letter below the line represents the
proposition which is the conclusion of the argument. Note that this logical

rule only mentions whole propositions. It does not go into details concerning the various parts of propositions, e.g. it does not mention names or predicates. It is a very simple rule. In the units that follow, we will present further logical rules, so that a more complete picture can be given of the whole process of rational calculation in interesting cases.

Summary Logic deals with meanings in a language system (i.e. with propositions, etc.), not with actual behaviour, although logical calculations are an ingredient of any rational behaviour. A system for describing logical thinking contains a notation for representing propositions unambiguously and rules of inference defining how propositions go together to make up valid arguments.

Because logic deals with such very basic aspects of thought and reasoning, it can sometimes seem as if it is 'stating the obvious'. The thing to remember is that one is not, in the end, interested in individual particular examples of correct logical argument (for, taken individually, such examples are usually very obvious and trivial), but rather in describing the whole system of logical inference, i.e. one is trying to build up a comprehensive account of all logical reasoning, from which the facts about the individual examples will follow automatically. One only looks at individual examples in order to check that the descriptive system that one is building does indeed match the facts.

Logic, with its emphasis on absolute precision, has a fascination for students who enjoy a mental discipline. Thus, in addition to its contribution to our understanding of the 'Laws of Thought', it can be good fun.

Unit 12 Study Guide and Exercises

Directions After you have read Unit 12 you should be able to tackle the following questions to test your understanding of the main ideas raised in the unit.

1 You should understand these terms and concepts from this unit:
logic
connectives
logical notation

2 What aspect of rational behaviour does **logic** (in our narrow semantic sense) refer to?

3 Describe some of the ways in which logical connectives such as *and, or,* and *not* differ from other word types (such as names and predicates).

4 What is the purpose of developing a logical notation for semantics? Why not just use ordinary English? You should mention at least three different general points made in this unit which address this question.

5 Here is an example similar to one in the text in which a difficulty arises when we attempt to state the rules for logical calculation (such as entailment of truth) in terms of ordinary language sentences.

a A piece of furniture is in the living room

b A table is a piece of furniture

c A table is in the living room

d A piece of furniture can be used to furnish a house

e A table is a piece of furniture

f A table can be used to furnish a house

Does the truth of sentence (c) follow necessarily from the truth of sentences (a) and (b)? Does the truth of sentence (f) follow necessarily from the truth of sentences (d) and (e)? Explain why or why not in each case.

6 What two components must a system of logic, like a system of arithmetic, have?

7 Which of the following arguments (i.e. logical calculations) reach **logically** valid conclusions, and which do not? Which argument utilizes the logical rule of **modus ponens**?

a If Fred got an A in the course, then he must have done all the work. Fred did get an A in the course, so therefore he didn't do all the work.

b If Fred got an A in the course, then he must have done all the work. Fred did get an A in the course, so therefore he must have done all the work.

c If Fred got an A in the course, then he must have done all the work. Fred did do all the work in the course, so therefore he did get an A.

d If Fred got an A in the course, then he must have done all the work. Fred didn't get an A in the course, so therefore he must not have done all the work.

e If Fred got an A in the course, then he must have done all the work. Fred didn't do all the work, so therefore he must not have got an A.

UNIT 13 A NOTATION FOR SIMPLE PROPOSITIONS

Entry requirements PROPOSITION (Unit 2), REFERRING EXPRESSION (Unit 4) and
PREDICATE (Unit 5). It will also help if you have gone through the previous
unit (Unit 12 'About logic'). Take the entry test below before continuing with
this unit.

Entry test (1) Are proper names referring expressions (*R*) or predicates (*P*)?   *R / P*

(2) Circle the proper names in the following list: *Confucius,
Birmingham, Japan, Scott, prophet, city, nation, author*

(3) Bracket the predicates in the above list.

(4) Circle the two-place predicates in the list below: *attack* (verb),
die (verb), *father, between, put, love* (verb), *in, cat, elephant,
forget*

(5) Can a proposition be ambiguous?   *Yes / No*

(6) Do sentences with similar grammatical
form have similar logical form?   *Always / Sometimes / Never*

Feedback (1) R (2) *Confucius, Birmingham, Japan, Scott* (3) *prophet, city, nation,
author* (4) *attack, father, love, in, forget* (5) No (6) sometimes, but not
always
If you got at least 5 out of 6 correct, continue to the introduction.
Otherwise, review the relevant unit.

Introduction Logic provides a notation for unambiguously representing the essentials
of propositions. Logic has in fact been extremely selective in the parts of
language it has dealt with; but the parts it has dealt with it has treated in
great depth.

Comment The notation we adopt here is closer to English, and therefore easier for
beginners to handle, than the rather more technical notations found in
some logic books and generally in the advanced literature of logic.

We assume that simple propositions, like simple sentences, have just one
predicator (recall Unit 5), which we write in CAPITAL LETTERS. The
arguments of the predicator we represent by single lower-case letters, putting
one of these letters before the predicator (like the subject of an English

sentence) and the others (if there are others) after the predicator, usually in the preferred English word order. Anything that is not a predicator or a referring expression is simply omitted from logical notation.

Example *Abraham died* would be represented by the formula **a DIE:**
Fido is a dog by **f DOG;**
Ted loves Alice by **t LOVE a;**
Phil introduced Mary to Jack by **p INTRODUCE m j**

Practice Translate the following into this simple notation:

(1) *Arthur dreamed* ....

(2) *Bill gulped* ....

(3) *Charlie swore* ....

(4) *Patrick cursed* ....

(5) *Ben cycles* ....

Feedback (1) **a DREAM** (2) **b GULP** (3) **c SWEAR** (4) **p CURSE** (5) **b CYCLE**

Comment These formulae are very bare, stripped down to nothing but names and predicators. The reasons for eliminating elements such as forms of the verb *be*, articles (*a, the*), tense markers (past, present), and certain prepositions (e.g. *to* in *Phil introduced Mary to Jack*) are partly a matter of serious principle and partly a matter of convenience. The most serious principle involved is the traditional concentration of logic on truth.

Articles, *a* and *the*, do not affect the truth of the propositions expressed by simple sentences. Accordingly, they are simply omitted from the relatively basic logical formulae we are dealing with here. This is an example of the omission of material from logical formulae on principled grounds. In the case of some, but not all, prepositions, e.g. *at, in, on, under*, there are similar principled reasons for not including them in logical formulae.

Practice (1) Are the following sentences paraphrases of each other?
Margaret is looking for Billy
Margaret is looking after Billy
Margaret is looking at Billy   *Yes / No*

(2) Are the following sentences paraphrases of each other?
Sidney put his hat under the table
Sidney put his hat on the table
Sidney put his hat beside the table   *Yes / No*

(3) Do the prepositions in questions (2) and (3) contribute to the senses of the sentences concerned?   *Yes / No*

153

(4) Are the following sentences paraphrases?
Humphrey envies Maurice
Humphrey is envious of Maurice   *Yes / No*

(5) In the second sentence above, could *of* be replaced by any other
preposition, thus giving the sentence a different sense?   *Yes / No*

(6) In the sentence *Teddy is the uncle of Franklin,* could the
preposition *of* be replaced by any other preposition, thus
changing the sense of the sentence?   *Yes / No*

(7) In *Charlene is crazy about horses* could the preposition *about*
be replaced by any other preposition, thus changing the sense
of the sentence?   *Yes / No*

Feedback   (1) No (2) No (3) Yes (4) Yes (5) No (6) No (7) No

Comment   Some prepositions contribute substantially to the sense of the sentence they
occur in, e.g. *Sidney put his hat ON the table,* whereas in other cases,
prepositions seem merely to be required by the grammar of the language
when certain verbs and adjectives are used, e.g. *present someone WITH
something,* or *be envious OF someone.* In these cases, the verb (e.g. *present*) or
the adjective (e.g. *envious*) can be regarded as making the crucial
contribution to the sense of the sentence, and the preposition can be
disregarded from the point of view of the logic of the proposition involved. It
should be understood that by disregarding such prepositions from the logical
representation of the sentence we are not saying that they have no meaning
whatsoever, but rather that whatever meaning they do have does not seem to
be particularly relevant to the logical aspects of meaning that we are
currently focusing on.

Prepositions like these which appear to make no significant contribution
to the logical sense of a sentence are omitted from the logical formulae
representing the proposition concerned. Prepositions which do make a
contribution, on the other hand, must be included in logical formulae for
propositions.

Example   *Winston is a nephew of Randolph*   **w NEPHEW r**

Stanley is crazy about Beethoven   **s CRAZY b**

Ellen is envious of James   **e ENVIOUS j**

Margaret is looking for Billy   **m LOOK-FOR b**

Margaret is looking at Billy   **m LOOK-AT b**

Walter is beside Harriet   **w BESIDE h**

Comment In effect, we treat expressions like *look for, look at, look after* as single predicates when they contain prepositions that contribute in an important way to the sense of the sentence. This is natural, as many such expressions are indeed synonymous with single-word predicates, e.g. *seek, regard, supervise.*

Practice Write formulae for the following:

(1) *Freda is shorter than Ellen* ....

(2) *Gill is proud of Keith* ....

(3) *Ireland is to the west of Scotland* ....

(4) *Dublin is the capital of Eire* ....

Feedback (1) **f SHORTER e** (2) **g PROUD k** (3) **i WEST s** (4) **d CAPITAL e**

Comment Tense (e.g. past, present) is not represented in our logical formulae, and neither is any form of the verb *be*. We also omit the word *than* in comparative sentences like that in (1) immediately above. The omission of tense is actually not justifiable on the grounds that tense does not contribute to the sense of a sentence, as shown below.

Practice Are the following pairs of sentences paraphrases?

(1) *It's raining*
     It was raining   Yes / No

(2) *Fred is going to Madrid*
     Fred went to Madrid   Yes / No

(3) *Charles is very angry*
     Charles was very angry   Yes / No

Feedback (1) No (2) No (3) No

Comment We omit any indication of tense from our logical formulae here for the quite arbitrary reason that a logic for tenses has only recently been developed, and it involves a number of complications which would be out of place in an elementary text such as this. In a full logical theory, tenses (and any other indications of time) must be dealt with.

Now, given that we are not representing tense in any way in our logical formulae, is there any need to include anything corresponding to the various forms of the verb *be* found in simple English sentences? Recall the distinction between equative and non-equative sentences (Unit 4).

Practice (1) Are the following sentences equative (*E*) or non-equative (*N*)?

(a) *Clark Kent is Superman*   *E / N*

(b) *Superman is Clark Kent*   *E / N*

(c)   *Clark Kent is mild-mannered*   *E / N*

(d)   *Clark Kent is a reporter*   *E / N*

(2)   In which of the above sentences did a form of the verb *be*
express the IDENTITY predicate?   ....

(3)   Does the word *is* in the sentences carry the information
'present tense'?   *Yes / No*

(4)   In sentence (c) above, does the word *is*, besides carrying
'present tense', actually make any contribution to the sense
of the sentence in addition to that made by the referring
expression *Clark Kent* and the predicate *mild-mannered*?   *Yes / No*

(5)   In sentence (d) above, does the word *is*, besides carrying the
information 'present tense', make any contribution to the sense
of the sentence not already made by either *Clark Kent* or *reporter*?   *Yes / No*

Feedback   (1) (a) E (b) E (c) N (d) N (2) sentences (a) and (b) (3) Yes (4) No (5) No

Comment   Besides its use as a 'carrier' of tense, the verb *be* sometimes expresses the
identity predicate (i.e. the predicate relating the referents of two referring
expressions in an equative sentence), and sometimes makes no contribution
to the sense of a sentence at all that is relevant for determining the truth
value of the proposition expressed by the sentence. In our logical formulae,
we will represent the identity predicate with an 'equals' sign $=$, and we will
simply omit anything corresponding to any other use of the verb *be*.

Example   *Clark Kent is Superman*   **ck = s**

   Clark Kent is a reporter   **ck REPORTER**

Practice   Write logical formulae for the following, using $=$ to represent the identity
predicate where appropriate. Where it is useful, use sequences of lower-case
letters for names, e.g. **dj** for Dr Jekyll.

(1)   *Dr Jekyll was a gentleman*   ....

(2)   *Mr Hyde was a villain*   ....

(3)   *Dr Jekyll was Mr Hyde*   ....

(4)   *Jack the Ripper was the Duke of Clarence*   ....

(5)   *Mary Clark was a sister of Clark Kent*   ....

Feedback   (1) **dj GENTLEMAN** (2) **mh VILLAIN** (3) **dj = mh** (4) **jr = dc**
(5) **mc SISTER ck**

Comment   We have been using lower-case letters (or sequences of letters), such as **s** and
ck, as names in logical formulae. We assume here that the semantics of names

is very straightforward, indeed nothing more than a direct association between the name itself and its referent in the real or imaginary world (that is, the universe of discourse assumed in connection with any particular example). (Modern logicians have proposed that the semantics of names is in fact more complicated than this, but we adopt a simple version of the logic of names here.) Logical formulae should be unambiguous, and in a well worked out system of notation, no two different individuals should have the same name. We have, for convenience, ignored this detail. We have, for instance, used the same name, **b**, in our formulae for both Bill and Beethoven. This will cause no problems in this text. Simply assume, for each particular example, that each logical name identifies an individual unambiguously. But remember that a single individual can have more than one name, even in a logical system (e.g. **ck** (Clark Kent) and **s** (Superman)). The existence of different names for the same individual is just what makes the identity predicate necessary.

Logical formulae for simple propositions are very simple in structure. It is important to adhere to this simple structure, as it embodies a strict definition of the structure of simple propositions. The definition is as follows:

Definition   Every SIMPLE proposition is representable by a single PREDICATOR, drawn from the predicates in the language, and a number of ARGUMENTS, drawn from the names in the language. This implies, among other things, that no formula for a simple proposition can have TWO (or more) predicators, and it cannot have anything which is neither a predicate nor a name.

Example   **j LOVE m** is a well-formed formula for a simple proposition
j m is not a well-formed formula, because it contains no predicator
j IDOLIZE ADORE m is not a well-formed formula for a simple proposition, because it contains two predicators
j and h LOVE m is not a well-formed formula for a simple proposition because it contains something ('and') which is neither a predicator nor a name

Practice   Are the following formulae well-formed for simple propositions?

(1) **j SEND h m**   *Yes / No*

(2) **j SEND BOOK m**   *Yes / No*

(3) **j UNCLE f**   *Yes / No*

(4) **j BROTHER f FATHER**   *Yes / No*

Feedback   (1) Yes (2) No (3) Yes (4) No

Comment   The implication of this is that many apparently simple sentences correspond to propositions which are not logically simple. Indeed, we would claim that,

157

for example, *John met Harry* is simpler in its logical structure than *John met a man*, because the latter contains a referring expression in which a predicate is embedded (see Unit 6). We shall not develop a notation in this book for representing referring expressions which contain predicates embedded in them, like *the man in the corner*. Consequently, all the referring expressions in our examples will be either proper names like *John* and *Harry* or pronouns like *she, him, itself.*

Logical notation is no more illuminating than Chinese to a person who knows neither. So what is the advantage of developing a new 'language', i.e. logical notation, to explain meaning, if one only has then to go on and explain what IT means? The answer is that logical notation has been designed to be perspicuous. Not only are logical formulae unambiguous, but also the structure of each formula reflects, in a direct and unconfused way, the type of situation in the world that it describes. The idea behind logical notation is that each different type of situation in the real world should be described by a different type of formula. Natural languages, such as English and Chinese, often use sentences of the same grammatical type to describe quite different situations.

Practice   (1) Can a generic sentence in English have the grammatical
                 structure 'subject-verb-object'?   *Yes / No*

           (2) Can a non-generic sentence in English have the grammatical
                 structure 'subject-verb-object'?   *Yes / No*

           (3) Do the following sentences all describe the same situation?
                 (They may emphasize different aspects of the situation, but is
                 it the same situation that is being described in all cases?)   *Yes / No*
                 Lightning struck the house
                 The house was struck by lightning
                 What struck the house was lightning
                 What was struck by lightning was the house
                 It was the house that was struck by lightning
                 What happened was that lightning struck the house

Feedback   (1) Yes (2) Yes (3) Yes, and one can think of many more paraphrases
           beside these.

Comment   Logical notation provides one type of formula (which we shall not meet
           here) for generic sentences, and a different type of formula for non-generic
           sentences. One can see from the formula itself what type of meaning it has.
           One does not need to appeal to the context, as one often does in interpreting
           a sentence in a natural language. Logical notation is austere, in that it does
           not provide the rich variety of structures seen in question (3) above.

Corresponding to each of these sentences, and all their other paraphrases, there would only be one formula in logical notation. There are no stylistic variants of formulae in logic.

What type of situation in the world is described by the type of formula which consists of a name followed by a one-place predicate? (This is the simplest type of logical formula.) The answer draws on the notions of referent (Unit 3) and extension (Unit 9).

Rule   A simple formula consisting of a name and a one-place predicate is true of a situation in which the referent of the name is a member of the extension of the predicate.

Example   Below is a picture of a tiny fragment of a universe of discourse (a situation). In the picture we have labelled individuals with their names (*Al, Ed, Mo*, etc.).

The formula **ed STAND** (corresponding to the sentence *Ed is standing*) is true of this situation.

The formula **mo CAT** is false of this situation.

Practice   In relation to the situation depicted above, are the following formulae true (*T*) or false (*F*)?

(1) **al MAN**   *T / F*

(2) **al WOMAN**   *T / F*

(3) **al STAND**   *T / F*

(4) **mo SLEEP**   *T / F*

(5) **ed SIT**   *T / F*

Feedback   (1) T (2) F (3) T (4) F (5) F

Comment A system of logic must have its own 'semantics', a set of principles relating its formulae to the situations they describe. The rule given above for simple formulae consisting of a name and a one-place predicate is part of such a set of principles, a 'semantics for logic'. Logicians use the term 'semantics' in a much narrower way than we do in this book; for a logician, the semantics of logic consists only in relating (parts of) formulae to entities outside the notational system, e.g. to referents and extensions.

It is very important to have this extensional component in a logical system, as it provides a constant reminder that logical formulae can only be fully understood to the extent that they are systematically related to some world (universe of discourse) external to the notational system itself. We shall not give explicit rules (such as the one above) for relating simple formulae with two-place and three-place predicates to the situations they describe. We shall rely on the reader's own intuitive grasp of the meanings of such predicates. Apply your intuitions to the practice below.

Practice Look at the situation shown in this picture and say whether the formulae below are true (*T*) or false (*F*) of this situation. Assume that the labels in the picture are the names of the individuals involved, and that the predicates in the formulae have their usual English meanings.

(1) **r BITE j**   *T / F*

(2) **g TOUCH k**   *T / F*

(3) **a ON r**   *T / F*

(4) **r UNDER a**   *T / F*

(5) **g BETWEEN k a**	*T / F*
(6) **k BETWEEN g a**	*T / F*
(7) **k BESIDE g**	*T / F*
(8) **k UNDER g**	*T / F*

Feedback   (1) T (2) T (3) T (4) T (5) F (6) T (7) T (8) F

Comment   The assignment of the truth values T (for 'true') and F (for 'false') is intuitively most straightforward in the case of simple propositions. In subsequent units, we shall describe how these values are used in 'calculating' the truth values of more complex propositions.

Summary   We have presented a logical notation for simple propositions. A well-formed formula for a simple proposition contains a single predicator, drawn from the predicates in the language, and a number of arguments, drawn from the names in the language. The notation we have given contains no elements corresponding to articles such as *a* and *the*, certain prepositions, and certain instances of the verb *be*, as these make no contribution to the truth conditions of the sentences containing them. We have also, for convenience only, omitted any representation of tense in our logical formulae.

The introduction of a notation for propositions (to be refined in subsequent units) fills a gap left empty since Unit 2, where we introduced a way of representing sentences and utterances, but not propositions. We now have (the beginnings of) a way of representing items at all three levels:

Utterance	Sentence	Proposition
'Jesus wept'	*Jesus wept*	**j WEEP**

Unit 13 Study Guide and Exercises

Directions   After you have read Unit 13 you should be able to tackle the following questions to test your understanding of the main ideas raised in the unit.

1 You should understand these terms and concepts from this unit:
logical formula
simple proposition

2 Translate the following sentences into the simple logical notation developed in this unit.
a   Bonnie cried
b   Fred is walking
c   Tom paid Mary
d   I sent Jack to Barney
e   Mary hates Fred

161

3 What is the reason for eliminating such linguistic elements as some instances of the verb *be*, articles (*a, the*), tense markers, and certain prepositions from logical notation?

4 We have claimed (along with many other semanticists) that the preposition *of* which co-occurs with certain adjectives and nouns in sentences like the following does not contribute to the senses of the sentences, but is merely required by the grammar.

a Tipper is envious of Hillary
b Teddy is the uncle of Franklin

We justified this by observing that the preposition *of* in these sentences could not be replaced by any other preposition that would give the sentence a different sense. This contrasts with sentence pairs like the following, where changing the prepositions does seem to change the sense.

c Jane is looking for Billy   e Fred is waiting for Tom
d Jane is looking at Billy   f Fred is waiting with Tom

While this simplifies the translation of sentences into logical notation (and does not conflict with the reason you should have given in question 3 above about why these prepositions can be omitted), does it seem right to claim that prepositions like these do not contribute at all to the senses of the sentences in which they occur? Is it really a matter of a strict distinction between sense vs no sense, or is the situation in fact more complex than was indicated in the text? Try to explain your thoughts about this in a short essay.

5 Translate each sentence (a–f) in question 4 above into the logical notation presented in this unit.

6 Now translate the following English sentences into well-formed logical notation (formulae) for simple propositions. You can use abbreviations such as **gwb** for multi-word referring expressions like George W. Bush.

a George W. Bush is the President of the United States
b Bill Clinton is a jogger
c Max is taller than Fred
d Wilma loves Max
e I'm waiting for Fred
f Fred will send Mike to Mary

7 Identify which of the following are wellformed formulae for simple propositions, and which are not wellformed (according to the definition of a simple proposition given in this unit). In each case explain why the propositions are, or are not, wellformed. For the wellformed propositions give an English sentence which the proposition could represent.

a   **m LOVE j**
b   **f m**
c   **m HATE DETEST b**
d   **m HATE b and s**
e   **f SEND m c**

f   **m AUNT k**
g   **j BROTHER m SISTER**
h   **m GENIUS**
i   **f or l SEE b**
j   **f SEE b**

8   Give one formula in logical notation which could be used to represent the situation described by ALL of the following sentences.
   a   What happened was that Jane saw Bill
   b   It was Bill who(m) Jane saw
   c   Jane saw Bill
   d   Bill was seen by Jane
   e   What Jane did was see Bill

9   How do logicians use the term **semantics**? Is their use of the term broader or narrower than that used in the rest of this textbook?

10   Consult the situation (picture) on page 159 in this unit with the individuals Al, Ed, and Mo, and determine whether the following formulae are true (T) or false (F) of the situation. Let **c** represent the name *cat*.
   a   **al LEFT mo**
   b   **ed BETWEEN al mo**
   c   **c BEHIND mo**
   d   **ed FRONT c**

   e   **c STAND**
   f   **c SLEEP**
   g   **c RUN**
   h   **ed BALD**

11   We noted at the end of this unit that, with the introduction of logical notation, we now have a way of systematically representing sentences, utterances, and propositions. Go back to the examples in question 2 above and represent each item systematically in this way.

12   Be sure you know how to interpret a simple logical formula in relation to the world which is its assumed universe of discourse. In this respect indicate how to interpret these simple logical formulae:
   a   **f CAT**
   b   **b CAR**

UNIT 14 CONNECTIVES: *AND* AND *OR*

Entry requirements   A good understanding of the preceding unit. If you are confident that you grasped the main points of the previous unit, take the entry test below. Otherwise, review Unit 13.

Entry test   (1) One of the following statements is correct, and two are incorrect. Which one is correct? Circle your choice.

     (a) A sentence can be thought of as the meaning of a proposition.

     (b) A formula such as **b RUN** represents a simple proposition.

     (c) Utterances never express propositions.

(2) Two of the sentences below express simple propositions and two express complex propositions for which no notation has been presented. Write down formulae for the two simple propositions.

     (a) *Nixon resigned*   ....

     (b) *Pat and her husband bought a chicken ranch*   ....

     (c) *Khomeini thwarted Carter*   ....

     (d) *If Maggie wins again, I'm emigrating*   ....

(3) Does logical analysis concentrate on considerations of the truth of propositions?

(4) Which of the following statements correctly expresses how the simple logical formula **j MAN** is to be interpreted in relation to the world which is its assumed universe of discourse?

     (a) The extension of the predicate **MAN** is a member of the extension of the name **j**.

     (b) The individual named **j** is a member of the extension of the predicate **MAN**.

     (c) The extension of the name **j** is identical to the extension of the predicate **MAN**.

Feedback   (1) (b) (It seems reasonable to say that utterances can express propositions, although in a sense indirectly, via the act of assertion – see Units 2 and 22) (2) (a) **n RESIGN** (c) **k THWART c** (3) Yes (4) (b)

164

If you got this test completely right, or only got part of one question wrong, continue to the introduction. Otherwise, review Unit 13.

Introduction The English words *and* and *or* correspond (roughly) to logical connectives. Connectives provide a way of joining simple propositions to form complex propositions. A logical analysis must state exactly how joining propositions by means of a connective affects the truth of the complex propositions so formed. We start with the connective corresponding to *and*, firstly introducing a notation for complex propositions formed with this connective.

Rule Any number of individual wellformed formulae can be placed in a sequence with the symbol **&** between each adjacent pair in the sequence: the result is a complex wellformed formula.

Example Take the three simple formulae:

c COME g   (*Caesar came to Gaul*)
c SEE g   (*Caesar saw Gaul*)
c CONQUER g   (*Caesar conquered Gaul*)

From these, a single complex formula can be formed:

(c COME g) & (c SEE g) & (c CONQUER g)

Comment The parentheses help visually to make the structure of the formula clear. Parentheses are not absolutely necessary in this case, although we shall see cases where parentheses are necessary for ensuring that logical formulae are unambiguous. Only formulae for whole propositions can be connected with **&**. Predicates and names cannot be connected with **&**.

Practice (1) Suggest an English translation for: **j TALL & m SMALL**.

....

(2) Translate the following into logical notation:
(a) *Andy entered and Mary left*

....

(b) *John loves Mary and Mary loves Bill*

....

(c) *John and Mary are Irish*

....

Feedback (1) E.g. *John is tall and Mary is small* (2) (a) **a ENTER & m LEAVE** (b) **j LOVE m & m LOVE b** (c) **j IRISH & m IRISH**

Comment Sometimes English can express a compound proposition in an apparently simple sentence.

Example   *Adolfo and Benito are Italian* would be represented by the complex formula **a ITALIAN & b ITALIAN**. This brings out clearly the fact that it is a paraphrase of *Adolfo is Italian and Benito is Italian*. (Again, **a & b ITALIAN** would not be a wellformed formula, because we have stipulated earlier that in our system of logical notation only propositions can be conjoined with **&**.)

Practice   Write logical formulae for the following (to avoid confusion, use **ad** as your logical name for Adam and **ab** as your logical name for Abel):

(1)   *Adam ploughed and Eve sewed*

....

(2)   *God created Adam and Eve*

....

(3)   *Adam and Eve are both parents of Cain*

....

(4)   *Eve bore Cain and Abel*

....

(5)   *Cain attacked and slew Abel*

....

Feedback   **(1) ad PLOUGH & e SEW (2) g CREATE ad & g CREATE e (3) ad PARENT c & e PARENT c (4) e BEAR c & e BEAR ab (5) c ATTACK ab & c SLAY ab**

Comment   What you have been doing above is called 'unpacking' the meanings of apparently simple sentences. In examples (1)–(5) the meaning of each sentence is a conjunction of two simple propositions. The logical symbol **&**, corresponding roughly to English *and*, expresses the logical conjunction of propositions. Not all simple sentences can have their meanings unpacked in exactly the same way as examples (1)–(5).

Practice   Consider *Adam and Eve are a happy couple.*

(1)   Does *Adam is a happy couple* make sense?   *Yes / No*

(2)   Does *Eve is a happy couple* make sense?   *Yes / No*

Feedback   (1) No (2) No

Comment   This illustrates that not all English sentences with *and* involve the logical conjunction of propositions, expressed by **&**.

      An analysis of this fact would involve going into the meaning of the predicate *couple*. We will not pursue such problems here.

      We consider next what rules of inference can be formulated involving formulae containing the connective **&**.

Practice (1) Is *God punished Adam and Eve* a paraphrase of *God punished Eve and Adam?*   Yes / No

      (2) Are the logical formulae for the above equivalent, i.e. is
g PUNISH a & g PUNISH e equivalent to
g PUNISH e & g PUNISH a?   Yes / No

Feedback   (1) Yes: it might appear as if there was a difference in the temporal order of punishment, e.g. Adam before Eve. However, neither sentence necessarily implies a temporal order. (2) Yes

Comment   We can say that **g PUNISH a & g PUNISH e** and **g PUNISH e & g PUNISH a** are equivalent, at least in terms of their truth values. This equivalence follows from a general rule of inference stating that from the conjunction of two propositions in a given order one can infer the conjunction of the same two propositions in the opposite order. This rule of inference, called 'Commutativity of Conjunction' is given in the form of a diagram below. In this diagram **p** and **q** are variables ranging over propositions, that is, **p** and **q** stand for any propositions one may think of.

Rule   Commutativity of conjunction:

$$\frac{\mathbf{p \, \& \, q}}{\mathbf{q \, \& \, p}}$$
     (premiss)
     (conclusion)

Comment   If it should seem to you that this rule is merely a statement of the obvious, you are right. Remember that one of the goals of logic is to describe explicitly the fundamental 'Laws of Thought'. The logician, like the mountaineer who climbs mountains, describes extremely basic rules of inference such as this 'because they are there'. Notice that, because the premiss and the conclusion in this rule are exact mirror images of each other, the conclusion (**q & p**) can be 'fed into' the rule as the premiss, in which case the original premiss (**p & q**) will 'emerge' as the conclusion. This complete interchangeability of premiss and conclusion amounts to their logical equivalence. The relationship between formulae and propositions can be seen in a way somewhat parallel to the relationship between names and their referents. We shall say that equivalent formulae actually stand for the same proposition, just as different (though equivalent) names stand for the same individual. (The rule of commutativity of conjunction demands the postulation of some additional principle to the effect that temporally ordered events are most helpfully described in an order which reflects the order of their occurrence. This seems a quite natural principle.)

    There are several other, equally obvious, rules of inference involving logical conjunction. In the practice below, answer the questions by trying to think whether the rules given really do describe your own understanding of the meaning of *and*.

Practice Some of the rules of inference proposed below are correct, and some are incorrect. Say which are correct (*C*) and which incorrect (*I*).

(1)

p	(premisses)	*C / I*
q		
p & q	(conclusion)	

(2)

p & q	(premiss)	*C / I*
p	(conclusion)	

(3)

p	(premiss)	*C / I*
p & q	(conclusion)	

Feedback (1) C (2) C (3) I

Comment Rule (3) above is incorrect, because, for example, one cannot draw the conclusion that John and Mary are here simply from the premiss that John is here. On the other hand, rule (2) above is correct because one can legitimately conclude, for example, that John is here from the premiss that John and Mary are here.

Formulating correct rules of inference like this is one way of specifying the meaning of the logical connective **&**, and hence indirectly (and approximately) of the English word *and*, which corresponds approximately to it. To the extent that logical **&** corresponds with English *and*, valid rules of inference such as (2) and the rule of Commutativity of Conjunction can be seen as describing very general entailment relations involving sentences containing *and*.

Practice Given below are pairs consisting of a sentence and a rule of inference. Using the given sentence as a premiss, write down the conclusion warranted by the given rule of inference. We have done the first one for you.

(1) *Melanie is pregnant and Mike is in Belgium*   **p & q**
     Mike is in Belgium and Melanie is pregnant   **q & p**
     ....

(2) *Lorna left and Bill stayed*   **p & q**

     ....   **p**

(3) *Frances sang and Harry tapdanced*   **p & q**

     ....   **q**

(4) Now, what is the sense relation that holds between each of the sentences given above and the answer you have written under it?

Feedback (2) Lorna left (3) Harry tapdanced (4) entailment

Comment   This establishes how logical rules of inference can be seen to play a part in the semanticist's overall task of specifying all the sense relations that hold between items (words and sentences) in a language. The rules of inference so far given probably seem trivial: indeed they do not do an impressive amount of work. But as we proceed we shall build up a larger set of inference rules, involving other logical connectives, and other sorts of logical element. Taken as a whole, the entire system of inference may escape the charge of triviality. (We shall also, later in this unit, give a completely different method for describing the meanings of the logical connectives.)

    The joining of propositions by the logical connective **&** is called 'conjunction'. Next we will deal with the joining of propositions by the logical connective **V**, corresponding to English *or*. This is called 'disjunction'. (The letter **V** can be thought of as standing for the Latin *vel*, meaning 'or'.)

Rule   Any number of wellformed formulae can be placed in a sequence with the symbol **V** between each adjacent pair in the sequence: the result is a complex wellformed formula.

Example   **h HERE**   (*Harry is here*)
          c DUTCHMAN   (*Charlie is a Dutchman*)
From these, a single complex formula can be formed:
(h HERE) V (c DUTCHMAN) (*Harry is here or Charlie is a Dutchman*)

Practice   Unpack the following into logical formulae:

(1)   *Dorothy saw Bill or Alan*

....

(2)   *Either Dunfermline or Kirkcaldy is the capital of Fife*

....

(3)   Does *Bernard or Christine strangled Mary* mean the same thing
as *Christine or Bernard strangled Mary*?   *Yes / No*

(4)   Are **b STRANGLE m V c STRANGLE m** and
c STRANGLE m V b STRANGLE m equivalent formulae?   *Yes / No*

(5)   Is every formula of the form **p V q** (where **p** and **q** stand for
any propositions) equivalent to one of the form **q V p**?   *Yes / No*

(6)   Give a rule of inference, in diagram form, accounting for this
equivalence.

....

Feedback   (1) **d SEE b V d SEE a** (2) **d CAPITAL f V k CAPITAL f**

$$\frac{\textbf{p V q}\ \text{(premiss)}}{\textbf{q V p}\ \text{(conclusion)}}$$

(3) Yes (4) Yes (5) Yes (6)

Comment | This last rule of inference is the rule of 'Commutativity of Disjunction'. This rule shows a similarity between the meaning of **&** (roughly corresponding to English *and*) and **V** (roughly, English *or*). Of course, there are important differences between *and* and *or*, and these can be seen from other rules of inference involving **V**.

Practice | (1) Is it correct to conclude that John is here simply from the premiss that either John or Mary is here? *Yes / No*

(2) Is the following a valid rule of inference? $\dfrac{p \lor q}{p}$ *Yes / No*

(3) Is a rule of exactly the same form, but with **&** instead of **V**, valid? *Yes / No*

Feedback | (1) No (2) No (3) Yes

Practice | Consider the following sentence:

Alice went to Birmingham and she met Cyril or she called on David

(1) Is it possible to take this sentence in such a way that we understand that Alice definitely went to Birmingham but did not necessarily meet Cyril? *Yes / No*

(2) Is it possible to take this sentence in such a way that we understand that Alice did not necessarily go to Birmingham, but that, if she did, she definitely met Cyril? *Yes / No*

Feedback | (1) Yes (2) Yes

Comment | This sentence is grammatically ambiguous (see Unit 11). The two meanings can be expressed by using brackets to group together the propositions differently in each logical formula.

Example | **a GO b & (a MEET c V a CALL-ON d)**
vs
(a GO b & a MEET c) V a CALL-ON d

Comment | The ambiguity here can be resolved by placing the word *either* in one of two positions.

Practice | (1) Which of the two formulae just given expresses the meaning of *Either Alice went to Birmingham and she met Cyril or she called on David*?

....

(2) Where would you put *either* in the original sentence to get the meaning expressed by **a GO b & (a MEET c V a CALL-ON d)**?

....

(3) Is the following sentence grammatically ambiguous?
Adam will take Lucy or Cathy and Diana   *Yes / No*

(4) Write down the two logical formulae corresponding to the two meanings of the sentence just given.

....

....

(5) Could the ambiguity of this sentence be resolved by a
strategic placement of *either*?   *Yes / No*

(6) Could the ambiguity of this sentence be resolved by a
strategic placement of the word *both*?   *Yes / No*

Feedback   (1) **(a GO b & a MEET c) V a CALL-ON d** (2) *Alice went to Birmingham and either she met Cyril or she called on David* (3) Yes (4) **a TAKE 1 V (a TAKE c & a TAKE d); (a TAKE 1 V a TAKE c) & a TAKE d** (5) No (6) Yes, but the results sound rather unnatural: *Adam will take Lucy or both Cathy and Diana* vs *Adam will take both Lucy or Cathy and Diana*. These could be made more acceptable by suitable intonations and stress.

Practice   (1) In relation to the examples in the last practice what can you say about the position of the words *either* or *both* in relation to the position of the brackets in the corresponding logical formulae?

....

....

(2) Write down two logical formulae corresponding to the two meanings of the following sentence: *Angela is Ben's mother or David's grandmother and Charlie's aunt.*

....

....

....

....

(3) Which of the two formulae in your answer to (2) definitely asserts that Angela is Charlie's aunt?

....

....

(4) Which of the two formulae in your answer to (2) definitely asserts that Angela is Ben's mother?

....

....

Feedback (1) The position of *either* and *both* roughly indicates the position of the left-hand bracket in the logical formula. (2) **a MOTHER b V (a GRANDMOTHER d & a AUNT c); (a MOTHER b V a GRANDMOTHER d) & a AUNT c** (3) **(a MOTHER b V a GRANDMOTHER d) & a AUNT c** (4) Neither. Can you explain why?

Comment Rules of inference, which can be seen as contributing to a description of the meanings of connectives such as **&** and **V**, can be interpreted in terms of truth. A rule of inference states, in effect, that a situation in which the premiss (or premisses) is (are) true is also a situation in which the conclusion is true. But rules of inference do not explicitly operate with the terms 'true' and 'false', and do not, either explicitly or implicitly, state any relationships between propositions which happen to be false.

A full account of the contribution that a connective such as **&** or **V** makes to the truth or falsehood of a complex proposition can be given in the form of a truth table.

Example Truth table for **&**:

p	q	p & q
T	T	T
T	F	F
F	T	F
F	F	F

Comment This table conveys the core of the meaning of the English word *and*. English *and* behaves in a slightly more complicated and subtle way than is indicated here, but the central features of the meaning of *and* are all reflected in this table.

In this table, **p** and **q** are, as before, variables standing for any proposition. The rows in the left-hand column list all possible combinations of the values T (for true) and F (for false) that can be assigned to a pair of propositions. The corresponding values in the right-hand column are the values of the formula **p & q** for those combinations of values.

The following practice, in terms of sentences rather than logical formulae, takes you through all the combinations in this truth table in the order given.

Practice (1) In a situation in which *Henry died* and *Terry resigned* are both true, is *Henry died and Terry resigned* true or false? *T / F*

(2) In a situation where *Henry died* is true, but *Terry resigned* is false, is *Henry died and Terry resigned* true or false? *T / F*

(3) Where *Henry died* is false, but *Terry resigned* is true, is *Henry died and Terry resigned* true or false? *T / F*

(4) Where *Henry died* and *Terry resigned* are both false, is
     Henry died and Terry resigned true or false?   *T / F*

Feedback (1) T (2) F (3) F (4) F

Comment English *and,* as we have said, is not exactly equivalent to the logical
connective **&,** whose meaning is defined solely in terms of truth. It is
interesting to ask about the meaning of the related English word *but.*

Practice (1) Make a quick, intuitive judgement here. Do the English
              words *and* and *but* mean the same thing?   *Yes / No*

          (2) Now we will work out a truth table for *but.* Remember that we
               are only concerned with the TRUTH in given situations of the
               sentences we cite.

               (a) In a situation where *Henry died* and *Terry resigned* are both
                    true, is the sentence *Henry died but Terry resigned* true or false? *T / F*

               (b) Where *Henry died* is true, but *Terry resigned* is false, is
                    Henry died but Terry resigned true or false?   *T / F*

               (c) Where *Henry died* is false, but *Terry resigned* is true, is
                    Henry died but Terry resigned true or false?   *T / F*

               (d) Where *Henry died* and *Terry resigned* are both false, is
                    Henry died but Terry resigned true or false?   *T / F*

          (3) On the basis of your answers to questions (a)–(d) above, fill in the values
               (T or F, as appropriate) in the right-hand column of the truth table for
               but below.

p	q	p *but* q
T	T	
T	F	
F	T	
F	F	

          (4) Does the truth table that you have filled out differ in any way
               from the truth table given for the logical connective **&**?   *Yes / No*

          (5) Considered only from the point of view of their effect on the
               truth of complex sentences containing them, do *and* and *but*
               differ in meaning?   *Yes / No*

Feedback (1) No (2) (a) T (b) F (c) F (d) F (3) T, F, F, F (reading down the column)
(4) No (5) No

Comment The conclusion reached about *and* and *but* need not be perplexing, so long as
one bears in mind that truth-conditional meaning, of the kind described in

truth tables, may be only a part of the meaning, in a wider sense, of a word. From the point of view of truth alone, *and* and *but* make the same contribution to meaning; but they differ in other aspects of meaning. In particular, the word *but* is preferred when the speaker wishes to indicate some kind of contrast between the two propositions involved. If the second proposition, but not the first, gives an unexpected piece of information, for instance, the use of *but*, rather than *and*, is appropriate. The logical connective **&** captures the truth-conditional aspects of the meanings of both *and* and *but*.

A truth table can also be given for **V**, corresponding approximately to English *or* (or *either . . . or*). We get you to construct one in practice below.

Practice (1) In a situation where *Henry died* and *Terry resigned* are both true, is
(*Either*) *Henry died or Terry resigned* true or false?   *T / F*

(2) Where *Henry died* is true, but *Terry resigned* is false, is (*Either*)
Henry died or Terry resigned true or false?   *T / F*

(3) Where *Henry died* is false, but *Terry resigned* is true, is (*Either*)
Henry died or Terry resigned true or false?   *T / F*

(4) Where *Henry died* and *Terry resigned* are both false, is (*Either*)
Henry died or Terry resigned true or false?   *T / F*

(5) Using your answers to (1)–(4) above as a basis, fill in the values (T or F, as appropriate) in the right-hand column of the table below.

p	q	p V q
T	T	
T	F	
F	T	
F	F	

Feedback (1) T (2) T (3) T (4) F (5) T, T, T, F (reading down the column)

Comment The values T and F which appear in truth tables are the same values as those assigned to simple propositions in relation to the situations in the world which they describe (recall the previous unit). In the case of simple propositions, the values T and F 'come from' the world. In the case of complex propositions with connectives such as **&** and **V**, the combinations of the values of the component simple propositions are 'looked up' in the appropriate truth table, and the value of the whole complex proposition (either T or F) is arrived at. Thus in the case of complex propositions, their truth values 'come from' the truth values of their constituent simple propositions.

Example Metaphorically, the truth value of a complex proposition is like the trunk of a tree whose roots reach down into the world. Truth values flow from the world upwards through the roots, being affected in various ways where the roots connect with each other, and eventually arriving at the trunk of the tree.

The following practices will give you additional experience in working with complex propositions. Try to work through them completely before checking the answers in the feedback sections.

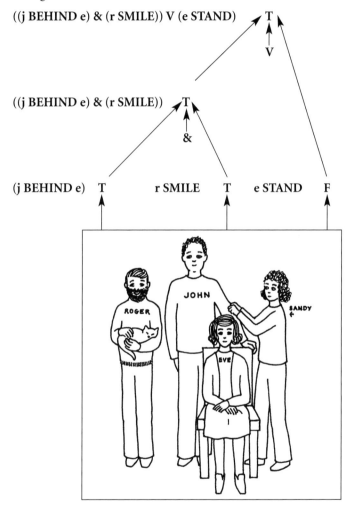

((j BEHIND e) & (r SMILE)) V (e STAND)   **T**

V

((j BEHIND e) & (r SMILE))   **T**

&

(j BEHIND e)   **T**   **r SMILE**   **T**   **e STAND**   **F**

Practice Using the world shown in the picture above as the source of truth values for simple propositions, and calculating the values of complex propositions from truth tables, fill in the values T and F, as appropriate, in the boxes in the diagrams below.

175

(1) ((e STAND) & (s PULL j)) V (e BEHIND j)

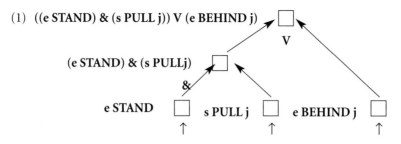

(2) (In this example, the boxes are on the left-hand side of their propositions, simply to make the diagram neater.)

Feedback

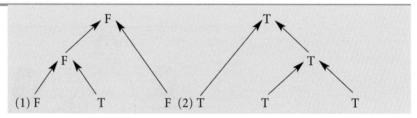

Practice Use the map overleaf as a 'world' to determine the truth values of the formulae (some simple, some complex) listed. We have used unabbreviated logical names, for convenience. Assume that the predicates have their usual English meanings. Boldface is not used in this practice.

(1) mumbai IN India   *T / F*

(2) karachi IN iran   *T / F*

(3) tibet BORDER afghanistan   *T / F*

(4) (tashkent IN iran) & (kabul IN tibet)   *T / F*

(5) (karachi IN pakistan) V (iran BORDER india)   *T / F*

(6) (karachi SOUTH tashkent) & ((tashkent EAST tehran) &
     (nepal BORDER tibet))   *T / F*

(7) ((chennai IN india) V (tehran IN tibet)) V (mumbai IN iran)   *T / F*

(8) ((chennai IN iran) V (tibet WEST iran)) & (kabul IN afghanistan)   *T / F*

Feedback   (1) T (2) F (3) T (4) F (5) T (6) T (7) T (8) F

Comment   Truth values of complex propositions are derived from the truth values of their constituent simple propositions. This is an example of what has been called the compositionality of meaning.

Definition   The thesis of COMPOSITIONALITY of meaning is that the meaning of any expression is a function of the meanings of the parts of which it is composed.

Comment   The truth tables we have given for **&** and **V** are in fact functions of the kind mentioned in this definition.

Summary   The logical connectives **&** (corresponding to English *and* and *but*) and **V** (roughly English *or*) are used to form complex propositional formulae by connecting simple propositional formulae. Rules of inference can be given involving these connectives, and they can be defined by means of truth tables.

Unit 14   Study Guide and Exercises

Directions   After you have read Unit 14 you should be able to tackle the following questions to test your understanding of the main ideas raised in the unit.

1   You should understand these terms and concepts from this unit:
    logical conjunction (with **&**)
    logical disjunction (with **V**)
    rules of inference
        commutativity of conjunction
        commutativity of disjunction
    compositionality of meaning
    truth tables

2   Translate the following into logical notation using either **&** or **V** (or both as required).
    a   Fred arrived and Mary left
    b   Either Fred is a Republican or Mary is a Democrat
    c   Max and Erma are happy
    d   Bill visited Jim and Mary
    e   Max saw Mary or Fred
    f   Jim briefed Jane and he saw Mary or he met Fred
        (disambiguate by means of different bracketing)
    g   Either Mary briefed Fred and she saw Jane or she saw David
        (is this ambiguous?)
    h   Mary briefed Fred and either she saw Jane or she saw David
        (is this ambiguous?)

3   What can be connected with the logical connectives **&** and **V**?
    What CANNOT be connected with these connectives in our logical system?

4   Do all English sentences with *and* involve the logical conjunction of propositions (expressed by **&**)? If not, give one or two examples different from those given in the text.

5   What are **rules of inference**? What does such a rule state in general?

6   Give an example in which a rule of inference involving **&** is valid but the corresponding rule with **V** is invalid.

7   Below are some examples in which a conclusion has been drawn from premises involving either logical conjunction or disjunction. Identify which conclusions follow logically from the given premises and which do not. Explain why in either case. Then translate the logically valid inferences into logical notation, letting the variables **p** and **q** stand for each proposition (e.g. let **p** = Bill signed a bill, etc.).

    a   **Premiss:** George signed a bill and Hillary gave a speech
        Conclusion: Hillary gave a speech
    b   **Premiss:** Max baked a pie or Mary baked a cake
        Conclusion: Max baked a pie

    c **Premiss**: George signed a bill or Hillary gave a speech

       Conclusion: Hillary gave a speech or Bill signed a bill

    d **Premiss**: Al made a trip

       Conclusion: Al made a trip or Tipper attended a hearing

    e **Premiss**: Socks chased a mouse and Millie was envious

       Conclusion: Millie was envious and Socks chased a mouse

8 Suppose it is true that *Tipper laughed* but *Al yawned* is false. Is the sentence *Tipper laughed and Al yawned* TRUE or FALSE?

9 Suppose that the sentences *Tipper laughed* and *Al yawned* are both true. Then is the sentence *Tipper laughed but Al yawned* TRUE or FALSE?

10 Based solely on their truth table values, do *and* and *but* have the same or different meanings? What aspects of meaning do these two words seem to share, and how do they appear to differ? Do their truth table 'meanings' fully characterize their complete senses? Briefly explain.

11 Calculate the truth values of the following complex propositions by referring to the world with the individuals Roger, John, Eve, and Sandy shown on page 175 in this unit. Pay special attention to the bracketing.

    a **(e STAND) & ((s PULL j) V (j BEHIND e))**

    b **(s STAND) V ((s PULL j) & (j BEHIND e))**

    c **((e SIT) & (j BETWEEN r s)) & (s PULL j)**

    d **((e STAND) V (s PULL j)) V (r BETWEEN s j)**

12 Explain the idea of **compositionality of meaning**. Are the truth tables for **&** and **V** developed in this unit examples of this notion? Explain briefly.

UNIT 15 MORE CONNECTIVES

Entry requirements CONJUNCTION, DISJUNCTION, RULE OF INFERENCE, and TRUTH TABLE (all from Unit 14), and a fluency in reading and writing logical formulae (Units 13 and 14). If you are confident of your grasp of these matters, take the entry test below. Otherwise, review Units 13 and 14.

Entry test (1) Which of the following does the English word *but* express?
    (a) logical conjunction
    (b) logical disjunction
    (c) logical negation

(2) Is the table given below a truth table for **p & q**, or for **p V q**, or for neither?

p	q	
T	T	T
T	F	F
F	T	T
F	F	T

(3) Write a logical formula for *Either Jim is Pat's cousin or Sue is Jim's wife and Pat's cousin.* (Use brackets.)

....

(4) Write a logical formula for *Sue is Jim's wife and either Sue or Jim is Pat's cousin.*

....

(5) Are the following two formulae logically equivalent? Why or why not?
((k BEAT f) & (f LOSE-TO k)) V (s WIN)
(s WIN) V ((f LOSE-TO k) & (k BEAT f))   *Yes / No*

(6) Is the following a valid rule of inference?
    $\dfrac{\textbf{p V q}}{\textbf{q \& p}}$ (premiss)   *Yes / No*
          (conclusion)

Feedback (1) (a) (2) neither (3) **(j COUSIN p) V ((s WIFE j) & (s COUSIN p))** (4) **(s WIFE j) & ((s COUSIN p) V (j COUSIN p))** (5) Yes, by commutativity of conjunction and disjunction. (6) No

180

> If you got at least 5 out of 6 right, continue to the introduction.
> Otherwise, review Unit 14.

Introduction Unit 14 introduced connectives of conjunction and disjunction. In this unit you will meet three more connectives: implication →, equivalence ≡ and negation ~.

Comment The connective ~ used in propositional logic is paraphrasable as English *not*. Strictly speaking, ~ does not CONNECT propositions, as do **&** and **V**. ~ is prefixed to the formula for a single proposition, producing its negation. ~ is sometimes called the 'negation operator', rather than the 'negation connective'. But it is traditional to group the negation operator with the other connectives, and we will do so here.

Example If **b SLEEP** stands for *Bill slept,* then
~ **b SLEEP** stands for *Bill didn't sleep.*

Practice Write formulae for the following:

(1) *Alice didn't sleep*

....

(2) *Cardiff is not between Edinburgh and Aberdeen*

....

(3) *Claire is not married to Bill*

....

(4) *Alice didn't come and Bill didn't come*

....

Feedback (1) ~ **a SLEEP** (2) ~ **c BETWEEN e a** (3) ~ **c MARRY b**
(4) (~ **a COME**) & (~ **b COME**)

Comment The brackets used in the answer to (4) above need to be inserted to prevent the formula being read as ~ (**a COME** & ~ **b COME**). This would be expressed in English as *It is not the case that Alice came and that Bill didn't come.*

Practice Write formulae for the following:

(1) *Alice didn't come and Bill didn't, either*

....⁻

(2) *Alice didn't come and nor did Bill*

....⁻

(3) *Neither Alice nor Bill came*

....

181

Feedback	(1) (~ a COME) & (~ b COME) (2) (~ a COME) & (~ b COME) (3) (~ a COME) & (~ b COME)

Comment The conjunction of two negatives can be expressed in English in a variety of ways, including using the *neither . . . nor* construction. You may think this odd, as intuitively *neither . . . nor* is the negation of *either . . . or*.

Practice Let **COME** stand for *came* and **a** and **b** for the names *Alice* and *Bill*. Also assume we are not speaking of anyone else besides Alice and Bill.

    (1) If *neither Alice nor Bill came* is true, how many of the people we are speaking of came? ....

    (2) If **a COME V b COME** is true, how many people came? ....

    (3) If ~ **(a COME V b COME)** is true, how many people came? ....

    (4) Is *Alice didn't come and Bill didn't come* a paraphrase of *Neither Alice nor Bill came?*   *Yes / No*

    (5) Do **(~ a COME) & (~ b COME)** and ~ **(a COME V b COME)** represent equivalent propositions?   *Yes / No*

Feedback	(1) none (2) either one or two (3) none, i.e. neither one nor two (4) Yes (5) Yes

Comment The equivalence of the two propositions in (5) above is an instance of one of a set of logical laws known as 'De Morgan's Laws'. We now turn to an instance of another of De Morgan's Laws, which neatly parallels the one we have just dealt with.

    If we take these two formulae **(~ a COME) & (~ b COME)** and ~ **(a COME V b COME)** and substitute **&** for **V** and vice versa, then the resultant formulae also represent equivalent propositions.

Practice (1) What English sentence most closely corresponds to the formula **(~ a COME) V (~ b COME)**?

    ....

    (2) If the formula given in Question (1) is true, how many people came? ....

    (3) Complete the following sentence to produce the sentence that most closely corresponds to the formula ~ **(a COME & b COME)**.

    It is not the case that ....

    (4) Is the answer to Question (3) a paraphrase of *It is not the case that both Alice and Bill came?*   *Yes / No*

    (5) If the sentences mentioned in Questions (3) and (4) above are true, how many people came? ....

(6) Is *Either Alice didn't come or Bill didn't come* a paraphrase of
Alice and Bill didn't both come?   *Yes / No*

(7) Do (~ **a COME**) **V** (~ **b COME**) and ~ (**a COME & b COME**)
represent equivalent propositions?   *Yes / No*

Feedback   (1) *Either Alice didn't come or Bill didn't come* (This might be used, for
example, by someone finding that a part of some food left out for Alice
and Bill has not been touched.) (2) none or one (3) *It is not the case that
Alice came and Bill came* (4) Yes (5) none or one (6) Yes (7) Yes

Comment   When negation interacts with conjunction or disjunction, a single meaning
can often be represented by two different logical formulae. Give two logical
formulae for each of the following:

Practice   (1) *Anne saw neither Ben nor Clara*

....

....

(2) *Anne didn't see both Ben and Clara*

....

....

(3) *Fred is neither boastful nor proud*

....

....

(4) *Fred is not both boastful and proud*

....

....

Feedback   (1) ~ (**a SEE b V a SEE c**); (~ **a SEE b**) **&** (~ **a SEE c**)

(2) ~ (**a SEE b & a SEE c**); (~ **a SEE b**) **V** (~ **a SEE c**)

(3) ~ (**f BOAST V f PROUD**); (~ **f BOAST**) **&** (~ **f PROUD**)

(4) ~ (**f BOAST & f PROUD**); (~ **f BOAST**) **V** (~ **f PROUD**)

Comment   These examples are particular cases of general rules which can be stated as
follows:

~ (**p V q**) is equivalent to (~ **p**) **&** (~ **q**)

~ (**p & q**) is equivalent to (~ **p**) **V** (~ **q**)

These equivalences can be seen as rules of inference, either with the left-hand sides as premisses and the right-hand sides as conclusions, or vice versa. In practice below, we get you to work out a truth table definition for the negation operator and also show you another rule of inference involving negation.

Practice (1) If *Henry died* is true, is *Henry didn't die* true or false?   T / F

(2) If *Henry died* is false, is *Henry didn't die* true or false?   T / F

(3) The truth table for ~ is simpler than those for the genuine connectives, since it only affects one proposition at a time. Fill in the appropriate values (either T or F) in the right-hand column of the table below.

p	~p
T	
F	

(4) Given the premiss that Henry died, is it correct to conclude that it is not the case that Henry didn't die?   Yes / No

(5) Give a rule of inference corresponding to the answer to the previous question.

....

(6) Is the converse of this rule of inference also a valid rule of inference?   Yes / No

Feedback   (1) F (2) T (3) F, T (reading down the column) (4) Yes

(5) $\dfrac{p}{\sim\sim p}$ (premiss) (conclusion)   (6) Yes

Comment   These logical relationships between truth and falsehood allow one to construct a nice little puzzle. We give it as practice below, with the advice that the answer may take you five or ten minutes hard thought to arrive at, so don't rush too impatiently to look at the feedback.

Practice   A prisoner is kept in a room with two jailers. The room has two doors, one to freedom, and the other to certain death. The prisoner knows this, but he does not know which door is which. He also knows that one of his jailers always tells the truth, and that the other always tells lies, but he does not know which jailer is the truth-teller and which is the liar. He is allowed to ask just ONE question of one of the jailers: he may choose which jailer to ask, and he may decide what question to ask. (Both jailers know which door is which, and each knows the other's lying or truthful disposition.) What single question can the prisoner ask in order to find out for certain which door leads to freedom?

Feedback
The question the prisoner should ask, of either jailer, is 'What would the other jailer say if I asked him which was the door to certain death?' Depending on which jailer he asks, the prisoner will either get a truthful report of a lying answer, or a lying report of a truthful answer. These are both equivalent to a lie, so the prisoner can be certain that the report he gets reflects the opposite of the truth about the doors. Armed with this certainty, he walks to freedom out of the door which the first jailer told him that the second jailer would say led to certain death.

Comment
We leave negation now. The logical connective symbolized by → corresponds roughly to the relation between an '*if*' clause and its sequel in English. The linking of two propositions by → forms what is called a conditional.

Example
The meaning of *If Alan is here, Clive is a liar* would be represented by the formula **a HERE → c LIAR**.

Practice
Give logical formulae for the following:

(1) *If the knight takes the bishop, Alice will lose*

....

(2) *Alice will lose if the knight takes the bishop*

....

Feedback
(1) **k TAKE b → a LOSE** (2) **k TAKE b → a LOSE**

Comment
In English, conditional sentences can be expressed with the clauses in either order, but the logical proposition remains the same.

Practice
Express the meanings of the following sentences in logical formulae:

(1) *If Adam trusts Eve, he's stupid*

....

(2) *Adam's stupid if he trusts Eve*

(3) *If David is Alice's brother, then Fanny's his aunt*

....

(4) *Fanny is David's aunt if he is Alice's brother*

....

Feedback
(1) **a TRUST e → a STUPID** (2) **a TRUST e → a STUPID**
(3) **d BROTHER a → f AUNT d** (4) **d BROTHER a → f AUNT d**

Comment   When we get combinations of → and the other connectives, we sometimes get cases of ambiguity in the corresponding English sentence. (We will use brackets as before to indicate different interpretations.)

Practice   Unpack the two meanings of the following sentences into two logical formulae. (If you can't spot the ambiguity at once, try uttering the sentences aloud with pauses in different places.)

If David is Alice's brother, then Fanny's his aunt or Bob's his uncle

....

....

Feedback   **(d BROTHER a → f AUNT d) V b UNCLE d**
d BROTHER a → (f AUNT d V b UNCLE d)

Practice   (1) At what point in the sentence in the previous practice can one insert the word *either* in order to make it convey:

d BROTHER a → (f AUNT d V b UNCLE d)?

....

....

(2) In what way could one rearrange the parts of the sentence mentioned to make it convey ONLY:

(d BROTHER a → f AUNT d) V b UNCLE d?

Either...

....

Feedback   (1) *If David is Alice's brother, then either Fanny's his aunt or Bob's his uncle*

(2) *Either Bob is David's uncle or, if David is Alice's brother, Fanny is his aunt*

Practice   (1) Unpack the ambiguity of the following sentence into two different logical formulae:

Claire will marry Burt and Ethel will resign if David goes to Glasgow

....

....

(2) Which of your formulae asserts that Claire will marry Burt in any case?

....

(3) How can the parts of the sentence mentioned be rearranged to convey only the meaning which asserts that Claire will marry Burt in any case?

....

(4) Using both the *if . . . then* construction and the *not only . . . but also* construction, rearrange the sentence mentioned so that it conveys that both Claire's marrying Burt and Ethel's resignation are conditional upon David's going to Glasgow.

....

Feedback (1) **c MARRY b & (d GO g → e RESIGN); d GO g → (c MARRY b & e RESIGN)** (2) **c MARRY b & (d GO g → e RESIGN)** (3) *Claire will marry Burt and if David goes to Glasgow, Ethel will resign* (4) *If David goes to Glasgow, then not only will Claire marry Burt but Ethel will also resign*

Comment We have introduced the logical connective → in an informal intuitive way as a 'translation' of English *if . . . then*. We have not defined the meaning of this connective in any formal way, either by truth table or by rule of inference. Our goal in this book is to present a system of logic in which elements of the logical notation correspond fairly closely with elements in ordinary language. In the case of **&** and **V**, whose meanings can be defined by truth tables, there is a satisfactorily close relationship with the English words *and* and *or*. But it is not possible to give a truth table definition of → which satisfactorily corresponds to the meaning English speakers intuitively grasp for *if . . . then*. To illustrate this, we pose below the questions which would be relevant to the construction of a truth table for *if . . . then*.

Practice (1) In a situation in which both *Henry died* and *Terry resigned* are true, is the sentence *If Henry died, then Terry resigned* true or false? *T / F*

(2) In a situation where *Henry died* is true, but *Terry resigned* is false, is *If Henry died, then Terry resigned* true or false? *T / F*

(3) In a situation where *Henry died* is false, but *Terry resigned* is true, is *If Henry died, then Terry resigned* true or false? *T / F*

(4) In a situation where *Henry died* and *Terry resigned* are both false, is *If Henry died, then Terry resigned* true or false? *T / F*

(5) Did you find these questions as easy to answer as the similar questions in the previous unit relating to truth tables for **&** and **V**? *Yes / No*

Feedback (1) The sentence with *if . . . then* could be true, but if there was no necessary connection in the situation concerned between Henry's death and Terry's resignation, English speakers would usually judge it to be false. (2) In this case, it seems clear that the sentence with *if . . . then* must be false. (3) The judgement of most English speakers is that, in this situation, the sentence with *if . . . then* does not apply, and so cannot be said to be either true or false. (4) Again, one might say that in this situation the sentence with *if . . . then* does not apply, and so cannot be true or false. On the other hand, if there was felt to be some necessary connection between the idea of Henry's death and that of Terry's resignation, one might judge the sentence to be true. (5) Presumably not

Comment   The concept of a necessary connection between propositions expressed by sentences in the *if . . . then* construction is not one that can be captured by a truth table. (In fact, logicians do define a connective, which they symbolize with → or alternatively ⊃, by means of a truth table (actually, the truth table given in Question (2) of the entry test for this unit). This connective is known as 'material implication'; but it is clear that material implication does not correspond closely with English *if . . . then*. Put simply, English *if . . . then* is not a truth-functional connective. One can, however, formulate rules of inference which capture the essence of the meaning of English *if . . . then*.

Practice   (1) Given the premiss that if Henry died, then Terry resigned, and given further the premiss that Henry did in fact die, would it be correct to conclude that Terry resigned?   *Yes / No*

(2) Symbolizing *if . . . then* by →, is the following rule of inference valid?

p → q   (premisses)
p   *Yes / No*
_____
q   (conclusion)

(3) Have you seen this rule of inference somewhere before?   *Yes / No*

(4) Given the premiss that if Henry died then Terry resigned, and given further the premiss that Terry did not in fact resign, would it be correct to conclude that Henry did not die?   *Yes / No*

(5) Is the following a correct rule of inference (involving both the conditional and negation)?

p → q   (premisses)
~q   *Yes / No*
_____
~p   (conclusion)

Feedback   (1) Yes (2) Yes (3) Yes, it is Modus Ponens, mentioned in Unit 12. (4) Yes (5) Yes, this rule of inference is known as 'Modus Tollens'.

Comment   A further logical connective is indicated with the symbol ≡. This expresses the meaning of *if and only if* in English. The linking of two propositions by ≡ produces what is called a 'biconditional'.

Example   The meaning of *Ada is married to Ben if and only if Ben is married to Ada* could be represented as **(a MARRY b) ≡ (b MARRY a)**

Practice   (1)   Express the meaning of the following sentence as a logical formula:

Alex is Bill's son if and only if Bill is Alex's father

....

(2)   Does the sentence just mentioned entail the following one?

Alex is Bill's son if Bill is Alex's father   Yes / No

(3)   Give a logical formula (using →) for the sentence in Question (2)

....

(4)   Does the sentence mentioned in Question (1) entail

*Alex is Bill's son only if Bill is Alex's father (and perhaps not
even then)*?   Yes / No

(5)   Give a logical formula (again using →) for the sentence mentioned in Question (4). (Nothing in your formula need correspond to the material after *and perhaps* in this sentence, which is included just to clarify its meaning.)

....

(6)   Could the sentence in Question (1) be represented logically as
((a SON b) → (b FATHER a)) & ((b FATHER a) → (a SON b))?   *Yes / No*

Feedback   (1) **(a SON b) ≡ (b FATHER a)** (2) Yes (3) **(b FATHER a) → (a SON b)**
(4) Yes (5) **(a SON b) → (b FATHER a)** (6) Yes

Comment   The biconditional connective is aptly named, because it is equivalent to the conjunction of two conditionals, one 'going in each direction'. In other words, there is a general rule.

Rule   **p ≡ q** is equivalent to **(p → q) & (q → p)**

Comment   The combination of the biconditional with *and* and *or* produces ambiguities of the kind we have seen before, but these are not quite so easily detectable as was the case with earlier examples. The English phrase *if and only if* is not current in everyday language, and so the question of defining the connective ≡ in such a way that it corresponds closely with the meaning of this phrase is not easy. Following from its relationship to the conditional connective →, a number of inference rules involving it can be stated.

189

Practice Are the following correct rules of inference or not?

(1) $\dfrac{p \equiv q}{q \equiv p}$ *Yes / No*

(2) $\dfrac{\begin{array}{c} p \equiv q \\ p \end{array}}{q}$ *Yes / No*

(3) $\dfrac{\begin{array}{c} p \equiv q \\ q \end{array}}{\sim p}$ *Yes / No*

(4) $\dfrac{\begin{array}{c} p \equiv q \\ \sim p \end{array}}{\sim q}$ *Yes / No*

(5) $\dfrac{\begin{array}{c} p \equiv q \\ \sim q \end{array}}{\sim p}$ *Yes / No*

Feedback (1) Yes (2) Yes (3) No (4) Yes (5) Yes

Comment We will not give a truth table definition for ≡.

Summary The logical negation operator ~ corresponds fairly closely with English *not* or *n't* in meaning, and can be defined both by truth table and by rules of inference. The logical connectives → (conditional) and ≡ (biconditional) cannot be defined by truth table in any way which closely reflects the meanings of English *if . . . then* and *if and only if*. However, rules of inference can be given for them which fairly accurately reflect valid inferences in English involving *if . . . then* and *if and only if*.

Now that you are familiar with these connectives, the conjunction and disjunction connectives of the previous unit, and the negation operator, you have met all the formal apparatus that together forms the system known as 'propositional logic', or 'propositional calculus'. This branch of Logic deals with the ways in which propositions can be connected (and negated) and the effect which these operations (of connection and negation) have in terms of truth and falsehood. This establishes a solid foundation for more advanced work in logic.

Unit 15 Study Guide and Exercises

Directions After you have read Unit 15 you should be able to tackle the following questions to test your understanding of the main ideas raised in the unit.

1 You should understand these terms and concepts from this unit:
implication (→)
conditional sentence

negative operator ($\sim$)
more rules of inference
    de Morgan's Laws
        $\sim$(p V q) $\equiv$ $\sim$p & $\sim$q
        $\sim$(p & q) $\equiv$ $\sim$p V $\sim$q
    double negation
        p $\equiv$ $\sim\sim$p
    modus ponens
    modus tollens
    biconditional (**$\equiv$**)
propositional calculus (or propositional logic)

2 Write logical formulae for the following, using brackets where necessary. You only need to give one formula to describe the given situation (though in some cases more than one may be possible).
  a Hillary didn't leave and Bill slept
  b Pontiac is not between Auburn Hills and Rochester
  c Tipper didn't leave and Al didn't arrive
  d It is not the case that Tipper left and Al didn't arrive
  e Hillary will win if Bill signs the bill
  f If Bill signs the bill, Hillary will win

3 Write two different logical formulae for each of the following (where each fomula is related to the other via one of de Morgan's Laws).
  a Bill is neither overweight nor lazy
  b Hillary is not both busy and lazy

4 Give two English sentences that correspond to the following logical formulae.
  a (**$\sim$a SLEPT**) **V** (**$\sim$b WORKED**)
  b (**$\sim$h STUDY**) & (**$\sim$t READ**)

5 Unpack the two meanings of the following ambiguous sentences into two logical formulae.
  a If Hillary is happy then Bill is content or Tipper is sad
  b Chelsea will feed Socks and Tipper will nap if Hillary goes to Little Rock

6 How could we rearrange the parts of the sentences in 5 above to make them convey ONLY one of the meanings expressed by the formulae you wrote for each sentence?

7 Is the English *if . . . then* construction generally understood by English speakers as a logical truth-functional connective? Why or why not?

8 Consider the following premisses and conclusion. Decide in each case whether the conclusion follows from the given premisses by means of a valid rule of inference, show the application of the rule in the manner described in the text (i.e. by letting a variable such as **p** or **q** stand for each proposition), and name the rule involved.

a If Mary bought a house, then she had to make payments. Mary didn't have to make payments, so therefore she didn't buy a house.

b If Tipper bought the record, then she wanted to hear it. Tipper wanted to hear the record, so therefore she bought it.

c If Bill signed the bill, then he caused a controversy. He signed the bill, so therefore he caused a controversy.

d Hillary fed Socks. Therefore, it is not the case that Hillary did not feed Socks.

e Either Bill didn't sign the bill or Hillary didn't write the law. Therefore, it is not the case that Bill signed the bill and Hillary wrote the law.

f Either Bill didn't sign the bill or Hillary didn't write the law. Therefore, it is not the case that Bill signed the bill or that Hillary wrote the law.

9 The biconditional connective is equivalent to the conjunction of two conditionals. Express the meaning of the following sentences in logical formulae in two ways: one with the biconditional connective and one with the (logically) equivalent conjunction of two conditionals.

a George is the president if and only if Laura is the first lady.

b Mary is Jane's mother if and only if Jane is Mary's daughter.

10 Which of the following are correct rules of inference? Name the correct ones and explain why the incorrect ones are incorrect. Understand the variables **p** and **q** to stand for propositions.

a	Premisses:	$p \rightarrow q, \sim q$
	Conclusion:	$\sim p$
b	Premiss:	$p \& q$
	Conclusion:	q
c	Premiss:	$p \lor q$
	Conclusion:	p
d	Premiss:	q
	Conclusion:	$p \lor q$
e	Premiss:	$\sim(p \& q)$
	Conclusion:	$\sim p \lor \sim q$
f	Premiss:	$\sim p \& \sim q$
	Conclusion:	$\sim q \& \sim p$

g Premiss: p
  Conclusion: p & q
h Premisses: p → q, q
  Conclusion: p

11 What is a **propositional logic**? What does this branch of Logic deal with?

5 Word meaning

UNIT 16 ABOUT DICTIONARIES

Entry requirements   None.

Introduction   A dictionary is a central part of the description of any language. A good ordinary household dictionary typically gives (at least) three kinds of information about words: phonological information about how the word is pronounced, grammatical (syntactical and morphological) information about its part of speech (e.g. noun, verb) and inflections (e.g. for plural number or past tense), and semantic information about the word's meaning.

Practice   Given below are some (slightly edited) entries extracted from the *Random House Dictionary of the English Language* (College edition 1968). In each case (a) underline the phonological information, (b) bracket [thus] the grammatical information, and (c) leave the semantic information unmarked.

(1) **green**   (grēn), *adj.* of the color of growing foliage
(2) **must**   (must), *auxiliary verb* to be compelled to, as by instinct or natural law
(3) **oak**   (ōk), *noun* any fagaceous tree or shrub of the genus *Quercus*, bearing the acorn as fruit
(4) **squirt**   (skwûrt), *intransitive verb* to eject liquid in a jet, as from a narrow orifice

Feedback   (1) (grēn) [*adj.*] of the color of growing foliage (2) (must) [*auxiliary verb*] to be compelled to, as by instinct or natural law (3) (ōk) [*noun*] any fagaceous . . . as fruit (4) (skwûrt) [*intransitive verb*] to eject liquid . . . narrow orifice

Comment   (If you are familiar with a phonetic alphabet typically used by linguists, such as the International Phonetic Alphabet (IPA), you will notice that Random House, regrettably, uses an idiosyncratic 'imitated pronunciation' instead of a proper phonetic alphabet.)

From now on we will suppress phonological information about the words we use as examples, and we will only refer to grammatical information in order to distinguish between various semantic senses of a word (e.g. between the sense of *carp*, the verb, and that of *carp*, the noun). We shall concentrate our attention on the semantic aspects of the kind of dictionary of a language

194

that a linguist would wish to present. It should be kept in mind as we investigate dictionaries and word meaning that, from the standpoint of modern linguistics, the dictionary constructed by a semanticist is supposed to represent important aspects of the mental knowledge about meaning that any typical native speaker of the language would have.

A dictionary tells you what words mean. The semanticist dictionary-writer and the ordinary dictionary-writer have quite similar goals, but they differ markedly in their style of approach and the emphasis which they place on their various goals. In order to illustrate the kind of dictionary that a semanticist tries to devise, we will first take a look at some properties of a good ordinary household dictionary.

We will give you some exercises based on samples extracted from the *Concise Oxford Dictionary* (6th edition, 1976), given below. (We have edited these samples from the dictionary so as to give only information that is relevant to the following exercises.)

animal	1	Organized being endowed (more or less perceptibly) with life, sensation, and voluntary motion; (esp.) such being other than man
female	1	Of the sex that can bear offspring or produce eggs; (of plants or their parts) fruit-bearing, having pistil and no stamens . . .
Homo	1	(Name of the genus including) man
human	1	Of or belonging to man; that is a man or consists of men
	2	Of man as opp. to God
	3	Having or showing the qualities distinctive of man as opp. to animals, machines, mere objects, etc.
husband		Married man, esp. in relation to his wife
join	1	Put together, fasten, unite . . .; unite (persons, one *with* or *to* another) in marriage, friendship, alliance, etc.
male	1	Of the sex that can beget offspring by performing the fertilizing function; (of plants) whose flowers contain only fecundating organs . . . of men or male animals or plants
man	1	Human being, individual of genus *Homo*, distinguished from other animals by superior mental development, power of articulate speech, and upright posture
	4	Adult, human male, opp. to woman, boy, or both
marriage	1	Condition of man and woman legally united for purpose of living together and usu. procreating lawful offspring
marry	1	. . . (of person) take as wife or husband in marriage
sex	1	Being male or female or hermaphrodite
unite		Join together, make or become one, consolidate, amalgamate
wife		Married woman esp. in relation to her husband
woman	1	Adult human female

195

Note   *Man* is given two separate senses here (numbered 1 and 4) and *human* is given three senses (1, 2, and 3). We will treat each sense as a different item, representing them as *man*₁, *man*₄, *human*₁, *human*₂, and *human*₃.

Comment   The first point to note about all dictionaries is that their definitions are necessarily interconnected.

Practice   (1) Below we have started to draw a diagram showing the interconnectedness of the definitions in the above sample. The rule for drawing arrows is: If the definition of X includes Y, draw an arrow from X to Y. You complete the diagram by drawing in the remaining three arrows.

(2) Now draw another such set of arrows to show the interconnectedness of the *Concise Oxford Dictionary*'s definitions of the terms below. Treat grammatically related pairs of words, such as *unite* and *united*, *marry* and *married*, as single items. There should be eleven arrows in the diagram in total.

Feedback

Comment   This interconnectedness of dictionary definitions is unavoidable, and indeed desirable. In the kind of dictionary that a semanticist would propose, as part of the semantic description of a language, there would be the same interconnectedness between the definitions of various predicates, because the semantic dictionary-writer's main interest is in representing as completely as possible the knowledge a native speaker has about all of the sense relations between predicates. (But notice that the ordinary dictionary's definitions are not usually phrased in terms of the specific, precisely defined sense relations, e.g. hyponymy, antonymy, etc., which the semanticist is interested in.) Clearly, our sample from the *Concise Oxford Dictionary* shows a high degree of circularity. This arises, probably, from the commonly accepted idea that the goal of a dictionary is to define everything. One cannot define absolutely everything without a degree of circularity in one's definitions. The linguistic semanticist, on the other hand, is more inclined than the ordinary dictionary-writer to leave some terms undefined. Such undefined terms are called semantic primes. The nearest equivalent in the ordinary dictionary to the semanticist's idea of undefined semantic primes is the use of rather technical, even sometimes abstruse, terms in its definitions.

Practice Go through the dictionary sample above and make a list of about seven or eight words used in the definitions that have a rather technical or academic flavour, words whose meanings uneducated people would perhaps not know. Write out your list in order of remoteness from ordinary language.

....

....

Feedback Our list would be as follows: *fecundate, genus, Homo, pistil, stamens, procreate, beget, hermaphrodite.*

Comment The use of such technical terms can be seen as an attempt to break out of the circularity which we have noted: an attempt to define the words of ordinary language in another language, e.g. Latin in the case of *Homo* (which is the Latin word for *man*), or the technical language of science, as in the case of *fecundate*. This is not a strategy which the descriptive semanticist adopts. But the descriptive semanticist's dictionary does use a few technical devices specifically designed (by semanticists) for the purpose of describing meaning. Beside some undefined semantic primes, the main technical device used is the framework of logic, with its notation using →, &, etc. and a small set of technical semantic terms, like hyponym, clearly defined within this logical framework. We will introduce further such terms gradually in subsequent units.

In connection with the use of technical language in ordinary dictionaries, we mention that they operate a small bias in favour of educated usage. This educated bias of dictionaries should not lead to misunderstanding about the nature of the semanticist's task. We, just as the ordinary dictionary-writer, are concerned with describing meaning, and not with prescribing meaning (that is, we are not concerned with making value judgements about any aspects of meaning). Academic semanticists tend to be well-educated people, and most speak a language in which, for example, both *bird* and *mammal* are hyponyms of *animal*. Semanticists aim to describe the sense relations between predicates, as they understand them, in their own everyday language.

There is one notable area in which descriptive semanticists are prepared to abandon ordinary language and to allow a few terms which do not actually occur in the language to be regarded as predicates entering into sense relations with other, actually occurring, predicates. We explain this below.

197

Example *Sibling* is not a word in the everyday English vocabulary, but is a technical term used to refer to someone who is either a brother or a sister. *Sibling* is to *brother* and *sister* what *parent* is to *father* and *mother*. The meaning of *sibling* contains no concept of sex. Clearly, the two predicates *brother* and *sister* form a natural class (that is, they share some component of meaning with each other); it is useful in our description of the relationships between predicates to have a term corresponding to such a natural class and so semanticists adopt one. In our descriptions, we will mark such 'theoretical' or 'technical' predicates with an asterisk, e.g. *sibling.

Comment Such theoretical predicates must be used sparingly and only to collect together under one heading a set of predicates that share a common conceptual element. Thus, *sexed can justifiably be used because *male* and *female* are, so to speak, 'two sides of the same coin', and the predicates grouped together under *locomote, such as *walk*, *run*, *crawl*, and *roll*, all have in common the fact that they contain an element of 'change of place', an element not contained in predicates such as *shake*, *twitch*, and *sway*. We now give you some practice in identifying such natural classes of predicates.

Practice Given below are sets of predicates. In each case, there is one 'odd man out', a predicate not belonging to the same natural class as all the others. (a) Identify the odd man out and (b) describe as concisely as you can the common conceptual element in the remaining predicates.

(1) *sing, talk, dance, speak, shout, whisper, mutter*

    (a) .... (b) ....

(2) *ooze, trickle, drip, seep, slide, gush, squirt*

    (a) .... (b) ....

(3) *rub, scratch, graze, wipe, scrape, brush, push* (all transitive verbs)

    (a) .... (b) ....

(4) *at, of, in, on, under, below, near*

    (a) .... (b) ....

(5) *square, circular, triangular, spherical, hexagonal, rectangular, polygonal*

    (a) .... (b) ....

Feedback (1) (a) *dance* (b) deliberate noise-making activity with the vocal tract (2) (a) *slide* (b) movement made by liquids (3) (a) *push* (b) movement of a solid body across and in contact with a surface (4) (a) *of* (b) physical location (5) (a) *spherical* (b) plane (two-dimensional) shape

Comment We now come to an essential property of any good dictionary, namely its precision. Good ordinary dictionaries achieve a high standard of precision, but we shall show that by the descriptive semanticist's criteria, even such a good dictionary as the *Concise Oxford Dictionary* fails to define the meanings of words with enough exactness.

Practice   To do these exercises you will need to refer back to the sample of definitions from the *Concise Oxford Dictionary* given above, p. 195.

(1) The definition of *marriage* includes the word *man*. How many senses of *man* have we given in the above sample?   ....

(2) Does the definition of *marriage* state explicitly which sense of *man* is intended?   *Yes / No*

(3) If one genuinely did not know the meaning of *marriage*, could one get the impression from this dictionary that it could mean 'condition of a woman and any other human being legally united for purpose of living together and usu. procreating lawful offspring'?   *Yes / No*

(4) Is this in fact what *marriage* means, at least traditionally?   *Yes / No*

(5) Would this difficulty be avoided if the dictionary marked (e.g. with subscript numbers) the senses of words used in its definitions, e.g. '*marriage*: Condition of man$_4$ and woman legally united . . .'?   *Yes / No*

(6) The word *man* (or *men*) occurs three times in the definition of the first sense of *human*. Which sense of *man* is intended, that of *man$_1$* or *man$_4$*?   ....

(7) In the definition of *husband*, which sense of *man* is intended?   ....

Feedback   (1) two (2) No (3) Yes (4) No (5) Yes (6) *man$_1$* (7) *man$_4$*

Comment   In fact the *Concise Oxford Dictionary* does use superscript numbers on the words in some of its definitions, but generally only in cases of homonymy, as opposed to polysemy (see Unit 11). The distinction between homonymy and polysemy is in many cases rather arbitrarily drawn, and, as we have seen in the above practice, it would increase the precision of the dictionary to use a device for distinguishing even closely related senses of the same word (i.e. cases of polysemy, as with *man$_1$* and *man$_4$*). Another way in which an ordinary dictionary lacks precision is by its frequent use of vague terms, such as 'etc.', 'more or less', 'especially', and 'usually'. You can check that all of these vague terms are used in the sample we took from the *Concise Oxford Dictionary*.

So far the criticisms we have made of the ordinary dictionary may not seem very condemning. One difficulty can be avoided by simply using subscript or superscript numbers to indicate each separate sense of a word. And it can well be argued that the use of such vague terms as 'etc.', 'more or less', 'especially', and 'usually' is unavoidable, because meanings simply cannot be pinned down with absolute precision. This is a perfectly valid point: as we noted in Unit 9, it is usually not possible to give complete sets of necessary and sufficient conditions corresponding to the senses of predicates. But for the present, we will indicate some areas where it is quite clear that a degree of precision can realistically be achieved which the *Concise Oxford Dictionary* happens not to achieve.

Practice   Answer the following questions about the sense relations between words and sentences as you understand them:

(1) Is *male* compatible with *female*?   Yes / No

(2) Does *John is married to Mary* entail *Mary is married to John*?   Yes / No

(3) Does *The bench is joined to the table* entail *The table is joined to the bench*?   Yes / No

(4) Is *man* (in either sense given) a hyponym of *animal*?   Yes / No

Feedback   (1) No (2) Yes (3) Yes (4) Yes

Comment   Now we will see whether this information is clearly presented, or indeed presented at all, in the ordinary dictionary. To do the following exercises, you must put yourself in the position of someone who really does not know the actual meanings of the words defined and is genuinely using the *Concise Oxford Dictionary* to try to discover what the words mean.

Practice   (1) In the definition given for *female* is there any mention of the predicate *male*?   Yes / No

(2) In the definition given for *male* is there any mention of *female*?   Yes / No

(3) In the definition of *sex* is it explicitly stated that one cannot be both male and female?   Yes / No

(4) In the definition of *join*, is there any explicit indication that *join* is a so-called symmetric predicate, i.e. that if X is joined to Y, then Y must also be joined to X?   Yes / No

(5) In the definition of *man*, does the use of 'other animals' imply that human beings are in fact animals?   Yes / No

(6) Would it be reasonable to infer from the definition of *human* that human beings are not animals?   Yes / No

Feedback   (1) No (2) No (3) No (4) No (5) Yes (6) Yes

Comment   We see that some quite clear facts about sense relations in English, i.e. the incompatibility of *male* and *female*, the symmetry of *join* and of *marry*, and the hyponymy of *man* to *animal*, are either not explicitly stated or left unclear in this ordinary dictionary. It may be objected that these facts are too obvious to mention. But the semanticist's goal is to be able to account for every sense relation, whether obvious or not, because he is interested in achieving the linguist's goal of describing and representing as much as possible about what any typical native speaker knows about meaning.

Traditionally, the linguistic semanticist is interested in the meanings of words and not in non-linguistic facts about the world. He has often made the assumption that non-linguistic facts are not particularly relevant to the study of linguistic meaning (that is, the meanings conveyed by the sense relations of the words within the language itself as opposed to meaning conveyed by information from the context or situation in which the language is used). Correspondingly, he attempts to make a strict demarcation between a dictionary and an encyclopaedia. (This attempt is actually highly problematic, but many linguists have assumed that the goal is worth pursuing.)

Definition A DICTIONARY describes the senses of predicates.

An ENCYCLOPAEDIA contains factual information of a variety of types, but generally no information specifically on the meanings of words.

Comment The stereotype of a predicate (Unit 9) contains, strictly speaking, only encyclopaedic information, although the importance of stereotypes in the use and understanding of words fuzzes the distinction between dictionary and encyclopaedia. Most ordinary dictionaries occasionally stray into the domain of encyclopaedias, giving information not strictly relevant to the bare senses (as opposed to stereotypes) of words. To illustrate this point, we will compare some entries from the *Concise Oxford Dictionary* with the corresponding entries in *Webster's New Collegiate Dictionary* (1959 edition).

Practice (a) Which of the two dictionaries quoted below is the more encyclopaedic?

....

(b) In the dictionary entries quoted below underline the information (in one or both entries) that seems not strictly relevant to the sense of the word defined.

Concise Oxford	*Webster's New Collegiate*
(1) **beret** Round flat felt or cloth cap	**beret** A round, flat, visorless cap of soft material, originally worn by Basque peasants
(2) **walrus** Large amphibious carnivorous arctic long-tusked mammal (*Odobenus rosmarus*) related to seal and sea-lion	**walrus** A very large marine (*Odobenus rosmarus*) of the Arctic Ocean allied to the seals, but forming a distinct family (*Odobenidae*). In the male the

201

upper canine teeth form greatly
elongated protruding tusks. The
skin makes valuable leather, the
tusks are fine ivory, and the
blubber yields oil.

Feedback (a) Webster's in both cases (b) The information that we would judge to be
not relevant to the sense of the words defined is as follows: (1) originally
worn by Basque peasants; (2) carnivorous; In the male, upper canine; The
skin makes . . . yields oil.

Comment There is room for some disagreement over the correct answers here, but
we expect you to have agreed with our judgements to a great extent. To show
you the basis of our judgements, and the criteria used by the theoretical
semanticist, we now relate the above cases to judgements about sense
properties, particularly drawing upon the notions of analytic and synthetic
(Unit 9).

Practice Say whether each of the following sentences is analytic (*A*), or synthetic (*S*).

(1) *Basque peasants used to wear berets*   *A / S*

(2) *A beret is a form of headgear*   *A / S*

(3) *This walrus is a mammal*   *A / S*

(4) *The skin of the walrus makes valuable leather*   *A / S*

Feedback (1) S (2) A (3) A (4) S

Comment From a traditional point of view, the descriptive semanticist is basically
interested in that information about words which can give rise to sentences
containing them being either analytic (e.g. *The walrus is an animal*) or
contradictions (e.g. *The walrus is not an animal*). Any other information is
not strictly semantic but encyclopaedic, at least under the assumption that
such a distinction can indeed be made.

It should be noted that the very issue of whether the analytic–synthetic
distinction can be coherently drawn (or even should be drawn) is
controversial, and has been receiving increasing attention in recent years.
You might notice that, in some ways, this distinction mirrors the distinction
made earlier between a narrower sort of dictionary information and a
broader sort of encyclopaedic information in characterizing the meaning of
a linguistic expression. There is disagreement among linguists in general
(and semanticists in particular) as to whether such a distinction is realistic or
even relevant to the study of meaning in language. Many semanticists are
coming to the realization that the study of meaning has to include the study

of encyclopaedic information in some way along with dictionary information in order to represent more adequately the knowledge a speaker has about the language. In this book we will continue to take the position that such a distinction can be drawn, even though there may be many instances which are unclear. But you should be aware that, as is often the case with human language, the situation is not as simple and clear-cut as it might seem to be at first glance. In most of our examples, we shall concentrate on the clear cases. You probably agreed with all our judgements in the above practice.

To end this unit we will mention one final goal that both ordinary dictionary-writers and descriptive semanticists may try to achieve, namely completeness of coverage. In this area the ordinary dictionary easily outstrips the semanticist's. It is not possible at this stage in our text to give exercises to show in detail why this is so, but it is a relevant fact that ordinary, informal dictionary writing has a centuries-long tradition to build upon, whereas the devising of dictionaries by semantic theorists working to exacting standards of logical rigour is an enterprise begun within the last century.

Summary We have illustrated in this unit certain important properties of dictionaries, namely interconnectedness, the use of certain technical or theoretical terms and devices, and precision, showing points of similarity and dissimilarity between the approaches of the ordinary dictionary-writer and the theoretical linguistic semanticist. The linguistic semanticist's approach is traditionally characterized by a strict insistence on describing just those properties of a word that relate to its sense (to the extent that this is possible), but we have seen that there is a tendency in recent years to pay more attention to encyclopaedic information as well.

Unit 16 Study Guide and Exercises

Directions After you have read Unit 16 you should be able to tackle the following questions to test your understanding of the main ideas raised in the unit.

1 You should understand these terms and concepts from this unit:
dictionary vs encyclopaedia
types of dictionary
  a linguistic semanticist's dictionary
  an ordinary dictionary-writer's dictionary
semantic primes
technical (theoretical) predicates

2 What kind of information about words is found in a typical (i.e. collegiate) dictionary?

3 What does it mean to say that all dictionary definitions are **interconnected**? How is this related to the various kinds of sense relations we studied in

Units 10 and 11? Is this sort of interconnectedness desirable? Why or why not?

4   Why is a certain degree of **circularity** necessary in dictionary entries? How do dictionaries occasionally try to avoid such circularity?

5   How do the goals, style of approach, etc., of a semanticist dictionary-writer differ from those of an ordinary dictionary-writer? How are they the same?

6   What is the main interest of the semanticist dictionary-writer?

7   What are **technical predicates** (such as *sibling) and what is the advantage in proposing them? Try to think of some additional examples not mentioned in the text which meet the criteria proposed in this unit for such predicates.

8   For each of the following sets of predicates indicate the one which does NOT belong to the same natural class as the others and WHY it does not belong. Then indicate the common conceptual element(s) the others share. Note that in some cases this element of meaning may be quite abstract.
    a   pine, elm, ash, oak, dandelion, sycamore, fir
    b   table, stone, book, glass, ship, soup, tree
    c   computer, paper, idea, lamp, car, highway, tractor
    d   walk, skip, run, jump, ride, swim, hop
    e   ask, tell, whisper, say, speak, talk, converse
    f   alive, tall, asleep, dead, married, pregnant

9   In what ways do ordinary dictionaries lack the sort of **precision** required by a linguistic semanticist? Give an example of how this lack of precision can lead to difficulties, especially for someone who does not know the actual meanings of the words being looked up. How can such lack of precision be remedied (or can it)?

10   Why do you think most ordinary dictionaries usually leave out reference to the kinds of sense relations we studied in Units 10 and 11? Why are they included in the linguistic semanticist's dictionary?

11   Do you think it is reasonable (or even possible) for the linguistic semanticist to try to omit encyclopaedic information from his dictionary? Why or why not? How does this issue relate to the distinction between **analytic** and **synthetic** sentences?

UNIT 17 MEANING POSTULATES

Entry requirements SENSE RELATIONS (Unit 10). If you feel you understand these, take the entry test below.

Entry test Answer the following questions:

(1) Which is the superordinate term in the following list:
man, stallion, male, boy, bull, boar ....

(2) Is *stallion* a hyponym of *horse*? Yes / No

(3) Is *This ram is female* a contradiction? Yes / No

(4) Is *This parrot is a bird* a contradiction? Yes / No

(5) Which of the following statements is correct?

(a) The propositional connective **&** corresponds roughly to
if . . . then.

(b) The propositional connective → corresponds roughly to
if . . . then.

(c) The propositional connective → corresponds roughly to *and*.

Feedback (1) *male* (2) Yes (3) Yes (4) No, it's analytic. (5) (b)
If you have scored less than 4 correct out of 5, you should review Unit 10 or Unit 15, as appropriate. Otherwise, continue to the introduction below.

Introduction In this unit we outline the shape of a linguistic semanticist's dictionary, that is, we investigate in greater detail how the semantic information in the dictionary can be represented. Such a dictionary is a list of predicates and their senses. For each sense of a predicate there is a dictionary entry which lists the sense properties of that predicate and the sense relations between it and other predicates.

We will begin with an informal example in order to give you a more concrete idea of the shape of the dictionary.

Example HUMAN BEING: One-place
synonym of MAN$_1$

MAN$_1$: One-place
synonym of HUMAN BEING

205

MAN$_2$:	One-place
	hyponym of MALE
	hyponym of ADULT
	hyponym of HUMAN BEING
MARRY$_1$:	Two-place
	symmetric
WOMAN:	One-place
	hyponym of FEMALE
	hyponym of ADULT
	hyponym of HUMAN BEING

Comment In our dictionary we adopt a notation in keeping with that used for predicates in our units on logic, i.e. we write predicates in capital letters. Note that the above example avoids a difficulty mentioned in the previous unit by carefully distinguishing between different senses of the same word, e.g. the entry for *human being* states that it is a synonym of *man$_1$*.

This unit will be devoted to elaborating the bare outline of a dictionary started in Unit 16. We begin by introducing the central idea of a meaning postulate.

Definition A MEANING POSTULATE is a formula expressing some aspect of the sense of a predicate. It can be read as a proposition necessarily true by virtue of the meaning of the particular predicates involved.

Example x MAN$_1$ ≡ x HUMAN BEING

Comment This example expresses the fact that *man* (in sense 1) is a synonym of *human being*. It is a generalization covering anything to which the predicate *man$_1$* is applied.

Practice Six hyponymy relations are mentioned in the informal dictionary sample above. In the space below, write out the six corresponding meaning postulates in the notation we have introduced. (Remember that the connective → expresses entailment, just as ≡ expresses paraphrase.)

(1) ....

(2) ....

(3) ....

(4) ....

(5) ....

(6) ....

Feedback (1) x MAN$_2$ → x MALE (2) x MAN$_2$ → x ADULT (3) x MAN$_2$ →
x HUMAN BEING (4) x WOMAN → x FEMALE (5) x WOMAN →
x ADULT (6) x WOMAN → x HUMAN BEING

Comment Not everything that we know about these predicates is represented
directly in these meaning postulates, but much can be arrived at simply
by process of deduction from the information actually given. The predicates
of a language all fit into an enormously complicated network of
interrelationships. A predicate may be indirectly related through this
network to thousands of other predicates. The semanticist wants the
presentation of information in his dictionary to be economical, and so only
includes the minimum number of meaning postulates from which it is
possible to deduce all the (direct or indirect) sense relations between
predicates.

Practice Given below is a sample set of (partial) dictionary entries. In this, two
hyponymy relations between predicates are directly represented. A further
hyponymy relation, not directly represented, may be deduced from these
entries. Write it down in the notation for meaning postulates.

METAL: x METAL → x MINERAL

MINERAL: x MINERAL → x SUBSTANCE

....

Feedback   x METAL → x SUBSTANCE

Comment In short, if it is stated that *metal* is a hyponym of *mineral*, and that *mineral* is
a hyponym of *substance*, there is no need to state explicitly that *metal* is a
hyponym of *substance*. This example illustrates a basic principle in the
organization of the dictionary, namely that the information explicitly stated
in it is less than the information that can be deduced from it. This is no
excuse for lack of precision; the information that is not stated explicitly in
dictionary entries must be deducible by the strict, simple, and clear laws of
logical inference. Any of the logical connectives **&**, **V**, and ~ (Units 14 and 15)
can be used in meaning postulates to express the various sense relations that
occur in language. The negative connective ~ can be used to account for
relations of binary antonymy.

Example **ASLEEP: x ASLEEP → ~ x AWAKE**

Practice Write partial dictionary entries for *male*, *abstract*, *open* (adj.), and *right* with
meaning postulates accounting for the binary antonymy between these
predicates and *female*, *concrete*, *closed*, and *wrong* respectively.

(1) MALE ....

(2) ABSTRACT ....

(3) OPEN ....

(4) RIGHT ....

Feedback **(1) x MALE → ~x FEMALE (2) x ABSTRACT → ~x CONCRETE**
(3) x OPEN → ~x CLOSED (4) x RIGHT → ~x WRONG

Comment We draw attention now to a formal similarity between the hyponymy relation
and another kind of semantic information about predicates, known as
selectional restrictions. We bring out the intuitive notion of a selectional
restriction in the following exercise.

Practice (1) Can an idea be red? *Yes / No*

(2) Can pain be red? *Yes / No*

(3) Can a lump of metal be red? *Yes / No*

(4) Is it true to say that the predicate *red* can only be applied
to concrete (i.e. non-abstract) things? *Yes / No*

(5) Is it true to say that if something is red, then it must be
concrete (in the sense of non-abstract)? *Yes / No*

Feedback (1) No (2) No (3) Yes (4) Yes (5) Yes

Comment The restriction of the predicate *red* to things satisfied by the predicate
concrete is a selectional restriction.

Practice (1) Formulate a partial dictionary entry for *red*, expressing its relationship
to *concrete*, using the meaning postulate notation.

....

(2) An idea is a kind of abstraction, i.e. ideas are necessarily abstract.
Write a meaning postulate expressing this relation between *idea*
and *abstract*.

....

(3) Are the two meaning postulates you have just written in any
way distinguishable from each other by their formats as
different types of meaning postulate? *Yes / No*

Feedback **(1) RED: x RED → x CONCRETE (2) x IDEA → x ABSTRACT (3)** No

Comment Intuitively, the hyponymy relation between predicates is often naturally
expressed by the phrase ' . . . *is a kind of* . . . ', e.g. *An idea is a kind of*

abstraction, A parrot is a kind of bird. The arrow → in the meaning postulates of dictionary entries can be used to express both the '. . . *is a kind of* . . .' relationship traditionally identified with hyponymy and the sort of relationship between *red* and *concrete* that we have called a selectional restriction.

In connection with the distinction traditionally drawn between hyponymy and selectional restrictions, we mention a corresponding distinction made between contradiction and anomaly.

Definition   CONTRADICTION is most centrally a logical term. The basic form of a logical contradiction is **p & ~p**. Anything that is clearly an instance of this basic logical contradiction, e.g. *John is here and John is not here*, can be called a contradiction.

ANOMALY is semantic oddness (as opposed to grammatical oddness) that can be traced to the meanings of the predicates in the sentence concerned. Thus *Christopher is killing phonemes* is anomalous because the meanings of the predicates *kill* and *phoneme* cannot be combined in this way. Anomaly involves the violation of a selectional restriction.

Practice   For each sentence below, say whether it is a basic contradiction (*C*), anomalous (*A*), or semantically acceptable (*OK*).

(1)	*Hilda's cow is a beautiful animal*	*C / A / OK*
(2)	*Jack's courage chewed the bone*	*C / A / OK*
(3)	*James sliced the idea*	*C / A / OK*
(4)	*John is neither here nor not here*	*C / A / OK*
(5)	*This contradictory sentence is not contradictory*	*C / A / OK*

Feedback   (1) OK (2) A (3) A (4) C (5) C

Comment   In this area, as indeed everywhere where one is dealing with the traditional notion of sense, one has to ignore metaphorical and figurative interpretations of sentences, even though such interpretations provide interesting insights into how meaning works. But we are dealing here with the strictly literal meanings of predicates.

In this book, we present a synthesis of the work of logicians and linguists interested in word meaning. We see the meanings of predicates and the meanings of the logical connectives as part of a single framework. We describe the meanings of predicates in logical terms (with meaning postulates) and so it is possible for us to reduce anomaly and contradiction to the same phenomenon. We treat anomaly as a special, indirect case of contradiction. That is, it is possible to deduce (by logical rules) a basic contradiction from an anomaly.

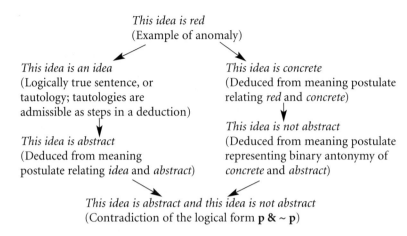

This idea is red
(Example of anomaly)

This idea is an idea
(Logically true sentence, or
tautology; tautologies are
admissible as steps in a deduction)

This idea is concrete
(Deduced from meaning postulate
relating *red* and *concrete*)

This idea is abstract
(Deduced from meaning
postulate relating *idea* and *abstract*)

This idea is not abstract
(Deduced from meaning postulate
representing binary antonymy of
concrete and *abstract*)

This idea is abstract and this idea is not abstract
(Contradiction of the logical form **p & ~ p**)

Comment Study the above chain of deduction carefully. Note that each step (apart from
the introduction of the tautology) is a direct interpretation of a meaning
postulate. We will now get you to construct a similar chain of deduction,
reducing a case of anomaly to a basic logical contradiction. (Actually the
following exercise on deduction, though we have made it fairly precise and
rigorous, is still informal and skirts around several technical problems
involving logic and reference. We think it best to avoid these problems in an
introductory text.)

Practice Given below are three partial dictionary entries.

ABSTRACT: x ABSTRACT → ~ x CONCRETE
IDEA: **x IDEA → x ABSTRACT**
SLEEP: **x SLEEP → x CONCRETE**

We now give an incomplete chain of deduction reducing the anomalous
sentence *the idea sleeps* to a basic contradiction. Your task is to fill in the
omitted stages in the deduction.

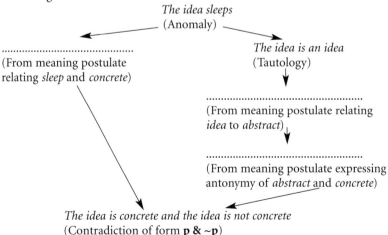

The idea sleeps
(Anomaly)

....
(From meaning postulate
relating *sleep* and *concrete*)

The idea is an idea
(Tautology)

....
(From meaning postulate relating
idea to *abstract*)

....
(From meaning postulate expressing
antonymy of *abstract* and *concrete*)

The idea is concrete and the idea is not concrete
(Contradiction of form **p & ~p**)

Feedback	The omitted stages are:

The idea is abstract
↓
The idea is not concrete

The idea is concrete

Comment So far, all our examples of meaning postulates have involved one-place predicates. Hyponymy relations between two-place predicates can also be expressed by meaning postulates.

Example x FATHER y → x PARENT y

Comment This is paraphraseable as: *If X is Y's father, then X is Y's parent.*

Practice Write meaning postulates to account for the hyponymy between the following pairs of two-place predicates.

(1) *son, child* ....

(2) *kick, strike* ....

(3) *hear, perceive* ....

(4) *brother, relation* ....

Feedback (1) x SON y → x CHILD y (2) x KICK y → x STRIKE y
(3) x HEAR y → x PERCEIVE y (4) x BROTHER y → x RELATION y

Comment Cases of binary antonymy between two-place predicates can also be handled.

Practice Write meaning postulates, using the negative connective ~ to account for the antonymy between the following pairs:

(1) *same, different* ....

(2) *inside, outside* ....

(3) *ignore, pay attention to* ....

(4) *friend, enemy* ....

Feedback (1) x SAME y → ~ x DIFFERENT y (2) x INSIDE y → ~ x OUTSIDE y
(3) x IGNORE y → ~ x PAY ATTENTION TO y
(4) x FRIEND y → ~ x ENEMY y

Comment The converse relationship can also be expressed in terms of meaning postulates.

Practice Write meaning postulates, using ≡, to account for the synonymy of the following pairs:

(1) *own, belong to* ....

(2) *above, below* ....

211

(3) *before, after*   ....

(4) *parent, child*   ....

Feedback   (1) **x OWN y ≡ y BELONG TO x** (2) **x ABOVE y ≡ y BELOW x**
(3) **x BEFORE y ≡ y AFTER x** (4) **x PARENT y ≡ y CHILD x**

Comment   Selectional restrictions apply to two-place predicates. Restrictions may affect
the expression in the 'subject position' (the x slot) or the expression in the
'object position' (the y slot).

Example   *Strike* is restricted to concrete objects. *John struck the table* is fine, but *John
struck motherhood* is not.
        A meaning postulate to express this fact can be formulated as follows:
x STRIKE y → y CONCRETE

Practice   Formulate meaning postulates to account for the following selectional
restrictions:

(1) *Heat* requires a concrete object.

....

(2) *Nourish* requires an animate object.

....

Feedback   (1) **x HEAT y → y CONCRETE** (2) **x NOURISH y → y ANIMATE**

Comment   The important thing when formulating meaning postulates involving two-
place predicates is to remember that in our notation the variable x
conventionally stands in subject position and y stands in object position. In
the case of three-place predicates, we use z to indicate the third position.
Hyponymy, converseness, and selectional restrictions affecting the three-place
predicates can all be expressed using the meaning postulate notation. We will
now mention a couple of types of phenomena that cannot easily be handled
by meaning postulates. We take these problem areas in ascending order of
seriousness.

Practice   The question of the time at which a predicate applies to an individual is an
important matter that we have so far neglected. Consider how it is relevant to
some sense relations.

(1) Are *dead* and *alive* binary antonyms in just the same way
     as *open* and *closed*?   *Yes / No*

(2) Can anything be dead without first having been alive?   *Yes / No*

(3) Does *This object is dead* entail *This object was once alive
     but is no longer alive*?   *Yes / No*

(4) Have you met in the logical notation used for meaning postulates any way of expressing the temporal notions contained in *once* and *no longer?*   *Yes / No*

Feedback (1) No (See next question.) (2) No (This is how we, and most English speakers, understand *dead.*) (3) Yes (4) No

Comment The factor of time is involved in a large number of other sense relations between predicates. Any predicate whose meaning involves a change of state (as *die*, *buy*, and *sell* do) will need some mention of time in its dictionary entry.

Practice For each of the sentences below, write down a complex sentence containing a *before* and an *after* (or equivalent) that is entailed by the first sentence. We have done the first one for you.

(1) *John arrived at my house at noon* entails
John was not at my house before noon and he was at my house after noon

....

(2) *The Normans conquered England in 1066* (Hint: use the verb *control*)

....

(3) *Harry has forgotten the combination of his safe*

....

(4) *Etienne learned to play the piano while he was in Paris*

....

Feedback (2) *The Normans did not control England before 1066 and they did control it after 1066* (3) *Harry once knew the combination of his safe and does not know it now* (4) *Etienne could not play the piano before he was in Paris but he could play it after he was in Paris*

Comment The need to mention time in descriptions of the senses of some predicates could be overcome by developing a more elaborate logic with the capacity to represent temporal relations and formulating meaning postulates within this more elaborate logical framework. We shall not investigate this possibility here, but move on to a problem with gradable antonymy (Unit 11).

The problem is that gradable predicates like *tall* and *short* do not have absolute meanings that can be conveniently summarized by meaning postulates. The context in which *tall* is used also contributes to its meaning. *Tall* in one context (e.g. of jockeys) means something different from *tall* in another context (e.g. of basketball players).

213

What we can say is that in a single context, i.e. applied to the same individual (e.g. Basil) with implicit comparison being made to just one set of individuals (e.g. Europeans), *tall* is the antonym of *short*.

Practice (1) Have any of the meaning postulates formulated so far
               in this and the previous units been related to the notion
               of context?   *Yes / No*

          (2) Once we introduce the notion of context are we talking about
               utterances or sentences?   ....

          (3) Could one speaker truthfully say 'Maggie is tall' and another
               speaker simultaneously, and referring to the same Maggie,
               truthfully say 'Maggie is short'?   *Yes / No*

Feedback (1) No (2) utterances (3) Yes, because the two speakers might be making implicit comparisons with different standards (e.g. Europeans or Pygmies). Also implicit standards are not stable and constant; what is short for one person may be tall for another.

Comment The example of gradable predicates like *tall*, *short*, *large*, *small*, *thin*, *thick*, etc. presents a problem for the enterprise of trying to represent all the semantic relations of a word in terms of meaning postulates. Meaning postulates are designed to account for necessary truths, i.e. truths which hold in all contexts.

Intuitively *tall* and *short* are just as clearly antonyms as *male* and *female*. Probably we should conclude that context plays a larger part in meaning than we have so far admitted, but this raises a difficulty for our whole framework. Maintaining the strict distinction between sentences and utterances, we cannot talk of the context of a sentence, for a sentence is an element in an abstract system of relationships. Meaning postulates are conceived within a framework for describing contextless sentences, and they work quite well when they are restricted to this kind of use. But as we saw in the previous unit, it is often difficult to draw the line between encyclopaedic (contextual) knowledge and dictionary knowledge (involving sense relations) in characterizing the relevant aspects of the meanings of words and other linguistic expressions. So, while contextual information is often relevant in representing the meaning of a word, it is not readily statable in the logical notation characteristic of meaning postulates.

Summary We have seen that meaning postulates play a central part in the traditional approach to constructing a semantic dictionary. Meaning postulates can be used to deduce information about sense relations, including hyponymy and some forms of antonymy, and about selectional restrictions and anomaly. Hyponymy relations and selectional restrictions are expressed by meaning postulates that look formally alike. Anomaly is seen as an indirect case of contradiction. Areas not easily handled by meaning postulates include change-of-state verbs and gradable predicates which require some kind of statement about the context in which the predicates are used.

Unit 17 Study Guide and Exercises

Directions   After you have read Unit 17 you should be able to tackle the following questions to test your understanding of the main ideas raised in the unit.

1   You should understand these terms and concepts from this unit:
meaning postulate
selectional restrictions
contradiction
anomaly

2   What are **meaning postulates** and why are they an important part of the linguistic semanticist's dictionary? Give an example. What specific kinds of truths are they designed to account for? What role (if any) does context play in their use?

3   Why do you think that we avoided including metaphor and figurative language in our discussion of dictionaries?

4   What does it mean to say that **anomaly** (not specifically a logical term) can be treated as a special case of logical **contradiction** (i.e. anomaly can be reduced to a case of logical contradiction)? Try to give an example other than one found in this unit.

5   Based on your intuitive knowledge of the meanings of the following predicates, write a meaning postulate for each (using the notation introduced in the text) which explicitly sets forth some part of the sense of the predicate. The first is done for you (note that predicates are written in upper-case letters). Note that in some cases two-place predicates are involved, and that the notation → represents the entailment relation.

a **WALK:**   x WALK → x USE LEGS

b **SWIM:**   ....

c **CHILD:**   ....

d **DEAD:**   ....

e **TRUE:**   ....

f **FOOD:**   ....

g **UNCLE:**   ....

h **GUEST:** ....

i **NEAR:** ....

6 What hyponymy relation (not directly stated) may be deduced from these partial dictionary entries? Write it down in meaning postulate notation. For item (d) think of your own example. Why does a linguist's dictionary omit explicit reference to all such deductively possible information?

| a | **WATER:** | x WATER → x LIQUID |
| | **LIQUID:** | x LIQUID → ~x SOLID |

....

| b | **GLASS:** | x GLASS → x BRITTLE |
| | **BRITTLE:** | x BRITTLE → x BREAKABLE |

....

| c | **WOMAN:** | x WOMAN → x HUMAN |
| | **HUMAN:** | x HUMAN → x MORTAL |

....

d ....

....

....

7 Examine each anomalous sentence below, in which one word has been italicized (the anomaly is designated by the * notation). Using the meaning postulate notation, formulate a partial dictionary entry for the italicized predicates based on the anomaly. Each partial entry you formulate is a **selectional restriction** for that predicate that has been violated in the sentence. In all cases assume that only the literal meanings of the predicates are involved (i.e. ignore figurative and/or metaphorical interpretations).

a *The idea *slept* soundly ....

b *I just *killed* the desk ....

c *This table is *understandable* ....

d *Your conclusion is *orange* ....

e *My *child* is a reptile ....

f *The burning *fire* was wet ....

g *The window *dripped* to the floor ....

h *The car *hopped* to a stop ....

i *My fish *danced* a tango ....

j *Fred *touched* the dream ....

k *Joan *bathed* in the hydrogen ....

8 How are the notions of the **hyponymy** relation and **selectional restrictions** related?

9 Show how the following anomalous sentences (designated again by the * notation) can be reduced to cases of basic logical contradiction, following the procedure outlined in this unit. Indicate what meaning postulates you have to invoke to make the deductions follow through.
   a *The reptile speaks
   b *The glass walked

10 What kinds of phenomena cannot be handled easily by meaning postulates? Why?

UNIT 18 PROPERTIES OF PREDICATES

Entry requirements   ANALYTIC SENTENCE, CONTRADICTION, and ENTAILMENT (Units 9 and 10). If you feel you understand these notions, take the entry test below.

Entry test   Assume constancy of reference of names in all questions.

(1) Is *John is similar to himself* analytic (*A*), synthetic (*S*),
     or a contradiction (*C*)?   *A / S / C*

(2) Is *John is different from himself* analytic (*A*), synthetic (*S*),
     or a contradiction (*C*)?   *A / S / C*

(3) What sense relation holds between these sentences?
     John is married to Mary
     Mary is married to John   ....

(4) What sense relation holds between these sentences?
     John is the father of Henry
     Henry is the father of John   ....

(5) What sense relation holds between the following two sentences?
     Jim is fatter than Kathleen and Kathleen is fatter than Neil
     Jim is fatter than Neil   ....

Feedback   (1) A (2) C (3) paraphrase (4) They contradict each other. (5) The first
           entails the second.
           If you scored at least 4 correct out of 5, continue to the introduction below.
           Otherwise, review Units 9 and 10.

Introduction   In this unit we shall illustrate sense properties of predicates, i.e. information
               about the meanings of predicates that makes no mention of other predicates.
               You can think of these sense properties as aspects of the meanings of each
               predicate that would be part of each predicate's dictionary entry in the mind
               of a native speaker of the language. We shall illustrate six sense properties
               that predicates may have. These six properties fall neatly into three groups of
               two, groups which might come under the headings of 'symmetry', 'reflexivity',
               and 'transitivity'. The two properties in each group are related to each other
               in exactly parallel ways. All of these properties are properties of two-place
               predicates.

Definition Given a two-place predicate *P*, if, for any pair of referring expressions *X* and *Y*, the sentence *XPY* ENTAILS the sentence *YPX*, then *P* is SYMMETRIC.

Example *Same* is a symmetric predicate, since, for any *X* and *Y*, *X is the same as Y* entails *Y is the same as X*. (In other words, if *X* is the same as *Y*, then *Y* must be the same as *X*.)

Practice (1) Do the following pairs of sentences entail each other?
Tanzania is different from Kenya
Kenya is different from Tanzania Yes / No

(2) Is *different* a symmetric predicate? Yes / No

(3) Does *Mary is married to Hans* entail *Hans is married to Mary*? Yes / No

(4) Is *married to* a symmetric predicate? Yes / No

(5) Does *Mary is devoted to Hans* entail *Hans is devoted to Mary*? Yes / No

(6) Is *devoted to* a symmetric predicate? Yes / No

Feedback (1) Yes (2) Yes (3) Yes (4) Yes (5) No (6) No

Comment The dictionary can give the information that a predicate is symmetric, in the form of a meaning postulate. Alternatively one might simply use the expression 'Symmetric' as a shorthand for a meaning postulate conveying this information. We illustrate the two possible notations below with a partial dictionary entry for *different*.

Example **DIFFERENT: x DIFFERENT y ≡ y DIFFERENT x**
DIFFERENT: Symmetric

Comment We now come to the property of asymmetry, which is in a sense the opposite of symmetry.

Definition Given a two-place predicate *P*, if the sentence *XPY* is a CONTRADICTORY of *YPX*, then *P* is an ASYMMETRIC predicate.

Example *John is taller than Bill* is a contradictory of *Bill is taller than John*. Therefore *taller than* is an asymmetric predicate.

Practice (1) Is *John is under the table* a contradictory of *The table is under John*? Yes / No

(2) Is *under* asymmetric? Yes / No

(3) Is *father of* as in *Alphonso was the father of Benito* asymmetric? Yes / No

(4) Is *admire* as in *Jimmy Carter admires Norman Mailer* asymmetric? Yes / No

Feedback (1) Yes (2) Yes (3) Yes (4) No

Comment Asymmetry can be expressed as a meaning postulate in dictionary entries (or the term 'Asymmetric' can be used as a shorthand for a meaning postulate giving this information).

Example **UNDER: x UNDER y → ~ y UNDER x**

UNDER: Asymmetric

Practice Are the following predicates symmetric (*S*), asymmetric (*A*), or neither (*N*)?

(1) *Servant* as in *The Vizier is a servant of the Caliph*   *S / A / N*

(2) *Love* (verb)   *S / A / N*

(3) *Resemble*   *S / A / N*

(4) *To the north of*   *S / A / N*

(5) *Simultaneous with*   *S / A / N*

Feedback (1) A (2) N (3) S (4) A (5) S

Comment We now move to the second group of sense properties, which might go under the heading of 'reflexivity'.

Definition Given a two-place predicate *P*, if for any single referring expression *X* (or for any pair of referring expressions *X* and *Y* which have the same referent, e.g. *John* and *himself*), the sentence *XPX* (or the sentence *XPY*) is ANALYTIC, then *P* is a REFLEXIVE predicate.

Example The predicate *as tall as* is reflexive, because whenever we form a sentence with one referring expression as its subject and put another with the same referent after *as tall as*, as in *John is as tall as himself*, the result is an analytic sentence.

Practice (1) Do *I* and *myself* have the same referent in *I am as old as myself*? *Yes / No*

(2) Is *I am as old as myself* analytic?   *Yes / No*

(3) So is the predicate *be as old as* reflexive?   *Yes / No*

(4) Are the capitalized predicates in the following sentences reflexive?

(a) *John's doorkey is IDENTICAL TO itself*   *Yes / No*

(b) *John LOVES himself*   *Yes / No*

Feedback (1) Yes (2) Yes (3) Yes (4) (a) Yes (b) No

Comment The example sentences above tended to be somewhat artificial. This is because the definition of reflexivity rests on that of analyticity, and analytic sentences are rare in everyday language, since they are, by definition, uninformative, even though they convey important information about the structure of the fundamental knowledge of the sense relations known by every native speaker. We move on now to the property of irreflexivity, which corresponds to reflexivity in the same way that asymmetry corresponds to symmetry.

Definition Given a two-place predicate P, if for any single referring expression X (or for any pair of referring expressions X and Y which have the same referent, e.g. *John* and *himself*) the sentence XPX (or the sentence XPY) is a CONTRADICTION, then P is an IRREFLEXIVE predicate.

Example The predicate *is taller than* is IRREFLEXIVE, because any sentence *X is taller than Y*, where X and Y have the same referent, is bound to be a contradiction.

Practice (1) Do *Mary* and *herself* have the same referent in *Mary is different from herself*?   *Yes / No*

(2) Is *Mary is different from herself* a contradiction?   *Yes / No*

(3) So is the predicate *is different from* irreflexive?   *Yes / No*

(4) Are the capitalized predicates in the following sentences irreflexive?
    (a) *Mary LOVES herself*   *Yes / No*
    (b) *Fred is SHORTER THAN himself*   *Yes / No*

Feedback (1) Yes (2) Yes (3) Yes (4) (a) No (b) Yes

Practice Are the following predicates reflexive (R), irreflexive (I), or neither (N)?

(1) *distrust* $R / I / N$

(2) *identical to* $R / I / N$

(3) *co-extensive with* $R / I / N$

(4) *married to* $R / I / N$

(5) *contiguous with* $R / I / N$

Feedback (1) N (2) R (3) R (4) I (5) I

Comment We move finally to the third group of sense properties, which might go under the heading of 'transitivity'.

Definition Given a two-place predicate P, if for any trio of referring expressions X, Y, and Z the compound sentence XPY *and* YPZ ENTAILS the sentence XPZ, then P is TRANSITIVE.

Example *The King is in his counting house and his counting house is in his castle* entails *The King is in his castle*. So the predicate *in* is transitive.

Practice (1) Is *above* in the following sentence a two-place predicate?
    John's flat is above mine and mine is above Mary's   *Yes / No*

(2) What does the above sentence entail concerning the relation between John's flat and Mary's?

John's flat is ....

(3) Is *above* transitive?...Yes / No

(4) Are the capitalized predicates in the following sets of sentences transitive?

    (a) *Socrates was WISER THAN Plato and Plato was*
        WISER THAN Aristotle
        Socrates was WISER THAN Aristotle   Yes / No

    (b) *Mary's cat is the FATHER OF Gill's cat and*
        Gill's cat is the FATHER OF Gerald's cat
        Mary's cat is the FATHER OF Gerald's cat   Yes / No

Feedback   (1) Yes (2) *above Mary's* (3) Yes (4) (a) Yes (b) No

Comment   Just as asymmetry and irreflexivity correspond to symmetry and reflexivity, so intransitivity corresponds to transitivity.

Definition   Given a two-place predicate *P*, if for any trio of referring expressions *X*, *Y*, and *Z*, the compound sentence *XPY and YPZ* is a CONTRADICTORY of *XPZ*, then *P* is INTRANSITIVE.

Example   *John is the father of Bill and Bill is the father of Sue* is incompatible with *John is the father of Sue*, so *father of* is intransitive.

Practice   Are the following predicates intransitive?

    (1) *enemy of*   Yes / No

    (2) *dislike*   Yes / No

    (3) *grandchild of*   Yes / No

    (4) *two inches taller than*   Yes / No

    (5) *jealous of*   Yes / No

Feedback   (1) No (2) No (3) Yes (4) Yes (5) No

Practice   Are the following predicates transitive (*T*), intransitive (*I*), or neither (*N*)?

    (1) *loves*   T / I / N

    (2) *respects*   T / I / N

    (3) *to the north of*   T / I / N

    (4) *lower than*   T / I / N

    (5) *the immediate superior of*   T / I / N

Feedback (1) N (2) N (3) T (4) T (5) I

Practice The relationships between the six terms you have learned can be summarized in the following table. Write the words *transitive, reflexive, symmetric, intransitive, irreflexive,* and *asymmetric* in the appropriate boxes below.

	Definition involves one sentence	Definition involves two sentences	Definition involves three sentences
Definition involves a necessary truth			
Definition involves a necessary falsehood			

Feedback

reflexive	symmetric	transitive
irreflexive	asymmetric	intransitive

Practice Classify the following predicates for each of the types of formal property dealt with above. Use the abbreviations R, S, T, IR, AS, IT. The first two are done for you.

(1) *same as*   R, S, T
(2) *different from*   IR, S
(3) *parent of*   ....
(4) *ancestor of*   ....
(5) *above*   ....
(6) *in*   ....
(7) *similar to*   ....

Feedback (3) IR, AS, IT (4) IR, AS, T (5) IR, AS, T (6) IR, AS, T (7) R, S

Definition Any relation expressed by a predicate that is reflexive, symmetric, and transitive is called an EQUIVALENCE RELATION.

Example *same as* expresses an equivalence relation.
different from does not.

Practice Do the following predicates express equivalence relations?

(1) *is the same height as*   Yes / No
(2) *is identical to*   Yes / No
(3) *is similar to*   Yes / No
(4) *is married to*   Yes / No

Feedback (1) Yes (2) Yes (3) No, *similar* is not transitive. (4) No

Summary The formal properties of predicates defined and illustrated in this unit
constitute part of the information given in the semanticist's dictionary and, as
a result, are meant to represent part of what any native speaker knows about
the meanings of such predicates. These formal properties, all involving two-
place predicates, can be represented in the notation for meaning postulates.

Unit 18 Study Guide and Exercises

Directions After you have read Unit 18 you should be able to tackle the following
questions to test your understanding of the main ideas raised in the unit.

1 You should understand these terms and concepts from this unit:
sense properties of two-place predicates
  symmetric vs asymmetric predicates
  reflexive vs irreflexive predicates
  transitive vs intransitive predicates
equivalence relation

2 What does it mean to say that the sense properties introduced in this unit
(listed above) make no mention of other predicates?

3 What sense property of a sentence does the definition of **reflexivity** rest
upon?

4 Classify the following predicates for each of the following types of formal
properties: **symmetric, asymmetric, reflexive, irreflexive, transitive**, or
intransitive. If none of the properties holds, state that as well. Give an
example of each predicate as the predicator in a sentence to illustrate its
adherence (or nonadherence) to the properties.

a offspring of   g jealous of
b a friend of   h depends on
c near   i be the same age as
d younger than   j live with
e looks like   k on
f hate

5 Which of the predicates in question 4 above express the **equivalence**
relation? For those which do NOT express equivalence relations, explain
why not (i.e. identify which requisite sense property the predicate lacks).

6 Be sure you understand the relationships between the six terms summarized
in the chart near the end of this unit.

UNIT 19 DERIVATION

Entry requirements A prior understanding of MEANING POSTULATES (Unit 17) is useful, but not essential, for this unit.

Introduction So far we have treated the dictionary of a language simply as a static list of predicates. We have made the tacit assumption that, in order for a predicate to be able to bear meaning, it must in some sense already be present in the dictionary of the language concerned. But this neglects the obvious fact that words that we have never heard before, and which have perhaps never even been used before, can have clear meanings.

Practice Below are sentences containing nonce-words (words coined on the spur of the moment), not found in a dictionary. The nonce-words are capitalized. Give a paraphrase of each nonce-word.

(1) *We'll need to HIGHER this shelf a bit*

....

(2) *I find SCREWDRIVING with my left hand difficult*

....

(3) *We don't have a butcher: we have a BUTCHERESS*

....

(4) *John was DECOBWEBBING the ceiling with a long-handled mop*

....

Feedback (1) make higher (2) using a screwdriver (3) female butcher (4) removing the cobwebs from

Comment You were most likely able to give a paraphrase for each of these nonce-words that was very close (if not exactly the same) to the answers given in the feedback, even though you have most likely never heard any of them before. If you think about it, this ability is really quite remarkable. What does it tell us about how our mental dictionaries, the dictionaries that the semanticist is trying to investigate, are structured?

It is intuitively clear that people somehow create new words from old ones. The dictionary writer has the difficult task of shooting at a moving target.

If he includes in his dictionary only words that have been attested until today, his dictionary will soon be out of date, as new words will have been coined and perhaps added to the everyday vocabulary of the language. Here's an example of how this can be done.

Practice   Invent new English words synonymous with the following expressions.
(Base your new words on existing words and try to ensure that the meaning of the new word is transparent, i.e. easily guessed at. Resist the temptation to be humorous.)

(1) *instrument for making things blunt*   ....

(2) *the property of being easy to please*   ....

(3) *the process of making something transparent*   ....

(4) *having to do with giraffes* (adjective)   ....

Feedback   (1) *blunter* (2) *pleasability* (3) *transparentization* (4) *giraffish, giraffy*

Comment   Although ordinary dictionary writers do not take the risk of actually predicting or anticipating new forms before they are attested, it is clear that there exist certain quite clear, regular, rule-governed processes by which new words are born from old ones. These processes are often called processes of derivation and the rules that describe them may be referred to as derivational rules, word formation rules, or morphological rules. In order to fully understand the process of word derivation and its rule-governed behaviour we need to define some terms so we can be somewhat more precise about exactly what we are dealing with.

Definition   DERIVATION is the process of forming new words according to a (fairly) regular pattern on the basis of pre-existing words.

Comment   New words may be formed by combining existing words with meaningful units smaller than words, or with other existing words, according to derivational patterns or rules that are part of every speaker's mental knowledge of the language. There is a special technical term used by linguists to describe the basic components that make up derived words.

Definition   A MORPHEME is a minimal unit of word building that combines a minimal unit of meaning with a minimal linguistic form that carries this meaning. (The word MORPHOLOGICAL is an adjective derived from this term.)

Comment   Morphemes are the building blocks of word derivation in language. Note that, according to this definition, the class of morphemes in a language is not restricted to just the class of free-standing words. The definition has to be general enough to include units smaller than actual words, such as prefixes

226

and suffixes, that also combine minimal forms with minimal units of meaning and can be used to construct new words.

Examples   An existing word such as *dog* is a morpheme because it combines a minimal unit of meaning (i.e. whatever it is we understand the word *dog* to mean) with a minimal linguistic form, consisting of three speech sounds represented here by the letters used to spell the word. The form is minimal because it is not possible to convey the meaning of *dog* by any smaller set of sounds than the three sounds that make up the word as we know it. For example, we can't suddenly start referring to a dog as an **og* (by leaving off the initial consonant sound represented by the letter *d*) or as a **do* (by leaving off the final consonant sound represented by the letter *g*). Similarly, the meaning is minimal because it is also not possible to somehow divide the meaning of the word form *dog* into smaller parts which would have anything to do with dogs as we know them.

    A unit smaller than an actual word, such as the suffix *-er* in the word *builder*, is also a morpheme, because it combines a minimal meaning (something like 'an entity that engages in the activity described by the verb that it attaches to') with a minimal linguistic form, consisting of the two speech sounds represented by the letters used to spell the suffix.

    Another unit smaller than an actual word, such as the prefix *re-* in the word *replay*, is also a morpheme, because it combines a minimal meaning (something like 'repeat the activity described by the verb that it attaches to') with a minimal linguistic form, consisting of the two speech sounds represented by the letters used to spell the prefix.

Comment   We say that the derived word *builder* is formed by attaching the suffix *-er* after the root word *build* and the derived word *replay* is formed by attaching the prefix *re-* before the root word *play*. The root words in each case clearly convey the core, fundamental meanings of the derived words. Prefixes always attach before the root morpheme and suffixes attach after the root morpheme.

Definition   A derived word formed by combining two pre-existing words in a language is called a COMPOUND word.

Example   Derived words such as *bluebird*, *spaceship*, *babysit*, and *bittersweet* (to name just a few) are compounds, because they consist of two pre-existing root words in the language rather than a root word together with either a prefix or suffix.

Practice   Divide each word in the following list into its constituent morphemes. Some words may contain only one morpheme, while others may contain two or more morphemes. Identify whether each morpheme is a root, a prefix, or a

227

suffix. Also identify any derived word that is a compound. You should focus on how the words are pronounced rather than on how they are spelled. Don't be surprised if morphemes, especially root morphemes, may sometimes be spelled differently when they occur as a component of a derived as opposed to when they occur by themselves.

(1) *greatness*	(9) *sincerity*
(2) *homework*	(10) *revitalize*
(3) *unpopular*	(11) *father*
(4) *windy*	(12) *inalienable*
(5) *intolerant*	(13) *unthoughtful*
(6) *friendships*	(14) *sleepwalk*
(7) *childishly*	(15) *clearance*
(8) *widen*	(16) *sunrise*

Feedback (1) *great-ness* (2) *home-work* (compound) (3) *un-popular* (4) *wind-y* (5) *in-tolerant* (6) *friend-ship-s* (7) *child-ish-ly* (8) *wide-en* (9) *sincere-ity* (10) *re-vital-ize* (11) *father* (only one morpheme) (12) *in-alien-able* (13) *un-thought-ful* (14) *sleep-walk* (compound) (15) *clear-ance* (16) *sun-rise* (compound)

Comment We start to analyse the processes of derivation in more detail by noting that a step in a derivation is usually actually not one process, but three simultaneous processes, namely:

a morphological process (e.g. changing the shape of an existing word by adding a prefix or suffix morpheme to an existing root morpheme)

a syntactic process (changing the part of speech of a word, e.g. from verb to noun)

and

a semantic process (producing a new sense)

Example

	Morphological process	Syntactic process	Semantic process
laugh:laughter	add suffix *-ter*	change verb to noun	produce word denoting an act or an activity
teach:teacher	add suffix *-er*	change verb to noun	produce word denoting an agent
red:redness	add suffix *-ness*	change adjective to noun	produce word denoting a property

Practice Given below are pairs of words, one derived from the other. Fill in details of the morphological and syntactic processes involved in the derivation, as in the example chart above. For the moment we will not deal with the semantic details.

	Morphological process	Syntactic process
(1) *wide : widen* (intransitive verb, as in *The road widened*)	....	....
(2) *wasp : waspish*	....	....
(3) *table : tabulate*	....	....
(4) *bake : bakery*	....	....
(5) *avoid : avoidable*	....	....
(6) *honest : honesty*	....	....

Feedback (1) Add suffix -*en*; change adjective to verb. (2) Add suffix -*ish*; change noun to adjective. (3) Add suffix -*ate* and modify the pronunciation of the original root word somewhat; change noun to verb. (4) Add suffix -*ery*; change verb to noun. (5) Add suffix -*able*; change verb to adjective. (6) Add suffix -*y*; change adjective to noun.

Comment Note that all the conceivable syntactic changes involving the three major parts of speech (noun, verb, adjective) actually occur. In English, though not in some other languages, the morphological process of suffixation is more common than that of prefixation.

We give now some examples of derivation involving no morphological process at all, or 'zero-derivation', as it is sometimes called. In such cases a root morpheme is converted from one part of speech to another without the addition of either a prefix or suffix to the root.

Example *Cook* (agent noun) is derived from *cook* (transitive verb) just as *painter* (agent noun) is derived from *paint* (transitive verb). We just happen not to have a word *cooker*, meaning a person who cooks, in English. The lack of such a form which would otherwise be derivable according to regular word formation patterns is sometimes referred to as a 'lexical gap'. *Cook* (noun) is an example of zero-derivation.

Practice The capitalized words in the sentence below are examples of zero-derivation. In each case: (a) give the part of speech of the capitalized word (including transitive or intransitive for verbs), arriving at your answer on the basis of its use in the given sentence; (b) give the part of speech of the word from which the example word is derived (the 'source word'); and (c) give an example sentence using the source word. We have done the first one for you.

(1) *The workmen will WIDEN the road*

    (a) *transitive verb* ....   (b) *intransitive verb* ....

    (c) *The road WIDENS here* ....

(2) *A window cannot OPEN by itself*

    (a) ....   (b) ....

    (c) ....

(3) *We're going to PAPER the wall at the far end of the room*

    (a) ....   (b) ....

    (c) ....

(4) *I'm going for a SWIM*

    (a) ....   (b) ....

    (c) ....

(5) *We met some really FUN people at Jake's party*
(acceptable in many dialects)

    (a) ....   (b) ....

    (c) ....

(6) *The children are building a PRETEND house in the garden*

    (a) ....   (b) ....

    (c) ....

Feedback
(2) (a) intransitive verb (b) adjective (c) He jumped through the OPEN window
(3) (a) transitive verb (b) noun (c) The patterned PAPER on the wall is peeling off
(4) (a) noun (b) intransitive verb (c) Sue can't SWIM very well
(5) (a) adjective (b) noun (c) We had a lot of FUN at Jake's party
(6) (a) adjective (b) verb (c) Let's PRETEND to build a house

Comment Such examples show that processes of derivation can often be 'invisible', because no morphological process is involved. When what is apparently the 'same' word is used in two different parts of speech, as in these examples, there is usually a semantic process involved as well, i.e. a change of sense of some sort. Thus, for example, *open* (the adjective) denotes a state, whereas *open* (the derived intransitive verb) denotes an action. The difference between states and actions is a difference in meaning, a semantic difference. It is simply a difference that is not reflected in a morphological change in the root word.

    Just as derivation can sometimes involve both semantic and syntactic processes, but no morphological process, cases also occur of morphological and semantic processes without an accompanying syntactic process, i.e. without a change in part of speech.

Example A comparative adjective, such as *larger*, is derived, by adding a suffix, from the adjective *large*. Even though both the source word and the derived form are adjectives, they have clearly distinct semantic properties, as we will now see.

Practice (1) A how-many-place predicate is *large?* ....

(2) A how-many-place predicate is *larger* (*than*)? (Assume that the word *than* automatically gets supplied by the grammatical rules of the language when necessary.) ....

(3) What is the normal antonym of *large?* ....

(4) In terms of our classification of antonyms (Unit 11) are *large* and *small* binary antonyms (*B*) or gradable antonyms (*G*)? *B / G*

(5) What is the normal antonym of *larger than?* ....

(6) In terms of our classification of antonyms (Unit 11) are *larger than* and *smaller than* converses? *Yes / No*

(7) Is *larger than* a transitive predicate? (recall Unit 18) *Yes / No*

(8) Is *larger than* a symmetric predicate? *Yes / No*

(9) Is *larger than* an irreflexive predicate? *Yes / No*

(10) Can a one-place predicate, such as *large*, have such properties as transitivity, asymmetry, and irreflexivity? *Yes / No*

Feedback (1) one-place (2) two-place (3) *small* (4) G (5) *smaller than* (6) Yes (7) Yes (8) No, it's asymmetric. (9) Yes (10) No

Comment This is a good clear example of the kind of semantic differences that can exist between a derived word and its source word. The differences that we have just illustrated between *large* and *larger than* are found quite generally between gradable adjectives and their comparative forms: whenever a one-place gradable adjective is converted into its comparative form, the derived form is a two-place converse form.

Unfortunately, it is not always possible to describe differences in meaning between derived words and their sources in as clear terms as we could in the case of comparative adjectives derived from gradable adjectives. As a step towards developing a full account of these meaning differences, semanticists have invented a number of classificatory labels for the various kinds of derivation found in languages. These labels include such terms as 'inchoative', 'causative', and 'resultative'. We will define these terms and give examples of the derivations labelled with them.

Definition   An INCHOATIVE form denotes the beginning, or coming into existence, of some state.

Example   *Dark* (adjective) denotes a state. *Darken* (intransitive verb), as in *The sky darkened*, is the corresponding inchoative form, because it denotes the beginning of a state of darkness.

Practice   For each of the words below (all of which denote states), give (a) the corresponding derived inchoative form, and (b) an example sentence containing the derived form. Remember that some derived forms may be morphologically identical to their sources, through zero-derivation.

(1) *dry*   (a) ....   (b) ....
....

(2) *clear*   (a) ....   (b) ....
....

(3) *hard*   (a) ....   (b) ....
....

(4) *flat*   (a) ....   (b) ....
....

(5) *soft*   (a) ....   (b) ....
....

Feedback   (1) (a) *dry* (b) My hair dried in the sun
(2) (a) *clear* or *clarify* (b) The sky cleared or The liquid clarified
(3) (a) *harden* (b) The clay hardened
(4) (a) *flatten* (b) The landscape flattened
(5) (a) *soften* (b) The tar on the road softened in the sun

Comment   Examples such as these confirm that the morphological process most commonly used in English to derive an inchoative form is the suffixation of -*en*. Obviously, however, suffixation of -*en* is not the only device used. Zero-derivation is quite common with inchoatives.

Definition   A CAUSATIVE form denotes an action which causes something to happen.

Example   *Open* (transitive verb) is the causative form corresponding to *open* (intransitive verb). If one opens a door, for example, one causes it to open (in the intransitive sense of *open*). In English zero-derivation is the commonest device for producing causative forms, although causatives are also frequently formed by adding the suffix -*en* to the non-causative root.

Practice   For each of the words below (all intransitive verbs) give (a) the corresponding causative form and (b) an example sentence containing it.

232

(1) *redden* (a) .... (b) ....

....

(2) *freeze* (a) .... (b) ....

....

(3) *move* (a) .... (b) ....

....

(4) *roll* (a) .... (b) ....

....

(5) *break* (a) .... (b) ....

....

Feedback
(1) (a) *redden* (b) John reddened his hands
(2) (a) *freeze* (b) We'll freeze these strawberries for Christmas
(3) (a) *move* (b) Someone has moved my desk
(4) (a) *roll* (b) Fiona rolled her pencil across the table
(5) (a) *break* (b) Be careful not to break the lampshade

Definition A RESULTATIVE form denotes a state resulting from some action.

Example *Broken* (used as an adjective) is the resultative form corresponding to *break* (transitive verb). The state of being broken results from the action of breaking.

Practice For each of the words below (all transitive verbs), give (a) the corresponding resultative form and (b) an example sentence containing it, with the derived form used as an attributive adjective, i.e. before a noun.

(1) *melt* (a) .... (b) ....

....

(2) *flatten* (a) .... (b) ....

....

(3) *freeze* (a) .... (b) ....

....

(4) *carve* (a) .... (b) ....

....

(5) *dry* (a) .... (b) ....

....

Feedback   (1) (a) *molten* (or *melted*) (b) This crucible contains molten steel
(2) (a) *flattened* (b) They live in huts made of flattened oil-drums
(3) (a) *frozen* (b) Ice is frozen water
(4) (a) *carved* (b) There is an intricately carved fireplace in his room
(5) (a) *dried* (b) The roof was thatched with dried grass

Comment   The notions inchoative, causative, and resultative take one 'round in a circle', from words denoting states, through words denoting processes, through words denoting actions, and back to words denoting states. This relationship is shown diagrammatically below.

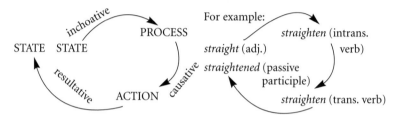

The derived resultative word describing a state (e.g. *straightened*) usually has a more specific meaning than the source word of the inchoative (*straight*).

In some cases, e.g. *straight – straightened, flat – flattened*, there are distinct state-denoting forms, one resultative and the other not. But in other cases, e.g. *bent, curved*, a single form has both a resultative and a non-resultative sense.

You should not get the impression from our diagrams above that it is easy to find foursomes of words like *straight – straighten – straighten – straightened* exemplifying the whole circular derivational process through inchoatives, causatives, and resultatives. Usually there is at least one gap.

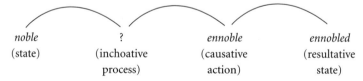

noble   ?   *ennoble*   *ennobled*
(state)   (inchoative   (causative   (resultative
             process)   action)   state)

Comment   In this case, there happens to be no inchoative form corresponding to the state-denoting *noble* and the causative *ennoble*.

When we talk of 'gaps', we do not mean that the language simply has no way at all of expressing the meaning concerned. In the case of *noble*, for instance, one could use a phrase, such as *become noble*, to convey the inchoative meaning. What we mean by a gap is that, in some cases, a morphologically derived form with the indicated meaning, which could be created by means of an existing derivational process in the language, is simply not used.

The existence of 'gaps' brings us to the notion of the productivity of various derivational processes.

Definition A derivational process is completely PRODUCTIVE if it can be used to produce an existing derived word from EVERY appropriate source word.

Comment It is doubtful whether any derivational process is actually completely productive, but some are very productive and others hardly productive at all.

Example The resultative derivational process (e.g. *pierce – pierced*) is more productive than the inchoative derivational process. Picking at random any verb denoting a transitive action, one has a relatively good chance of identifying a corresponding resultative form, whereas the chances of finding an inchoative corresponding to a randomly picked state-denoting form are, by comparison, poorer.

Practice Listed below are pairs of derivational processes with examples. By trying to think of further examples of each derivational process, make an informed guess about which member of each pair is the more productive.

(1) Adverbial -*ly* (e.g. *happy – happily, bumpy – bumpily, quick – quickly*)
Female -*ess* (e.g. *sculptor – sculptress, actor – actress*)

....

(2) Nominal -*ness* (e.g. *red – redness, empty – emptiness*)
Nominal -*y* (e.g. *honest – honesty*) (Only consider the derivation of nouns from adjectives by suffixation of -*y*, i.e. we're not concerned here with, e.g. *beef – beefy*, where an adjective is derived from a noun.)

....

(3) Adjectival -*ine* (e.g. *elephant – elephantine, crystal – crystalline*)
Adjectival -*y* (e.g. *cat – catty, sport – sporty*)
(Ignore the fact that this particular derivational process is somewhat colloquial or 'slangy'.)

....

(4) Agentive -*er* (e.g. *bake – baker, train – trainer*)
Locative -*ery* (e.g. *bake – bakery, bind – bindery*)

....

(5) Negative adjectival *dis*- (e.g. *honest – dishonest, ingenuous – disingenuous*)
Negative adjectival *un*- (e.g. *happy – unhappy, welcome – unwelcome*)

....

Feedback (1) Adverbial -*ly* is more productive than female -*ess*. (2) Nominal -*ness* is more productive than nominal -*y*. (3) Adjectival -*y* is more productive than adjectival -*ine*. (4) Agentive -*er* is more productive than locative -*ery*. (5) Negative adjectival *un*- is more productive than negative adjectival *dis*-.

Comment   In the above practice we have identified derivational processes by at least two terms, typically a syntactic term (e.g. adverbial) and a morphological term (e.g. -*ly*), and sometimes a semantic term (e.g. agentive). It is necessary to do this because often the same morphological process can correlate with different semantic and/or syntactic processes. We illustrate this in practice below.

Practice   The suffix -*ry* (or -*ery*) is associated with a number of different semantic classes of words. The most important of these can be labelled as

(a)   occupation/activity/behaviour (as in *archery* or *tomfoolery*)
(b)   physical location (as in *bakery*)
(c)   collection of objects (as in *cutlery*)

   For each of the words listed below, say which of these three semantic classes it belongs to. Use the letters (a), (b), (c), as above, to label the classes.

(1)   *crockery*   ....

(2)   *dentistry*   ....

(3)   *finery*   ....

(4)   *forestry*   ....

(5)   *grocery*   ....

(6)   *gunnery*   ....

(7)   *jewelry*   ....

Feedback   (1) (c) (2) (a) (3) (c) (4) (a) (5) (b) (6) (a) (7) (c)

Comment   Strictly speaking, there are at least three separate derivational processes involving three separate suffix morphemes -*ry* involved here, which we may label as (a) Activity -*ry*, (b) Location -*ry*, and (c) Collection -*ry*. None of these three processes is particularly productive. The third, Collection -*ry*, is less productive in modern English than the other two. Each suffix morpheme -*ry* appears to have its own separate, individual meaning, and it is possible that these meanings might be related to each other in some way. If this is true, then the suffix -*ry* might be polysemous, but we won't pursue this further here.

   We might think that, because there are rule-governed processes for deriving new words from existing morphemes in a language, it is unnecessary to list these new words separately in the dictionary. According to this line of reasoning, whenever such words are used they could simply be created by using the appropriate word formation processes. As a result, the total inventory of words in the semanticist's dictionary, which is supposed to reflect the organization of the speaker's mental dictionary, would be greatly reduced, since so many words in everyday use are clearly the result of derivational processes. But most linguists feel that words which are the product of derivational processes are best described within the dictionary with their own individual dictionary entries, which include information about the nature of the derivational processes involved.

One reason for this is that derived words seem to have a certain degree of semantic independence and psychological stability once they are created. Derived words often take on individualized idiosyncratic meanings that are not clearly predictable from the meanings of the component morphemes which were combined to form them. In other words, they take on their own unique semantic identity. A good example of this is what can happen when two roots are combined to form a compound. Consider such compounds as *houseboat, housecoat,* and *housecat.* The meanings of the roots *house, boat, coat,* and *cat* are individually clear to a native speaker. But the meanings of each derived compound cannot be completely predicted from the meanings of the component root words according to a simple semantic rule. While a *houseboat* is a boat that can be used like or as a house (i.e. you can live in it), a *housecoat* is not a coat that can be used like a house (i.e. you can't live in it, though you usually wear it inside the house), and a *housecat* is certainly not a cat that can be used like a house, but a cat that lives inside the house. While the derived compounds have meanings that have something to do with the meanings of the component root morphemes, it's not possible to predict exactly what the actual relationship between them is in each case. Consequently, it seems desirable to list them separately in the dictionary.

Another reason for listing derived words with their own individual dictionary entries is that nearly all word formation processes are only partially productive. Consequently, it is not possible to predict which new words will be derived from a particular word formation rule. Because we want our dictionary representation of the speaker's knowledge to be as accurate as possible and to avoid making erroneous predictions about potential new words which are never actually produced, it is better to list each derived word separately in the manner described above.

We give examples below of the kind of (partial) dictionary entries that we envisage for derived forms.

Example **LARGER: COMPARATIVE of LARGE**

WIDEN$_1$: INCHOATIVE of WIDE

WIDEN$_2$: CAUSATIVE of WIDEN$_1$

Practice Using terms drawn from *causative, inchoative, resultative, comparative, feminizer, negative,* formulate partial dictionary entries along the above lines for the following words, showing their relationships with other words.

(1) *unpleasant* ....

(2) *tigress* ....

(3) *burnt* ....

(4) *smellier* ....

(5) *shake* (transitive verb) ....

Feedback (1) **UNPLEASANT: NEGATIVE of PLEASANT** (2) **TIGRESS: FEMINIZER of TIGER** (3) **BURNT: RESULTATIVE of BURN** (4) **SMELLIER: COMPARATIVE of SMELLY** (5) **SHAKE$_2$: CAUSATIVE of SHAKE$_1$** (where *shake$_1$* is the intransitive verb)

Comment Terms like *negative, inchoative, feminizer*, as used here, have a similar function to other technical terms which may be used in dictionary entries, such as *symmetric, transitive, reflexive*, etc. Whereas these latter terms describe sense properties of predicates, terms like *negative, inchoative*, etc. describe complex sense relations between predicates. Thus these terms are parallel to the technical semantic terms *hyponym* and *converse*, which also describe sense relations between predicates. And just as the terms *symmetric, transitive*, etc. can be regarded as shorthand for information spelled out in exact detail in meaning postulates, so too terms like *causative, negative*, etc. stand for somewhat complex sense relations whose details can be made explicit by meaning postulates.

Example The dictionary entry given above for *shake$_2$*, namely

    SHAKE$_2$: CAUSATIVE of SHAKE$_1$

can be formulated alternatively as

    SHAKE$_2$: x SHAKE$_2$ y → x CAUSE (y SHAKE$_1$)

Here CAUSE represents the English predicate *cause*. This meaning postulate captures the entailment relation between sentences such as *Patrick shook the table* and *Patrick caused the table to shake*. (It is to be understood that the predicate *cause* will have in its own dictionary entry a meaning postulate as follows:

    x CAUSE p → p

This accounts for the possibility of the inference *The table shook* from *Patrick caused the table to shake*.)

Comment It is possible in principle to give definitions in logical terms of any semantic relationship between a 'source' predicate and a derived predicate. Such definitions would in many cases be quite complex, and some would even involve devising extensions to the basic logical notation we have adopted in this book (e.g. to account for time and degree). We will not pursue the matter of such definitions further, and we will also not look at any different types of derivational process in addition to those we have already discussed (i.e. inchoative, etc.), even though there are many further such processes to be found. We hope to have established the basic point that the meanings of derived forms can be represented in dictionary entries in relatively straightforward ways along the general lines adopted in this book.

Finally in this unit we take up a matter suggested by the above discussion, that of suppletion.

Definition SUPPLETION is a process whereby, in irregular and idiosyncratic cases, substitution of a MORPHOLOGICALLY UNRELATED form is associated with the specific semantic and/or syntactic processes normally accompanying a morphological process.

Example *Bad – worse* is a case of suppletion. *Worse* is clearly semantically related to *bad* in exactly the same way as, for example, *larger* is related to *large*, but there is no morphological relationship between the two words, i.e. there is no phonetic similarity between them.

Practice Give the suppletive forms indicated in each case below:

(1) The ordinal numeral corresponding to the cardinal
numeral *one* (as, for example, *seventh* corresponds to *seven*)   ....

(2) The ordinal numeral corresponding to the cardinal *two*   ....

(3) The superlative form of *good* (as *largest* is the superlative
of *large*)   ....

(4) A plural form of *person* (a more colloquial form than *persons*)   ....

Feedback (1) *first* (2) *second* (3) *best* (4) *people*

Comment The format of dictionary entries and the method of stating semantic relationships between predicates in no way require semantically related predicates to be morphologically related also. Thus it is just as easy to state a semantic relationship between morphologically unrelated forms (i.e. *bad – worse*) as between morphologically related forms (e.g. *large – larger*). Where we see a semantic relationship between morphologically unrelated forms, dictionary entries can express this, as in the examples below.

Example **WORSE: COMPARATIVE of BAD**

KILL: CAUSATIVE of DIE

Practice Suggest (partial) dictionary entries for the first word in each of the pairs below, making clear its semantic relationship with the second word of the pair.

(1) *melt* (intransitive verb), *liquid*   ....

(2) *create, exist*   ....

239

(3) *petrify* (intransitive verb), *stone* (adjective)   ....

(4) *bring, come*   ....

(5) *take, go*   ....

Feedback | (1) **MELT: INCHOATIVE of LIQUID** (2) **CREATE: CAUSATIVE of EXIST** (3) **PETRIFY: INCHOATIVE of STONE** (4) **BRING: CAUSATIVE of COME** (E.g. *John brought Liz to our house* entails *John caused Liz to come to our house.*) (5) **TAKE: CAUSATIVE of GO** (E.g. *Jim took his car to Egypt* entails *Jim caused his car to go to Egypt.*)

Comment | We have only given partial dictionary entries here. The senses of words like *bring* and *take* are in fact quite complex, and we have merely drawn attention to one aspect of their meanings, namely their relationships with the meanings of *come* and *go*, respectively.

Summary | We have defined and illustrated the notion of derivation in this unit, emphasizing its morphological, syntactic, and semantic components and the issue of productivity. We have only drawn our illustrations from a relatively small (and relatively well-understood) set, concentrating on the notions inchoative, causative, resultative, and comparative. There are many other derivational processes relating pairs of words: we have only skimmed the surface of this topic. The semantic relationship between a 'source' word and a derived word can be shown in dictionary entries.

Unit 19 Study Guide and Exercises

Directions After you have read Unit 19 you should be able to tackle the following questions to test your understanding of the main ideas raised in the unit.

1 You should understand these terms and concepts from this unit:

derivation	causative form
morphology	resultative form
morphological process	suppletion
zero derivation	productivity
inchoative form	

2 Invent single **new** English words that are synonymous with the following expressions by making use of your knowledge of English derivational morphology (word formation processes). In each case derive the new word directly from the word given in italics (since there are often existing words with the indicated meanings which are not directly derived from the words given). There may be more than one possible suitable derivation.

a instrument for making things *narrow* ....

b the result of being *terrified* ....
   (cf. signify/signification)

c the property of being easy to *fool* ....

d to make something *green* ....

e the result of making something *green* ....

f the process of making something *green* ....

g having to do with *hamsters* (adjective) ....

h the property of being *electric* ....

3 What are the three steps involved in the **derivation** of new words? Show
   how these steps are involved in the derivation of the new words you coined
   in the preceding exercise.

4 Try to identify the component morphemes in the following English words
   and then describe the steps (rules) involved in their derivation.

   a leathery   i jittery
   b privatize   j implausibility
   c watertight   k inconceivable
   d tabulation   l flatten
   e redden   m unhappier
   f intensity   n deemphasize
   g befriended   o endearment
   h washable   p girlfriend

5 We noted in this unit that some sorts of derivation can be **invisible**. Explain
   this with respect to the sort of derivation process involved with the
   italicized words in the following sentences.

   a I have to *book* a flight tomorrow
   b The batter got a *hit*
   c The committee *tabled* the issue until tomorrow
   d The pages of the old book had *yellowed* with age

6 Describe the kind of **semantic** differences found between the derived words
   (or expressions) and their sources below. If the particular sort of semantic
   change which results from the given derivation process has a name, then
   give that as well. In most cases additional information is given in order to
   make clear the intended syntactic category (part of speech) of both the
   source and derived words in this exercise.

SOURCE WORD	DERIVED WORD
a cold	colder than
b red (Adj.)	redden (intransitive V)
c cool (Adj.)	cool (intransitive V)

d melt (intransitive V)   melt (transitive V)
e freeze (transitive V)   frozen
f crush (transitive V)   crushed
g fly (intransitive V)   fly (transitive V)

7 Now make up separate sentences for both the source and derived words in question 6, in which each word is used in its intended sense.

8 Starting with each of the following forms denoting **states**, supply the English derived forms which express the other indicated semantic notions, according to the pattern described earlier in this unit. If there is a **gap** (i.e. no form in English corresponding to one of the notions), then leave it blank, but be ready to say how the notion is otherwise expressed in English. The first is done for you, repeated from an example given in this unit.

	STATE	PROCESS	ACTION	RESULTANT STATE
a	noble	....	ennoble	ennobled
b	sad	....	....	....
c	tired	....	....	....
d	long	....	....	....
e	moist	....	....	....
f	deep	....	....	....

9 Explain the notion of **productivity** as it pertains to derivational morphology.

10 We noted that the following suffixes and prefixes are relatively unproductive in comparison to other derivational morphemes in English. Demonstrate this by writing, next to the given English words that CAN be formed with each morpheme, a few which CANNOT be formed with the morpheme (where the morpheme is intended to be attached to the same part of speech and to contribute the same kind of meaning as in the sample words).

			CANNOT BE FORMED
a	*-ess*:	sculptress/actress	....
b	*-y*:	honesty/modesty	....
c	*-ine*:	elephantine/crystalline	....
d	*-ery*:	bakery/bindery	....
e	*dis-*:	dishonest/disloyal	....
f	*-en*:	redden/thicken	....
g	*a-*:	atypical/asymmetric	....

11 Formulate partial dictionary entries for the following words, showing their relationships with the words from which they were derived (use the format and terminology given in this unit). Do not formulate these as meaning postulates here.

   a shattered   ....

   b break (transitive)   ....

   c longer   ....

   d replay   ....

   e soften (intransitive)   ....

   f freeze (transitive)   ....

12 Reformulate the dictionary entries you wrote in question 11 for the following verbs as **meaning postulates**.

   a break (transitive)   ....

   b freeze (transitive)   ....

13 Give the **suppletive** forms indicated in each case below. Find another example (not in the textbook) for item (f).

   a The comparative form of *good*:   ....

   b The plural form of *child*:   ....

   c The first person singular of *be*:   ....

   d The superlative form of *bad*:   ....

   e The past tense form of *go*:   ....

   f ....

UNIT 20 PARTICIPANT ROLES

Entry requirements A grasp of logical formulae for SIMPLE PROPOSITIONS (Unit 13), MEANING POSTULATES (Unit 17), DERIVATION (Unit 19). If you feel familiar with these, take the entry test below. Otherwise, review the relevant units.

Entry test (1) Give a logical formula for *The workmen spoiled the carpet with their boots* (using **w**, **c**, and **b** as logical names).

....

(2) Similarly, give a logical formula for *The boots spoiled the carpet.*

....

(3) What is the relationship between the two predicates *boil* (*boil$_1$* and *boil$_2$*) in *The liquid boiled* and *John boiled the liquid?*

....

(4) Which of the following meaning postulates correctly describes the relationship between the two predicates *boil?* Circle your choice.

(a) **x BOIL$_2$ y → x CAUSE (y BOIL$_2$)**
(b) **x BOIL$_2$ y → y CAUSE (x BOIL$_1$)**
(c) **x BOIL$_2$ y → x CAUSE (y BOIL$_1$)**

Feedback (1) **w SPOIL c b** (2) **b SPOIL c** (3) *boil$_2$* is the causative of the inchoative *boil$_1$* (4) (c)

If you got at least 3 out of 4 correct, proceed to the introduction. Otherwise, review the relevant unit(s).

Introduction The basic semantic ingredients of a common type of simple sentence, as we have analysed it, are (1) a predicate, and (2) a number of referring expressions. The referring expressions correspond to actual things, persons, etc. in the world more or less directly, *via* the device of reference. The function of the predicate is to describe the specific relationship between the things, persons, etc. referred to, i.e. to describe how the things and/or people participate in the particular situation described. In this unit, we shall investigate a proposed way of being more precise about the different ways in which things and people participate in some of the real-world situations described by sentences.

244

Practice   We start with a well-known example.

(1) Which are the referring expressions in the sentence *John opened the door with the key?*

....

(2) What is the predicate which relates these referring expressions in the sentence concerned?

....

(3) Picture to yourself the situation described by *John opened the door with a key*. Could the sentence *The key opened the door* also be used to describe this same situation (even though giving less information about it, by not mentioning John)?   *Yes / No*

(4) Could this same situation also be described (even less informatively) by the bare sentence *The door opened?*   *Yes / No*

(5) In the situation described there is a door.
(a) Is it opening? (b) Or is it being opened? (c) Or both opening and being opened?

(6) There is a key in this situation, too.
(a) Is it opening the door? (b) Or is it being used to open the door? (c) Or is it both opening the door and being used to open the door?

Feedback   (1) *John, the door, the key* (2) *open* (3) Yes (4) Yes (5) (c) (6) (c)

Comment   In all three sentences

John opened the door with the key
The key opened the door
The door opened

the roles played by the participant objects (door, key) and people (John) do not vary. In this example, the roles played by the participants are labelled as follows:

John	AGENT
the door	AFFECTED
the key	INSTRUMENT

We give rough definitions of these terms below, but you should be warned that it will not be easy to apply these definitions in all cases.

Definition   The AGENT of a sentence is the person deliberately carrying out the action described, e.g. John in *John opened the door*.
    The AFFECTED participant is the thing (not usually a person, although it may be) upon which the action is carried out, in many cases the thing

245

changed by the action in the most obvious way, the door in our example.
Some semanticists refer to the affected participant as the PATIENT.

The INSTRUMENT is the thing (hardly ever a person) by means of which
the action is carried out, the key in our example.

Practice (1) Identify the Agents in the following sentences by circling them as in (a).
    (a) (A burglar) ransacked my house
    (b) *My mother's Imari bowl was broken by a thief*

(2) Identify the Affected objects (or persons) in the following:
    (a) *Muriel dealt the cards carefully to each player*
    (b) *The tree was felled by a single blow from Paul's axe*

(3) Identify the Instruments in the following:
    (a) *Seymour sliced the salami with a knife*
    (b) *Hamish used a screwdriver to open the tin*

Feedback (1) (b) *a thief* (2) (a) *the cards* (b) *the tree* (3) (a) *a knife* (b) *a screwdriver*

Comment The notion of role (e.g. Agent, Instrument, etc.) adds a new dimension to our
view of the meanings of sentences. In rough logical formulae, we could
represent *John opened the door with the key* as **j OPEN d k**, treating *open* as a
three-place predicate. *The key opened the door* would be **k OPEN d** (with *open*
as a two-place predicate), and *The door opened* would be **d OPEN** (*open* as
one-place predicate). This notation fails to show that in all three cases the
door is involved in exactly the same way in the action of opening, and it also
fails to show that in the first two cases the key's participation in the action is
the same.

One could augment the logical formulae with this information in the
following way:

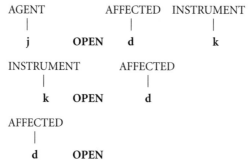

This makes it clear, for example, that no matter whether *the door* appears
before or after the verb *opened* (or whether its logical name **d** is mentioned
first or second in the logical formula), the way in which the door participates
in the act of opening described is the same: the door is the object AFFECTED
in this situation.

246

Practice For each of the sentences given below, write out an augmented logical formula as in the examples just given, indicating what objects or persons play the roles of Agent, Affected, and Instrument. (Use the abbreviations AG, AF, IN. We have done the first one for you.)

(1) *Floyd smashed the glass with the hammer*
    AG   **AF IN**
     f SMASH g h
....

(2) *The hammer smashed the glass*

....

(3) *The glass smashed*

....

(4) *Crippen dissolved the body with the acid*

....

(5) *The acid dissolved the body*

....

(6) *The body dissolved*

....

Feedback (2) **IN**   **AF** (3) **AF**   (4) **AG**   **AF IN**
     h SMASH g   **g SMASH**   **c DISSOLVE b a**
(5) **IN**   **AF** (6) **AF**
    a DISSOLVE b   **b DISSOLVE**

Comment The position of a referring expression in a sentence is only very loosely correlated with the role of its referent in the situation described. Let us distinguish three different grammatical positions in the sentence, as follows:

Subject position – preceding main verb
Object position – immediately following main verb
Complement – after the verb, but not immediately, often after a preposition

Example SUBJECT   OBJECT   COMPLEMENT
     | | |
  John   opened   the door   with the key

Practice The following chart provides a box for each logically possible combination of role and grammatical position. For instance, the top left-hand box corresponds to the occurrence of an Agent in subject position.

	Subject	Object	Complement
Agent			
Affected			
Instrument			

Among the sentences below, you will find examples illustrating some of these possibilities. Put the numbers of the sentences in the appropriate boxes above. (Some numbers will go in more than one box; some boxes will remain blank.)

(1) *The dynamite blew the safe open*
(2) *The hut was set alight by vandals*
(3) *Alfred burnt the cakes*
(4) *Charles built Emily a mahogany bookcase*
(5) *Sidney swatted the fly with his hat*

Feedback

3, 4, 5		2
2	1, 3, 5	4
1		5

Comment Certain clear tendencies in the relationship between grammatical position and participant role emerge from this chart (which is quite representative of the general situation). We get you to identify these trends below.

Practice (1) Which two combinations of participant role with grammatical position are the most common?

....

(2) Which two combinations are not represented in the chart, and are generally rare in the language at large?

....

(3) Which grammatical position, or positions, is, or are, the most versatile, i.e. which position(s) can be used for the greatest variety of different participant roles (as far as we have seen)?

....

(4) Which grammatical position is least versatile?

....

Feedback (1) Agent – Subject and Affected – Object are the most frequent correlations. (2) Agent in Object position, and Instrument in Object position (3) Subject position and Complement position are the most versatile. (This is partly, but only partly, the result of our rather broad definition of Complement position.) (4) Object position is the least versatile.

Comment We emphasize that participant roles, such as Agent, Affected, and Instrument are defined semantically, in terms of the meanings of sentences, and not grammatically, in terms of position in sentences. Grammatical positions in a sentence and the participant roles which occupy these positions are independent kinds of linguistic notions and should be kept distinct from one another. Clearly, there is some systematic relationship between the semantic roles and the grammatical positions, but it is evidently a complicated relationship.

We will now mention several further roles that have been identified in the semantic literature: location and beneficiary. We want to make it clear that we are not going to attempt to describe every kind of role that has been proposed, but just focus on the ones that seem to occur most frequently.

Definition The role of LOCATION is played by any expression referring to the place where the action described by a sentence takes place.

The BENEFICIARY is the person for whose benefit or to whose detriment the action described by the sentence is carried out. It is usually assumed that the Beneficiary, if mentioned, is distinct from both the Agent and the Affected. Note that the word 'beneficiary' as used in semantic theory has a special technical sense that differs from the way it is used in everyday English. This is clear from the fact that the Beneficiary of an action might not always be positively affected by that action, but could be negatively affected, depending on the action in question.

Example AFFECTED   LOCATION
| | | | | | | | | | | | | | |
Caesar was assassinated in Rome

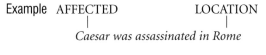

AGENT   BENEFICIARY   AFFECTED
Keith   gave   Gill   a replica of the Venus de Milo

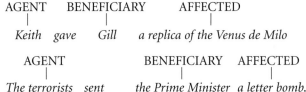

    AGENT   BENEFICIARY   AFFECTED
The terrorists sent   the Prime Minister a letter bomb.

Practice (1) Identify the Locations in the following sentences by circling them:
    (a) *It is windy in Edinburgh*
    (b) *I'm meeting Dick at Waverley Station*
    (c) *Tallahassee is humid in summer*

    (2) Identify the Beneficiaries in the following:
    (a) *Ruth knitted Bryan a sweater*
    (b) *Alan was sent a special offer from the Reader's Digest*
    (c) *Glenn bought a micro-computer for his son*

Feedback (1) (a) in Edinburgh (b) at Waverley Station (c) Tallahassee (2) (a) Bryan (b) Alan (c) his son

Comment   With these two new roles, we again see the versatility of Subject position and Complement position. Both roles are found correlated with both grammatical positions. Note further that in Complement position each role has one or more characteristic prepositions that is used to signal it. We will bring these facts out in the following practice.

Practice   (1)   In sentences in the previous section, two different prepositions are used in connection with the expression of Location. What are they?

....

(2)   Write down three other prepositions that can be used to express Location.

....

(3)   In sentence (2) (c) above, what preposition is used to express the Beneficiary role?

....

(4)   Give another preposition that can be used to express the Beneficiary role. (Think of paraphrases of the examples used above.)

....

(5)   When the Instrument role is expressed in the Complement of a sentence, what preposition is typically used to express it?

....

(6)   When the Agent role is expressed in the Complement of a sentence (as in passive sentences) what preposition expresses this role?

....

Feedback   (1) *in, at* (2) *on, under, near, by, above*, etc. (3) *for* (4) *to* (5) *with* (and sometimes *by*) (6) *by*

Comment   We have so far given definitions and examples of five different roles. Some proponents of the theory of roles envisage that it is necessary to define further roles, perhaps bringing the total of roles to about a dozen or so. But all agree on the need to postulate relatively few roles: the more roles one postulates, the weaker is the theory of roles, because the proliferation of roles makes it more difficult to capture broad generalizations on how participant roles work. Agreeing on what roles are necessary, exactly how many there are, and how to define them with respect to one another has proved very difficult. We illustrate some interesting cases in this respect below, in which we find data with referring expressions that don't seem to fit any of the roles we have considered so far.

Practice (1) In the situation described by *Napoleon saw Josephine*,
              is any action necessarily taking place?   *Yes / No*

          (2) Can we infer from *Napoleon saw Josephine* that Napoleon
              deliberately saw her?   *Yes / No*

          (3) And can we infer that Josephine deliberately involved
              herself in this event of seeing?   *Yes / No*

          (4) Is it obvious who, if anyone, is Agent in *Napoleon
              saw Josephine*?   *Yes / No*

          (5) Who, if anyone, is Affected in *Napoleon saw Josephine*?   ....

          (6) Do any of the roles Location, Beneficiary, or Instrument
              fit the part played by Josephine in this episode?   *Yes / No*

Feedback (1) No (2) No (3) No (4) No (5) If anyone, it is Napoleon, but his role
          does not really fit the notion of Affected as defined earlier. (6) No

Comment What such examples show is that in the area of participant roles, as
         everywhere else in semantics, there are cases which require further analysis
         and further elaboration of the theoretical and descriptive framework. Let's
         dig a little deeper into how we might go about expanding the inventory of
         roles somewhat to account for examples like the one immediately above. A
         sentence like *Napoleon saw Josephine* suggests the need to posit at least two
         additional roles beyond the ones considered so far. Semanticists have called
         these roles 'experiencer' and 'theme'.

Definition The EXPERIENCER is typically a person who is mentally aware of, perceives,
           or experiences the action or state described by the sentence, but who is not in
           control of the situation. (Experiencer characteristics can also sometimes be
           attributed to animals.)
               The THEME participant is a thing or person whose location is described,
           or a thing or person that is perceived by an Experiencer.

Example EXPERIENCER   THEME
              | |
         The children heard *the loud noise*

Practice (1) Identify the Experiencers in the following:
              (a) *Jane saw a movie last night*
              (b) *Janice became sick when she heard the news*
              (c) *The thunder was heard by everyone*

          (2) Identify the Themes in the following:
              (a) *My computer is sitting on that desk*
              (b) *Jack saw a play last week*
              (c) *The Honda belongs to Jim*

Feedback	(1) (a) Jane (b) Janice (c) everyone (2) (a) My computer (b) a play (c) The Honda

Comment   As was the case with other participant roles we have examined, we also see that the Experiencer and Theme roles are not restricted to Subject position. To make this clearer, try to answer the following questions.

Practice   (1)   What role other than Agent can be expressed in the Complement of a sentence (as in passive sentences) after the preposition *by*?

....

(2)   Which two positions can be occupied by the Theme role?

....

(3)   In the examples given in this practice, does the Theme ever appear in Complement position?

....

....

Feedback	(1) Experiencer (2) Subject and Object (3) No

Comment   Note that the need to posit the additional roles of Experiencer and Theme does not necessarily invalidate the notion of roles altogether. Though, as mentioned earlier, we would like to hold down the total number of roles as much as possible, we have to be prepared to posit new ones where the facts clearly call for it, as we have just seen. Later in this unit we shall mention other areas where the roles as we have defined them cannot be assigned clearly. Meanwhile we look at another interesting case that provokes thought in relation to the idea of roles.

Practice   (1)   Do the sentences *Ahmed bought a camel from Abdullah* and *Abdullah sold a camel to Ahmed* describe the same event?   *Yes / No*

(2)   In the event described by these sentences, there are three participants, Ahmed, Abdullah, and the camel. Which one is the Agent?   ....

(3)   Might it be more satisfactory to relate the notion of Agent, not to the actual situation described, but rather to some specific sentence chosen to describe it?   *Yes / No*

(4)   Following this line of thought, would one then say that *Abdullah* was the Agent in the sentence with *buy*, and *Ahmed* the Agent in the sentence with *sell*?   *Yes / No*

(5)   Now, granting that *Ahmed* is the Agent in one sentence, but not in the other, is there still not some role which we feel Ahmed is playing in both sentences? What might this role be?   ....

Feedback (1) Yes (2) Not the camel, certainly, but either Ahmed or Abdullah (or both) could be thought of as the Agent. (3) Yes, if we insist on there only being one Agent per case. (4) No, the other way around (*Ahmed* the Agent in the sentence with *buy*, and *Abdullah* in the sentence with *sell*). (5) Yes, it seems that *Ahmed* could be regarded as the Beneficiary in both cases (and so, actually, could *Abdullah*).

Comment   Cases such as this raise the question of whether a referring expression can bear more than one role relation to the verb in a particular sentence. This question has played an important part in the issue of how meaning and grammar are interrelated in recent linguistic theories, but we will not go further into this matter here.

We will now show how information about participant roles can be included in the dictionary. Proponents of the notion of role envisage that in the dictionary entry for each verb in the language there will be a 'role-frame', indicating what roles must be, and what roles may be, mentioned in connection with the verb. These role frames are considered to be part of the semantic representation of each verb.

Example   OPEN: (AGENT) AFFECTED (INSTRUMENT)
This is part of the dictionary entry for the verb *open*. The parentheses indicate that the roles shown within them (i.e. Agent and Instrument) are optional with this verb, and the role not enclosed by parentheses, Affected, is obligatory. I.e. when describing some act of opening, one must mention what gets opened, and one may also mention who did the opening and what he did it with. Recall that in

John opened the door
The key opened the door
The door opened

the door is mentioned in all three sentences, but John and the key are not mentioned in all three sentences.

Practice   (1) What two roles are mentioned in *Julia planted a tree*?   ....

(2) What further role is mentioned in *Julia planted a tree in the garden*?   ....

(3) What single role is mentioned in *A tree was planted*?   ....

(4) Is the Agent role mentioned in some, but not all, of these examples?   *Yes / No*

(5) Is the Location role mentioned in some, but not all, of these examples?   *Yes / No*

(6) Is the Affected role mentioned in all of these examples?   *Yes / No*

(7) Which of the following role-frames captures these facts correctly?
 (a) (AGENT) (AFFECTED) (LOCATION)
 (b) AGENT AFFECTED (LOCATION)
 (c) (AGENT) AFFECTED (LOCATION)
 (d) (AGENT) AFFECTED LOCATION

Feedback (1) Agent and Affected (2) Location (3) Affected (4) Yes (5) Yes (6) Yes (7) (c)

Practice Listed below are a number of verbs, with some example sentences containing them. On the basis of what occurs in all of the example sentences, and what only occurs in some of them, formulate a role-frame for the dictionary entry of each verb.

(1) BLOW UP: ....
 Vacek blew up the tank with a hand grenade
 The hand grenade blew up the tank
 The tank blew up

(2) RAIN: ....
 It's raining in Paris
 It's raining

(3) CHASE: ....
 John chased the ball to the bottom of the hill
 The ball was chased to the bottom of the hill
 The ball was chased

(4) GIVE: ....
 John gave Mary a book
 Mary was given a book
 A book was given to Mary

(5) PUT: ....
 Lucy put a log on the fire with the tongs
 Lucy put a log on the fire
 A log was put on the fire

Feedback (1) BLOW UP: (AGENT) AFFECTED (INSTRUMENT) (2) RAIN: (LOCATION) (3) CHASE: (AGENT) AFFECTED (LOCATION) (4) GIVE: (AGENT) AFFECTED BENEFICIARY (5) PUT: (AGENT) AFFECTED (INSTRUMENT) LOCATION

Comment The Affected role, when it is permitted at all, is obligatory in these examples. The Agent role is frequently permitted, though never obligatory, in these examples. These two facts reflect a quite general trend in the language.

254

We will now point out a certain economy in the dictionary that the role-frame notation makes possible in the case of verbs which, like *blow up* and *open*, can appear in a non-passive form even when no Agent is mentioned.

Practice (1) A how-many-place predicate is *shake* in *Patrick shook the table*? ....

(2) A how-many-place predicate is *shake* in *The table shook*? ....

(3) Does *Patrick shook the table* entail *The table shook*? Yes / No

(4) Would this entailment be accounted for in an analysis which assumed two separate verbs *shake*, one a two-place predicate and the other a one-place predicate, with (partial) dictionary entries as follows?

SHAKE$_2$: two-place, **x SHAKE$_2$ y** $\rightarrow$ **y SHAKE$_1$**, . . .

SHAKE$_1$: one-place . . . Yes / No

(5) Is it more economical to postulate a single verb *shake* with an optional Agent in its role-frame, as in

SHAKE: (AGENT) AFFECTED? Yes / No

Feedback (1) two-place (2) one-place (3) Yes (4) Yes (5) The role-frame notation is slightly more economical.

Comment We have compared the role-frame approach to dictionary entries with the logical, meaning postulate approach in order to show that, as far as we have seen, the two approaches are not incompatible. The two approaches have different emphases. Whereas logical approaches emphasize entailment relations between sentences, the role-frame approach concentrates more on the semantic relationships between referring expressions inside a sentence, that is, on the way in which the action denoted by a verb can be said to involve participants in a number of different roles.

Some of the differences between the two approaches are rather accidental. Thus the role-frame approach pays more attention to the roles typically expressed by adverbial phrases, such as Location and Instrument, which logical approaches frequently neglect. On the other hand, the role-frame approach generally pays little attention to the logician's insight that not only verbs, but also nouns, adjectives and prepositions are all semantically predicates. The role approach concentrates almost exclusively on verbs. We show below some of the difficulties which arise when one tries to generalize the idea of role to all predicates.

We consider first prepositions, which we take to be two-place predicates (three-place in the case of *between*).

Practice (1) What is the predicator in *The bull is in the 40-acre field*? ....

(2) Stretching the definition of Location (p. 249) to include states as well as actions, would it seem reasonable to say that *the 40-acre field* played the role of Location in the above sentence? *Yes / No*

(3) Granted that we can assign Location to *the 40-acre field*, which of the other roles that we have seen (Agent, Instrument, Beneficiary, Affected, Experiencer, Theme) seems to be played by *the bull*? ....

(4) What is the predicator in *This book is for Louise*? (Again, assume that there is a predicator here.) ....

(5) Allowing Beneficiary to be applied in the case of states as well as actions, could one assign the Beneficiary role to *Louise* in this sentence? *Yes / No*

(6) If so, what role could one plausibly assign to *this book*? ....

Feedback (1) *in* (2) Yes (3) Theme seems to fit reasonably well according to its definition given earlier. (4) *for* (5) Yes (6) In this case none seems to fit well.

Comment We see that the Theme role fits the case of the referring expression *the bull* in Subject position in the sentence *The bull is in the 40-acre field*, because, according to our definition of Theme, a referring expression whose location is described relative to some other entity can be regarded as fulfilling this role. But none of the roles that we have mentioned so far seems to fit the case of the referring expression *this book* in Subject position in the example *This book is for Louise*. Now let's look at some one-place predicates.

Practice (1) What is the predicator in *That animal is a cow*? ....

(2) Does the referring expression *that animal* here seem to be in an Agent relationship with the predicate *cow*? *Yes / No*

(3) Does it seem to be in an Instrument relationship with the predicate *cow*? *Yes / No*

(4) Or Beneficiary perhaps? *Yes / No*

(5) Location? *Yes / No*

(6) What is the predicator in *This poppy is red*? ....

(7) Does the referring expression *this poppy* seem to bear any of the role relationships that we have mentioned to the predicate *red*? *Yes / No*

Feedback (1) *cow* (2) No (3) No (4) No (5) No (6) *red* (7) No

Comment These examples show that none of the roles mentioned so far (Agent, Instrument, Beneficiary, Location, Affected, Experiencer, Theme) fit the relation borne by a grammatical Subject to a noun, adjective, or preposition predicate. One way to deal with this problem that has been suggested by some semanticists would be to extend the notion of Theme to include situations such as these in which a referring expression is essentially inert or neutral with respect to the predicator in the sentence. If this is accepted, then the Theme role becomes a kind of default or catch-all role that is invoked when none of the more specific ones fit. While such a solution will work, it is unsatisfactory to a certain extent due to its lack of precision. So there is clearly room for more research in this area of semantics.

Summary The notion of participant role adds a new dimension to the study of sense relations. Participant roles indicate relationships between a verb (and possibly other predicators) and the referring expressions in a sentence. We have illustrated a number of such roles that have been proposed, namely Agent, Affected, Instrument, Location, Beneficiary, Experiencer, and Theme. We have seen how dictionary information involving roles can be presented and we have mentioned several problems with the notion of participant role.

Unit 20 Study Guide and Exercises

Directions After you have read Unit 20 you should be able to tackle the following questions to test your understanding of the main ideas raised in the unit.

1 You should understand these terms and concepts from this unit:
some participant (semantic) roles
   Agent
   Affected (Patient)
   Instrument
   Location
   Beneficiary
   Experiencer
   Theme
role frame of a verb
grammatical positions in the sentence
   Subject position
   Object position
   Complement position

2 What are **participant (semantic) roles**? Is there any current fixed number of such roles accepted by linguists?

3 Translate each of the following sentences into an augmented logical formula, indicating which entities play the roles of **Agent, Affected**, and **Instrument**.

a The worker moved the beam with a crane

b The crane moved the beam

c The beam moved

d The arsonist burned the house with fire

e The fire burned the house

f The house burned

4 In each of the following sentences identify the participant role and the grammatical position (i.e. either Subject, Object, or Complement) of each referring expression. Possible semantic roles include **Agent, Affected, Instrument, Location, Beneficiary, Experiencer**, and **Theme**.

a Mary roasted the duck

b Jane smelled the burning dinner

c The duck was roasted by Mary

d The bomb destroyed the building

e Jane kicked the tyre with her foot

f Fred saw a comedy show in that club

g I saw Mortimer in Detroit

h Jane gave Mary the book

i Mary was given the book by Jane

j Jerry did the favour for me

k Detroit is a big city

l Jane gave the book to Mary

5 What problem arises when we try to assign semantic roles such as Agent and Affected (Patient) to the participants in a sentence like *Mortimer saw Millie* (as opposed to sentences such as *Mortimer chased Millie* or *Fred broke the glass*)? How was this problem dealt with?

6 In a sentence such as *Mortimer kicked the bully*, is it possible that *the bully* might have more than one semantic role? If so, which ones? Explain briefly, and justify your choices. Can you give another example where a given participant could conceivably have more than one role assigned to it?

7 Formulate a **role frame** for each of the following verbs which would be part of its dictionary entry. To do this think of several sentences involving the verb in which you try to leave out various arguments (in much the same way as was done in this unit). Which role always seems to be present if it is permitted at all?

a *set* ....

b *snow* ....

c *donate*   ....

d *melt*   ....

8 How does the role frame approach to dictionary entries compare and contrast with the logical, meaning postulate approach? What are the strengths and weaknesses of each?

9 We claimed that a problem with the role frame approach is that it is difficult to propose a suitable semantic role for the italicized referring expressions in Subject position in sentences like the following:

a *This book* is for Louise

b *The car* is red

c *The movie* is interesting

What exactly is the difficulty, given how we have defined the roles presented in this unit? We suggested that we might be able to extend the Theme role somehow to deal with this problem, but we didn't provide any details as to how this might be done. Another possibility, not mentioned previously, would be to propose a different role, in addition to those described in this unit, which could account for these examples. See if you can sketch out a way of elaborating the theory of participant roles to deal with these issues.

6 Interpersonal and non-literal meaning

UNIT 21 SPEECH ACTS

Entry requirements SENTENCES and UTTERANCES (Unit 2). If you feel you are familiar with these notions, take the entry test below.

Entry test Answer the following questions

(1) If Fred and Jack both greet each other one morning with
'How are you today?', have they both made the same utterance?   *Yes / No*

(2) How many different sentences are involved when Jack
and Fred greet each other as above?   ....

(3) Is it conceivable to give the exact time, date, and place of an
utterance?   *Yes / No*

(4) Is a sentence an event?   *Yes / No*

(5) Can it be said in the case of the English sentence *The man
hit the bust of Stalin with a hammer*, used out of context as
an example, which particular person in the world is the
referent of *the man*?   *Yes / No*

(6) In making the utterance 'Elvis is great', would a speaker
normally be carrying out an act of referring, i.e. referring
to some particular person?   *Yes / No*

Feedback (1) No (2) One (3) Yes (4) No (5) No (6) Yes
If you have scored less than 5 correct out of 6, you should review Unit 2.
Otherwise, continue to the introduction below.

Introduction 'Actions speak louder than words' is a well-known proverb. But we will show in this unit that the alleged distinction between acts and speech is a misleading oversimplification. We will show how, to a large extent, speech is action, and that language can actually be used to do things.

Comment When a speaker, in appropriate circumstances, makes an utterance containing a referring expression, he carries out a certain act, an act of referring. Referring is typically a linguistic act, but we shall see that it is possible to carry out all sorts of other acts using language. We will start with another obviously linguistic act, that of stating or asserting.

260

Definition   An ACT of ASSERTION is carried out when a speaker utters a declarative
              sentence (which can be either true or false), and undertakes a certain
              responsibility, or commitment, to the hearer, that a particular state of
              affairs, or situation, exists in the world.

Example   If I say, 'Simon is in the kitchen', I assert to my hearer that in the real world a
              situation exists in which a person named Simon is in a room identified by the
              referring expression *the kitchen*.

Comment   There was once a strong tendency among semanticists to assume that there
              was not much more to the meanings of sentences (and utterances) than this
              kind of correspondence between sentences (and utterances) and the world.
              This view has been called the Descriptive Fallacy. We give a simple version of
              this below.

Definition   The DESCRIPTIVE FALLACY is the view that the sole purpose of making
              assertions is to DESCRIBE some state of affairs.

Example   According to the Descriptive Fallacy view, my only purpose in uttering
              'Simon is in the kitchen' would be to describe a particular state of affairs,
              and nothing more.

Comment   The Descriptive Fallacy view is not wholly wrong. An element of description
              is involved in many utterances. But description is not indulged in only for its
              own sake. There is usually a more basic purpose behind an utterance.

Practice   Would the main purpose of making the following assertions normally be
              simply to describe some existing state of affairs in the world?

              (1) 'There is a wasp in your left ear'   *Yes / No*

              (2) 'Someone has broken the space-bar on my typewriter'   *Yes / No*

              (3) 'This gun is loaded'   *Yes / No*

              (4) 'You are a fool'   *Yes / No*

              (5) 'I love you'   *Yes / No*

Feedback   It is doubtful whether one's main purpose in making an assertion is ever
              simply to describe an existing state of affairs in the world. So we would
              suggest that the answer in all the above cases is No.

Practice   For each of the above five utterances state one or two purposes that the
              speaker may have had in mind when uttering them. As a guide, we have done
              the first one for you.

              (1) To warn the hearer of the danger of being stung, or to shock him (or both)
                   ....

                   ....

(2) ....

....

(3) ....

....

(4) ....

....

(5) ....

....

Feedback   (2) To complain about the damage, or to apologize to someone about to borrow the machine, etc. (3) As a warning during an armed robbery, or as an example during an elementary weapon-training lesson for soldiers, etc. (4) To insult the hearer, or, between intimates, to tease him, or to impress a bystander with one's directness of manner, etc. (5) To reassure the hearer, or to console him, or to make him feel indebted, or to please him, etc.

Comment   All of these answers mention acts of one kind or another. Thus warning, shocking, complaining, apologizing, insulting, reassuring, etc. are all acts. They are all things that we DO, using language. An important part of the meaning of utterances is what speakers DO by uttering them. Acts such as teasing, insulting, etc. are aspects of utterance meaning and not of sentence meaning. We reinforce this conclusion below.

Practice   Take a sentence such as *There's a piece of fish on the table.*

(1) Could this sentence be uttered as a means of complaining to a waiter in a restaurant that a table had not been cleared properly?   *Yes / No*

(2) Could it, in other circumstances, be uttered to warn one's husband or wife not to let the cat in the kitchen?   *Yes / No*

(3) Could it, in still other circumstances, be uttered to reassure one's husband or wife that his or her lunch has not been forgotten?   *Yes / No*

(4) Could it, in a different situation, be used to incriminate a child who had raided the refrigerator?   *Yes / No*

(5) Are individual sentences generally identifiable with single specific acts that are carried out by uttering them?   *Yes / No*

Feedback (1) Yes (2) Yes (3) Yes (4) Yes (5) No, one sentence can generally be uttered to perform a wide variety of different acts, depending on who utters it and where, when, and why it is uttered.

Comment Quite contrary to the popular belief that actions and words are entirely distinct, many actions can actually be performed with words. Now we will look at some actions, usually, but not always, involving human objects, that can be performed either by physical means, such as a gesture, or by making an appropriate utterance.

Practice (1) Can you congratulate someone by a pat on the back, or a hug?   *Yes / No*

(2) Can you congratulate someone by uttering 'Well done'?   *Yes / No*

(3) Can you bid at an auction by nodding?   *Yes / No*

(4) Can you bid at an auction by saying 'Eleven pounds'?   *Yes / No*

(5) Can you promise someone something by a nod?   *Yes / No*

(6) Can you promise someone something with an utterance beginning 'I promise . . .'?   *Yes / No*

Feedback (1)–(6) Yes

Comment A large number of acts, then, can be performed either by means of an utterance or by some other means. We have also seen two rather special kinds of acts that can only be performed by means of an utterance; these are the specifically linguistic acts of referring and asserting.

We will now spend a little time on an interesting distinction that can be made now that we have established the basic point that assertive utterances do not merely describe some state of affairs, but also carry out acts. This is the distinction between performative utterances (and sentences) and constative utterances (and sentences).

Definition A PERFORMATIVE utterance is one that actually describes the act that it performs, i.e. it PERFORMS some act and SIMULTANEOUSLY DESCRIBES that act.

Example 'I promise to repay you tomorrow' is performative because in saying it the speaker actually does what the utterance describes, i.e. he promises to repay the hearer the next day. That is, the utterance both describes and is a promise.

By contrast, the utterance 'John promised to repay me tomorrow', although it describes a promise, is not itself a promise. So this utterance does not simultaneously do what it describes, and is therefore not a performative.

Practice (1) If I say to you, 'I warn you not to come any closer', do I, by so saying, actually perform the act of warning you not to come any closer?   *Yes / No*

(2) Does the utterance 'I warn you not to come any closer'
     describe an act of warning by the speaker?   *Yes / No*

(3) Is the utterance 'I warn you not to come any closer' a
     performative utterance?   *Yes / No*

(4) If Sam says to Rachel, 'I admit that I took 50p from the coffee
     money', does he, by so saying, actually perform the act of
     admitting that he took the money?   *Yes / No*

(5) And does Sam's utterance describe an act of admission?   *Yes / No*

(6) Is 'I admit that I took 50p from the coffee money'
     performative?   *Yes / No*

(7) If someone says, 'I'm trying to get this box open with a
     screwdriver', does that utterance itself constitute an act of
     trying to open a box with a screwdriver?   *Yes / No*

(8) Is 'I'm trying to get this box open with a screwdriver'
     performative?   *Yes / No*

Feedback   (1) Yes (2) Yes (3) Yes (4) Yes (5) Yes (6) Yes (7) No, although it does
           describe such an act. (8) No

Comment   Opposed to performative utterances are constative utterances. These can be
          defined very simply.

Definition   A CONSTATIVE utterance is one which makes an ASSERTION (i.e. it is
             often the utterance of a declarative sentence) but is NOT performative.

Example   'I'm trying to get this box open with a screwdriver' is a constative utterance,
          because it makes an assertion about a particular state of affairs, but is not
          performative, i.e. the utterance does not simultaneously describe and
          perform the same act.

Practice   Are the following utterances performative (*P*) or constative (*C*)?

           (1) 'I name this ship Hibernia'   *P / C*

           (2) 'I believe in the dictatorship of the Proletariat' *P / C*

           (3) 'I admit I was hasty'   *P / C*

           (4) 'I think I was wrong'   *P / C*

           (5) 'I hereby inform you that you are sacked'   *P / C*

           (6) 'I give you supper every night'   *P / C*

Feedback   (1) P (act of naming) (2) C (only describes belief) (3) P (act of admission)
           (4) C (only describes mental state) (5) P (act of informing) (6) C (only
           describes a state of affairs)

Comment You will have noticed that many performative utterances contain the 1st person pronoun 'I', followed by a certain type of verb in the present tense. E.g. 'I promise . . ', 'I admit . . ', 'I congratulate . . ', etc. These are all verbs which describe speech acts. We classify them as performative verbs.

Definition A PERFORMATIVE VERB is one which, when used in a simple positive present tense sentence, with a 1st person singular subject, can make the utterance of that sentence performative.

Example *Sentence* is a performative verb because, for example, 'I sentence you to be hanged by the neck' is a performative utterance.

Punish is not a performative verb because, for example, 'I punish you' is not a performative utterance.

Practice Are the following performative verbs, or not?

(1)	*apologize*	Yes / No
(2)	*authorize*	Yes / No
(3)	*argue*	Yes / No
(4)	*condemn*	Yes / No
(5)	*squeal*	Yes / No

Feedback (1) Yes (2) Yes (3) No (4) Yes (5) No

Comment Note that although all of the above verbs describe acts carried out in speech, they are not therefore necessarily performative. Thus although I can argue with you verbally, simply saying 'I argue' does not of itself constitute an argument. On the other hand, simply saying 'I warn you' is of itself enough to administer a warning.

Naturally enough, there are some borderline cases, in which it is hard to say whether some particular verb is, or is not, performative. Many good examples of performative verbs occur in standardized and stereotyped formulae used in public ceremonies, such as *pronounce* in 'I pronounce you man and wife' in a marriage ceremony.

Practice Think of three or more examples of performative verbs used in the formulae of conventionalized public and social occasions.

....

....

Feedback *name* (e.g. 'I name this ship Titanic'); *baptize*; *object* (e.g. 'I object, your Honour'); *declare* (e.g. 'I declare this bridge open'); *plead* (e.g. 'I plead Not Guilty')

Comment   As noted above, performative utterances contain a performative verb, and
many have 1st person singular subjects and are in the present tense. But
there are exceptions to this pattern.

Practice   Some of the following utterances are exceptions to the statement that
all performative utterances have 1st person singular subjects. Which
utterances are the exceptions? (Indicate your answer by underlining the
exceptions.)

(1) 'You are hereby forbidden to leave this room'

(2) 'All passengers on flight number forty-seven are requested to proceed to
gate ten'

(3) 'I suggest that you see a psychiatrist as soon as possible'

(4) 'This ship is called Titanic'

(5) 'We thank you for the compliment you have paid us'

Feedback   (1) exception, because performative, but with a 2nd person subject (2)
exception, because performative but with 3rd person plural subject (3) not
an exception (4) not an exception, because not performative (5) exception,
because performative but with 1st person plural subject

Comment   Although most performative utterances have 1st person singular subjects,
there are exceptions. In fact, the most reliable test to determine whether an
utterance is performative is to insert the adverbial word *hereby* immediately
before the verb and see if the modified utterance is acceptable.

Practice   Can *hereby* be acceptably inserted in the space indicated in the following
utterances?

(1) 'I ( ) give notice that I will lock these doors in sixty seconds'   *Yes / No*

(2) 'Listeners are ( ) reminded that BBC wireless licences expire
on April 4th'   *Yes / No*

(3) 'It ( ) gives me great pleasure to open this building'   *Yes / No*

(4) 'I ( ) warn you not to talk to my sister again'   *Yes / No*

(5) 'I ( ) believe in God the Father Almighty, Creator of Heaven
and Earth'   *Yes / No*

Feedback   (1) Yes (2) Yes (3) No (4) Yes (5) No

Comment   If a sentence can be accompanied by *hereby* without seeming odd, then
the utterance of that sentence (in normal circumstances) constitutes a
performative utterance.

Practice   Indicate whether the following sentences are odd or not odd.

(1) *I hereby warn you that you will fail*   *Odd / Not odd*

(2) *They hereby warn her that she will fail*   *Odd / Not odd*

(3) *I hereby promised him that I would be at the station at*
     three o'clock   *Odd / Not odd*

(4) *The management hereby warn customers that mistakes*
     in change cannot be rectified once the customer has left
     the counter   *Odd / Not odd*

(5) *Spitting is hereby forbidden*   *Odd / Not odd*

(6) *I hereby sing*   *Odd / Not odd*

Feedback   (1) Not odd (2) Odd (3) Odd (4) Not odd (5) Not odd (6) Odd

Summary   Words and sentences when uttered are used to do things, to carry out
           socially significant acts, in addition to merely describing aspects of the
           world. The notion of a performative illustrates this point in some rather
           special cases.
               In subsequent units, we will analyse in more detail the various
           characteristics of speech acts. (The original developer of modern theories
           of speech acts was the Oxford philosopher J.L. Austin.)

Unit 21 Study Guide and Exercises

Directions After you have read Unit 21 you should be able to tackle the following
           questions to test your understanding of the main ideas raised in the unit.

1 You should understand these terms and concepts from this unit:

   speech acts   performative utterance
   act of referring   constative utterance
   act of assertion   performative verb
   descriptive fallacy

2 Explain what it means to say that actions and words are not entirely
   distinct. Give an example.

3 What does it mean to say that actions can be performed with words
   (i.e. with an utterance)? What are such acts called?

4 For each of the following utterances state one or two purposes that the
   speaker may have had in mind when uttering them. Explain how such
   utterances exemplify the **descriptive fallacy**.
   a 'The car is dirty.'
   b 'Is it right to allow skateboarding on our sidewalks?'
   c 'Look at the mess you just made!'
   d 'Some of the pages have been torn out.'

5   Try to identify the kind(s) of acts mentioned in your answer to question 4 above (such as warning, requesting, ordering, complaining, apologizing, etc.).

6   Identify whether the following utterances are **performative** or **constative**. If an utterance is performative, describe the act being performed, as well as the act being described.
  a 'I order you to pay the bill.'
  b 'I pronounce you man and wife.'
  c 'I promise to drop by tomorrow.'
  d 'The minister pronounced them man and wife.'
  e 'I promised to drop by tomorrow.'
  f 'I sweep the floor every Tuesday.'
  g 'I believe you were wrong.'

7   Identify which of the following is a performative verb and use it in a sentence as a performative. Use the *hereby* test to help you make your decision. Think of three additional performative verbs not listed here, and also use them performatively in a sentence.
  a declare   e write
  b warn   f approve ('to OK something')
  c think   g remind
  d promise   h consider

8   Performative verbs follow certain conventions. What are they? Are there exceptions? Give an example or two of each.

9   Identify which of the following utterances are performative. Also identify the utterances which are **exceptions** to the conventions you mentioned in the answer to the previous question. Explain why they are exceptions.
  a 'Students are asked to keep noise to a minimum.'
  b 'You are hereby allowed to enter the vault.'
  c 'You must enter quietly.'
  d 'We apologize for our mistake.'
  e 'I admit that I made a mistake.'
  f 'The text was written by two authors.'
  g 'Wearing hats inside is forbidden.'

10 Why do we talk about **utterances** being performative (rather than sentences or propositions)?

UNIT 22 PERLOCUTIONS AND ILLOCUTIONS

Entry requirements SPEECH ACTS (Unit 21). If you feel you understand this idea, take the entry test below. Otherwise, review Unit 21.

Entry test (1) Which of the following acts can be performed through the use of language? Underline your choices.

kicking, asserting, warning, promising, running, referring, insulting

(2) Which of the following statements is correct? Circle your choice.
  (a) There are no acts which can be performed either linguistically (e.g. with an utterance) or non-linguistically (e.g. with a gesture).
  (b) There are no acts which cannot be performed linguistically.
  (c) Some acts can be performed either linguistically or non-linguistically.

(3) Can the same sentence be uttered on different occasions to perform different acts?   *Yes / No*

(4) Is the sentence *I hereby command you to teach first-year Semantics* performative (*P*), constative (*C*), or neither (*N*)?   *P / C / N*

Feedback (1) asserting, warning, promising, referring, insulting (2) (c) (3) Yes
(4) P
If you got at least 3 out of 4 correct, continue to the introduction. Otherwise, review Unit 21.

Introduction In Unit 21 we made the point that a part of the meaning of an utterance is what that utterance does. This kind of meaning is essentially different from, and adds a new dimension to, the kind of meaning associated with declarative sentences by semantic theories of sense relations and logic. The view of meaning as involving acts also leads away from the emphasis placed by theories of sense relations and logic on truth. In this unit we shall begin to explore these consequences of the speech act view of meaning.

Comment The study of sense relations and logic has concentrated almost exclusively on the meaning of only one type of sentence, i.e. declaratives. Actually, attempts have been made recently to extend logic to cover imperatives and interrogatives, but these suggestions have not been generally accepted as identifying the correct way to analyse non-declaratives. In this unit we will begin to show how the notion of speech acts could provide a link between the senses of declarative and non-declarative sentences.

To start with, imperative and interrogative sentences, when uttered, clearly perform acts, just as declaratives do.

Practice (1) Could the utterance 'Don't come a step nearer!' be an act of warning? *Yes / No*

(2) Could the utterance 'Get lost' be an act of dismissing? *Yes / No*

(3) Could the utterance 'Why don't you try looking in Woolworths?' be an act of making a suggestion? *Yes / No*

(4) Could the utterance 'Do you think I'm an idiot?' be an act of rejecting a suggestion? *Yes / No*

(5) Just as the linguistic act of asserting can be seen as typifying utterances of declarative sentences, what linguistic act typifies interrogative utterances, i.e. what act is typically performed by uttering an interrogative sentence?

....

(6) And, similarly, what act is most typically carried out by an imperative utterance?

....

Feedback (1) Yes (2) Yes (3) Yes (4) Yes (5) the act of asking a question (6) the act of ordering someone to do something

Comment These answers show that the speech act approach to meaning promises a unified account of the utterance of sentences of all types, declarative, interrogative, and imperative. All perform acts of some kind or other. And, furthermore, sentences of each type, when uttered, tend to carry out typical linguistic acts. The pattern is summarized in the chart below. The very names of the sentence types (declarative, interrogative, and imperative) contain thinly disguised Latin allusions to the acts of asserting, asking, and ordering. So one might think that a straightforward matching of sentence types to acts was all that was needed to account for this aspect of meaning. But a little thought shows that this simple scheme will not work. Language is used in more complicated ways.

Sentence type	Typical linguistic act performed by uttering a sentence of this type
declarative	asserting
interrogative	asking
imperative	ordering

Practice In the following situation, does the act carried out by the utterance seem to be primarily one of asserting, asking, or ordering? In each case, note the sentence type, whether declarative, interrogative, or imperative. We have done the first one for you.

(1) Lady at ticket office in railway station: 'I'd like a day return to Morecambe, please'

Sentence type: declarative   *Act:*   requesting or ordering

(2) Speaker at a meeting on a hot political issue: 'Is it right to condone thuggery?'

Sentence type: ....   *Act:* ....

(3) The Duke of Omnium, to his butler, who sees to his every need: 'It's cold in here, Hives'

Sentence type: ....   *Act:* ....

(4) To companion on a country walk, while climbing a fence: 'My skirt is caught on the barbed wire'

Sentence type: ....   *Act:* ....

(5) Biology teacher: 'Note that the female cell has two X-shaped chromosomes'

Sentence type: ....   *Act:* ....

(6) Mother to child who is eating untidily: 'Look at the mess you've made under your chair'

Sentence type: ....   *Act:* ....

Feedback (2) interrogative; asserting (= 'It is not right') (3) declarative; ordering (= 'close the window') (4) declarative; requesting or ordering (= 'Please help me') (5) imperative; asserting (= 'The female cell has two X-shaped chromosomes') (6) imperative; asserting (= 'You've made a mess')

Comment Obviously the simple matching of acts with sentence types has plenty of exceptions, and we need to develop a more subtle theory than that given in the table. So far, we have been rather crude in our labelling of acts, as assertions, warnings, threats, etc. More careful distinctions need to be made between various different types of speech act, in order to begin to make sense of this area of meaning. We now introduce the technical distinction between perlocutionary act and illocutionary act.

Definition The PERLOCUTIONARY ACT (or just simply the PERLOCUTION) carried out by a speaker making an utterance is the act of causing a certain effect on the hearer and others.

271

Example If I say 'There's a hornet in your left ear', it may well cause you to panic, scream and scratch wildly at your ear. Causing these emotions and actions of yours is the perlocution of my utterance, or the perlocutionary act I perform by making that utterance.

Comment The perlocution of an utterance is the causing of a change to be brought about, perhaps unintentionally, through, or by means of, the utterance (Latin *per* 'through, by means of'). The point of carefully distinguishing the perlocutionary aspect of the speech act from others is that perlocutions can often be accidental, and thus bear a relatively unsystematic relationship to any classification of sentence types.

Practice Describe at least two possible perlocutionary effects of each of the utterances in the following situations. We have done the first one for you.

(1) Neighbour to recently bereaved widow: 'I was so sorry to hear about your loss'

Possible effect: Awareness of her grief floods back into hearer's mind and she begins to weep. Another possible effect: Hearer, expecting the utterance, gives a prepared reply: 'Thank you. It was a shock, but I must get used to it.'

(2) Lecturer to student: 'You'll find the book on Swahili infinitives quite fascinating'

....

....

....

(3) Child to playground supervisor: 'Miss, Billy just swore at me. He told me to piss off'

....

....

....

(4) One chess player to another: 'I just made a bad move'

....

....

....

(5) Policeman to man in street: 'Good evening, Sir. Do you live around here?'

....

....

....

Feedback (2) The student is amused at the lecturer's enthusiastic naivety *or* the student is annoyed at what he takes to be obvious sarcasm *or* nothing: the student hasn't heard the utterance. (3) The playground supervisor is shocked at Billy's bad language and goes to reprimand him *or* she tells the child to go away and sort out his own problems with Billy. (4) The other player wonders quietly whether his opponent is trying to lull him into a false sense of security *or* whether he really is now in an advantageous position *or* the other player realizes his opponent has indeed made a mistake, grunts unchivalrously, and captures his opponent's queen. (5) The man says, aggressively: 'It's none of your business' and walks on *or* the man says, embarrassed: 'Yes, I suppose you're wondering what I'm doing with this brick.'

Comment It is important to remember that the perlocutionary acts involved in examples such as these are not the effects of the original utterances. Rather, the perlocutionary act involved in making an utterance is that part of the total act which causes such effects. We will return to this point later. Meanwhile, we move to the notion of illocutionary act.

Definition The ILLOCUTIONARY ACT (or simply the ILLOCUTION) carried out by a speaker making an utterance is the act viewed in terms of the utterance's significance within a conventional system of social interaction. One way to think about the illocutionary act is that it reflects the intention of the speaker in making the utterance in the first place. Illocutions are acts defined by social conventions, acts such as accosting, accusing, admitting, apologizing, challenging, complaining, condoling, congratulating, declining, deploring, giving permission, giving way, greeting, leavetaking, mocking, naming, offering, praising, promising, proposing marriage, protesting, recommending, surrendering, thanking, toasting.

Example Saying: 'I'm very grateful to you for all you have done for me' performs the illocutionary act of thanking, which appears to be the speaker's intention in making the utterance.

Practice Selecting your answers from the list of illocutions given in the above definition, say what illocutionary acts are performed by the following utterances, assuming normal circumstances.

(6) 'Would you like a cup of coffee?'

....

(7) 'After you' (said to someone wishing to go through the same door as the speaker)

....

(8) 'I'm awfully sorry I wasn't at the meeting this morning'

....

(9) 'You can play outside for half an hour'

....

(10) 'Good evening'

....

(11) 'Good night'

....

Feedback | (6) offering (7) giving way (8) apologizing (9) giving permission (10) greeting (and sometimes, but not often, leavetaking) (11) leavetaking (not greeting)

Comment | As a further indication of the notion of illocutionary act, we contrast it with that of perlocutionary act. The perlocution of an utterance is often quite different from its illocution. We can see this using the last two sets of examples again.

Practice | In questions (2)–(5), on p. 272, you were asked to suggest perlocutionary effects for given utterances. Now state the illocution of each of those utterances, selecting from the list given in the above definition, and assuming normal circumstances.

(1) ....

(2) ....

(3) ....

(4) ....

(5) ....

In questions (6)–(11) on pp. 273–4, you were asked for the illocutions of certain utterances. Now suggest a possible perlocution for each. Use the same general form of words for each answer, i.e. begin with 'Causing the hearer to . . .'

(6) ....

....

(7) ....

....

(8) ....

....

(9) ....

....

(10) ....

....

(11) ....

....

Feedback (1) condoling (2) recommending (3) complaining (4) admitting (5) accosting (6) e.g. causing the hearer to start suddenly, as she had not realized anybody else was in the room (7) e.g. causing the hearer to smile, bow, extend his hand, and say 'No, after you' (8) e.g. causing the hearer to lift his eyes heavenwards, and 'tut' disgustedly (9) e.g. causing the hearer to race out of the room, picking up his football on the way (10) e.g. causing the hearer to reply 'Good evening' (11) e.g. causing the hearer to smile and wonder why the speaker is being so polite

Comment Illocutionary acts form a kind of social coinage, a complicated currency with specific values, by means of which speakers manipulate, negotiate, and interact with other speakers. To continue the metaphor, social encounters involve the exchange of illocutions.

Example speaker A: 'Hello' (greeting)
speaker B: 'Hello' (greeting)
speaker A: 'You took the last biscuit' (accusation)
speaker B: 'No, I didn't' (denial)

Practice Do each of the following pairs of illocutions seem appropriate sequences (*Yes*) or not (*No*)?

(1) greeting – greeting		*Yes / No*
(2) accusation – denial		*Yes / No*
(3) greeting – denial		*Yes / No*
(4) protest – apology		*Yes / No*
(5) congratulation – apology		*Yes / No*
(6) compliment – leavetaking		*Yes / No*

Feedback   (1) Yes (2) Yes (3) No (4) Yes (5) No (6) No

Practice   Consider again the following example:

Utterance: 'Would you like a cup of coffee?'

Illocutionary act: Offering

Perlocutionary act: (e.g.) causing the hearer to think the speaker is more generous than he thought

(1) Is the illocutionary act something the speaker intends to
    do in making the utterance?   *Yes / No*

(2) Is the perlocutionary act something the speaker intends
    to do in making the utterance?   *Yes / No*

(3) Is it evident what illocutionary act has been performed
    (in this case offering) as soon as the utterance is made?   *Yes / No*

(4) Is it evident what perlocutionary act has been performed
    as soon as the utterance is made?   *Yes / No*

(5) Is the illocutionary act performed something that is
    within the full control of the speaker?   *Yes / No*

(6) Is the perlocutionary act performed something that is
    within the full control of the speaker?   *Yes / No*

Feedback   (1) Yes (2) sometimes, perhaps, but by no means always (3) Yes (4) No
            (5) Yes (6) No

Comment   Generally speaking, the illocutionary act inherent in an utterance is intended
            by the speaker, is under his full control, and if it is evident, it is so as the
            utterance is made, whereas the perlocutionary act performed through an
            utterance is not always intended by the speaker, is not under his full control,
            and is usually not evident until after the utterance is made.
                It is much more usual to talk of a speaker 'trying' to carry out a
            perlocutionary act (e.g. trying to amuse, or shock, or annoy someone) than it
            is to talk of a speaker 'trying' to carry out an illocutionary act (e.g. trying to
            apologize, or to offer someone something, or to complain about something).
            In the latter case, but not the former, there is the strong implication that one
            is being actually prevented from speaking. Because of these differences, it is
            possible in very many cases to classify acts as either illocutionary or
            perlocutionary.

Examples   The act of addressing someone is illocutionary because it is something that
            a speaker can decide for himself to do, and be sure of doing it when he
            decides to do it. The hearer (the addressee) in a speech situation cannot
            decide whether to be addressed or not (although he may ignore the fact

276

that he is being addressed, or possibly not realize that he is being addressed).

The act of persuading someone of something, on the other hand, is perlocutionary, because the speaker cannot be sure of persuading the hearer, no matter how hard he tries. The hearer can decide whether to be persuaded or not.

Practice Using the criteria just outlined, classify the following acts as either illocutionary (*I*) or perlocutionary (*P*).

(1) distracting someone   *I / P*

(2) claiming   *I / P*

(3) denying something   *I / P*

(4) hurting someone   *I / P*

(5) predicting something   *I / P*

(6) mocking someone   *I / P*

Feedback (1) P (2) I (3) I (4) P (5) I (6) I

Comment The existence of an unclear case, such as contradicting, which seems to have some features of an illocutionary act and some of a perlocutionary act, shows that the actual application of this distinction is somewhat fuzzy, but nevertheless, it is plain that for a large number of acts carried out in, or by, utterances, the distinction between illocution and perlocution is quite clear. The above practice and observations highlight the somewhat accidental and haphazard character of the relationship between sentences when uttered and perlocutionary acts.

Obviously there is more hope of being able to discover neat systematic relationships between speech acts and utterance types (and hence sentence types) if we concentrate on the illocutions of utterances, rather than on their perlocutions. In short, making the careful distinction between illocutionary acts and perlocutionary acts enables us to simplify the problem of relating speech to acts, by excluding (temporarily at least) perlocutionary acts. Accordingly, we concentrate in later units on the illocutions of utterances.

Finally, we introduce two further terms, 'phonic act' and 'propositional act'.

Definition The PHONIC ACT involved in an utterance is the physical act of making certain vocal sounds.

The PROPOSITIONAL ACT involved in an utterance consists in the mental acts of REFERRING (to certain objects or people in the world) and of PREDICATING (i.e. coupling predicates to referring expressions).

Practice   A parrot says 'Fire'

(1) Is a phonic act involved?   *Yes / No*

(2) Is a propositional act involved?   *Yes / No*

(3) Is an illocutionary act involved?   *Yes / No*

(4) Is a perlocutionary act involved?   *Yes / No*

Feedback   (1) Yes (2) No, a parrot doesn't understand the meaning of what it says.
(3) No (4) It could be, if someone didn't realize it was a parrot speaking,
and took the utterance seriously.

Summary   The simple notion of speech act, introduced in Unit 21, has been refined
by making the distinction between illocutions and perlocutions. Our
attention in subsequent units will be directed exclusively to illocutionary
acts, and we shall make some further distinctions between types of
illocutions.

Unit 22   Study Guide and Exercises

Directions   After you have read Unit 22 you should be able to tackle the following
questions to test your understanding of the main ideas raised in the unit.

1 You should understand these terms and concepts from this unit:

declarative sentence   perlocutionary act (perlocution)
interrogative sentence   illocutionary act (illocution)
imperative sentence   phonic act
propositional act

2 What basic kinds of acts are typically performed by the utterance of
declarative, interrogative, and imperative sentences, respectively?

3 For each of the following situations, identify both the **sentence type** of the
utterance and the **act carried out** by the utterance (from among asserting,
asking, or ordering).

a Father to his son: 'The car is dirty.'

b Irate citizen to the city council: 'Is it right to allow skateboarding on our
sidewalks?'

c Mother to small child: 'Look at the mess you just made!'

d Student to a friend on a windy day: 'Some of my papers have blown
away.'

e Photographer to a client: 'Stand right there and say cheese!'

f Student to a teacher: 'What is the correct answer to question 2?'

g Student to a teacher: 'I had trouble with question 2.'

h Teacher to a student: 'Question 2 has not yet been answered.'

4 What basic principle is exemplified by data like that in question 3 above?

5 Make sure you understand the difference between **perlocutionary** and **illocutionary** acts.

6 Identify some of the possible **perlocutionary** effects of each utterance given in question 3 above. Must such effects necessarily follow with the utterance of the sentences involved, or are they accidental? Then do the same for the following additional utterances.

    a Policeman to a loiterer: 'I'm afraid you'll have to move on.'

    b Parent to a child: 'It's time for bed now.'

    c Teacher to a student: 'You're going to flunk math.'

    d Doctor to a patient: 'You have only 3 minutes to live.'

    e Auto mechanic to car owner: 'I'll have to replace the engine.'

    f Auto mechanic to car owner: 'There's nothing wrong with your car, so there'll be no charge.'

    g Sales clerk to customer: 'This coat costs £900.'

    h Official to contest winner: 'You just won £5,000,000!'

7 Identify the **illocutionary** act performed by uttering each of the following (you may want to consult the list given in this unit):

    a 'Could you pass the salt?' (Would 'Yes' be an appropriate answer?)

    b 'I'm afraid the cake didn't turn out too well.'

    c 'What a despicable movie!'

    d 'I've had enough to drink for now.'

    e 'But there are too many books to read in this class!'

    f 'You have written a beautiful critique of the problem.'

    g 'I don't see any way out of this trap, Darth Vader.'

    h 'Hi, how are things going?'

8 Now go back to question 6 and state the **illocution** of each utterance there, then go back to question 7 and suggest a few possible **perlocutions** for each utterance there.

9 Which of the following pairs of illocutions seem to be appropriate sequences? For those which are appropriate, make up a pair of utterances which exemplify them.

    a offering – declining

    b praising – thanking

    c congratulation – toasting

    d congratulation – declining

    e accosting – condoling

    f accusing – admitting

    g leavetaking – mocking

    h deploring – agreeing

10 Classify the following acts as either **illocutionary (I)** or **perlocutionary (P)**.

a persuading someone   f irritating someone

b bothering someone   g pleasing someone

c apologizing to someone   h protesting to someone

d upsetting someone   i helping someone

e accosting someone   j impressing someone

11 Why do linguistic semanticists concentrate on illocutionary acts rather than perlocutionary acts?

UNIT 23 FELICITY CONDITIONS

Entry requirements SPEECH ACT (Unit 21) and ILLOCUTION (Unit 22). If you feel you are familiar with the notions explained in the above units, take the entry test below. If not, review the relevant unit.

Entry test Answer the following questions:

(1) Name three performative verbs.

    ....

(2) Complete the following definition:
     A performative utterance is one that .... some act and

     .... that act.

(3) Note down the sentence type and the main illocutionary act performed in the following utterances.
     (a) Man in pet shop: 'Is that parrot expensive?'

          Sentence type: ....   *Act*: ....
     (b) Teacher to class: 'I don't want to hear noise at the back of the class'

          Sentence type: ....   *Act*: ....
     (c) Man helping a blind man across a road: 'Watch the step'

          Sentence type: ....   *Act*: ....
     (d) Man in argument: 'Do you take me for a fool?'

          Sentence type: ....   *Act*: ....

Feedback (1) *promise, beg, admit*, etc. (2) A performative utterance is one that describes some act and simultaneously performs that act.
(3) (a) interrogative; enquiry (b) declarative; command (c) imperative; warning (d) interrogative; assertion
If you have more than one wrong answer, you should review Units 21 and 22. Otherwise, continue to the introduction.

Introduction So far, we have outlined a way of looking at speech as action. Utterances can be seen as significant acts on a social level, e.g. accusations, confessions, denials, greetings, etc. The question we now pose is: by what system do speakers know when such social moves are appropriate? That is, in what circumstances are illocutions used? A further technical notion, that of felicity

281

condition, needs to be introduced in order to give a plausible answer to this question.

Definition The FELICITY CONDITIONS of an illocutionary act are conditions that must be fulfilled in the situation in which the act is carried out if the act is to be said to be carried out properly, or felicitously.

Examples One of the felicity conditions for the illocutionary act of ordering is that the speaker must be superior to, or in authority over, the hearer. Thus, if a servant says to the Queen 'Open the window', there is a certain incongruity, or anomalousness, or infelicity in the act (of ordering) carried out, but if the Queen says 'Open the window' to the servant, there is no infelicity.

A felicity condition for the illocutionary act of accusing is that the deed or property attributed to the accused is wrong in some way. Thus one can felicitously accuse someone of theft or murder, but normally only infelicitously of, say, being a nice guy, or of helping an old lady to cross the road.

Practice Given below are illocutionary acts, and for each act there are four suggested felicity conditions. In each case only two of the felicity conditions are actually correct. Indicate the correct felicity conditions by circling your choices.

(1) promising:
  (a) The speaker must intend to carry out the thing promised.
  (b) The speaker must be inferior in status to the hearer.
  (c) The thing promised must be something that the hearer wants to happen.
  (d) The thing promised must be morally wrong.

(2) apologizing:
  (a) The speaker must be responsible for the thing apologized for.
  (b) The thing apologized for must be (or must have been) unavoidable.
  (c) The thing apologized for must be morally wrong.
  (d) The hearer must not want the thing apologized for to happen (or to have happened).

(3) greeting:
  (a) The speaker and the hearer must be of different sex.
  (b) The speaker and the hearer must not be in the middle of a conversation.
  (c) The speaker must believe the hearer to have recently suffered a loss.
  (d) The speaker feels some respect and/or sense of community (however slight) with the hearer.

(4) naming:
  (a) The thing or person named must not already have a recognized name known to the speaker.

    (b) The speaker must be recognized by his community as having authority to name.

    (c) The thing or person named must belong to the speaker.

    (d) The thing or person named must be held in considerable respect by the community.

(5) protesting:

    (a) The speaker and the hearer must have recently been in conflict with each other.

    (b) The speaker must disapprove of the state of affairs protested at.

    (c) The state of affairs protested at must be disapproved of by the community generally.

    (d) The hearer must be held to be responsible (by the speaker) for the state of affairs protested at.

Feedback (1) (a), (c) (2) (a), (d) (3) (b),(d) (4) (a), (b) (5) (b), (d) (Some of the analyses given here may be debatable. You may debate them with your instructors and fellow-students.)

Comment In other units (13 and 14) we have mentioned the notion of truth conditions. Truth conditions are conditions that must be satisfied by the world if an utterance (of a declarative sentence) is true. For example, the utterance 'There is a cat on the table' is only true if in the world at the time of the utterance there actually is a table with a cat on it. Correspondingly, felicity conditions are conditions that must be satisfied by the world if an illocutionary act is felicitous (or 'appropriate').

Practice Label the illocutionary acts in the following situations felicitous or infelicitous, applying normal everyday criteria. In each case also name the illocutionary act concerned. We have done the first one for you.

(1)

Thanking. Infelicitous.
....

(2)

....

(3)

....

(4)

....

(5)

....

Feedback   (2) marrying; felicitous (3) reprimanding (telling off); infelicitous
(4) promising; infelicitous (5) dismissing, or giving permission;
infelicitous

Comment   These exercises bring out some similarities and differences between truth
conditions and felicity conditions. Another obvious difference between
them is that felicity conditions are of wider application than truth
conditions. Only declarative sentences may be true or false, but all types of
sentence, declarative, interrogative, and imperative, can be uttered to carry
out illocutionary acts that may be felicitous or infelicitous.

Practice   Name the illocutionary acts carried out in the following examples, and state
whether they are, as far as you can see, felicitous or infelicitous. In each case
state the sentence type involved.

(1)

....

(2)

....

(3)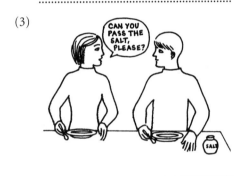

....

Feedback   (1) imperative; offering; infelicitous (2) imperative; ordering; infelicitous
(3) interrogative; requesting; felicitous

Comment   A good way of discovering the felicity conditions of an illocutionary act is
to imagine a situation in which a speaker carries out such an act, or attempts
to, but something in the situation makes the act 'misfire', or not come off
appropriately. For example, in question (1) above, the speaker is definitely
carrying out an act of offering a cigarette, but there is something odd, or
infelicitous, about the offer, as the hearer already has the cigarette. This shows
that one of the felicity conditions for the act of offering is that the hearer
must not already have the thing offered.

   Next, we will look at the case of a particular subtype of felicity condition,
namely sincerity conditions.

Definition   A SINCERITY CONDITION on an illocutionary act is a condition that must
be fulfilled if the act is said to be carried out SINCERELY, but failure to meet
such a condition does not prevent the carrying out of the act altogether.

285

Example   A sincerity condition on apologizing is that the apologizer believes that the thing apologized for is wrong in some way. Thus, if John enters a room at a certain time, believing that to do so is wrong in some way (e.g. impolite, tactless, sacrilegious) and he says 'I'm sorry to come in here at this moment', then he has apologized, and apologized sincerely. But if he says the same thing in the same circumstances, except that he does not believe that what he has done is wrong in any way, then he has still apologized, but insincerely.

Practice   (1) If Helen says to me 'Congratulations on passing your driving test', has she thereby congratulated me?   *Yes / No*

(2) If Helen, in the above scene, believes that I only got through my driving test by bribing the examiner, is her congratulation sincere?   *Yes / No*

(3) Is it a sincerity condition on congratulating that the speaker believe the thing on which he congratulates the hearer to be praiseworthy in some way?   *Yes / No*

(4) If I say 'I bet you can't beat my computer at chess', have I thereby carried out an act of challenging?   *Yes / No*

(5) But if I know that my computer has actually been programmed to lose at chess, is my challenge sincere?   *Yes / No*

(6) Is it a sincerity condition on challenging that the speaker believe that what he challenges the hearer to do is difficult in some way?   *Yes / No*

(7) Is it a sincerity condition on thanking that the speaker approve of the thing for which he thanks the hearer?   *Yes / No*

(8) Is it a sincerity condition on criticizing that the speaker approve of the thing he criticizes?   *Yes / No*

Feedback   (1) Yes (2) No (3) Yes (4) Yes (5) No (6) Yes (7) Yes (8) No

Comment   Some of these sincerity conditions were mentioned earlier as examples of felicity conditions generally, i.e. sincerity conditions are simply a special case of felicity conditions.

We have emphasized the difference between sentence meaning and utterance meaning, but of course there must be a linking relationship between them. The link exists through the capacity of languages to describe anything, including acts (like speech acts) which make use of language itself (i.e. language can be used as its own metalanguage). (A metalanguage is the language one uses to talk about a particular subject.)

Thus we find that almost any illocutionary act has a predicate word describing it. For example, the act of accusing is described by the English predicate *accuse*. The parallel is obvious. If an act is significant in a society (as illocutionary acts are), then it is not surprising that the society should have coined a word to describe it. Just as illocutionary acts can be described with English words and sentences, so can their felicity conditions.

There is an essential circularity that we are involved in when doing semantics. We want to formulate precise statements about utterance meaning, including statements about the felicity conditions on illocutionary acts, and we must do so in English (or some other language), using English words and sentences. But another concern of semantics is to make precise statements about the meanings of English words and sentences. Thus, for instance, formulating sincerity conditions helps us to form a precise picture of how utterance meaning works, but simultaneously it sheds light on the meaning of the word *sincere* itself.

Summary This unit has explored the notion of felicity conditions, including that of sincerity condition. The notion of felicity condition will be made use of in the next unit. We have also mentioned an aspect of the relationship between utterance meaning and sentence meaning, a relationship which we will also explore further in later units.

Unit 23 Study Guide and Exercises

Directions After you have read Unit 23 you should be able to tackle the following questions to test your understanding of the main ideas raised in the unit.

1 You should understand these terms and concepts from this unit:
   felicity conditions
   sincerity conditions

2 List the felicity conditions for the following speech acts:
   a promising
   b admitting
   c declining
   d offering

3 Name the **illocutionary** acts involved in each of the following situations and label them as being either **felicitous** or **infelicitous** (assuming normal everyday criteria). Make sure you indicate why the act in question is either felicitous or infelicitous (i.e. say how it either agrees with or contradicts the felicity conditions for the act). Also state the sentence type involved.
   a Waiter to customer: 'I don't like this food!'
   b Contest official to winner: 'I'm sorry I gave you the prize money.'
   c Customer to waiter: 'I've had enough, thanks.'
   d Victor to the loser: 'I give up!'
   e Prospective picnicker to his friends: 'I promise to bring only stale food to the picnic.'

f One zoo worker to another: 'Can I carry that elephant for you?'

g A non-chessplayer to another: 'I bet I can beat you at chess.'

h Father to child: 'You can stay up another hour.'

4 What are some similarities and differences between **truth conditions** and **felicity conditions**? What does it mean to say that felicity conditions are of wider application than truth conditions?

5 Why are **sincerity conditions** classified as a subtype of felicity conditions (and not the other way around)? What is the difference between the two types of conditions?

6 Identify whether each of the following conditions given for a particular speech act is a **felicity** condition or a **sincerity** condition, and be able to explain why. If it is difficult to choose, try to explain why.

a apologizing: the thing apologized for must have been unavoidable

b apologizing: the speaker must be responsible for the thing apologized for

c accusing: the speaker must think that the person accused actually did the deed

d accusing: the speaker is aware that something bad, illegal, etc., has occurred

e offering: the hearer must not already have the thing that is offered

f offering: the speaker wants to give the thing offered to the hearer

g congratulating: the hearer has either accomplished something good, or something good has happened to her

h congratulating: the speaker thinks the event accomplished by the hearer is very good or noteworthy

i thanking: the hearer(s) must have done something on behalf of the speaker

j thanking: the speaker approves of what the hearer(s) did for her

7 Give a few sincerity conditions for the speech acts you provided felicity conditions for in question 2 above.

8 What sincerity condition(s) are likely to be present in the following utterances? Identify the type of illocutionary act, as well.

a 'I'm sorry to barge in like this.'

b 'Pass the grapes, please.'

c 'There are too many ants at this picnic!'

9 Does the lack of sincerity necessarily prevent the speech acts in question 8 from being carried out? Suppose, for example, that (b) were uttered to someone even if the speaker doesn't want the grapes, or that (c) were uttered by someone who loves ants.

10 At the end of this unit we discussed how sentence meaning and utterance meaning are linked, despite their differences. What is this link?

UNIT 24 DIRECT AND INDIRECT ILLOCUTIONS

Entry requirements ILLOCUTIONS (Unit 22) and FELICITY CONDITIONS (Unit 23). If you feel you understand these notions, take the entry test below. Otherwise, review the relevant unit.

Entry test (1) Consider the utterance 'Excuse me, you're standing on my dress'. In normal circumstances, which of the following statements about this utterance is true? Circle your choice.

(a) The perlocution of the utterance is an excuse.
(b) One of the illocutions of the utterance is an act of informing.
(c) The proposition of the utterance is an act of reminding.

(2) Which appears to be the more systematic, the relationship between utterances and their illocutions (*I*), or the relationship between utterances and their perlocutions (*P*)?   *I / P*

(3) Can an illocution normally be carried out unintentionally?   *Yes / No*

Are the following utterances, whose illocutions are requests, felicitous (*F*) or infelicitous (*I*) in normal circumstances?

(4) Bus passenger to another passenger, 'Would you mind opening the window slightly?'   *F / I*

(5) Hospital visitor to patient with arms in plaster, 'Pass the grapes, please'   *F / I*

(6) Which of the following is a felicity condition on requests?
(a) that the speaker be able to carry out the action described
(b) that the hearer be able to carry out the action described
(c) that the hearer want to carry out the action described

Feedback   (1) (b) (2) I (3) No (4) F (5) I (6) (b)
If you have scored less than 5 out of 6, you should review Units 22 and 23. Otherwise, continue to the introduction below.

Introduction The main problem we will concentrate on in this unit is that of trying to discover some systematic way of telling from the form of an uttered sentence what illocutionary act is performed in uttering it. There must be some such system, because language users are able to tell with great (though not total) reliability from the form of an uttered sentence what illocutionary act is performed.

Practice   According to the conventions of everyday usage, could the utterance, in a normal situation, of 'Would you like a cup of coffee?' be an act of:

(1) warning?
(2) thanking?
(3) apologizing?
(4) offering?
(5) enquiring?
(6) questioning?

Feedback   (1) No (2) No (3) No (4) Yes (5) Yes (6) Yes

Comment   English speakers generally agree about facts such as these. The interesting question is: HOW do English speakers extract from the specific words used in 'Would you like a cup of coffee?' the information that this utterance definitely is an act of offering, enquiring, and asking, and that it is not an act of thanking, warning, or apologizing? We pursue this question below, but one reservation should be mentioned straight away. This is that the facts are not always as clear as in the example just given. We will reinforce this point with some practice.

Practice   Do each of the following situations indicate a clear understanding on the part of both participants of what illocutionary acts are involved?

(1)	Factory inspector:	'I'll come back and see this machine tomorrow'	
	Foreman:	'Is that a threat or a promise?'	*Yes / No*
(2)	Amateur astrologer:	'I'm trying to cast your horoscope. Let's see, now – you were born under Aquarius'	
	Sceptic:	'Are you asking me or telling me?'	*Yes / No*
(3)	A:	'You deserve a trip to Alaska for what you've done'	
	B:	'You mean as a punishment, or as a reward?'	*Yes / No*

Feedback   (1) No (It is not clear to the hearer whether the illocution of the first utterance is a threat or a promise.) (2) No (similarly) (3) No (The first utterance could have the illocution of praising or deprecating.)

Comment   Despite the existence of such unclear cases, in which there may be doubt about what illocutionary act actually is carried out in an utterance, we shall concentrate on the clear cases as far as possible. Note that one utterance may have several illocutions at the same time.

Practice The utterances in the following examples actually carry out several illocutionary acts simultaneously. Give two illocutions in each case. We have done the first one for you.

(1) 'Can I remind everybody that we meet here again at 6 pm?'

Asking, reminding, and informing

(2) 'Can you pass the salt?'

....

(3) To a car salesman who has just mentioned a price of £950 for a car: 'O.K. I'll take it at that price'

....

(4) Young man in crowd addressed by the Prime Minister, shouting loudly: 'What are you going to do about the three million unemployed?'

....

(5) Shopgirl, handing over a packet of razor blades and two bars of soap: 'That will be 88p, please'

....

(6) Museum attendant, to visitor: 'I'm afraid we're closing now, Sir'

....

Feedback (2) asking, requesting (3) accepting, agreeing (4) protesting, asking (5) informing, requesting (6) apologizing, informing, requesting

Comment Now that we have seen that an utterance can have more than one illocution, it is useful to introduce the distinction between direct and indirect illocutions.

Definitions The DIRECT ILLOCUTION of an utterance is the illocution most directly indicated by a LITERAL reading of the grammatical form and vocabulary of the sentence uttered.

The INDIRECT ILLOCUTION of an utterance is any further illocution the utterance may have.

Example The direct illocution of 'Can you pass the salt?' is an enquiry about the hearer's ability to pass the salt. The indirect illocution is a request that the hearer pass the salt.

Practice Give the direct and indirect illocutions of the following utterances. We have done the first one for you.

(1) 'Why don't we go to Portugal this summer?'

Direct illocution: Asking why speaker and hearer do not (or will not)

go to Portugal

> Indirect illocution: Suggesting that the speaker and the hearer go to
>
> Portugal

(2) 'Let me say immediately that I endorse the chairman's ruling'

Direct illocution: ....

Indirect illocution: ....

(3) 'I believe you may have been looking for me'

Direct illocution: ....

Indirect illocution: ....

(4) 'I must ask you to leave'

Direct illocution: ....

Indirect illocution: ....

(5) 'Don't you think you ought to phone your mother?'

Direct illocution: ....

Indirect illocution: ....

Feedback (2) Direct: Ordering hearer to permit speaker to say . . .; Indirect: Endorsing chairman's ruling (3) Direct: Asserting that speaker believes hearer may have been looking for speaker; Indirect: Asking whether hearer has been looking for speaker (4) Direct: Asserting that speaker is obliged to ask hearer to leave; Indirect: Asking hearer to leave (5) Direct: Asking whether hearer thinks he ought to phone his mother; Indirect: Suggesting that hearer should phone his mother

Comment The difference between direct and indirect illocutions is seen through the fact that a pedantic or deliberately unhelpful reply can be given to an utterance which has both kinds of illocutions. For example, in reply to 'I must ask you to leave' one might say, thwarting the intentions of the first speaker: 'Must you?'

Practice Suggest pedantic, unhelpful, but literally correct, replies to the utterances in (2), (3), and (5) above, alongside more natural, helpful replies.

(2) Unhelpful: ....

Helpful: ....

(3) Unhelpful: ....

Helpful: ....

(5) Unhelpful: ....

Helpful: ....

Feedback (2) Unhelpful: 'No. You may not say that'; Helpful: 'Thank you for
your endorsement' (3) Unhelpful: 'Do you?'; Helpful: 'Yes. I have
been' (5) Unhelpful: 'Yes. I think I ought to'; Helpful: 'Yes. I'll do it
straight away'

Comment The notion of speakers being helpful in conversations is important and will
be developed in Unit 26. Returning now to our main theme, the search for a
correct statement of the systematic relationship between the form of an
uttered sentence and the illocution carried out in uttering it, it is clear that
for direct illocutions the relationship is quite straightforward. This follows
from our definition of direct illocution. (The straightforward facts can be
summarized as in the table given on p. 270.) The immediate task now facing
us is to try to find some systematic way of relating the indirect illocutions of
utterances to the direct illocutions. Put simply, the question facing us is this:
By what rules can a language user work out the indirect illocution of an
utterance from its direct illocution? For example, if you ask me if I can pass
the salt, how do I know that you are requesting me to pass the salt rather
than enquiring about my physical ability to pass it?

The notion of felicity condition, dealt with in the previous unit, turns out
to be crucial in answering this question.

Practice (1) Given below are four suggested felicity conditions for the act of
enquiring (or asking a question). Only two of them are actually correct.
Which two? Circle your choice.
(a) The hearer must believe that the speaker knows the answer to the
question.
(b) The hearer must not know the answer to the question.
(c) The speaker must believe that the hearer knows the answer to the
question.
(d) The speaker must not know the answer to the question.

(2) In normal everyday circumstances, is it reasonable to
assume that almost anyone one speaks to will be physically
capable of such a trivial act as picking up a salt-shaker
and passing it? *Yes / No*

(3) Given your answers to questions (1) and (2), if at a normal
everyday lunch table I say to you, 'Can you pass the salt?'
would it be reasonable to judge my utterance infelicitous
as an act of enquiring? *Yes / No*

(4) Is it one of the felicity conditions of the act of requesting
that the speaker must believe that the hearer is physically
able to do the thing that he (the hearer) is requested to do? *Yes / No*

(5) The direct way of requesting the salt is to say 'Please pass the salt'. 'Can you pass the salt?' is an indirect way of requesting it. Give three other utterances whose indirect illocution is a request for the salt.

....

....

Feedback   (1) (c), (d) (2) Yes (3) Yes (4) Yes (5) 'Would you mind passing the salt', 'I'd be grateful if you would pass the salt', 'Can I trouble you for the salt?'

Comment   The question 'Can you pass the salt?' overtly draws attention to one of the felicity conditions of the act of requesting. It is as if the speaker goes about getting the salt passed to him by carefully ensuring that the necessary preconditions for having his request granted are fulfilled. (Of course, the hearer will then usually cut the proceedings short by actually passing the salt.) From this example we can state the following approximate rule about direct and indirect illocutions.

Rule   Where the direct illocution of an utterance is deliberately infelicitous, the indirect illocution is an act to which the hearer's attention is drawn by mentioning one of its felicity conditions.

Comment   This rule is merely a suggestive beginning. It is by no means the whole story. For the rest of this unit, we will investigate in greater detail the possible methods by which speakers recognize the indirect illocutions of utterances. For this purpose, it has been found useful to classify all illocutionary acts into different categories, depending on the type of interaction between speaker and hearer that they bring about. Two classes of illocutionary acts that we shall mention are directives and commissives.

Definition   A DIRECTIVE act is any illocutionary act which essentially involves the speaker trying to get the hearer to behave in some required way.

Example   Ordering and suggesting are directive acts. Apologizing and promising are not.

Definition   A COMMISSIVE act is any illocutionary act which essentially involves the speaker committing himself to behave in some required way.

Example   Promising and swearing (in one sense) are commissive acts. Ordering and thanking are not.

Comment   There are other classes of illocution which we do not mention here. Thus thanking and apologizing, for example, do not belong to either of the groups that we have mentioned.

Practice Say whether the following acts are directive (*D*), commissive (*C*), or neither (*N*).

(1)	volunteering	*D / C / N*
(2)	advising	*D / C / N*
(3)	forbidding	*D / C / N*
(4)	accepting	*D / C / N*
(5)	requesting	*D / C / N*
(6)	congratulating	*D / C / N*
(7)	insulting	*D / C / N*
(8)	undertaking	*D / C / N*

Feedback (1) C (2) D (3) D (4) C (5) D (6) N (7) N (8) C

Comment Do not confuse the terms 'direct' and 'directive', which mean quite different kinds of things. The term 'direct' denotes how an illocution is carried out, i.e. whether directly or indirectly. The term 'directive' denotes the kind of act carried out, i.e. getting (directing) someone to do something. Thus there can be direct directives (e.g. 'Pass the salt') and indirect directives (e.g. 'Can you pass the salt?'). Naturally there can also be both direct and indirect commissives.

Practice Locate the following utterances (using their numbers) in the appropriate box on the following diagram.

	Directive	Commissive
Direct		
Indirect		

(1) 'Can I help you?' (offering)
(2) 'I could do with a drink'
(3) 'Stop'
(4) 'I promise to be there promptly'
(5) 'Go away'
(6) 'I would appreciate it if you went away'
(7) 'If you need me at any time, just call'

Feedback

3,5	4
2,6	1,7

Practice (1) Think of five or more examples of directive illocutionary acts.
(2) Think of three or more examples of commissive illocutionary acts.

Feedback (1) admonishing, appealing, begging, bidding (in an old-fashioned sense of *bid*), commanding, counselling, demanding, directing, enjoining, exhorting, imploring, insisting, instructing, inviting, pleading, urging, etc.

> (2) binding oneself, committing oneself, giving one's word, guaranteeing, offering, pledging, vowing

Comment Getting other people to do things and undertaking to do things oneself are two of the most important activities in maintaining the social fabric of our everyday lives. Society as we know it could not exist without the availability of a range of directive and commissive acts.

Asserting and questioning certain of the felicity conditions of a directive are (more or less polite and more or less reliable) ways of carrying out an indirect directive. We will look at the effects of asserting and questioning the general felicity condition on directives which concerns the hearer's ability to carry out the required action.

Practice (1) Could the utterance 'You can shut up' actually be a command to the hearer to shut up? *Yes / No*

(2) Could the utterance 'You can make me a cup of coffee while we're waiting for John' be a request? *Yes / No*

(3) Could the utterance 'You can try wrapping it in greaseproof paper' be a suggestion? *Yes / No*

(4) Could 'Can you shut up?' be a command? *Yes / No*

(5) Could 'Can you make me a cup of coffee while we're waiting for John?' be a request? *Yes / No*

(6) Could 'Can you try wrapping it in greaseproof paper?' be a suggestion? *Yes / No*

(7) Do these examples tend to show that asserting or questioning the hearer's ability to carry out an action are ways of achieving an (indirect) directive? *Yes / No*

Feedback (1) Yes (2) Yes (3) Yes (4) Yes (5) Yes (6) Yes (7) Yes

Practice Imagine that you are the first person mentioned in each of the situations below, and compose (a) an assertion of the hearer's ability to carry out the desired action and (b) an enquiry about the hearer's ability to carry out the desired action, each having an indirectly directive illocution. We have done the first one for you.

(1) Businessman wanting his secretary to tell callers he is out:

   (a) 'You can tell callers I'm out' ....

   (b) 'Can you tell callers I'm out?' ....

(2) Father who wants son to turn down his record player:

   (a) ....

   (b) ....

(3) Customer who wants a car salesman to show him a convertible:

(a) ....

(b) ....

(4) Wife who wants husband to unscrew a stiff lid on a jam jar:

(a) ....

(b) ....

Feedback (2) (a) 'You can turn that record player down' (b) 'Can you turn that record player down?' (3) (a) 'You can show me a convertible' (b) 'Can you show me a convertible?' (4) (a) 'You can get this lid off for me' (b) 'Can you get this lid off for me?'

Comment It must be said that there is something rather odd (perhaps excessively indirect) about the assertions (though not about the questions) in these cases. We will not try to analyse this difficulty.

So far we have concentrated on indirect directives. We will now look briefly at indirect commissives, seeing how they also can be achieved by various kinds of assertions and questions.

Practice (1) Can a monolingual English speaker felicitously volunteer to translate a Welsh TV programme? *Yes / No*

(2) Can a non-swimmer felicitously guarantee that he will swim to the rescue of any bather in difficulties at the beach? *Yes / No*

(3) In the case of directives an important felicity condition concerns the ability of the hearer to carry out the action concerned. In the case of commissives, is there a general felicity condition on the ability of the speaker to perform the action he commits himself to? *Yes / No*

(4) Write down an utterance asserting the speaker's ability to buy the hearer a packet of cigarettes.

....

(5) Write down an utterance questioning the speaker's ability to buy the hearer a packet of cigarettes.

....

(6) Could your answer to (4) be an offer? *Yes / No*

(7) Could it be a promise? *Yes / No*

(8) Could it be an act of volunteering? *Yes / No*

(9) Could your answer to (5) be an offer? *Yes / No*

(10) Could it be a promise?   *Yes / No*

(11) Could it be an act of volunteering?   *Yes / No*

Feedback (1) No (2) No (3) Yes (4) 'I can buy you a packet of cigarettes' (5) 'Can I buy you a packet of cigarettes?' (6) Yes (7) No (8) Possibly – the answer is unclear. (9) Yes (10) No (11) Again the answer is unclear.

Comment Asserting or questioning the speaker's ability to perform some action can give rise to a commissive illocution. But only some commissive illocutions (e.g. offers) can be conveyed in this indirect way. Promises, for instance, apparently cannot be so made. Presumably promises, being more solemn and binding than offers, require a more deliberate and explicit means of expression. Acts of volunteering seem to fall between offers and promises in the degree of directness they require.

We will, lastly, examine a few more examples of asserting and questioning the speaker's ability to perform some action, to check that this method of carrying out indirect commissives is general.

Practice (1) Give an utterance asserting the speaker's ability to lend the hearer £5.

....

(2) Give an utterance questioning the speaker's ability to lend the hearer £5.

....

(3) Give an utterance asserting the speaker's ability to work harder.

....

(4) Give an utterance questioning the speaker's ability to work harder.

....

(5) Could your answer to (1) have a commissive illocution of some kind (e.g. offer, vow, etc.)?   *Yes / No*

(6) Could your answer to (2) have a commissive illocution of some kind?   *Yes / No*

(7) Could your answer to (3) have a commissive illocution of some kind?   *Yes / No*

(8) Could your answer to (4) have a commissive illocution of some kind?   *Yes / No*

Feedback (1) 'I can lend you £5' (2) 'Can I lend you £5?' (3) 'I can work harder' (4) 'Can I work harder?' (5) Yes, some commissive illocutions, but not all (e.g. an offer but not a promise) (6) Yes, as for (5) (7) Yes, as for (5) (8) In this case, it's not clear whether a commissive act really can be carried out with this utterance.

Summary   In this unit we have introduced the distinction between direct and indirect illocutions, and have begun to explore the methods by which speakers and hearers can identify the indirect illocutions of utterances. We introduced two major types of illocution, namely directives and commissives, and saw how they can be carried out by asserting or questioning certain of their felicity conditions. Several of these concepts will be revisited in the next unit.

Unit 24 Study Guide and Exercises

Directions After you have read Unit 24 you should be able to tackle the following questions to test your understanding of the main ideas raised in the unit.

1 You should understand these terms and concepts from this unit:
direct illocution
indirect illocution
two types of illocutionary act:
  directive act
  commissive act

2 Give an example of an utterance (not in the book) that carries out several illocutionary acts simultaneously, and identify them. How can one utterance have more than one illocution at the same time?

3 Briefly describe the difference between **direct** and **indirect** illocutions.

4 Give the **direct** and **indirect** illocutions of the following utterances.
   a 'Can you hand me the butter?'
   b 'The car is dirty.'
   c 'When do you plan to dust your room?'
   d 'Maybe we could go to the movies.'
   e 'This place is really dusty.'
   f 'I'd like the salt.'
   g 'The sugar is over there.'
   h 'Let me be the first to say that I'm glad you're back.'
   i 'Don't you think we ought to leave?'
   j 'Why can't you take out the garbage?'
   k 'I could clobber you for that.'
   l 'You took the last cookie!'
   m 'I wish you would wash the car.'
   n 'Is it right to condone murder?'
   o 'Why don't you take out the garbage?'

5 Suggest unhelpful, pedantic (but literally correct) replies to each of the utterances in question 4 above, alongside more natural helpful ones. The

possibility of both types of reply gives evidence that both direct and indirect illocutions are involved.

6 How are we able to relate the indirect illocutions of utterances to their direct illocutions – i.e. how are we able to figure out an utterance's indirect illocution(s) from its direct illocution? What previously studied notion plays a crucial role in this relationship? Be sure you fully understand this (the main point of the unit).

7 Give one or two additional utterances that have the same indirect illocutions as each of the utterances in question 4 above.

8 Briefly describe the difference between **directive** and **commissive** acts. What (if anything) do they have in common? Give several examples of each type (from the book if you like), and explain briefly why they belong to each type.

9 Why are such speech acts as apologizing, thanking, congratulating, insulting, etc. not examples of either directive or commissive acts? Can you think of additional types of speech acts which also do not fall into either of these two categories?

10 Classify the following acts as either **directive, commissive**, or neither, and be ready to explain your choice.

a	pledging	g	giving permission
b	accosting	h	surrendering
c	accusing	i	declining
d	imploring	j	praising
e	complaining	k	protesting
f	inviting	l	recommending

11 Classify the following utterances as belonging to one of the following categories: **direct** or **indirect directives**, **direct** or **indirect commissives**. For the indirect acts explain which felicity conditions are invoked.
   a 'Put on this sweater.'
   b 'It would be a good idea for you to stay here.'
   c 'I'll volunteer to feed the tiger.'
   d 'Could I get you a drink?'
   e 'Send back that package.'
   f 'I don't think I'll be able to go with you.'
   g 'Why don't you put on this sweater?'
   h 'Could you give me the answer?'
   i 'I accept your challenge.'

12 Comment on the importance of **directive** and **commissive** acts in our everyday lives. Would it be possible for us to get along without them?

13 Imagine you are the first person mentioned in each situation below, and compose (a) an assertion of the hearer's ability to carry out the desired action and (b) an enquiry about the hearer's ability to carry out the action. In each case you will have constructed an utterance with the illocutionary force of an indirect directive.
    a Professor asking the departmental secretary to take his calls
    b Parent who wants her child to wash the car
    c Person who wants help in lifting a heavy object

14 We noted that only some commissive illocutions can be conveyed indirectly by asserting or questioning the speaker's ability to perform the action. Thus it is possible to make an indirect offer by saying 'Can I get/offer you a cup of coffee?', but this utterance cannot be interpreted as an indirect promise, and you also can't say '*Can I promise you a cup of coffee?' (at least not with the force of an indirect promise). We suggested this is because a promise, in being more solemn and binding than an offer, requires a more direct means of expression (while volunteering is somewhere in-between). Consider now the commissive illocutionary acts you identified in question 10 above, as well as vowing, undertaking, guaranteeing, and decide whether each follows the pattern of promising, offering, volunteering, with respect to being able to be conveyed indirectly. Does our explanation above for promising account for these commissive acts, too?

15 The meaning of an individual predicate plays a role in whether it can acceptably be used to convey an indirect illocution. Assume the judgements indicated for each of the following pairs of utterances involving **commissives**, where the introductory question mark is meant to indicate that the utterance is probably less likely in most situations. Can you think of a reason why this could be so, given the meanings of the verbs and the context in which the utterances might occur?
    a 'I accept your offer.'
    b ?'Can I accept your offer?'
    c ?'I decline your offer.'
    d 'Can I decline your offer?'

16 In order for a speaker to utter a **request** felicitously each of the following felicity conditions must hold.
    a the speaker believes that the task has not yet been done
    b the speaker believes that the hearer is able to do the task
    c the speaker believes the hearer is willing to do the task
    d the speaker wants the task to be done
    Formulate four indirect requests, each of which invokes a different felicity condition (i.e. each of which asserts or questions a different one of the given felicity conditions for a request).

301

17 The following are indirect **questions**. Use them to formulate the three felicity conditions for questions (keeping in mind that indirect speech acts invoke or mention the felicity conditions for the act).

a 'I don't know the answer to that.'

b 'I'd like to know the answer to that.'

c 'Do you know the answer to that?'

UNIT 25 PROPOSITIONS AND ILLOCUTIONS

Entry requirements DIRECT and INDIRECT ILLOCUTIONS (Unit 24). If you feel you understand these notions, take the entry test below. If not, review Unit 24.

Entry test (1) Briefly define what is meant by a directive act.

A directive act is any illocutionary act which ....

....

....

(2) Give an example of a directive act.

....

(3) Briefly define what is meant by a commissive act.

A commissive act is any illocutionary act which ....

....

....

(4) Give an example of a commissive act.

....

(5) Is the sentence *I promise to fail you if you do not hand in your essay on time* literally used to promise? (Assume normal circumstances.)   *Yes / No*

Feedback (1) A directive act is any illocutionary act which essentially involves the speaker trying to get the hearer to behave in some required way.
(2) ordering, suggesting, requesting, etc. (3) A commissive act is any illocutionary act which essentially involves the speaker committing himself to behave in some required way. (4) promising, undertaking, accepting, etc. (5) No, a warning or threat
If you have scored less than 4 correct out of 5, review Unit 24. Otherwise, continue to the introduction below.

Introduction In this unit we will try to draw out some of the relationships between two large areas of meaning that we have mentioned so far in this book, namely sentence meaning and utterance meaning. The notion of proposition, and the closely related concepts of predication and reference, are crucial for sentence meaning.

The notion of illocution is crucial for utterance meaning. The two kinds of meaning are different, although they obviously interact in communication.

Definition SENTENCE MEANING is what a sentence means, regardless of the context and situation in which it may be used.

UTTERANCE MEANING is what a speaker means when he makes an utterance in a particular situation.

Practice Each of the following is a statement from an everyday context in which the word *meaning* or *means* or *mean* is used. Say whether the statement is about sentence meaning (*S*) or about utterance meaning (*U*).

(1) A statement by a tourist guide: The inscription above this door, translated into English, means *Those who enter here will live forever.*   *S / U*

(2) What did you mean by telling me you'd think twice about lending money to Gary?   *S / U*

(3) When George says that his gun is loaded, he means it as a threat.   *S / U*

(4) I think I understand the literal meaning of what you're saying, but I can't see why you should be saying it to me.   *S / U*

(5) Fred is very understanding; he knows what I mean even though I don't use the right words to say it.   *S / U*

(6) *No head injury is too trivial to ignore* actually, and surprisingly, means the opposite of what you first think.   *S / U*

Feedback (1) S (2) U (3) U (4) S (5) U (6) S

Comment The gap between sentence meaning and utterance meaning is least noticeable when speakers are being direct (i.e. not being ironic, or diplomatic, or polite). Politeness is one of the main motivations for using an indirect illocution in preference to a direct one (Unit 24). In the previous unit we saw how a speaker could carry out an indirect illocution by (directly) asserting or questioning certain of its felicity conditions. Now we will go through an exactly parallel exercise, illuminating one aspect of the relationship between propositions and illocutions.

Definition The PROPOSITIONAL CONTENT of a directive illocution can be expressed
(partial) by a declarative sentence describing the action that the speaker requires of the hearer. (This definition is partial because it only applies to directives. It does not apply to commissives, for instance, or other types of illocution.)

Practice Express the propositional content of each of the following directives with a declarative sentence.

(1) 'I would like you to feed my cat while I'm on holiday'

You will ....

(2) 'Forceps!' (uttered by a surgeon during an operation)

(3) 'Relax!'

....

(4) 'Don't give up!'

....

(5) In each of the above cases, would uttering the declarative
sentence you have given actually carry out (either more or less
directly) the same directive illocution as the original utterance?   *Yes / No*

(6) In general, does it seem that uttering a declarative sentence
describing an action required of the hearer actually carries
out a directive illocution?   *Yes / No*

(7) Is it polite (*P*) or rather impolite (*I*) to issue a directive with
an utterance beginning 'You will . . .'?   *P / I*

Feedback   (1) You will feed my cat while I'm on holiday (2) You will pass me the
forceps (3) You will relax (4) You will not give up (5) Yes (6) Yes (7) I

Comment   One way of carrying out an indirect directive is to (directly) assert that the
hearer will carry out the action required, i.e. to assert the propositional
content of the directive. But this method of getting people to do things is
hardly less blunt or more polite than simply issuing a direct directive. We
look now at a method that is (in some instances, at least) more polite.

Practice   (1) Give an interrogative sentence corresponding to sentence (1) in the
feedback above.

....

(2) Would uttering this sentence normally be a more or a less
polite way of carrying out the illocution involved?   *More / less*

(3) Give an interrogative sentence corresponding to sentence
(3) in the feedback above.

....

(4) Would uttering this sentence normally be a more or a less
polite way of carrying out the illocution involved?   *More / less*

(5) Give an interrogative sentence corresponding to sentence
(4) in the feedback above.

....

(6) Would uttering this sentence actually carry out the same
directive illocutionary act as uttering the corresponding
declarative sentence?   *Yes / No*

Feedback (1) Will you feed my cat while I'm on holiday? (2) More (3) Will you relax? (4) Perhaps slightly more polite, but only just (5) Won't you give up? or Will you not give up? (6) No. Uttering the declarative sentence has the illocution of a command (or a prediction that the hearer will not give up), whereas uttering either of the corresponding interrogatives has the illocution of a suggestion actually urging the hearer to give up.

Comment Thus another way of carrying out an indirect directive is to question the propositional content of the illocution. This method actually results in a more polite utterance than simply asserting the propositional content. But, as we have seen in the last two examples (*Will you relax?* and *Won't you give up?*), this method is not completely general. Sometimes uttering the interrogative is not more polite than uttering the corresponding declarative. And sometimes the interrogative form gives rise to a quite different illocution (as in the last example). These exceptions probably have something to do with the special nature of such items as *relax, give up*, and the effects of negation. We will not delve more deeply into such complications, but will turn to the case of indirect commissives.

Practice (1) In the case of directives, the actor who is to carry out the required action is the hearer of the utterance. Who is the actor to carry out the action concerned in the case of commissive illocutions?

....

(2) Could the propositional content of an offer to give the hearer a piece of gum be expressed with the sentence *I will give you a piece of gum*?   Yes / No

(3) In general, can the propositional content of any commissive illocution be expressed with a sentence of the form *I will . . .?*   Yes / No

Feedback (1) the speaker (2) Yes (3) Yes

Definition (partial) The PROPOSITIONAL CONTENT of a COMMISSIVE ILLOCUTION can be expressed by a declarative sentence describing the action which the speaker undertakes to perform.

Comment Now we will see whether asserting and questioning the propositional content of a commissive actually (indirectly) carries out that commissive, parallel to the case of directives.

Practice (1) In each of the following cases, give an assertion of the propositional content of the commissive illocution concerned. We have done the first one for you.

(a) Father promising to buy his son a rubber dinghy when he can swim:

'I will buy you a rubber dinghy when you can swim'
....

(b) Dinner guest, offering to help wash the dinner dishes:

....

(c) Soldier volunteering to cover his section's retreat:

....

(2) For each of the above cases (a)–(c), turn the assertion you gave as answer into a question.

(a) ....

(b) ....

(c) ....

(3) Could the utterances (assertions) given as answers to (1) (a)–(c) actually be commissive speech acts (i.e. acts of promising, offering, and volunteering)?   *Yes / No*

(4) Could the utterances (questions) that you gave as answers to (2) (a)–(c) actually be commissive speech acts?   *Yes / No*

Feedback (1) (b) 'I'll help wash the dishes' (c) 'I'll cover the section's retreat' (2) (a) 'Will I buy you a rubber dinghy when you can swim?' (b) 'Will I help wash the dishes?' (c) 'Will I cover the section's retreat?' (3) Yes, in all three cases (4) No, in all cases

Comment Commissives are like directives in that they can be indirectly carried out by asserting their propositional content, but they differ from directives in that they cannot generally be carried out by questioning their propositional content. (Actually there are several dialectal complications involving *shall* and *will* which we will not pursue here.) The situation can be summarized as in the table below. Considerations of politeness are among the main reasons for speakers preferring to get their message across by means of indirect, rather than direct, illocutions.

	Directives	Commissives
ASSERTION of propositional content	relatively impolite	moderately polite
QUESTIONING of propositional content	relatively polite	moderately polite but not appropriate in all cases

We leave the topic of politeness now and look at other aspects of the relationship between speech acts and the propositions they involve. The fact that one can talk about the propositional content of any speech act should not be taken to indicate that propositions necessarily 'precede' or 'underlie' speech acts. One can conceive of a speech act being committed without any thought of its propositional content passing through the mind of the speaker.

The relationship between propositions and illocutions is simply a special case of the age-old, and very thorny, question of the relationship between thought and action. There is no simple statement of this relationship. In rational behaviour, thought precedes and shapes action, but, as we all know, thoughtless actions occur and can be significant. Even thoughtless actions can be described, after the event, with declarative sentences, i.e. in terms of propositions. With these reservations in mind, we will continue to examine the relationship between sentences and utterances, concentrating on reference and predication.

Practice   If I say to you: 'Will you turn off the kitchen light?'

(1)   What is the direct illocution of the utterance (assertion, question or command)?

....

(2)   What is the indirect illocution of the utterance (e.g. apology, promise, . . .)? (Assume normal circumstances.)

(3)   Does the utterance use any referring expressions?   *Yes / No*

(4)   If there are any referring expressions used, list them.

(5)   In this utterance, is any predicate used to express a connection between the things or persons referred to?   *Yes / No*

(6)   What is this predicate?

....

(7)   In making this utterance, would I normally be carrying out one or more acts of reference?   *Yes / No*

(8)   In making this utterance, would I be carrying out an act of predicating some connection between the objects or persons referred to?   *Yes / No*

(9)   In this instance, does the predication apply to a past, present, or future connection between the objects or persons referred to?   *Past / Present / Future*

Feedback   (1) question (2) request (3) Yes (4) *you* and *the kitchen light* (5) Yes (6) The verb *turn off* (7) Yes, two separate acts of referring (8) Yes, predicating a relation of turning off between you and the kitchen light (9) a future connection

Comment   We see in the above example that even though an utterance is used primarily to do something, i.e. to perform a significant social act such as requesting, the notions of reference and predicate are crucially involved. This is the case in most instances; propositional meaning and interpersonal meaning are closely interwoven. We show below that in some cases, however, the principal participants in illocutionary acts are not explicitly referred to, and that, in a tiny minority of cases, an illocutionary act can even be carried out without any obvious use of reference and predication at all. The speaker and the hearer are the main parties involved in illocutionary acts. But note that a specific utterance may or may not explicitly refer to the speaker or the hearer.

Practice   For each of the following utterances, (a) name the most likely illocutionary act being carried out, (b) say whether the speaker is explicitly referred to, and (c) say whether the hearer is explicitly referred to.

(1) 'I am most grateful to you'

(a) .... (b)   *Yes / No*   (c)   *Yes / No*

(2) 'Thank you very much'

(a) .... (b)   *Yes / No*   (c)   *Yes / No*

(3) 'Thanks a lot'

(a) .... (b)   *Yes / No*   (c)   *Yes / No*

(4) 'Go away'

(a) .... (b)   *Yes / No*   (c)   *Yes / No*

(5) 'Please will you pass the sugar'

(a) .... (b)   *Yes / No*   (c)   *Yes / No*

(6) 'I hereby undertake to pay all my debts'

(a) .... (b)   *Yes / No*   (c)   *Yes / No*

Feedback   (1) (a) thanking (b) Yes (c) Yes (2) (a) thanking (b) No (c) Yes (3) (a) thanking (b) No (c) No (4) (a) ordering (or commanding) (b) No (c) No (5) (a) requesting (b) No (c) Yes (6) (a) promising (b) Yes (c) No

Comment   We see that for an illocutionary act to be carried out there is no need for either the speaker or the hearer to be referred to (although, in general, reference to the speaker or hearer makes the illocution of an utterance more explicit, and hence clearer). We will now look to see whether the linguistic device of predication is also in some cases dispensable. Can an illocutionary act be carried out without even the use of predication?

Practice   (1)   Would it seem reasonable to say that *I thank you* has as its meaning a proposition, involving two referring expressions and a (two-place) predicate *thank*?   *Yes / No*

(2)   What illocutionary act is normally carried out with the utterance 'Hello'?

....

(3) Is *Hello* a declarative sentence?   *Yes / No*

(4) Would it seem reasonable to call *hello* a predicate?   *Yes / No*

(5) What is the negative of *I thank you*?

....

(6) Is there a negative of *Hello*?   *Yes / No*

(7) Would it seem reasonable to analyse the meaning of *Hello* as a
      proposition?   *Yes / No*

Feedback (1) Yes (2) greeting (3) No (4) No (5) *I do not thank you* (6) No (7) No

Practice (1) What illocutionary act is normally carried out in uttering 'Hey!' ....

(2) Would it be reasonable to analyse the meaning of *Hey!* as a
      proposition, involving referring expressions and a predicate?   *Yes / No*

(3) What illocutionary act is normally carried out in uttering
      'Goodbye'?   ....

(4) Would it be reasonable to analyse the meaning of *Goodbye* as a
      proposition, involving referring expressions and a predicate?   *Yes / No*

Feedback (1) calling for attention (2) No (3) leavetaking (4) No

Comment Expressions like *Hello*, *Goodbye*, and *Hey!* belong to a tiny set that seem to
have purely non-propositional meaning. Although of course it is possible to
describe their effects with declarative sentences such as *I greet you* and *I take
my leave of you*, this is not an argument that *Hello*, *Goodbye*, and *Hey!*
themselves have propositions as their meanings, or that they contain referring
expressions or predicates. Such expressions are for this reason (verbal)
gestures, parallel in essential ways to non-verbal gestures such as waves, nods,
and handshakes. Rather than classing these expressions under categories of
meaning such as predicate or name, we will categorize them simply as
primary illocution indicators.

Practice Given below are some further utterances which could also be regarded as
using primary illocution indicators. For each one, state the illocutionary
act(s) normally indicated by it.

(1) 'Bravo!'   ....

(2) 'Please'   ....

(3) 'Hi'   ....

(4) 'Pardon?'   ....

(5) 'Hooray'   ....

(6) 'Eh?'   ....

Feedback   (1) congratulating (or expressing admiration) (2) requesting (or entreating) (3) greeting (4) requesting repetition of the hearer's previous utterance (5) expressing (exuberant) approval, congratulating (6) querying (or asking or enquiring)

Comment   Clearly, one-word primary illocution indicators such as these are a rather marginal part of language. Note that most of those given cannot be integrated into sentences, but can only be used on their own. An exception is *please*, which can occur in the middle of a sentence, as in *Will library users please return books to the shelves?* The use of *please* in an utterance makes it unambiguously a request. The use of *please* to indicate a particular illocution is highly conventionalized. No other English word can be so straightforwardly associated with one particular illocution, while at the same time being able to appear in the middle of sentences, as *please* can.

Summary   The study of speech acts adds a dimension to the study of meaning, in particular the interpersonal dimension. It gives us a way of describing how speakers use sentences in actual utterances to interact with other speakers in social situations, exchanging such socially significant illocutions as promises, requests, greetings, warnings, etc. But human communication is not purely interpersonal; people communicate about the world they live in, using reference and predication. In these units we hope to have given some idea of the complex ways in which all these semantic notions are related.

Unit 25   Study Guide and Exercises

Directions   After you have read Unit 25 you should be able to tackle the following questions to test your understanding of the main ideas raised in the unit.

   1   You should understand these terms and concepts from this unit:
sentence meaning
utterance meaning
propositional content of a directive illocution
propositional content of a commissive illocution
primary illocution indicators

   2   Express the propositional content of each of the following directives with a declarative sentence (that asserts this content). Do the declarative sentences you give also have the same directive illocution as the original? Comment on the relative politeness of each type of utterance.
     a 'Put on this sweater.'
     b 'Stay over there.'
     c 'I'd like you to do something for me.'
     d 'You have to stay here.'

3 Give interrogative sentences corresponding to each sentence in question 2 above (i.e. sentences that question the propositional content of the illocution). Does the utterance of each of these sentences carry out the same directive illocutionary act as uttering the corresponding declarative sentence? Comment on politeness.

4 In each of the following cases give an assertion of the propositional content of the commissive illocution concerned, with a sentence of the form *I will* . . . Then turn each assertion into a question (that questions the propositional content of the illocution). Comment on whether the assertions and questions you formulated are equally suitable as commissive speech acts of the intended type.

   a Student promising to finish his homework

   b Host offering to get her guests something to drink

   c General accepting the surrender of his army

   d Engineer undertaking a new project

5 What is perhaps the main reason for speakers preferring to communicate their messages by means of **indirect** rather than **direct** illocutions?

6 Consider an utterance like 'Can you take out the garbage?' and answer the following questions.

   a Identify the direct illocution of the utterance

   b Identify the indirect illocution of the utterance

   c Identify the referring expressions and predicator (if any)

   d Does the utterance carry out any acts of reference or predication?

7 For each of the following utterances identify the most likely illocutionary act involved and indicate whether the speaker or hearer is explicitly mentioned (and identify them if they are).

   a 'Here's the book.'

   b 'Here's the book you ordered.'

   c 'I appreciate the help.'

   d 'Scram!'

   e 'We'd like another helping.'

8 For each of the following utterances identify the most likely illocutionary act involved and indicate whether it contains any referring expressions or predicates. Can you think of any other similar utterances not already listed here or in the text?

   a 'So long.'

   b 'Over here!'

   c 'What's up?'

   d 'No.'

   e 'Ouch!'

   f 'Great!'

9 Is it necessary for the speaker and hearer to be referred to explicitly in order for an illocutionary act to be carried out? Explain briefly and give one or two examples not already given here.

10 What do expressions such as *bravo, hello, goodbye, hey!* (and the additional ones given in question 8 above) have in common? How are they classified in this unit? Are they similar to any non-linguistic behaviour? Explain briefly.

UNIT 26 CONVERSATIONAL IMPLICATURE

Entry requirements ENTAILMENT (Unit 10). If you feel you understand this notion, take the entry test below. Otherwise, review Unit 10.

Entry test Of the following pairs of sentences, say whether the one in column A entails the one in column B. (For brevity here, as elsewhere, we speak of entailment between sentences, rather than, more strictly, between the propositions underlying sentences.)

A	B	
(1) *John is a bachelor*	*John is a man*	*Yes / No*
(2) *Eliza plays the fiddle*	*Someone plays a musical instrument*	*Yes / No*
(3) *I've done my homework*	*I haven't brushed my teeth*	*Yes / No*
(4) *Some of the students came to my party*	*Not all of the students came to my party*	*Yes / No*
(5) *Mary owns three canaries*	*Mary owns a canary*	*Yes / No*
(6) *John picked a tulip*	*John didn't pick a rose*	*Yes / No*

Feedback (1) Yes (2) Yes (3) No (4) No (5) Yes (6) No

If you have scored less than 5 correct out of 6, review Unit 10. Otherwise, continue to the introduction below.

Introduction In this unit we will explain the notion of conversational implicature. Implicature (as we will call it for short) is a concept of utterance meaning as opposed to sentence meaning, but is parallel in many ways to the sense relation (i.e. sentence meaning concept) of entailment (Unit 10). Furthermore, implicature is related to the method by which speakers work out the indirect illocutions of utterances (Unit 24). We will do a little reviewing of these areas and then get across the idea of implicature.

Comment As a first step we need to draw out clearly the notion of entailment. The point to get across here is that entailment is based firmly on the notion of truth.

Definition If, when a proposition A is TRUE, a proposition B must therefore also be TRUE, then proposition A ENTAILS proposition B. (We extend this definition in a natural way to involve the SENTENCES expressed by two such propositions, A and B.)

Practice   Imagine that there are, say, six students who might or might not have come to my party. That is, we are concerned with a little world containing six students. Imagine their names are Philip, Ruth, Margaret, Louise, Andrew, and Jan.

(1) Does the expression *some of the students* specify any particular number of students, e.g. 4 or 5 or 6?   *Yes / No*

(2) Is the sentence *Some, in fact all, of the students came to the party* a contradiction?   *Yes / No*

(3) If *some of the students* is used as a referring expression, referring to just the group Philip, Ruth, and Margaret, does the sentence *Some of the students came to the party* say anything about Louise, Andrew, and Jan?   *Yes / No*

(4) If the sentence *Some of the students came to the party* is true, where the subject phrase of the sentence refers to some particular group of students, can we logically conclude anything about the group of students not referred to?   *Yes / No*

(5) So if *Some of the students came to the party* is true, is it conceivable that the other unreferred-to students also came to the party?   *Yes / No*

(6) If *Some of the students came to the party* is true, could it conceivably be the case that in fact ALL of the students came to the party?   *Yes / No*

(7) Does *Some of the students came to the party* entail *Not all of the students came to the party*?   *Yes / No*

Feedback   (1) No (2) No (3) No (4) No (5) Yes (6) Yes (7) No

Comment   We have taken you step by step through this example deliberately to tie down the strict use of the term 'entailment' that we insist on. Perhaps you felt some discomfort at our conclusion, feeling that our notion of entailment is drawn too narrowly or too strictly, and at odds with everyday conversation. The point we wish to make is that the entailment relationship between sentences is different from the other, more general notion of inference.

Definition   An INFERENCE is any conclusion that one is reasonably entitled to draw from a sentence or utterance.

Comment   All entailments are inferences, but not all inferences are entailments.
Implicature, which we are about to introduce, is another kind of inference, distinct from entailment.

315

Practice   (1) If I say 'Katie's father didn't give her any supper', would it be
               reasonable for you to conclude that Katie got no supper?   *Yes / No*

       (2) If a mother asks her son whether he has done his homework
            and brushed his teeth, and he replies 'I've done my homework'
            would it be reasonable for his mother to conclude that he
            hadn't brushed his teeth?   *Yes / No*

       (3) Does *I've done my homework* entail *I haven't brushed my teeth*?   *Yes / No*

       (4) If you ask me whether many students came to the party and
            I say 'Some of them came', would it be reasonable for you to
            infer that not all of the students came to the party?   *Yes / No*

       (5) In these circumstances is the proposition that not all of the
            students came to the party a reasonable inference from my
            utterance?   *Yes / No*

       (6) Does *Some of the students came to the party* entail *Not all of*
            the students came to the party?   *Yes / No*

Feedback   (1) Only if you have some specific knowledge that no-one other than
Katie's father gave her her supper. (2) Yes, in a normal household (3) No
(4) Yes (5) Yes (6) No (as dealt with before)

Comment   We have just seen some cases of reasonable inference which are not cases of
entailment. These were examples of (conversational) implicature. Note that
these examples involved conclusions drawn from utterances on particular
occasions and not from isolated sentences. Thus implicature is a matter of
utterance meaning, and not of sentence meaning. Implicature is not a form
of inference that can be predicted solely from a knowledge of the system of
sense relations between sentences. In this respect the problem of implicature
resembles the problem (dealt with in Unit 24) of how hearers arrive at the
indirect illocutions of utterances. How does a hearer make reasonable
inferences from an utterance when the actual sentence uttered does not in
fact entail some of the inferences he makes? To start to answer this question,
we explore some aspects of everyday conversation.

Practice   In normal conversation, does a helpful speaker try to:

       (1) Give relatively unspecific, even vacuous, answers to questions?   *Yes / No*

       (2) Give information that the hearer already knows?   *Yes / No*

       (3) Give information that is not relevant to the topic of
            conversation?   *Yes / No*

       (4) Give information in a way that is easy to understand?   *Yes / No*

       (5) Avoid ambiguity, or potentially misleading statements?   *Yes / No*

Feedback   (1) No (2) No (3) No (4) Yes (5) Yes

Comment   The answers reflect what has been called the Co-operative Principle, the
            overriding social rule which speakers generally try to follow in conversation.
            The Co-operative Principle can be stated simply as 'be as helpful to your
            hearer as you can'. The fact that speakers are assumed to follow this principle
            is used by hearers in making inferences from the utterances they hear, as we
            shall now see in detail.

Practice   In the following dialogues, say whether the second speaker is making an
            utterance that is fully co-operative (C) or one that is misleading (M) or
            unhelpful in some way (U).

            (1) Policeman at the front door: 'Is your father or your mother at home?'
                 Small boy (who knows that his father is at home):
                 'Either my mother's gone out shopping or she hasn't'   C / M / U

            (2) Traffic warden to motorist parked on double yellow line: 'Is
                 this your car, sir?'
                 Motorist (looking at the black clouds): 'I think it's going
                 to rain'   C / M / U

            (3) Customer in stationery shop: 'Could you tell me where I
                 could buy some felt-tip pens?'
                 Shop girl (who knows she has felt-tip pens in stock):
                 'Yes, you could get some at Woolworths, down the road'   C / M / U

            (4) Mother: 'Now tell me the truth. Who put the ferret in
                 the bathtub?'
                 Son (who knows who did it): 'Someone put it there'   C / M / U

Feedback   (1) U (2) U (3) M (therefore unhelpful) (4) U

Practice   Now in each of the above situations, say whether the second speaker,
            although clearly being unhelpful, is telling the truth or not (as far as you
            can tell).

            (1) *Yes / No*

            (2) *Yes / No*

            (3) *Yes / No*

            (4) *Yes / No*

Feedback   (1) Yes (2) Yes (3) Yes (4) Yes

Comment   Being co-operative in conversation obviously involves more than simply
            telling the truth, although truthfulness is part of co-operativeness.

We separate out the following further components of conversational co-operativeness.

(1) Relevance – keep to the topic of the conversation.

(2) Informativeness – tell the hearer just what he needs to know, no more and no less.

(3) Clarity – speak in a way that the hearer will understand.

These principles are called maxims. We shall refer to them as the maxim of relevance, the maxim of informativeness, and the maxim of clarity.

Practice Go back over the situations in questions (1)–(4) above and say whether the utterance of the second speaker in each case is irrelevant (*I*), less informative than it might have been (*LI*) or unclear, i.e. difficult for the hearer to understand (*U*).

(1) *U / LI / I*

(2) *U / LI / I*

(3) *U / LI / I*

(4) *U / LI / I*

Feedback (1) LI (2) I (3) LI (4) LI

Comment All the situations mentioned so far have been abnormal, in the sense that one of the speakers was deliberately being less than helpful. It is important to move to an analysis of normal situations, in which one or more of the maxims might seem to be being violated, but in fact the hearer's assumption that this is not the case leads him to a particular inference from the speaker's utterance. We will look now at some instances.

Practice (1) Does *Mary speaks French* entail *Mary is John's daughter*?   *Yes / No*

(2) If I asked 'Do any of John's daughters speak a foreign language?', and you replied 'Mary speaks French', would it be reasonable for me to conclude that Mary is John's daughter?   *Yes / No*

(3) Would I normally assume that you would make a relevant reply?   *Yes / No*

(4) In the above situation, if Mary were not in fact John's daughter, would your reply be relevant?   *Yes / No*

(5) Would it be sensible for me to reason as follows: If Mary were not John's daughter, his reply would not be relevant: I assume that his reply IS relevant and therefore Mary IS John's daughter.   *Yes / No*

Feedback (1) No (2) Yes (3) Yes (4) No (5) Yes

Comment The example we have just gone through is one of implicature. The proposition that Mary is John's daughter is an implicature of the utterance 'Mary speaks French' in this particular situation. What makes this a case of implicature is the crucial role played in the hearer's calculations by the assumption that the speaker is trying to be helpful. The hearer is entitled to draw the inference that Mary is John's daughter only if it can be safely assumed that the speaker is being helpful. A comparison between entailment and implicature can be shown in a diagram.

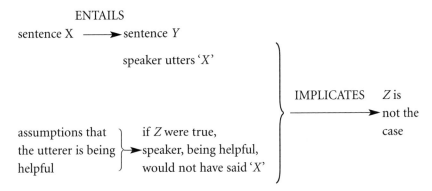

ENTAILS

sentence X ⟶ sentence Y

speaker utters 'X'

IMPLICATES Z is
⟶ not the
case

assumptions that   if Z were true,
the utterer is being ⟶ speaker, being helpful,
helpful   would not have said 'X'

The above example used the maxim of relevance. We will go through another example, this time using the maxim of informativeness.

Practice Consider the situation in which a speaker knows that all the students came to the party (assuming some given party and group of students). He is asked whether many students came to the party. In this situation:

(1) Is the utterance 'Some of the students came' true? *Yes / No*

(2) Is the utterance 'All of the students came' true? *Yes / No*

(3) Is the utterance 'Some of the students came' as informative as it could be? *Yes / No*

(4) Is the utterance 'All the students came' as informative as it could be? *Yes / No*

(5) Would the hearer normally assume that the speaker would try to be as informative as possible? *Yes / No*

(6) Would the hearer be reasonable to calculate as follows: If all the students had come, he would have said: 'All the students came'? *Yes / No*

(7) If the speaker in fact said 'Some of the students came', would it be reasonable for the hearer to calculate: He did not say 'All the students came' and therefore it is not the case that all the students came (otherwise he would have said so). *Yes / No*

(8)   Would the hearer, then, reasonably infer from the utterance
'Some of the students came' that not all of the students came?   *Yes / No*

Feedback   (1) Yes (2) Yes (3) No (4) Yes (5) Yes (6) Yes (7) Yes (8) Yes

Comment   The proposition that not all the students came is an implicature of the
utterance 'Some of the students came' in the above situation. It is an
implicature based on the maxim of informativeness. We will give next an
example of implicature based on the maxim of clarity. It must be said,
however, that examples of implicature involving the maxim of clarity are
not easy to find, and the example we are about to give could conceivably be
interpreted in other ways.

Practice   Consider the following conversation between Wayne and Sue.

Wayne: 'You and Jim really must come round to my place some evening'

Sue: 'Yes. We'd like to'

Wayne: 'Of course, you two don't drink, do you?'

Sue: 'Well, we don't not drink'

(1)   If Sue had meant to convey to Wayne just the simple proposition that
she and Jim drink, which utterance would have achieved that purpose
most directly:

(a) 'We drink' or (b) 'We don't not drink'?   *(a) / (b)*

(2)   Is 'We don't not drink' in any sense less clear than 'We drink'?
I.e. would it take a hearer a bit more thought to figure out
what is being conveyed?   *Yes / No*

(3)   Would it be reasonable of Wayne, in the circumstances, to
reason as follows:

If she had meant to tell me simply that they drink, she would
have said, in order to be as clear as possible, 'We drink'. Since
she did not say simply 'We drink', I assume she is trying to
convey something more complex, or subtle, to me.   *Yes / No*

(4)   Express in your own words the extra message that Sue might have been
trying to get across by deliberately using the rather unclear double
negative.

....

....

Feedback   (1) (a) (2) Yes (3) Yes (4) Possibly: We don't carry our lack of enthusiasm
for drinking to the extreme of not drinking. Or: We drink, in moderation.

Comment Sue's double negative here could also be an apparent violation of a maxim of brevity, according to which a speaker should try to be as brief as possible. A doubly negative sentence is not as brief as a simple positive sentence. The factors of clarity and brevity are hard to distinguish consistently. We will look at a few more examples of implicature.

Practice Consider the conversation:

A: 'Did you buy salt?'

B: 'I tried to'

(1) If B had bought salt, would it be reasonable to assume that this was because he had tried to do so? *Yes / No*

(2) If B had bought salt, would he be telling A more than was necessary by mentioning that he had tried to buy it? *Yes / No*

(3) Could A reason as follows: If he had bought salt, he would not tell me that he had tried to buy it; since he tells me specifically that he tried to buy it, I conclude that he did not buy salt. *Yes / No*

(4) Is the proposition that B did not buy salt an implicature of his utterance? *Yes / No*

Feedback (1) Yes (2) Yes (3) Yes (4) Yes

Practice Give an implicature of B's utterance in each of the situations below.

(1) A: 'Do you love me?'
B: 'I'm quite fond of you'

Implicature: ....

(2) A: 'Was there a fiddler at the bar last night?'
B: 'There was a man scraping a bow across a violin'

Implicature: ....

(3) A: 'Do you like my new carpet?'
B: 'The wallpaper's not bad'

Implicature: ....

Feedback (1) B does not love A. (2) The fiddler at the bar was not very good.
(3) B does not like A's new carpet.

Comment Remember that in a case of implicature the hearer crucially makes the assumption that the speaker is not violating one of the conversational maxims, of relevance, of informativeness, or of clarity (or brevity).

Practice Below are some conversations between two people, A and B. After each conversation an implicature from B's utterance is given. In each case, say whether the crucial assumption leading the hearer to this implicature involves the maxim of (*R*) relevance, (*I*) informativeness, or (*C*) clarity (or brevity). Circle your answer.

(1) A: (by an obviously immobilized car) 'My car's broken down'
    B: 'There is a garage round the corner'

Implicature: The garage is open and has a mechanic who might repair the fault.   *R / I / C*

(2) A: 'What subjects is Jack taking?'
    B: 'He's not taking Linguistics'

Implicature: B does not know exactly which subjects Jack is taking.   *R / I / C*

(3) A: 'Have you brushed your teeth and tidied your room?'
    B: 'I've brushed my teeth'

Implicature: B has not tidied his room.   *R / I / C*

(4) A: 'Who was that man you were talking to?'
    B: 'That was my mother's husband'

Implicature: B's mother's husband is not B's father.   *R / I / C*

(5) A: 'Is Betsy in?'
    B: 'Her light is on'

Implicature: Betsy's light being on is usually a sign of whether she is in or not.   *R / I / C*

Feedback   (1) R (2) I (3) I (or perhaps brevity, since B could have simply said 'Yes' if he had tidied his room) (4) C (or brevity) (5) R

Comment   To reinforce the contrast between implicature and entailment check that none of the implicatures from B's utterances above are actually entailed by the sentences uttered by B.

Practice   In the situations below, fill in an appropriate utterance for B, so that what he says implicates (but does not entail) the conclusion in the right-hand column. In other words, if you were B, what might you say in order to convey the given conclusion to A, without stating it directly?

(1) A: 'Let's try the new Arab restaurant round the corner'
    B: ....

Implicature: Arab restaurants are likely not to serve vegetarian food.

(2) A: 'Meet me at Piccadilly Circus at midnight'
    B: ....

Implicature: Piccadilly Circus is not a safe place to be at midnight.

(3) A: 'Do you use your local swimming pool very much?'

B: ....

Implicature: B's local swimming pool has salt water.

(4) A: 'How much do I owe you now?'

B: ....

Implicature: A's debts to B are large and complicated to work out.

Feedback Some possible replies from B are: (1) 'I'm a vegetarian' (2) 'I'll bring a large friend with me, in that case' or 'You like to live dangerously' (3) 'The salt water hurts my eyes' (4) 'I'll have to get my calculator'

Comment Finally in this unit, we mention the possibility of the explicit cancellation of implicatures.

Definition An implicature of one part of an utterance is said to be CANCELLED when another part of the utterance or a following utterance explicitly contradicts it.

Example In the utterance 'I tried to buy salt, and in fact I succeeded', the implicature (from the first half of the utterance) that the speaker did not in fact buy salt is explicitly cancelled by the assertion in the second half of the utterance.

Practice (1) Would the utterance 'Some of my friends are linguists' normally have as an implicature the proposition that not all of the speaker's friends are linguists?   *Yes / No*

(2) Would this implicature be cancelled if the utterance continued '. . . in fact, all of my friends are linguists'?   *Yes / No*

(3) Is the sentence *Some, in fact all, of my friends are linguists* actually a contradiction, i.e. necessarily false?   *Yes / No*

(4) If a teacher said 'The students who answered questions in section A have passed the test', might a reasonable implicature be that students who did not answer questions in section A have not passed the test?   *Yes / No*

(5) Suggest a continuation of the teacher's utterance cancelling this implicature.

....

(6) Is the sentence *The students who answered questions in section A have passed the test, just as the students who did not answer those questions have* a contradiction?   *Yes / No*

Feedback (1) Yes (2) Yes (3) No (4) Yes (5) '. . . in fact everyone passed the test' (6) No

Comment   Examples such as these illustrate the contrast between implicature and
           entailment. Entailments cannot be cancelled without contradiction. E.g.
           in *I killed Cock Robin and Cock Robin did not die*, where the second half
           contradicts an entailment of the first half, the whole is a contradiction.
           But a conversational implicature can be cancelled without resulting in a
           contradiction, as shown in the above practice.

Summary   This unit has outlined the notion of conversational implicature, a form of
           reasonable inference. Implicature, a notion of utterance meaning, contrasts
           with entailment, a notion of sentence meaning.
               Implicature exists by reason of general social conventions, the chief of
           which is the principle of co-operativeness between speakers. (The idea of
           implicature, which links logic and conversation, was developed by the
           philosopher Paul Grice.)

Unit 26 Study Guide and Exercises

Directions After you have read Unit 26 you should be able to tackle the
            following questions to test your understanding of the main ideas
            raised in the unit.

   1 You should understand these terms and concepts from this unit:
      inference
          entailment (logical)
          implicature (conversational)
      cancellation of implicatures
      co-operative principle (be as helpful as possible)
          maxim of relevance
          maxim of informativeness
          maxim of clarity (includes brevity, avoidance of ambiguity/obscurity)

   2 What do the notions **entailment** and **implicature** have in common? How
      do they differ? What does it mean to say that implicatures are non-truth-
      conditional inferences?

   3 An implicature can result through the **flouting** of one of the maxims by the
      speaker (B), in which the hearer (A) can infer something not explicitly said
      if the speaker (B) disregards one of the maxims (whether intentionally or
      not), though the hearer (A) assumes that the speaker is not doing so. Give
      an implicature of B's utterance in each of the following situations, and then
      identify the maxim(s) (i.e. relevance, informativeness, or clarity) that
      has/have been flouted (and thus which led the hearer to this implicature).
      Note that none of the implicatures from B's utterances are actually entailed
      by the sentences uttered by B.

  a A: 'Professor, will you write a letter of recommendation for me?'
     B: 'Certainly. I will say that you were always neatly dressed, punctual,
         and are unfailingly polite.'
  b A: 'How are you today?'
     B: 'Oh, Lansing is the capital of Michigan.'
  c A: 'I'm not feeling very well today.'
     B: 'There's a hospital across the street.'
  d A: 'What did you think of that new movie?'
     B: 'Well, the costumes were authentic.'
  e A: 'How did you get that car into the dining room?'
     B: 'It was easy. I made a left turn when I came out of the kitchen.'
  f A: 'What colour did you paint your living room?'
     B: 'I painted the walls off-white to match the black sofa. The trimming
         will be gray except by the door, which will be salmon to match the
         Picasso print I bought two years ago.'
  g. A: 'How's the weather?'
     B: 'It's 86.7 degrees Fahrenheit. The air is humid, muggy, and the
         pavement is so hot I can feel it through my shoes.'
  h. A: 'What's your recipe for a birthday cake?'
     B: 'It should have icing. Use unbleached flour and sugar in the cake and
         bake it for an hour. Preheat the oven to 325 degrees and beat in three
         fresh eggs.'
  i A: 'How do you like my new suit?'
     B: 'Well, your shoes look nice.'
  j A: 'Have you done your homework and taken out the garbage?'
     B: 'I've taken out the garbage.'
  k A: 'I may win the lottery for $83 million.'
     B: 'There may be people on Mars, too.'

4 For each of the following fill in an appropriate utterance for B which
   implicates (but does not entail) the indicated implicature. There may be
   several appropriate possibilities
   a A: 'Let's see if this store has what we are looking for.'
      B: ....
      Implicature: The store sells expensive merchandise
   b A: 'Why don't we have lunch in this restaurant?'
      B: ....
      Implicature: The food there is too fattening
   c A: 'Are the Browns at home?'
      B: ....
      Implicature: The Browns are usually home when their car is in the
      driveway

    d A: 'Should we turn right or left?'

        B: ....

        Implicature: B isn't sure which way to turn

    e A: 'How is your physics course going?'

        B: ....

        Implicature: B is having trouble in the course

5 Think about the meaning relationship between the following pair of sentences.

    a Most birds are on the lawn   b Many birds are on the lawn

Does (a) entail or merely implicate (b)? Remember that entailments cannot be cancelled without contradiction (because asserting a sentence and denying its entailment results in a contradiction), as in the following.

    c Jack managed to open the door, but he didn't open the door

Sentence (c) is a contradiction because the fact that Jack managed to open the door entails that he in fact did open the door, but then the second clause denies that this is true. Implicatures, on the other hand, can be cancelled without contradiction, as in the following sentence, where the original implicature of the sentence *I tried to buy food* – i.e. that I couldn't buy food – is cancelled by my saying that in fact I succeeded in doing so.

    d I tried to buy food, and in fact I succeeded

Therefore, if sentence (a) above entails sentence (b), then the following sentence (e) should be a contradiction, while if (a) only implicates (b), then the second part of (e) below (which negates the proposition in (b)) should merely cancel (b) without a contradiction.

    e Most birds are on the lawn, but in fact there are not many birds on the lawn

There may be a difference of opinion about these sentences. See if you can figure out what it is about the meanings of *most* and *many* which appears to contribute to your answer.

6 Consider the following exchange.

      A: I may win the lottery for $83 million

      B: There may be people on Mars, too

      A: What are you, some kind of astronomer?

B originally triggered an implicature in her response to A's original statement, which you provided earlier in question 3k above. What effect does A's retort then have on the implicature originally triggered by B?

UNIT 27 NON-LITERAL MEANING: IDIOMS, METAPHOR, AND METONYMY

Entry requirements There are no specific entry requirements for this unit, although you might want to review some previous topics that are relevant for the discussion to follow: the difference between SPEAKER (UTTERANCE) MEANING and SENTENCE MEANING discussed in Units 1 and 25, the notion of CONTEXT in Unit 7, and also the notions of COMPOSITIONALITY in Unit 14 and ANOMALY in Unit 17.

Introduction Now that you have completed the first twenty-six units of this book, you have acquired a solid introduction into most of the basic areas of traditional linguistic semantics. The first twenty units dealt primarily with what we have called 'literal' meaning, which evokes two main ideas: first, that the meanings of words and sentences are essentially independent of the context or occasion of use; and second, that the meaning of a composite expression is essentially compositional. As we described earlier in Unit 14, compositionality refers to the idea that a composite expression's overall meaning is clearly a function of the literal meanings of the parts of which it is composed. Perhaps the epitome of this kind of study is represented by the use of logic and the concept of truth conditions and truth values to represent the literal meanings of the propositions expressed by sentences in human languages. The study of literal meaning is very important and has long been the main focus of linguistic semantics, going all the way back to the ancient Greek philosophers Plato and Aristotle. This is why so much attention was paid to it in this book.

In Units 21–26 we began to expand the focus of our study of meaning somewhat beyond the classic issues of sense, reference, and logic by examining aspects of interpersonal meaning, such as speech acts and various kinds of inference, including conversational implicature. This sort of meaning goes beyond literal meaning and entailment relationships based on truth conditions, and involves aspects of the context of the utterance and intentions of the speaker. We have referred to this kind of meaning before as SPEAKER or UTTERANCE MEANING.

In this unit we will turn our attention to semantic phenomena that evoke what has traditionally been called 'figurative' or 'non-literal' meaning: in particular, idiomatic or fixed expressions, metaphor, and metonymy. The study of this kind of meaning has not traditionally been the focus of linguistic

327

semantics, partially because it is often difficult to distinguish it precisely from literal meaning, and also because non-literal meaning has sometimes been regarded as largely idiosyncratic and therefore as less principled and rule-governed than literal meaning. But the study of non-literal meaning, especially metaphor, has become much more important in recent years, partly because semanticists have begun to realize how prevalent it is in everyday language. They have also begun to discover that much, if not all, of its use is not totally haphazard or idiosyncratic, but subject to certain rules and principles that can be discovered and described. Consequently, we feel that a brief introduction to non-literal meaning is appropriate before wrapping up the presentation of topics in this introductory book. Let us begin with a look at idiomatic expressions, which are used quite frequently in everyday language.

Definition IDIOMATIC EXPRESSIONS (IDIOMS) are multi-word phrases whose overall meanings are idiosyncratic and largely unpredictable, reflecting speaker meanings that are not derivable by combining the literal senses of the individual words in each phrase according to the regular semantic rules of the language.

Comment It follows that the typical meanings of idioms are not fully compositional. Interestingly enough, however, most idioms also have possible, though unlikely, literal compositional interpretations along with their idiomatic senses. Which meaning is intended usually depends on the context in which the expression is used. Let's look at some examples.

Examples Expressions such as *let the cat out of the bag* and *take the bull by the horns* are commonly used idioms whose usual meanings are not fully compositional, but have to be learned as a whole. Any speaker of English knows, for example, that *let the cat out of the bag* is usually used to mean something like 'reveal a secret', though it also has a possible, though rarely intended, literal compositional meaning something like 'release a small feline animal from a sack'. Similarly, *take the bull by the horns* typically evokes the idea that someone 'takes charge of a situation', though it could also have the more literal compositional meaning 'grab a (real) bull by its horns'.

Practice Each sentence below is ambiguous, containing a phrase that could be understood either idiomatically (figuratively) or literally, depending upon the context in which the sentence is used. For each sentence (a) give a paraphrase that correctly evokes each sense and (b) suggest a context in which each sense might be appropriately used.

(1) *The people let their hair down*

    (a) Literal sense: ....

         Idiomatic sense: ....

   (b) Context for literal sense: ....

      Context for idiomatic sense: ....

   (2) *We hauled them over the coals*

      (a) Literal sense: ....

         Idiomatic sense: ....

      (b) Context for literal sense: ....

         Context for idiomatic sense: ....

   (3) *He put his foot in his mouth*

      (a) Literal sense: ....

         Idiomatic sense: ....

      (b) Context for literal sense: ....

         Context for idiomatic sense: ....

Feedback
(1) (a) Literal sense: people with long hair physically let their hair hang down from an up (constrained) position to fall around their shoulders. Idiomatic sense: the people relaxed their inhibitions and behaved less carefully. (b) Context for literal sense: perhaps the people were getting ready to wash their hair. Context for idiomatic sense: the people were in a relaxed mood at a party and behaved in a free and natural manner.

(2) Literal sense: we physically carried something over a pile of hot coals. Idiomatic sense: we disciplined some people. Context for literal sense: we had to carry something over actual hot coals, as in a burning building, in order to get it to safety. Context for idiomatic sense: we had to tell someone that they were behaving badly.

(3) Literal sense: he actually put one of his feet in his mouth. Idiomatic sense: he said something inappropriate. Context for literal sense: *he* could refer to a dog who is cleaning his feet by licking them. Context for idiomatic sense: a person is saying things that are inappropriate.

Comment
The fact that many, though perhaps not all, idioms are at least partly compositional tends to be obscured, because the compositional aspects of the figurative meanings conveyed by idioms are often metaphorical in nature. Let us look more closely at some additional examples of idiomatic expressions that more clearly evoke metaphors in order to understand better exactly what metaphors are and how they work in everyday language.

Examples
Examples of figurative language in idioms that evoke metaphors may be found in such sentences as *My car is a lemon* and *Dr Jones is a butcher*. It is immediately apparent that if we try to interpret these sentences literally they would typically sound anomalous or nonsensical, unless special

circumstances are taken into account. (For example, Dr Jones may indeed also work part of the time as an actual butcher.) But, as was the case in the previous examples, each sentence is a perfectly natural way of expressing a speaker meaning that does not seem to be immediately derivable from what is literally said. The first sentence is typically used, for example, to mean that my car is defective in some way, and the second means that Dr Jones is not a particularly good doctor.

Practice   Briefly explain for each of the following sentences what it is about them that makes them appear to be anomalous if they are interpreted literally. Then describe what kind of intended non-literal meaning they convey.

(1)   *Frank is a snake in the grass*

Anomaly: ....

Non-literal meaning: ....

(2)   *Jane lives in a cottage at the foot of the mountain*

Anomaly: ....

Non-literal meaning: ....

(3)   *Sam is a pig*

Anomaly: ....

Non-literal meaning: ....

(4)   *Marie is sitting at the head of the table*

Anomaly: ....

Non-literal meaning: ....

Feedback   (1)   Anomaly: Frank is being equated with (or classified as) being a particular kind of animal (a snake), which is literally untrue. Nonliteral meaning: something about Frank's behaviour is untrustworthy.

(2)   Anomaly: Jane lives in a cottage that is near a part of the mountain that actually looks like a foot of an animal (or human). Non-literal meaning: Jane lives near the bottom or lower part of the mountain.

(3)   Anomaly: Sam is being equated with (or classified as) being a particular kind of animal (a pig). Non-literal meaning: Sam is sloppy or disorganized.

(4)   Anomaly: Marie is sitting near the part of the table that looks just like the head of an animal or human being. Non-literal meaning: Marie is sitting at the end of a rectangular table usually reserved for an important person.

Comment   How do such non-literal meanings come about? One way of dealing with the problem has been to claim that such kinds of non-literal language are first interpreted as though they are actually literally true. Under such an analysis, when the hearer recognizes that the language is anomalous in some way when understood literally, various kinds of inference strategies are used to give the intended non-literal interpretation within the context in which the sentence is uttered. Note that this approach, the details of which we won't go into here, assumes that there is something defective about non-literal language that has to be repaired before communication can occur. Another approach is to assume that such expressions, essentially uninterpretable when understood literally in most contexts, can be interpreted as though they have a more literal equivalent that signifies or assumes a resemblance between two very different kinds of entities, as if the speaker were saying something like *My car is **like** a lemon* or *Dr Jones is **like** a butcher*. The corresponding simile induced with the word *like* would then be interpretable because, presumably, it would not be asserting or assuming an anomalous meaning as such, but rather a meaning in which two concrete entities are being compared to each other. Since such comparisons do not in principle appear to violate restrictions that might preclude any use of language that is not completely literal, they are interpretable and therefore acceptable.

Another way of looking at metaphor is the approach presented by George Lakoff and Mark Johnson (henceforth abbreviated as LJ) in their influential book *Metaphors We Live By* (1980). In the rest of this unit we will examine some of their ideas and give you the opportunity to work with them in the following practices and exercises. Let us first consider how LJ view metaphor in general.

Definition METAPHORS are conceptual (mental) operations reflected in human language that enable speakers to structure and construe abstract areas of knowledge and experience in more concrete experiential terms.

Comment According to this view of metaphor, speakers make use of a familiar area of knowledge, called the source domain, to understand an area of knowledge that is less familiar, the target domain. The source domain is typically understood through our experience in and with the physical world around us. There is a kind of conceptual mapping operation in which aspects of knowledge in the more familiar source domain are placed in correspondence with aspects of the less-familiar target domain in order to structure the target domain in a way that makes it more accessible to human understanding.

Example Consider our earlier examples of *My car is a lemon* and *Dr Jones is a butcher*. In each case a certain aspect of the more complex and/or abstract areas of knowledge involving what we generally know about cars and doctors has been explicitly highlighted in each metaphorical expression by linguistically linking the more abstract target domains of knowledge about cars and doctors to more particularized familiar concrete source domains (i.e. knowledge about lemons in the 'fruit' domain and butchers in the domain of possible professions, respectively) in order to specify that there is something *negative* about each. We know from experience, for example, that lemons are sour and that butchers can be messy and rough in their work. This familiar knowledge helps us understand certain negative aspects of car ownership and medical practice in a particularly immediate way via metaphor.

Comment   Even though conceptualizing a car as if it were a lemon or a doctor as if he or she were a butcher may be literally anomalous, these metaphorical expressions bring out certain pertinent aspects of each knowledge domain that might be relevant on some occasion. The metaphors evoked in these particular expressions have become standardized, i.e. 'fixed by convention' (LJ 1980: 54), and as such have become common ways of expressing negative judgements about cars and doctors in English. They are also very limited in scope, however, since we typically only compare cars with lemons in the familiar fruit domain, for example, to convey some kind of metaphorical meaning. With the possible exception of *My car is a peach* (meaning that it is an excellent car for some speakers of English), it is not possible, for example, to say such things as *My car is a pear* or *My car is an apple* without causing an anomaly. This is because a metaphor such as A CAR IS A PIECE OF FRUIT, like the metaphor A MOUNTAIN IS A PERSON cited by LJ as underlying the expression *foot of the mountain*, is 'marginal in our culture and our language', consisting of 'only one conventionally fixed expression of the language' (LJ 1980: 54).

Similarly, we cannot say things like *Dr Jones is a florist* or *Dr Jones is a baker* with anything other than the literal (and somewhat odd) compositional meanings in each case, because whatever metaphor might underlie the particular expression *Dr Jones is a butcher* (perhaps something like A DOCTOR IS A TRADESMAN) is also quite isolated and apparently limited to this one example. A further idiosyncratic aspect of this example is that it's not clear why knowledge about being a butcher (from the source domain) is construed negatively, since butchers are typically quite skilled at what they do. Apparently, there is more to the understanding of an idiomatic expression, even one that might be partly metaphorical in nature, than can be explained just by directly mapping aspects of the source domain to the target domain. Idiomatic expressions often take on a life of their own. (See Taylor 2002: Chapters 24 and 27 for more discussion about metaphors and idiomatic language.)

Expressions such as *My car is a lemon* and *Dr Jones is a butcher* now function essentially as idioms in the language, but as idioms that originally reflected metaphorical relationships which have become fixed (or frozen) over time. LJ refer to them as 'isolated instances of metaphorical concepts' or, in other words, as 'idiosyncratic metaphorical expressions that stand alone and are not used systematically in our language or thought' (LJ 1980: 54).

It should now be apparent that many of the examples in the preceding practices also evoke essentially frozen metaphors of various kinds, which we will give you the opportunity to explore in the exercises at the end of this unit.

A major contribution of LJ's work was their demonstration that our language is suffused with a large number of metaphorical expressions that are not frozen, but which reflect large-scale metaphorical systems which they divide into several subtypes. The first subtype we will examine here are structural metaphors.

Definition STRUCTURAL METAPHORS are abstract metaphorical systems in which an entire (typically abstract) complex mental concept is structured in terms of some other (usually more concrete) concept. They typically involve multiple individual linguistic expressions that evoke some aspect of the metaphor (as opposed to more restricted frozen metaphors which usually occur in only one expression). Another way of thinking about structural metaphors is that 'they allow us . . . to use one highly structured and clearly delineated concept to structure another' (LJ 1980: 61).

Example Consider such expressions as the following: (1) *Her point of view is indefensible.* (2) *They attacked everything we said.* (3) *I finally won/lost the argument.* (4) *She defended her claim that the moon is habitable.* (5) *We demolished their argument.* (6) *My strategy against their argument was weak.* (7) *Our criticism of his claim was right on target.*

According to LJ, the language in these everyday expressions is neither exceptional nor particularly figurative in nature, but reflects the usual way we talk about intellectual argument. But it is couched in the concrete language of warfare (i.e. actual physical combat), using such words from this area of experience as *defend, attack, win, lose,* etc. LJ suggest that such language provides evidence that we actually conceptualize argument in terms of war, and therefore that English has the structural metaphor ARGUMENT IS WAR.

Comment Notice that in expressing the metaphor in written terms, we state the more abstract domain (ARGUMENT) first, followed by a form of the verb *to be,* and then the concrete domain (WAR), with all parts in upper-case letters.

Practice Each item below contains several everyday English expressions that evoke a particular structural metaphor. Try to identify this metaphor using the format described above.

(1) Metaphor: ....
    (a) *John and Mary have come a long way together*
    (b) *Our lives have taken different paths*

(c) *I think she will go far in life*

(d) *We have come to a crossroads in our life*

(2) Metaphor: ....

(a) *Stop wasting my time*

(b) *We can save time by taking this shortcut*

(c) *This delay will cost us at least two hours*

(d) *She always spends too much time shopping*

(3) Metaphor: ....

(a) *Jane put in her two cents' worth*

(b) *John is rich in ideas*

(c) *That book is a treasure trove of ideas*

(d) *Mary has a wealth of new ideas*

Feedback   (1) LIFE IS A JOURNEY. (2) TIME IS MONEY. (3) IDEAS ARE MONEY.

Comment   We see in this practice that both the abstract TIME and IDEA domains are at least partially structured in terms of the more concrete MONEY domain. LJ observe that it is not unusual to find more than one abstract knowledge domain structured in terms of the same basic source domain. This probably occurs because some source domains, such as the MONEY domain, are very central and fundamental to our everyday experience as human beings. As such, our understanding of these basic domains makes them highly useful in helping us comprehend more abstract domains.

We also sometimes find the opposite situation in which a particular important abstract knowledge domain is structured by means of more than one structural metaphor. In other words, more than one concrete source domain may be used to structure various aspects of a more abstract target domain, if that domain is important enough in the conceptual system of the language. This is illustrated in the following practice.

Practice   Each set of sentences below evokes one particular structural metaphor in which a particular abstract target domain has been structured by means of a particular source domain. Identify each structural metaphor.

(1) Metaphor: ....

(a) *John's theory gave birth to a new way of thinking about physics*

(b) *He is the father of modern biology*

(c) *Fred's brainchild was that the moon is uninhabitable*

(d) *Her ideas spawned a number of new approaches in research*

(e) *That idea died off years ago*

(2) Metaphor: ....

(a) *That idea died on the vine*

(b) *His ideas have finally come to fruition*

334

(c) *That version of linguistics is an offshoot of an earlier theory*
(d) *Linguistics is a field with many branches*
(e) *I'd like to plant a novel idea in your mind*

Feedback   (1) IDEAS ARE PEOPLE. (2) IDEAS ARE PLANTS.

Comment   The addition of these two new examples to the earlier IDEAS ARE MONEY
example shows that there are at least three (if not more) structural
metaphors in common use in English that structure the domain of IDEAS.
    LJ also identify two additional general kinds of metaphor that are
commonly found in everyday language.

Definition   ORIENTATIONAL METAPHORS give concepts spatial orientation by
associating an abstract knowledge area with some aspect of experiential
knowledge grounded in how human beings understand their orientation
in physical space, i.e. up vs down, front vs back, etc.

Example   Expressions such as the following seem to relate the abstract notion of being
happy with being located in a physically UP position: *I'm feeling up today,*
That movie boosted my spirits, Her spirits rose at the news. LJ call this
metaphor HAPPY IS UP.

Comment   LJ observe that our metaphorical understanding of abstract domains of
knowledge in terms of their being situated UP in physical space is not limited
just to how we understand happiness, but that we comprehend several other
abstract domains using variations on the same orientational metaphor. Some
of these other metaphors are illustrated in the following practice.

Practice   Try to categorize the following expressions according to the particular kinds
of UP metaphor they reflect.

(1) *It's eight o'clock, time to wake up*
(2) *John is at the peak of health*
(3) *Jane is on top of the situation*
(4) *The number of articles on semantics seems to keep going up*
(5) *The dean of the college occupies a lofty position in the university*
(6) *Jack does high-quality work*
(7) *That teacher always sets high standards*

Feedback   These are the metaphors suggested by LJ: (1) CONSCIOUS IS UP.
(2) HEALTH IS UP. (3) HAVING CONTROL/FORCE IS UP.
(4) MORE IS UP. (5) HIGH STATUS IS UP. (6) GOOD IS UP. (7) VIRTUE
IS UP.

Comment   These examples of orientational metaphors reveal some interesting facts about
the language. First, they show that the use of metaphorical language is

systematic and not random or haphazard. There is 'external systematicity among the various spatialization metaphors' (LJ 1980: 18) in that all the metaphors involving UP are positive in some way or evoke general well-being when viewed against our cultural knowledge and understanding. In other words, the various metaphors are coherent with each other. Second, the systematic nature of the metaphors reflects the fact that they 'are rooted in physical and cultural experience' (LJ 1980: 18). We understand such metaphors because they are grounded in the way we experience the world. (We will leave it to you to explain in a later exercise what physical and cultural experience might cause the various abstract knowledge domains illustrated above to be associated with UP as opposed to some other orientation.)

Now that we have looked at orientational metaphors, let us briefly examine the second general kind of metaphor (in addition to structural metaphors) that LJ identified as frequently found in language.

Definition ONTOLOGICAL METAPHORS help structure our understanding of abstract concepts and experiences, such as events, activities, emotions, ideas, etc., in terms of our experience with actual physical objects and substances in the real world. (The term *ontological* is derived from the Greek root *onta* 'the things which exist' + -*logy* 'the science of'.)

Example LJ use the metaphor INFLATION IS AN ENTITY to illustrate how ontological metaphors work. They observe that by treating an abstract concept such as monetary inflation as though it were a physical object we can use the everyday language we typically use to talk about such objects to understand the concept better. Here are some ways in which we can talk about inflation: (1) *Inflation is lowering our standard of living.* (2) *Inflation is increasing every year.* (3) *The negative aspects of inflation far outweigh the positive ones.* (4) *Inflation is ruining our economy.* (5) *We have to fight inflation or it will conquer us.*

The metaphor allows us to refer to inflation in each sentence as though it were a physical entity. LJ note that we can also use the metaphor to quantify it (2), identify a particular aspect of it (3), see it as a cause (1,4), and act with respect to it (5), etc.

Comment LJ observe that the language has an enormous number of these metaphors and that they are so common that they are rarely even recognized as metaphors at all, but rather as simply part of the everyday ordinary language.

Practice Try to identify in what particular way the ontological metaphors in each sentence below treat an abstract concept as though it were a physical object. Choose from among the following options: referring, quantifying, identifying aspects, identifying causes, setting goals and/or motivating actions (from LJ 1980: 26–7).

(1) *John set out to seek his fame and fortune*
(2) *His fear of flying is getting better*
(3) *Mary has a lot of hostility toward her brother*
(4) *We thought that her suggestion was a bad idea*
(5) *His lack of moral fibre makes him weak*

Feedback
(1) Setting a goal (2) Referring (3) Quantifying (4) Identifying aspects (5) Identifying a cause

Comment
The ontological metaphors examined so far have been identified by LJ as entity and substance metaphors. Another kind of ontological metaphor treats abstractions as though they were physical containers of various kinds. Such metaphors are called container metaphors. An important way in which they are grounded in our everyday bodily experience is that we typically perceive our own bodies as containers with both an inside and outside aspect bounded off from each other, and we can project this knowledge onto abstract entities of various kinds.

Example
We often treat land areas as though they were physical containers with overt boundaries, as in such expressions as: *We live in a field by the lake, They travelled out of their home state, I'm going to drive to Kansas next week.* We also typically treat what we see within our visual field as though it were a kind of bounded container, as seen in such expressions as *The mountains came into view, The city is now out of sight,* etc.

Practice
LJ claim that all kinds of events, actions, activities, and states are typically conceptualized as though they were physical entities by means of ontological metaphors. Try to identify the relevant aspects of each ontological metaphor in each sentence below.

(1) *There were many runners in the race*
(2) *Jack got into car racing as a young man*
(3) *John and Mary are in love*
(4) *The girl fell into a deep depression*

Feedback
(1) The race is construed as a container object. (2) The activity of car racing is construed as a substance container. (3) The state of being in love is construed as a container. (4) The depression is construed as a container object.

Comment
There is another common type of ontological metaphor that allows us to impute various kinds of human qualities to non-human entities.

Definition
PERSONIFICATION is a particular subtype of ontological metaphor in which an abstract entity is construed as though it were a physical object which is then further specified as being a person.

Examples   Here are some examples of personification: (1) *That theory explains*
everything you need to know about metaphor. (2) *I think that life has cheated*
me out of any hope of happiness. (3) *Cancer finally caught up with him.*

Comment   Note that, literally speaking, a theory cannot explain anything (1), only a
person can. Similarly, only people can literally cheat someone (2) or catch
up with someone (3). But conceiving such non-human entities as *a*
theory, *life*, and *cancer* as though they are human entities enables us to
attribute motivations and characteristics to them that would not be
possible without personification. Conceptualizing entities in human
terms by means of personification makes them more accessible to
understanding.

Let us now examine one more example of non-literal language, metonymy,
that is somewhat different from the kinds of non-literal language we have
seen up to this point.

Definition   METONYMY is a kind of non-literal language in which one entity is used to
refer to another entity that is associated with it in some way. In other words,
metonymic concepts 'allow us to conceptualize one thing by means of its
relation to something else' (LJ 1980: 39).

Example   The following example of metonymy is frequently cited in the literature to
illustrate this concept:
The ham sandwich in the next booth is waiting for his bill

Comment   How do we understand this sentence? Clearly we cannot interpret it
literally, since we are not implying that an actual sandwich is waiting to get
its bill. Such an interpretation would lead to an anomaly. We rather
understand it to mean that the person who ordered the ham sandwich is
waiting for his bill. In the particular context in which this sentence would
be uttered, presumably a café or restaurant, the person uttering the sentence
would know that there was a close relationship between the thing ordered
and the person who ordered it. Because this relationship is so obvious in
the context, it is permissible to refer to the person by what he ordered. As a
matter of fact, this might be the preferred way of referring to the person,
because the people who wait on customers in a diner typically don't learn
the names of their customers, but they are well aware of what their
customers ordered.

Practice   Explain the metonymy in each sentence below.
(1)   *We enjoy watching Hitchcock more than Spielberg*
(2)   The Times *asked a pertinent question at the news conference*
(3)   *The White House refused to answer the question*

Feedback   (1) *Hitchcock* and *Spielberg* are used to represent the films they made. (2) *The Times* is used to represent the reporter who works for the newspaper. (3) *The White House* is used to refer to the spokesperson who works there who actually refused to answer.

Comment   LJ observe that there are in fact several different kinds of metonymy that are frequently found in everyday language. We will introduce them here by means of a practice. (Note that metonymies are written in the same way as metaphors.)

Practice   Each of the sentences given below exemplifies one of the following particular subtypes of metonymy: THE PART FOR THE WHOLE, THE FACE FOR THE PERSON, PRODUCER FOR PRODUCT, OBJECT USED FOR USER, CONTROLLER FOR CONTROLLED, INSTITUTION FOR PEOPLE RESPONSIBLE, THE PLACE FOR THE INSTITUTION, THE PLACE FOR THE EVENT. Match each sentence with the kind of metonymy that it represents.

(1)   *Watergate was an important scandal in American politics*
(2)   *The rancher needs some more hands during roundup time*
(3)   *The buses are on strike today*
(4)   *Hollywood keeps putting out mediocre movies*
(5)   *The art collector bought an expensive Picasso*
(6)   *Hitler conquered Poland in just a few days*
(7)   *The Army needs many new soldiers*
(8)   *She's just another pretty face*

Feedback   (1) THE PLACE FOR THE EVENT (2) THE PART FOR THE WHOLE (3) OBJECT USED FOR USER (4) THE PLACE FOR THE INSTITUTION (5) PRODUCER FOR PRODUCT (6) CONTROLLER FOR CONTROLLED (7) INSTITUTION FOR PEOPLE RESPONSIBLE (8) THE FACE FOR THE PERSON

Comment   As a matter of fact, multiple examples could be given for each subtype of metonymy in this practice, which you will be asked to do in a later exercise. This shows that examples of metonymy are rarely isolated and unrelated to each other. Moreover, it seems clear that the kinds of associations between entities that allow us to refer to one entity by means of another via metonymy are principled and not arbitrary, as was discussed earlier with respect to the ham sandwich example. It is easy to see the same kind of principled association in other cases, once the appropriate context is taken into account. For example, invoking the metonymy THE PLACE FOR THE EVENT by using *Watergate* to refer to the scandal that took place in the Nixon administration in the 1970s makes sense and is not arbitrary, because the sequence of events that led to the scandal started with a burglary in the apartment complex with that name in Washington DC.

These facts about metonymy show that it is highly structured and not random or haphazard. LJ note that, like metaphors, 'metonymic concepts structure not just our language but our thoughts, attitudes, and actions. And, like metaphoric concepts, metonymic concepts are grounded in our experience' (LJ 1980: 39).

Summary This unit has examined several kinds of non-literal or figurative language and has investigated the extent to which it might be structured in some way. Our survey has shown that, although non-literal language is often thought of as essentially random and idiosyncratic, in reality it tends to be more systematically organized than has usually been recognized. In spite of their apparent idiosyncratic nature, for example, many idiomatic expressions (such as *My car is a lemon*) probably originated as isolated metaphors which have become fixed or frozen over time. The fact that the metaphors on which they were based never became widely used in the language has led to their identification as frozen expressions.

But the language is replete with a number of different kinds of metaphorical expressions that are more elaborately entrenched in the culture and, consequently, are more highly systematic in nature. We have found ample evidence in English of numerous structural metaphors, orientational metaphors, and ontological metaphors which are by no means random, but highly structured and rule-governed. Finally, we have examined the role played by several different subtypes of metonymy in everyday language and have found, once again, that it, too, is systematic in nature.

We must now draw to a close our discussion of non-literal language, although we have barely scratched the surface of this vast topic and have glossed over some aspects of it that are too complex to pursue in an introductory text. If you are interested in reading further about non-literal language, including metaphor, metonymy, and related subjects, we encourage you to take a look at the references at the end of the book.

Unit 27 Study Guide and Exercises

Directions After you have read Unit 27 you should be able to tackle the following questions to test your understanding of the main ideas raised in the unit.

1 You should understand these terms and concepts from this unit:
literal vs non-literal language
idiom (idiomatic or 'fixed' expression)
compositional vs non-compositional expressions

metaphor
  isolated metaphor
  structural metaphor
  orientational metaphor
  ontological metaphor
    entity and substance metaphors
    container metaphors
    personification
metonymy (and its various subtypes)

2 **Idioms as isolated metaphors**. This exercise is a variation on an earlier one
in this unit. Each of the following sentences contains an italicized idiomatic
expression that would make it anomalous if it were interpreted literally (i.e.
compositionally). Briefly explain this anomaly for each sentence, and then
describe what kind of intended non-literal meaning the sentence typically
conveys. Finally, if possible, try to suggest what kind of isolated metaphor
each sentence might be an example of. If it's not possible to formulate an
appropriate metaphor in simple terms, try at least to explain to what extent
the expression might be partially analysable (i.e. compositional). The first
item, repeated from an earlier practice, is done for you.

a Frank is *a snake in the grass*
  Anomaly: Frank is being equated with (or classified as) being a particular
  kind of animal (a snake), which is literally untrue.
  Non-literal meaning: Something about Frank's behaviour is untrustworthy.
  Metaphor: PEOPLE ARE ANIMALS. (Note that this is not completely
  isolated, since we do have such expressions as *Frank is a tiger, Mary is a
  lamb*, etc.) In this case, Frank's apparent identification as a snake is
  meant to associate him with the popular idea that snakes are sneaky and
  underhanded.

b Jack *pulled my leg* when he told me that story

c Jim *painted the town red* when he returned from college

d The old horse finally *kicked the bucket*

e When we tried to solve that math problem we discovered that we were *up
  the creek (without a paddle)*

f The suggestion made by Mary makes me think that *she has a bee in her
  bonnet*

g Jerry *sold me down the river*

h If you can figure out how to do that, *I'll eat my hat*

i Fred always tried to *throw his weight around*

j Don't say a word! *Bite your tongue!*

k I *gave them a piece of my mind*

l Mary and John seem to have *hit it off with each other*

m *Eat your heart out*: I just won the lottery!

n *Jack is a pig*

o Mary *let the cat out of the bag* when she told me about Jane's marriage to Jake

p Jim *took the bull by the horns* when he decided to deal with the problem

q Mary *spilled the beans* when I asked her about the secret

3 Each of the following sets of sentences exemplifies a particular structural metaphor in English. Identify the particular words or phrases in each sentence that evoke the metaphor and then identify the metaphor itself. Then see if you can provide one or two (or possibly more) additional examples of the metaphor in English.

A a What is the foundation for your theory?

   b I think your theory needs more support

   c If that's all your theory consists of, it'll fall apart

   d His idea collapsed because it didn't have enough support

   e Every theory or idea needs a firm foundation

   f ....

   Metaphor: ....

B a His comments left a bad taste in my mouth

   b Her suggestion was nothing but a half-baked idea

   c There was a lot to digest in the professor's new theory

   d The class stewed over what the lecturer said for a while

   e You can really sink your teeth into that writer's ideas

   f ....

   Metaphor: ....

C a She was crazy about him

   b He nearly drove her out of her mind

   c Jack went mad over Mary when he first saw her

   d She's just wild about Fred

   e Fred nearly drove Mary insane

   f ....

   Metaphor: ....

D a The odds are against me, but I'll take my chances with this project

   b If I play my cards right, I may be able to succeed in life

   c Jack is a real loser. He's never around when the chips are down

   d My ace in the hole is that I know something they don't know

   e It's a toss up whether John is bluffing or not

   f ....

   Metaphor: ....

4 Now try to do the opposite of what you did in exercise 3. For each structural metaphor given below supply as many sentences as you can which evoke the metaphor.

a THE MIND IS A MACHINE
b LOVE IS A PHYSICAL FORCE
c LOVE IS A (MEDICAL) PATIENT
d LOVE IS WAR
e LIFE IS A CONTAINER

5 We have already seen that an important abstract concept, such as IDEA, can be structured by means of multiple metaphors, each of which gives a slightly different perspective on how the concept can be understood. This range of metaphors allows us to understand the concept better. The metaphors already illustrated structure the domain of IDEAS in terms of the more concrete source domains MONEY, PEOPLE, and PLANTS. Try to find one or two additional metaphors for structuring the abstract IDEA domain using other source domains and give several English examples for each.

6 We have seen that orientational metaphors are externally systematic. LJ note that they are also 'internally systematic' in that each metaphor 'defines a coherent system rather than a number of isolated and random cases'. In other words, all expressions involving UP evoke the same kind of experience. For example, *I'm feeling up* is another example of the HAPPY IS UP metaphor, but the metaphor would be incoherent if saying *My spirits rose* meant 'I became sadder.' In an earlier practice you categorized several isolated sentences according to the particular kind of UP orientational metaphor they reflected. See if you can come up with some additional examples that are internally systematic with the examples already given for some of the UP metaphors mentioned earlier.

a HEALTH IS UP   e GOOD IS UP
b HAVING CONTROL/FORCE IS UP   f VIRTUE IS UP
c MORE IS UP   g HIGH STATUS IS UP
d HAPPY IS UP

7 The opposite of UP is DOWN. For each of the UP metaphors in exercise 6 find one or two examples of the corresponding DOWN metaphor (if it exists) and name the metaphor. Here's an example: *John came down with the flu* (SICKNESS IS DOWN). (Note how odd it sounds to say that someone *came up with the flu*.)

8 We did not discuss the specific physical or experiential reasons why the language would have so many orientational metaphors in which UP is associated with positive notions such as being healthy, being good, having more of something, having higher status, etc. Can you explain why these positive notions are associated with UP instead of some other orientation (such as DOWN)?

9 Although most of the orientational metaphors involving UP are coherent with each other in evoking meanings that are positive in some way, there are

occasional expressions involving UP which appear not to be coherent with metaphors such as those listed in exercise 6. An example is the expression *The answer to that question is up in the air*, in which the UP orientation might be argued to be negative in some way. Can you propose the different metaphor that underlies this expression and suggest what experiential basis it has?

10 Try to identify in what particular way the additional ontological metaphors in each sentence below treat an abstract concept as though it were a physical object. Choose from among the following options: referring, quantifying, identifying aspects, identifying causes, setting goals and/or motivating actions.

   a I could see the intensity with which she worked
   b They did that out of compassion for the poor
   c There is too much hatred in the world
   d I'm looking forward to finding a solution to this problem
   e The brutality of aggression is a major factor in many conflicts
   f They are working toward peace in the world

11 In an earlier practice you matched an example sentence with the kind of metonymy it represented. For each kind of metonymy below give at least three additional sentences that represent it. For item (h) see if you can find another kind of metonymy and give some examples.

   a THE PLACE FOR THE EVENT
   b THE PART FOR THE WHOLE
   c OBJECT USED FOR USER
   d THE PLACE FOR THE INSTITUTION
   e PRODUCER FOR PRODUCT
   f CONTROLLER FOR CONTROLLED
   g INSTITUTION FOR PEOPLE RESPONSIBLE

   h ....

12 What kind of metonymy is reflected in the following sets of sentences?
   A a I have to fill the car with gas (*Hint*: what is literally being filled here?)
       b I need to use the bathroom
       c China won the championship

   Metonymy: ....

   B a The pot is boiling (*Hint*: what is literally boiling here?)
       b Room 44 needs more towels
       c The bus in front of us decided to turn left

   Metonymy: ....

SELECTED REFERENCES AND
RECOMMENDATIONS FOR FURTHER STUDY

References The material in Unit 8 dealing with prototype effects in the semantics of
color is from the following influential book.

> Brent Berlin and Paul Kay, *Basic Color Terms: Their Universality and
> Evolution*, Berkeley: University of California Press (1969).

Much of the material on metaphor and metonymy in Unit 27 is freely
adapted from the first few chapters of the following influential book.

> George Lakoff and Mark Johnson, *Metaphors We Live By*, Chicago:
> University of Chicago Press (1980).

Selected additional material for Unit 27 was adapted from and influenced by
the following introductory text on cognitive linguistics.

> John R. Taylor, *Cognitive Grammar*, New York: Oxford University Press
> (2002).

Further study Since the first edition of this textbook appeared in 1983 the number of
scholarly books, articles, and textbooks dealing with semantics has grown
immensely, and it is not possible or even appropriate to give an exhaustive
listing in an introductory textbook like this one. The intention here is simply
to indicate other books of interest that students can consult either for a
different approach to topics covered in this book or for information about
topics in Semantics that were not dealt with here. Of course, the references in
these additional books will lead interested students into other areas of the
subject, as well.

The following books are good elementary introductions to semantics,
covering much of the same material as this book, but in their own
different ways, and sometimes adopting somewhat different points of view
from ours.

> Allan Cruse, *Meaning in Language: An Introduction to Semantics and
> Pragmatics*, 2nd edition, New York: Oxford University Press (2004).
> Geoffrey N. Leech, *Semantics*, 2nd edition, Harmondsworth: Penguin
> Books (1981).
> Sebastian Löbner, *Understanding Semantics*, New York: Arnold/Oxford
> University Press (2002).

345

F. R. Palmer, *Semantics*, 2nd edition, Cambridge: Cambridge University Press (1982).

John Saeed, *Semantics*, 2nd edition, Oxford: Blackwell Publishing (2003).

The following books are also introductions, but at not quite such an elementary level as the ones recommended above. The books by Allan, Frawley, Kearns, Kempson, and Lyons deal in their own unique ways with roughly the same subject area as this book, while the books by Cruse, Leech, and Levinson concentrate on questions of the meanings of utterances in context, i.e. roughly the area we have labelled 'interpersonal meaning'.

Keith Allan, *Natural Language Semantics*, Oxford: Blackwell Publishers (2001).

D. A. Cruse, *Lexical Semantics*, Cambridge: Cambridge University Press (1986).

William Frawley, *Linguistic Semantics*, Hillsdale, NJ: Lawrence Erlbaum Associates (1992).

Kate Kearns, *Semantics*, New York: St Martin's Press (2000).

Ruth Kempson, *Semantic Theory*, Cambridge: Cambridge University Press (1977).

Geoffrey N. Leech, *Principles of Pragmatics*, London: Longman (1983).

Stephen C. Levinson, *Pragmatics*, Cambridge: Cambridge University Press (1983).

John Lyons, *Linguistic Semantics*, Cambridge: Cambridge University Press (1995).

The following books focus in particular on formal and logical aspects of meaning like those we treated in Units 12–15, but in much greater detail.

Jens Allwood, Lars-Gunnar Andersson, and Östen Dahl, *Logic in Linguistics*, Cambridge: Cambridge University Press (1977).

Gennaro Chierchia and Sally McConnell-Ginet, *Meaning and Grammar: An Introduction to Semantics*, Cambridge, MA: The MIT Press (1990).

Henriëtte de Swart, *Introduction to Natural Language Semantics*, Stanford, CA: CSLI Publications (1998).

The following is an encyclopaedic and authoritative work on semantics, not exactly bed-time reading, but indispensable for serious reference, especially on relatively standard and traditional issues.

John Lyons, *Semantics* (2 volumes), Cambridge: Cambridge University Press (1977).

INDEX

Page numbers in bold type indicate places in the text where definitions of terms are given. The index does not include material found in the exercises or study guide.